50% OFF
Online SHRM-CP Prep Course!

By Mometrix

Dear Customer,

We consider it an honor and a privilege that you chose our SHRM-CP Study Guide. As a way of showing our appreciation and to help us better serve you, we are offering **50% off our online SHRM-CP Prep Course.** Many courses cost hundreds of dollars and don't deliver enough value. With our course, you get access to the best SHRM-CP prep material, and **you only pay half price**.

We have structured our online course to perfectly complement your printed study guide. The SHRM-CP Prep Course contains **in-depth lessons** that cover all the most important topics, **1,200+ practice questions** to ensure you feel prepared, and over **300 digital flashcards**, so you can study while you're on the go.

Online SHRM-CP Prep Course

Topics Covered:

- Behavioral Competencies
  - Leadership
  - Interpersonal
  - Business
- Human Resources Expertise
  - People
  - Organization
  - Workplace

Course Features:

- SHRM-CP Study Guide
  - Get content that complements our best-selling study guide.
- 8 Full-Length Practice Tests
  - With over 1,200 practice questions, you can test yourself again and again.
- Mobile Friendly
  - If you need to study on the go, the course is easily accessible from your mobile device.
- SHRM-CP Flashcards
  - Our course includes a flashcard mode consisting of over 300 content cards to help you study.

To receive this discount, visit our website at mometrix.com/university/shrm or simply scan this QR code with your smartphone. At the checkout page, enter the discount code: **shrm50off**

If you have any questions or concerns, please contact us at support@mometrix.com.

Sincerely,

FREE Study Skills Videos/DVD Offer

Dear Customer,

Thank you for your purchase from Mometrix! We consider it an honor and a privilege that you have purchased our product and we want to ensure your satisfaction.

As part of our ongoing effort to meet the needs of test takers, we have developed a set of Study Skills Videos that we would like to give you for <u>FREE</u>. These videos cover our *best practices* for getting ready for your exam, from how to use our study materials to how to best prepare for the day of the test.

All that we ask is that you email us with feedback that would describe your experience so far with our product. Good, bad, or indifferent, we want to know what you think!

To get your FREE Study Skills Videos, you can use the **QR code** below, or send us an **email** at <u>studyvideos@mometrix.com</u> with *FREE VIDEOS* in the subject line and the following information in the body of the email:

- The name of the product you purchased.
- Your product rating on a scale of 1-5, with 5 being the highest rating.
- Your feedback. It can be long, short, or anything in between. We just want to know your impressions and experience so far with our product. (Good feedback might include how our study material met your needs and ways we might be able to make it even better. You could highlight features that you found helpful or features that you think we should add.)

If you have any questions or concerns, please don't hesitate to contact me directly.

Thanks again!

Sincerely,

Jay Willis
Vice President
<u>jay.willis@mometrix.com</u>
1-800-673-8175

SHRM CP

Exam Prep
2024-2025

4 Full-Length
Practice Tests

**SHRM CP Certification Secrets
Study Guide with Detailed
Answer Explanations**

4th Edition

Written and edited by the Mometrix Human Resources Certification Test Team

Printed in the United States of America

This paper meets the requirements of ANSI/NISO Z39.48-1992 (Permanence of Paper).

Mometrix offers volume discount pricing to institutions. For more information or a price quote, please contact our sales department at sales@mometrix.com or 888-248-1219.

Paperback
ISBN 13: 978-1-5167-2448-2

DEAR FUTURE EXAM SUCCESS STORY

First of all, **THANK YOU** for purchasing Mometrix study materials!

Second, congratulations! You are one of the few determined test-takers who are committed to doing whatever it takes to excel on your exam. **You have come to the right place.** We developed these study materials with one goal in mind: to deliver you the information you need in a format that's concise and easy to use.

In addition to optimizing your guide for the content of the test, we've outlined our recommended steps for breaking down the preparation process into small, attainable goals so you can make sure you stay on track.

We've also analyzed the entire test-taking process, identifying the most common pitfalls and showing how you can overcome them and be ready for any curveball the test throws you.

Standardized testing is one of the biggest obstacles on your road to success, which only increases the importance of doing well in the high-pressure, high-stakes environment of test day. Your results on this test could have a significant impact on your future, and this guide provides the information and practical advice to help you achieve your full potential on test day.

Your success is our success

We would love to hear from you! If you would like to share the story of your exam success or if you have any questions or comments in regard to our products, please contact us at **800-673-8175** or **support@mometrix.com**.

Thanks again for your business and we wish you continued success!

Sincerely,
The Mometrix Test Preparation Team

> **Need more help? Check out our flashcards at:**
> **http://mometrixflashcards.com/SHRM**

TABLE OF CONTENTS

Introduction

Thank you for purchasing this resource! You have made the choice to prepare yourself for a test that could have a huge impact on your future, and this guide is designed to help you be fully ready for test day. Obviously, it's important to have a solid understanding of the test material, but you also need to be prepared for the unique environment and stressors of the test, so that you can perform to the best of your abilities.

For this purpose, the first section that appears in this guide is the **Secret Keys**. We've devoted countless hours to meticulously researching what works and what doesn't, and we've boiled down our findings to the five most impactful steps you can take to improve your performance on the test. We start at the beginning with study planning and move through the preparation process, all the way to the testing strategies that will help you get the most out of what you know when you're finally sitting in front of the test.

We recommend that you start preparing for your test as far in advance as possible. However, if you've bought this guide as a last-minute study resource and only have a few days before your test, we recommend that you skip over the first two Secret Keys since they address a long-term study plan.

If you struggle with **test anxiety**, we strongly encourage you to check out our recommendations for how you can overcome it. Test anxiety is a formidable foe, but it can be beaten, and we want to make sure you have the tools you need to defeat it.

Secret Key #1 – Plan Big, Study Small

There's a lot riding on your performance. If you want to ace this test, you're going to need to keep your skills sharp and the material fresh in your mind. You need a plan that lets you review everything you need to know while still fitting in your schedule. We'll break this strategy down into three categories.

Information Organization

Start with the information you already have: the official test outline. From this, you can make a complete list of all the concepts you need to cover before the test. Organize these concepts into groups that can be studied together, and create a list of any related vocabulary you need to learn so you can brush up on any difficult terms. You'll want to keep this vocabulary list handy once you actually start studying since you may need to add to it along the way.

Time Management

Once you have your set of study concepts, decide how to spread them out over the time you have left before the test. Break your study plan into small, clear goals so you have a manageable task for each day and know exactly what you're doing. Then just focus on one small step at a time. When you manage your time this way, you don't need to spend hours at a time studying. Studying a small block of content for a short period each day helps you retain information better and avoid stressing over how much you have left to do. You can relax knowing that you have a plan to cover everything in time. In order for this strategy to be effective though, you have to start studying early and stick to your schedule. Avoid the exhaustion and futility that comes from last-minute cramming!

Study Environment

The environment you study in has a big impact on your learning. Studying in a coffee shop, while probably more enjoyable, is not likely to be as fruitful as studying in a quiet room. It's important to keep distractions to a minimum. You're only planning to study for a short block of time, so make the most of it. Don't pause to check your phone or get up to find a snack. It's also important to **avoid multitasking**. Research has consistently shown that multitasking will make your studying dramatically less effective. Your study area should also be comfortable and well-lit so you don't have the distraction of straining your eyes or sitting on an uncomfortable chair.

 The time of day you study is also important. You want to be rested and alert. Don't wait until just before bedtime. Study when you'll be most likely to comprehend and remember. Even better, if you know what time of day your test will be, set that time aside for study. That way your brain will be used to working on that subject at that specific time and you'll have a better chance of recalling information.

Finally, it can be helpful to team up with others who are studying for the same test. Your actual studying should be done in as isolated an environment as possible, but the work of organizing the information and setting up the study plan can be divided up. In between study sessions, you can discuss with your teammates the concepts that you're all studying and quiz each other on the details. Just be sure that your teammates are as serious about the test as you are. If you find that your study time is being replaced with social time, you might need to find a new team.

Secret Key #2 – Make Your Studying Count

You're devoting a lot of time and effort to preparing for this test, so you want to be absolutely certain it will pay off. This means doing more than just reading the content and hoping you can remember it on test day. It's important to make every minute of study count. There are two main areas you can focus on to make your studying count.

Retention

It doesn't matter how much time you study if you can't remember the material. You need to make sure you are retaining the concepts. To check your retention of the information you're learning, try recalling it at later times with minimal prompting. Try carrying around flashcards and glance at one or two from time to time or ask a friend who's also studying for the test to quiz you.

To enhance your retention, look for ways to put the information into practice so that you can apply it rather than simply recalling it. If you're using the information in practical ways, it will be much easier to remember. Similarly, it helps to solidify a concept in your mind if you're not only reading it to yourself but also explaining it to someone else. Ask a friend to let you teach them about a concept you're a little shaky on (or speak aloud to an imaginary audience if necessary). As you try to summarize, define, give examples, and answer your friend's questions, you'll understand the concepts better and they will stay with you longer. Finally, step back for a big picture view and ask yourself how each piece of information fits with the whole subject. When you link the different concepts together and see them working together as a whole, it's easier to remember the individual components.

Finally, practice showing your work on any multi-step problems, even if you're just studying. Writing out each step you take to solve a problem will help solidify the process in your mind, and you'll be more likely to remember it during the test.

Modality

Modality simply refers to the means or method by which you study. Choosing a study modality that fits your own individual learning style is crucial. No two people learn best in exactly the same way, so it's important to know your strengths and use them to your advantage.

For example, if you learn best by visualization, focus on visualizing a concept in your mind and draw an image or a diagram. Try color-coding your notes, illustrating them, or creating symbols that will trigger your mind to recall a learned concept. If you learn best by hearing or discussing information, find a study partner who learns the same way or read aloud to yourself. Think about how to put the information in your own words. Imagine that you are giving a lecture on the topic and record yourself so you can listen to it later.

For any learning style, flashcards can be helpful. Organize the information so you can take advantage of spare moments to review. Underline key words or phrases. Use different colors for different categories. Mnemonic devices (such as creating a short list in which every item starts with the same letter) can also help with retention. Find what works best for you and use it to store the information in your mind most effectively and easily.

3

Secret Key #3 – Practice the Right Way

Your success on test day depends not only on how many hours you put into preparing, but also on whether you prepared the right way. It's good to check along the way to see if your studying is paying off. One of the most effective ways to do this is by taking practice tests to evaluate your progress. Practice tests are useful because they show exactly where you need to improve. Every time you take a practice test, pay special attention to these three groups of questions:

- The questions you got wrong
- The questions you had to guess on, even if you guessed right
- The questions you found difficult or slow to work through

This will show you exactly what your weak areas are, and where you need to devote more study time. Ask yourself why each of these questions gave you trouble. Was it because you didn't understand the material? Was it because you didn't remember the vocabulary? Do you need more repetitions on this type of question to build speed and confidence? Dig into those questions and figure out how you can strengthen your weak areas as you go back to review the material.

 Additionally, many practice tests have a section explaining the answer choices. It can be tempting to read the explanation and think that you now have a good understanding of the concept. However, an explanation likely only covers part of the question's broader context. Even if the explanation makes perfect sense, **go back and investigate** every concept related to the question until you're positive you have a thorough understanding.

As you go along, keep in mind that the practice test is just that: practice. Memorizing these questions and answers will not be very helpful on the actual test because it is unlikely to have any of the same exact questions. If you only know the right answers to the sample questions, you won't be prepared for the real thing. **Study the concepts** until you understand them fully, and then you'll be able to answer any question that shows up on the test.

It's important to wait on the practice tests until you're ready. If you take a test on your first day of study, you may be overwhelmed by the amount of material covered and how much you need to learn. Work up to it gradually.

On test day, you'll need to be prepared for answering questions, managing your time, and using the test-taking strategies you've learned. It's a lot to balance, like a mental marathon that will have a big impact on your future. Like training for a marathon, you'll need to start slowly and work your way up. When test day arrives, you'll be ready.

Start with the strategies you've read in the first two Secret Keys—plan your course and study in the way that works best for you. If you have time, consider using multiple study resources to get different approaches to the same concepts. It can be helpful to see difficult concepts from more than one angle. Then find a good source for practice tests. Many times, the test website will suggest potential study resources or provide sample tests.

Practice Test Strategy

If you're able to find at least three practice tests, we recommend this strategy:

UNTIMED AND OPEN-BOOK PRACTICE

Take the first test with no time constraints and with your notes and study guide handy. Take your time and focus on applying the strategies you've learned.

TIMED AND OPEN-BOOK PRACTICE

Take the second practice test open-book as well, but set a timer and practice pacing yourself to finish in time.

TIMED AND CLOSED-BOOK PRACTICE

Take any other practice tests as if it were test day. Set a timer and put away your study materials. Sit at a table or desk in a quiet room, imagine yourself at the testing center, and answer questions as quickly and accurately as possible.

Keep repeating timed and closed-book tests on a regular basis until you run out of practice tests or it's time for the actual test. Your mind will be ready for the schedule and stress of test day, and you'll be able to focus on recalling the material you've learned.

Secret Key #4 – Pace Yourself

Once you're fully prepared for the material on the test, your biggest challenge on test day will be managing your time. Just knowing that the clock is ticking can make you panic even if you have plenty of time left. Work on pacing yourself so you can build confidence against the time constraints of the exam. Pacing is a difficult skill to master, especially in a high-pressure environment, so **practice is vital**.

Set time expectations for your pace based on how much time is available. For example, if a section has 60 questions and the time limit is 30 minutes, you know you have to average 30 seconds or less per question in order to answer them all. Although 30 seconds is the hard limit, set 25 seconds per question as your goal, so you reserve extra time to spend on harder questions. When you budget extra time for the harder questions, you no longer have any reason to stress when those questions take longer to answer.

Don't let this time expectation distract you from working through the test at a calm, steady pace, but keep it in mind so you don't spend too much time on any one question. Recognize that taking extra time on one question you don't understand may keep you from answering two that you do understand later in the test. If your time limit for a question is up and you're still not sure of the answer, mark it and move on, and come back to it later if the time and the test format allow. If the testing format doesn't allow you to return to earlier questions, just make an educated guess; then put it out of your mind and move on.

On the easier questions, be careful not to rush. It may seem wise to hurry through them so you have more time for the challenging ones, but it's not worth missing one if you know the concept and just didn't take the time to read the question fully. Work efficiently but make sure you understand the question and have looked at all of the answer choices, since more than one may seem right at first.

Even if you're paying attention to the time, you may find yourself a little behind at some point. You should speed up to get back on track, but do so wisely. Don't panic; just take a few seconds less on each question until you're caught up. Don't guess without thinking, but do look through the answer choices and eliminate any you know are wrong. If you can get down to two choices, it is often worthwhile to guess from those. Once you've chosen an answer, move on and don't dwell on any that you skipped or had to hurry through. If a question was taking too long, chances are it was one of the harder ones, so you weren't as likely to get it right anyway.

On the other hand, if you find yourself getting ahead of schedule, it may be beneficial to slow down a little. The more quickly you work, the more likely you are to make a careless mistake that will affect your score. You've budgeted time for each question, so don't be afraid to spend that time. Practice an efficient but careful pace to get the most out of the time you have.

Secret Key #5 – Have a Plan for Guessing

When you're taking the test, you may find yourself stuck on a question. Some of the answer choices seem better than others, but you don't see the one answer choice that is obviously correct. What do you do?

The scenario described above is very common, yet most test takers have not effectively prepared for it. Developing and practicing a plan for guessing may be one of the single most effective uses of your time as you get ready for the exam.

In developing your plan for guessing, there are three questions to address:

- When should you start the guessing process?
- How should you narrow down the choices?
- Which answer should you choose?

When to Start the Guessing Process

Unless your plan for guessing is to select C every time (which, despite its merits, is not what we recommend), you need to leave yourself enough time to apply your answer elimination strategies. Since you have a limited amount of time for each question, that means that if you're going to give yourself the best shot at guessing correctly, you have to decide quickly whether or not you will guess.

Of course, the best-case scenario is that you don't have to guess at all, so first, see if you can answer the question based on your knowledge of the subject and basic reasoning skills. Focus on the key words in the question and try to jog your memory of related topics. Give yourself a chance to bring the knowledge to mind, but once you realize that you don't have (or you can't access) the knowledge you need to answer the question, it's time to start the guessing process.

It's almost always better to start the guessing process too early than too late. It only takes a few seconds to remember something and answer the question from knowledge. Carefully eliminating wrong answer choices takes longer. Plus, going through the process of eliminating answer choices can actually help jog your memory.

Summary: Start the guessing process as soon as you decide that you can't answer the question based on your knowledge.

How to Narrow Down the Choices

The next chapter in this book (**Test-Taking Strategies**) includes a wide range of strategies for how to approach questions and how to look for answer choices to eliminate. You will definitely want to read those carefully, practice them, and figure out which ones work best for you. Here though, we're going to address a mindset rather than a particular strategy.

Your odds of guessing an answer correctly depend on how many options you are choosing from.

Number of options left	5	4	3	2	1
Odds of guessing correctly	20%	25%	33%	50%	100%

You can see from this chart just how valuable it is to be able to eliminate incorrect answers and make an educated guess, but there are two things that many test takers do that cause them to miss out on the benefits of guessing:

- Accidentally eliminating the correct answer
- Selecting an answer based on an impression

We'll look at the first one here, and the second one in the next section.

To avoid accidentally eliminating the correct answer, we recommend a thought exercise called **the $5 challenge**. In this challenge, you only eliminate an answer choice from contention if you are willing to bet $5 on it being wrong. Why $5? Five dollars is a small but not insignificant amount of money. It's an amount you could afford to lose but wouldn't want to throw away. And while losing $5 once might not hurt too much, doing it twenty times will set you back $100. In the same way, each small decision you make—eliminating a choice here, guessing on a question there—won't by itself impact your score very much, but when you put them all together, they can make a big difference. By holding each answer choice elimination decision to a higher standard, you can reduce the risk of accidentally eliminating the correct answer.

The $5 challenge can also be applied in a positive sense: If you are willing to bet $5 that an answer choice *is* correct, go ahead and mark it as correct.

Summary: Only eliminate an answer choice if you are willing to bet $5 that it is wrong.

Which Answer to Choose

You're taking the test. You've run into a hard question and decided you'll have to guess. You've eliminated all the answer choices you're willing to bet $5 on. Now you have to pick an answer. Why do we even need to talk about this? Why can't you just pick whichever one you feel like when the time comes?

The answer to these questions is that if you don't come into the test with a plan, you'll rely on your impression to select an answer choice, and if you do that, you risk falling into a trap. The test writers know that everyone who takes their test will be guessing on some of the questions, so they intentionally write wrong answer choices to seem plausible. You still have to pick an answer though, and if the wrong answer choices are designed to look right, how can you ever be sure that you're not falling for their trap? The best solution we've found to this dilemma is to take the decision out of your hands entirely. Here is the process we recommend:

Once you've eliminated any choices that you are confident (willing to bet $5) are wrong, select the first remaining choice as your answer.

Whether you choose to select the first remaining choice, the second, or the last, the important thing is that you use some preselected standard. Using this approach guarantees that you will not be enticed into selecting an answer choice that looks right, because you are not basing your decision on how the answer choices look.

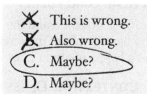

This is not meant to make you question your knowledge. Instead, it is to help you recognize the difference between your knowledge and your impressions. There's a huge difference between thinking an answer is right because of what you know, and thinking an answer is right because it looks or sounds like it should be right.

Summary: To ensure that your selection is appropriately random, make a predetermined selection from among all answer choices you have not eliminated.

Test-Taking Strategies

This section contains a list of test-taking strategies that you may find helpful as you work through the test. By taking what you know and applying logical thought, you can maximize your chances of answering any question correctly!

It is very important to realize that every question is different and every person is different: no single strategy will work on every question, and no single strategy will work for every person. That's why we've included all of them here, so you can try them out and determine which ones work best for different types of questions and which ones work best for you.

Question Strategies

☑ READ CAREFULLY

Read the question and the answer choices carefully. Don't miss the question because you misread the terms. You have plenty of time to read each question thoroughly and make sure you understand what is being asked. Yet a happy medium must be attained, so don't waste too much time. You must read carefully and efficiently.

☑ CONTEXTUAL CLUES

Look for contextual clues. If the question includes a word you are not familiar with, look at the immediate context for some indication of what the word might mean. Contextual clues can often give you all the information you need to decipher the meaning of an unfamiliar word. Even if you can't determine the meaning, you may be able to narrow down the possibilities enough to make a solid guess at the answer to the question.

☑ PREFIXES

If you're having trouble with a word in the question or answer choices, try dissecting it. Take advantage of every clue that the word might include. Prefixes can be a huge help. Usually, they allow you to determine a basic meaning. *Pre-* means before, *post-* means after, *pro-* is positive, *de-* is negative. From prefixes, you can get an idea of the general meaning of the word and try to put it into context.

☑ HEDGE WORDS

Watch out for critical hedge words, such as *likely, may, can, sometimes, often, almost, mostly, usually, generally, rarely,* and *sometimes*. Question writers insert these hedge phrases to cover every possibility. Often an answer choice will be wrong simply because it leaves no room for exception. Be on guard for answer choices that have definitive words such as *exactly* and *always*.

☑ SWITCHBACK WORDS

Stay alert for *switchbacks*. These are the words and phrases frequently used to alert you to shifts in thought. The most common switchback words are *but, although,* and *however*. Others include *nevertheless, on the other hand, even though, while, in spite of, despite,* and *regardless of*. Switchback words are important to catch because they can change the direction of the question or an answer choice.

☑ FACE VALUE

When in doubt, use common sense. Accept the situation in the problem at face value. Don't read too much into it. These problems will not require you to make wild assumptions. If you have to go beyond creativity and warp time or space in order to have an answer choice fit the question, then you should move on and consider the other answer choices. These are normal problems rooted in reality. The applicable relationship or explanation may not be readily apparent, but it is there for you to figure out. Use your common sense to interpret anything that isn't clear.

Answer Choice Strategies

☑ ANSWER SELECTION

The most thorough way to pick an answer choice is to identify and eliminate wrong answers until only one is left, then confirm it is the correct answer. Sometimes an answer choice may immediately seem right, but be careful. The test writers will usually put more than one reasonable answer choice on each question, so take a second to read all of them and make sure that the other choices are not equally obvious. As long as you have time left, it is better to read every answer choice than to pick the first one that looks right without checking the others.

☑ ANSWER CHOICE FAMILIES

An answer choice family consists of two (in rare cases, three) answer choices that are very similar in construction and cannot all be true at the same time. If you see two answer choices that are direct opposites or parallels, one of them is usually the correct answer. For instance, if one answer choice says that quantity x increases and another either says that quantity x decreases (opposite) or says that quantity y increases (parallel), then those answer choices would fall into the same family. An answer choice that doesn't match the construction of the answer choice family is more likely to be incorrect. Most questions will not have answer choice families, but when they do appear, you should be prepared to recognize them.

☑ ELIMINATE ANSWERS

Eliminate answer choices as soon as you realize they are wrong, but make sure you consider all possibilities. If you are eliminating answer choices and realize that the last one you are left with is also wrong, don't panic. Start over and consider each choice again. There may be something you missed the first time that you will realize on the second pass.

☑ AVOID FACT TRAPS

Don't be distracted by an answer choice that is factually true but doesn't answer the question. You are looking for the choice that answers the question. Stay focused on what the question is asking for so you don't accidentally pick an answer that is true but incorrect. Always go back to the question and make sure the answer choice you've selected actually answers the question and is not merely a true statement.

☑ EXTREME STATEMENTS

In general, you should avoid answers that put forth extreme actions as standard practice or proclaim controversial ideas as established fact. An answer choice that states the "process should be used in certain situations, if..." is much more likely to be correct than one that states the "process should be discontinued completely." The first is a calm rational statement and doesn't even make a definitive, uncompromising stance, using a hedge word *if* to provide wiggle room, whereas the second choice is far more extreme.

☑ BENCHMARK

As you read through the answer choices and you come across one that seems to answer the question well, mentally select that answer choice. This is not your final answer, but it's the one that will help you evaluate the other answer choices. The one that you selected is your benchmark or standard for judging each of the other answer choices. Every other answer choice must be compared to your benchmark. That choice is correct until proven otherwise by another answer choice beating it. If you find a better answer, then that one becomes your new benchmark. Once you've decided that no other choice answers the question as well as your benchmark, you have your final answer.

☑ PREDICT THE ANSWER

Before you even start looking at the answer choices, it is often best to try to predict the answer. When you come up with the answer on your own, it is easier to avoid distractions and traps because you will know exactly what to look for. The right answer choice is unlikely to be word-for-word what you came up with, but it should be a close match. Even if you are confident that you have the right answer, you should still take the time to read each option before moving on.

General Strategies

☑ TOUGH QUESTIONS

If you are stumped on a problem or it appears too hard or too difficult, don't waste time. Move on! Remember though, if you can quickly check for obviously incorrect answer choices, your chances of guessing correctly are greatly improved. Before you completely give up, at least try to knock out a couple of possible answers. Eliminate what you can and then guess at the remaining answer choices before moving on.

☑ CHECK YOUR WORK

Since you will probably not know every term listed and the answer to every question, it is important that you get credit for the ones that you do know. Don't miss any questions through careless mistakes. If at all possible, try to take a second to look back over your answer selection and make sure you've selected the correct answer choice and haven't made a costly careless mistake (such as marking an answer choice that you didn't mean to mark). This quick double check should more than pay for itself in caught mistakes for the time it costs.

☑ PACE YOURSELF

It's easy to be overwhelmed when you're looking at a page full of questions; your mind is confused and full of random thoughts, and the clock is ticking down faster than you would like. Calm down and maintain the pace that you have set for yourself. Especially as you get down to the last few minutes of the test, don't let the small numbers on the clock make you panic. As long as you are on track by monitoring your pace, you are guaranteed to have time for each question.

☑ DON'T RUSH

It is very easy to make errors when you are in a hurry. Maintaining a fast pace in answering questions is pointless if it makes you miss questions that you would have gotten right otherwise. Test writers like to include distracting information and wrong answers that seem right. Taking a little extra time to avoid careless mistakes can make all the difference in your test score. Find a pace that allows you to be confident in the answers that you select.

☑ KEEP MOVING

Panicking will not help you pass the test, so do your best to stay calm and keep moving. Taking deep breaths and going through the answer elimination steps you practiced can help to break through a stress barrier and keep your pace.

Final Notes

The combination of a solid foundation of content knowledge and the confidence that comes from practicing your plan for applying that knowledge is the key to maximizing your performance on test day. As your foundation of content knowledge is built up and strengthened, you'll find that the strategies included in this chapter become more and more effective in helping you quickly sift through the distractions and traps of the test to isolate the correct answer.

Now that you're preparing to move forward into the test content chapters of this book, be sure to keep your goal in mind. As you read, think about how you will be able to apply this information on the test. If you've already seen sample questions for the test and you have an idea of the question format and style, try to come up with questions of your own that you can answer based on what you're reading. This will give you valuable practice applying your knowledge in the same ways you can expect to on test day.

Good luck and good studying!

Four-Week SHRM-CP Study Plan

On the next few pages, we've provided an optional study plan to help you use this study guide to its fullest potential over the course of four weeks. If you have eight weeks available and want to spread it out more, spend two weeks on each section of the plan.

Below is a quick summary of the subjects covered in each week of the plan.

- Week 1: Behavioral Competencies: Leadership, Interpersonal, and Business
- Week 2: HR Expertise: People
- Week 3: HR Expertise: Organization and Workplace
- Week 4: Practice Tests

Please note that not all subjects will take the same amount of time to work through.

Two full-length practice tests are included in this study guide. We recommend saving any additional practice tests until after you've completed the study plan. Take these practice tests without any reference materials a day or two before the real thing as practice runs to get you in the mode of answering questions at a good pace.

Week 1: Behavioral Competencies: Leadership, Interpersonal, and Business

INSTRUCTIONAL CONTENT

First, read carefully through the Behavioral Competencies: Leadership, Interpersonal, and Business chapters in this book, checking off your progress as you go:

- ❏ Leadership and Navigation
- ❏ Ethical Practice
- ❏ Diversity, Equity, and Inclusion
- ❏ Relationship Management
- ❏ Communication
- ❏ Global Mindset
- ❏ Business Acumen
- ❏ Consultation
- ❏ Analytical Aptitude

As you read, do the following:

- Highlight any sections, terms, or concepts you think are important
- Draw an asterisk (*) next to any areas you are struggling with
- Watch the review videos to gain more understanding of a particular topic
- Take notes in your notebook or in the margins of this book

After you've read through everything, go back and review any sections that you highlighted or that you drew an asterisk next to, referencing your notes along the way.

14

Week 2: HR Expertise: People

INSTRUCTIONAL CONTENT

First, read carefully through the HR Expertise: People chapter in this book, checking off your progress as you go:

- ❏ HR Strategic Planning
- ❏ Talent Acquisition
- ❏ Employee Engagement and Retention
- ❏ Learning and Development
- ❏ Total Rewards

As you read, do the following:

- Highlight any sections, terms, or concepts you think are important
- Draw an asterisk (*) next to any areas you are struggling with
- Watch the review videos to gain more understanding of a particular topic
- Take notes in your notebook or in the margins of this book

After you've read through everything, go back and review any sections that you highlighted or that you drew an asterisk next to, referencing your notes along the way.

Week 3: HR Expertise: Organization and Workplace

INSTRUCTIONAL CONTENT

First, read carefully through the HR Expertise: Organization and Workplace chapters in this book, checking off your progress as you go:

- ❏ Structure of the HR Function
- ❏ Organizational Effectiveness and Development
- ❏ Workforce Management
- ❏ Employee and Labor Relations
- ❏ Technology Management
- ❏ Managing a Global Workforce
- ❏ Risk Management
- ❏ Corporate Social Responsibility
- ❏ US Employment Law and Regulations

As you read, do the following:

- Highlight any sections, terms, or concepts you think are important
- Draw an asterisk (*) next to any areas you are struggling with
- Watch the review videos to gain more understanding of a particular topic
- Take notes in your notebook or in the margins of this book

After you've read through everything, go back and review any sections that you highlighted or that you drew an asterisk next to, referencing your notes along the way.

Week 4: Practice Tests

Your success on test day depends not only on how many hours you put into preparing, but also on whether you prepared the right way. It's good to check along the way to see if your studying is paying off. One of the most effective ways to do this is by taking practice tests to evaluate your progress. Practice tests are useful because they show exactly where you need to improve. Every time you take a practice test, pay special attention to these three groups of questions:

- The questions you got wrong
- The questions you had to guess on, even if you guessed right
- The questions you found difficult or slow to work through

This will show you exactly what your weak areas are, and where you need to devote more study time. Ask yourself why each of these questions gave you trouble. Was it because you didn't understand the material? Was it because you didn't remember the vocabulary? Do you need more repetitions on this type of question to build speed and confidence? Dig into those questions and figure out how you can strengthen your weak areas as you go back to review the material.

PRACTICE TEST #1

Now that you've read over the instructional content, it's time to take a practice test. Complete Practice Test #1. Take this test with **no time constraints**, and feel free to reference the applicable sections of this guide as you go. Once you've finished, check your answers against the provided answer key. For any questions you answered incorrectly, review the answer rationale, and then **go back and review** the applicable sections of the book. The goal in this stage is to understand why you answered the question incorrectly, and make sure that the next time you see a similar question, you will get it right.

PRACTICE TEST #2

Next, complete Practice Test #2. This time, give yourself **3 hours and 40 minutes** to complete all of the questions. You should again feel free to reference the guide and your notes, but be mindful of the clock. If you run out of time before you finish all of the questions, mark where you were when time expired, but go ahead and finish taking the practice test. Once you've finished, check your answers against the provided answer key, and as before, review the answer rationale for any that you answered incorrectly and then go back and review the associated instructional content. Your goal is still to increase understanding of the content but also to get used to the time constraints you will face on the test.

As you go along, keep in mind that the practice test is just that: practice. Memorizing these questions and answers will not be very helpful on the actual test because it is unlikely to have any of the same exact questions. If you only know the right answers to the sample questions, you won't be prepared for the real thing. **Study the concepts** until you understand them fully, and then you'll be able to answer any question that shows up on the test.

Behavioral Competencies: Leadership

Leadership and Navigation

LEADERSHIP THEORIES

SITUATIONAL LEADERSHIP

A leader should consider the circumstances and his or her followers when planning and making decisions. To remain effective, a leader's style must adapt to the situation. **Situational leadership** is rooted in this adaptability—the theory purports that there is no universally applicable way to lead. Depending on the circumstances and the maturity and ability of the team, a leader may lead by directing, engaging, collaborating, or delegating.

INCLUSIVE LEADERSHIP

A leader should promote an atmosphere of respect, in which all employees have equal ability to share and utilize the skills they bring to the organization. It requires a willingness to listen with understanding and an ability to communicate with diverse populations across differences. **Inclusive leadership** requires remaining conscious of cultural values while bridging behavioral gaps and leveraging differences to increase performance. Some leadership traits that encourage inclusion are empowerment, accountability, courage, and humility. Inclusive leaders will do the following:

- Support staff development
- Demonstrate confidence
- Hold employees accountable
- Set personal interests aside
- Act on convictions and principles
- Admit mistakes
- Learn from criticism
- Seek contributions from others

PARTICIPATIVE LEADERSHIP

When a leader allows all employees to be fully informed and involved in the operations of the organization, he or she is demonstrating **participative leadership**. This type of leadership can be achieved by supporting employees when they make mistakes, treating them with consideration and respect, inviting them to recommend innovative ideas and suggestions, and providing training and development opportunities to help them advance.

TRANSFORMATIONAL LEADERSHIP

A leader should champion a shared vision with employees. **Transformational leadership** requires changing the attitudes and assumptions of the team while building commitment to the organization's mission, objectives, and strategies. Leaders inspire awareness of and dedication to the group's mission. Followers are empowered by facts, resources, and support so that they can then approach work in a committed, concerned, and involved way.

A transformational leader must be:

- **Charismatic:** gains buy-in for the vision and mission, earns respect and trust, and instills pride
- **Inspirational:** communicates heightened performance expectations and encourages big-picture thinking

17

- **Intellectually stimulating:** promotes learning and development and advocates for the use of logic and reason to solve problems
- **Considerate of individuality:** coaches followers, treats each person individually, and provides followers with personal attention

THEORY X AND THEORY Y OF LEADERSHIP

Douglas McGregor described two contrasting ways for leaders to view employees: Theory X and Theory Y. When a leader subscribes to **Theory X**, he or she sees employees as lazy and only motivated by disciplinary action. Conversely, when a leader believes in **Theory Y**, he or she views employees as willing, hard workers who only need to be shown the importance of their work to facilitate continued motivation.

PEOPLE MANAGEMENT

There are four stages of **people management**: directing, coaching, supporting, and delegating. **Directing** involves limited flexibility for the employee and is characterized by defining, planning, teaching, and monitoring. Individuals in this learning stage have high commitment but minimal skills, and need clear standards, goals, and timelines with regular feedback. **Coaching** involves supportive direction characterized by praise, encouragement, prioritizing, and feedback. Individuals in this stage have some commitment and skills but still need recognition and feedback while they try to develop more-effective ways to perform tasks. **Supporting** involves even less specific direction, and is characterized by listening, collaborating, and appreciating. Individuals in this stage are more confident, skilled, and self-reliant problem-solvers. **Delegating** involves a lot of flexibility with little direction, and is characterized by trusting, empowering, acknowledging, and challenging. Individuals in this final stage have high commitment and excellent skills. They are ready for trust, responsibility, authority, variety, and challenges.

MOTIVATION THEORIES
EXTRINSIC AND INTRINSIC MOTIVATION

Motivation is what propels a person to behave in a certain way.

Extrinsic motivation is derived from external factors. People can be externally motivated by money, gifts, and recognition.

Intrinsic motivation is derived from a person's own thoughts and beliefs. People can be internally motivated by the feeling of achievement, the excitement of learning something new, or their competitive nature.

TAYLOR'S SCIENTIFIC MANAGEMENT

Frederick Taylor ran a series of experiments within a manufacturing setting to better understand the nature of work. He found that people could be motivated by their working conditions and noted that employers should provide adequate safety measures, lighting, and tools to do the work. He concluded that employees will change their behavior when they know they are being observed.

SKINNER'S OPERANT CONDITIONING

B. F. Skinner contended that motivation is based on extrinsic factors such as reward and punishment. Employers can influence behavior through either positive reinforcement or negative reinforcement, which results in employees acting in certain ways to receive prizes or to avoid discipline.

MASLOW'S HIERARCHY OF NEEDS

Abraham Maslow said that people have a variety of **needs** that must be met in a particular order: physiological, safety, social, esteem, and self-actualization. **Physiological** needs are tied to the body, like taking care of thirst. **Safety** needs are based on having adequate shelter from harm. **Social** needs involve feeling a sense of acceptance by peers. **Esteem** needs entail feeling respected by peers. Last, **self-actualization** needs are tied to

feeling fulfilled by one's life. Maslow contended that lower-level needs have to be met first. For example, if someone is unsafe, he or she will not be concerned with feeling respected.

Review Video: <u>Maslow's Hierarchy of Needs</u>
Visit mometrix.com/academy and enter code: 461825

HERZBERG'S MOTIVATOR HYGIENE THEORY

Herzberg stated that an employee's motivation is affected by both hygiene factors and motivators. **Hygiene factors** are extrinsic, and include salary, benefits, and work environment. **Motivators** are intrinsic, and include growth and recognition. Both hygiene factors and motivators play roles in whether a person feels satisfied in his or her job; hygiene factors are also called **job dissatisfiers**, and motivators are also called **job satisfiers**.

Herzberg learned that job satisfaction and dissatisfaction are independent of one another. In other words, removing causes of dissatisfaction doesn't necessarily lead to job satisfaction. Similarly, adding causes of job satisfaction does not necessarily negate job dissatisfaction. For example, if an employee is underpaid and the work is dreadfully boring, the employee will still be dissatisfied even if given a substantial raise. The employee, although better paid, will still work in a role that has no room for growth. In essence, to keep employees satisfied with their jobs, employers need to eliminate the hygiene factor issues and increase the presence of motivators.

McCLELLAND'S ACQUIRED NEEDS THEORY

David McClelland saw motivation as primarily intrinsic and said that it arises from three main needs: achievement, affiliation, and power. The need for **achievement** involves embracing challenges, being goal-oriented, and taking calculated risks. The need for **affiliation** involves wanting to belong, yearning to be liked, and focusing on collaboration over competition. The need for **power** involves wanting to influence others, being competitive, and striving to attain a high status. Employees could be motivated by a blend of these needs. For example, an employee may be achievement-oriented and still want to be liked.

LOCKE'S GOAL-SETTING THEORY

Dr. Edwin Locke developed a **goal-setting theory** for motivation in the 1960s. Locke's research led him to conclude that employees are driven by explicit, measurable **goals** that are challenging but attainable. Locke suggested that if employees take part in **collaboratively** setting goals and objectives, they will be more vested in attaining those goals. However, individuals who have an internal drive may be more likely to succeed. Locke also noted that providing **feedback** to employees is critical. Locke tied goal-setting to task performance because having goals energizes employees and assists them with handling specific situations that arise. According to Locke, attaining a goal should provide both intrinsic and extrinsic **rewards** that result in employee satisfaction.

VROOM'S EXPECTANCY THEORY

Victor Vroom's **expectancy theory** assumes that rationality will drive employees toward the option that provides maximum pleasure and minimal pain. Although he noted that performance strength may be determined by an individual's personality, knowledge, experiences, skills, and abilities, Vroom believed that increased effort will eventually lead to better performance as long as employees have the tools necessary to get the job done. Moreover, employees will be motivated if they believe that favorable performance will return a desired reward, which will satisfy an important need and thus make the effort worthwhile. Vroom created the following formula to describe expectancy theory: Expectancy × Instrumentality × Valence = Motivation

Expectancy is the belief that one's best efforts will yield good performance. **Instrumentality** is the belief that good performance will yield a particular result. **Valence** is the value of an outcome to a given employee; this will fluctuate, as not all employees are motivated by the same things at the same time. If any of the multipliers are low, then the resulting **motivation** will also be low.

ATTRIBUTION THEORY

Fritz Heider's **attribution theory**, which was further developed by Bernard Weiner, identifies ability, effort, task difficulty, and luck as the most important factors for achieving success. This theory can help identify the root causes of an individual's behavior or performance. **Attribution** consists of **three stages**: 1) observing behavior, 2) determining whether the behavior is deliberate, and 3) concluding whether the behavior is due to internal or external factors. The **locus of causality** identifies outcomes based on internal controls such as ability and effort as well as external factors such as task difficulty and luck. The **locus of stability** identifies outcomes based on fixed, stable factors such as ability and task difficulty, along with variable factors such as effort and luck. Correctly identifying the source or rationale behind employees' behavior can help leaders effectively motivate them.

SELF-DETERMINATION THEORY

Based on work by Edward L. Deci and Richard M. Ryan, **self-determination theory** identifies three core intrinsic motivators: autonomy, competence, and relatedness. **Autonomy** in this context focuses on self-initiation and regulating one's behavior toward task selection, organization, and completion. **Competence** involves mastery of skills required to complete the work and interact with the environment effectively. **Relatedness** involves attachment to and a sense of belongingness within a group. Leaders should give employees opportunities to make decisions about their work, sharpen their skills, and connect with others in the organization whenever possible. Doing so will increase their internal drive and promote psychological wellness.

JOB CHARACTERISTICS MODEL

Richard Hackman and Greg Oldham found that five **job characteristics** affect job performance and satisfaction: task identity, task significance, skill variety, autonomy, and feedback. **Task identity** is when employees can see how their roles affect the entire organization so that they no longer feel like they operate in isolation. This knowledge can lead to greater job satisfaction. **Task significance** is when employees can understand the larger impacts of their work on other people or society, which can also lead to greater job satisfaction. **Skill variety** is when employees can use many different skills in their work, which reinforces that the job is important. **Autonomy** is when employees receive their manager's trust and have leeway in decision-making. This empowerment typically leads to higher levels of employee engagement and job satisfaction. **Feedback** is when employees receive commentary on their performance, enabling them to improve or encouraging them to stay the course. Regular feedback can also lead to higher levels of employee engagement and job satisfaction.

INFLUENCE AND PERSUASION TECHNIQUES

PERSONAL APPEAL

The **personal appeal** technique involves eliciting emotion to prompt behavior. It entails using strong language that conjures up specific imagery designed to lead the communication's recipient into making a certain decision or taking a certain action. If the recipient is more factually driven, this technique may not be as effective.

FORMING COALITIONS

The technique of **forming coalitions** is useful when a shared goal is identified. Like-minded people within an organization can come together to fight for or against a current cause. Their individual voices will carry more weight as a unified group, increasing the chance that they will achieve the desired outcome.

RATIONAL PERSUASION

Using **rational persuasion** involves employing facts, figures, and logic as the basis for an argument or case. It appeals to someone on a cognitive, rational level. A person who uses rational persuasion tries to garner consensus based on what is factually correct. If the recipient is more emotionally driven, this technique may not be as effective.

LEADING BY EXAMPLE

A leader that is **leading by example** models the attitudes, words, and behaviors that they would like to see exhibited by their followers. It shows the followers that the leader is not "above" doing what they are required to do and, in fact, personally endorses the task. Although this technique is somewhat indirect, followers may emulate the leader for a variety of reasons. They could admire the leader, fear retribution for not following, or desire to be on the "right" side of corporate policies, to name a few. Regardless of individual motivations, leading by example sets the tone for the team.

PERSONAL LEADERSHIP QUALITIES

VISION

A strong leader has **vision,** which is the ability to plan and to think about the future with imagination, determination, wisdom, and calculation. Having a clear idea of the desired destination or outcome allows leaders to consider challenges that may arise and how to respond to them. This helps maintain focus even when facing a potential issue. A path toward reaching goals is defined. Brainstorming, planning, and guidelines are then established to meet those goals. A visionary leader motivates others to challenge their thinking and their own plans. Vision provides purpose in tasks and activities, and creates meaning in things being done, answering the "why" behind various activities. Without vision, direction and motivation must be externally derived.

SELF-MOTIVATION

The ability to find passion for and interest in a particular goal or task and using that passion and interest as the driving force to accomplish the goal or task is called **self-motivation**. Self-motivation is most often driven by **intrinsic motivation** but can also be driven by **extrinsic motivation**. Self-motivation is a key leadership quality because those who are self-motivated do not rely on external motivation to get things accomplished. It is a beneficial quality, as it allows the individual to work harder in areas of interest because they have a desire to be better. Self-motivation is more fulfilling than purely external motivation, and can lead to a more-positive outlook on accomplishments and successes.

SELF-DISCIPLINE

The ability to stay motivated, be actionable, and continue forward despite the obstacles that may appear is known as **self-discipline**. Essentially, self-discipline means being able to do things that should be done, even when doing them is not desired. It is the determination and commitment needed to keep putting in the effort to accomplish an outcome. Self-discipline is critical in achieving goals because obstacles will arise, and self-discipline provides the "grit" needed to overcome the obstacles. This skill is highly important for leaders, because while different initiatives and challenges may seem daunting or impossible, a high level of self-discipline allows the individual to persevere and achieve the desired result. Leaders do not always have people behind them pushing them forward, so having the ability to push oneself forward is an important skill.

RISK-TAKING

Making progress and achieving goals often require an individual to take risks. Strong leaders understand that risks must be taken in order to move forward and be innovative. Taking risks requires making bold decisions, accepting uncertainty, and, at times, entering the unknown. Leaders will take calculated risks, which means that they consider the potential outcomes, costs, and benefits of the action. **Risk-taking** develops creativity, fosters an environment of continuous learning, and allows for the individual or team to adapt to changes. Risk-taking requires flexibility and being open to the possibility of failure.

COMMITMENT TO CONTINUOUS LEARNING

The ongoing practice of gaining new knowledge and developing skills and competencies through various formats, like education and training, is known as **continuous learning**. Having a strong commitment to continuous learning helps a person to develop different perspectives, adapt to unexpected changes, build confidence and capability, and find innovative approaches. Markets, technology, sociopolitical climates, and

21

ways of working are constantly changing and evolving. Continuous learning helps leaders stay ahead of changing trends and continue to push for success and achievement.

GROWTH MINDSET

Individuals with a **growth mindset** believe that skills, talents, and abilities can be developed and improved over time, with work and effort. Those with a growth mindset view challenges as opportunities rather than roadblocks. They are motivated to improve to reach a goal. They persist in their efforts and see that failure is part of learning and growing. This skill is particularly important for leaders, for whom resilience and motivation are key when faced with challenges or setbacks. The effort and positivity displayed through a growth mindset can facilitate effort and dedication among coworkers. Leaders with a growth mindset also foster an environment of collaboration where both efforts and successes are recognized. Team members are challenged to reach their highest levels of potential.

NAVIGATING THE ORGANIZATION

UNDERSTANDING THE ORGANIZATION'S POLITICAL ENVIRONMENT AND CULTURE

Every organization has its own distinct culture and political environment. **Organizational culture** can be described as the beliefs, values, communication patterns, rules, and shared assumptions that guide behaviors and actions in the workplace. Company culture can provide meaning and satisfaction to current employees and can be leveraged to attract talent. Culture can increase productivity and engagement, increasing the bottom line for the company. Companies also have distinct **political environments**. The political environment can be an important recruiting piece as well, because individuals who align with the political environment of an organization will more strongly desire employment with the company. It can also improve retention because employees will feel more value in working for an organization that shares their political values or contributes to the world in a meaningful way. Understanding the culture and political environment of the organization is important in accurately explaining what the company does and what it stands for, aiding with talent acquisition and reduction in turnover.

MANAGING HUMAN RESOURCE INITIATIVES

RESOURCE ALLOCATION AND PROJECT NEEDS

When beginning a project, a detailed project plan containing information about the **project needs**, budget, scheduling, and **resource allocation** should be created. Breaking the plan into smaller sections or phases may help make it more manageable. Once the plan is created and the project begins, the plan should be closely tracked and monitored. There are many areas of potential difficulties with resource allocation, including employee absences, multiple projects happening at once, equipment downtime, and snags with project supplies. Tracking the project plan can help with identifying a resource issue early on, allowing time to make changes to the plan or reorganize resources. The deadline and budget usually cannot be modified much, so an efficient project manager must be able to determine which resources can be stretched or moved to meet the project needs. Tracking and analyzing will continue through the life of the project, and several adjustments may be needed.

INFLUENCE

ADVANCING THE ORGANIZATION'S STRATEGIC GOALS

The role of human resources (HR) involves a balance between serving employees and protecting the needs of the business. HR should also serve to **advance the strategic goals and objectives of the organization**. HR may identify high-potential employees that can be developed and promoted into leadership roles to help move the organization toward those strategic objectives. This could also include designing or implementing different training and education activities in order to develop staff toward meeting goals. HR can also help guide departments and employees toward meeting specific metrics, such as reduced absenteeism or increased contact with customers, which will help guide the organization toward specific strategy goals. HR can be a strong strategic and thought partner, so working with various departments and levels of management can help ensure that organizational objectives are being met.

Ethical Practice

Ethics are the moral principles, values, and accepted standards of behavior that determine whether an action is right or wrong. The Society for Human Resource Management (SHRM) Competency Model defines **ethical practice** as "the knowledge, skills, abilities, and other characteristics needed to maintain high levels of personal and professional integrity and to act as an ethical agent who promotes core values, integrity, and accountability throughout the organization."

ETHICAL BUSINESS PRINCIPLES AND PRACTICES

TRANSPARENCY

Freely sharing nonconfidential information results in better-informed and more-engaged employees. Most employees appreciate when management is forthcoming with information such as healthcare costs, pay increase schedules, or future changes on the horizon. **Transparency** may be a tool for removing obstacles to diversity, as employees will be better able to understand one another. Being transparent and openly communicating with staff during decision-making processes can also build employee trust and be leveraged as a recruiting or retention tool. Various sources on the internet now provide job seekers with transparent information about a company's culture, benefits, average pay, and interview process. It is always better for employees to hear this information directly from the employer so that the firm can ensure accuracy and address any questions or concerns head-on.

AUTHENTICITY

Although it can have various definitions, at its core **authenticity** means remaining true to one's own values, personality, and goals despite whatever external pressures may exist to appear otherwise. This means being genuine, honest, and accountable, and acting in accordance with one's own beliefs. Authentic individuals demonstrate integrity and confidence in their decisions, because they do what they believe is right. Authentic individuals have a high level of control and realization of potential, because they dictate their own choices and actions versus letting others drive decision-making. Authenticity inspires trust through displaying consistency and openness. Open communication and transparency are byproducts of authenticity that help foster more-collaborative working environments.

CONFLICTS OF INTEREST

A **conflict of interest** occurs when someone with a responsibility to act in the best interest of the company may also be in a position to derive personal benefit at the expense of the company. Situations that involve a conflict of interests include:

- Utilizing company resources for personal financial gain
- Forming relationships or obligations that compromise objectivity when conducting duties
- Disclosing company information to interfere with bidding, negotiating, or contracting
- Exerting influence in business transactions that benefit the individual or a relative
- Traveling at vendors' or customers' expense
- Accepting gifts, services, or favors from company stakeholders

Conflicts of interest should be avoided. Clear policies regarding conflicts of interest should be in place, and all employees should be held to them.

PRIVACY PRINCIPLES AND PRACTICES

With technology now a part of every business transaction, it is essential that companies and employees adhere to strict confidentiality practices and **privacy principles**. From monitoring employees to asking interview questions, employers need to take care to avoid invading personal privacy. Legal regulations that inform best practices and internal privacy policies should be consulted regularly for guidance. In addition, companies should consider implementing **confidentiality or nondisclosure agreements** so that employees are aware

23

that databases, client lists, and other proprietary information must be protected and that the sharing of these records externally is strictly prohibited.

CONFIDENTIALITY

Keeping employees' private information private is vital in human resource (HR) practices. Maintaining the **confidentiality** of all employee records is imperative. Information to be safeguarded includes, but is not limited to, Social Security numbers, birth dates, addresses, phone numbers, personal email addresses, benefits enrollments, medical or leave details, garnishments, bank account information, disciplinary actions, grievances, and employment eligibility data. When employee record information is requested for legitimate purposes, a written release signed by the employee should be obtained and kept on file. Examples of these requests include employment verification for bank loans or mortgage applications.

Further, HR should internally disclose this sensitive data only to those who are authorized and if the scenario at hand is appropriate. For example, a supervisor should have knowledge of employees' disciplinary histories so that he or she can manage them more effectively. However, that supervisor does not need to know what benefit plan an employee elected or that an employee has a tax lien.

However, HR cannot always promise complete confidentiality. For example, if an employee makes an allegation of harassment, HR will move to investigate immediately. HR should inform the complainant and anyone involved in the investigation that the situation will be handled as discreetly as possible; however, the nature of an investigation dictates that information obtained during the process may be shared with third parties, including the accused, on a need-to-know basis.

COMMUNICATING SENSITIVE INFORMATION

Personal data or information that could possibly cause embarrassment, harm, or discrimination if used or disclosed improperly is referred to as **sensitive information**. HR has access to a breadth of sensitive information, and may have to, at times, communicate some of that information with a third party. Using discretion while doing so is key. When such communication must occur, HR should verify with the individual what information they are comfortable disclosing, and in what forum. For example, if an employee has a medical condition that requires specific accommodation, there should be a conversation on what level of detail can be discussed with the employee's immediate supervisor or others who may be affected.

There are specific instances in which information may need to be shared despite an individual's wish to keep it confidential. For example, if an applicant has a criminal record that could potentially violate company policy, that information needs to be shared with the appropriate decision-makers. If an employee reveals an instance of harassment, the complaint requires investigation, and confidentiality may not be possible at all levels, HR needs to assure the employee that confidentiality and privacy will be maintained unless necessary, and in those instances the information will be revealed only to appropriate parties.

ANONYMITY

On the same idea as confidentiality, **anonymity** provides employees with the ability to partake in activities without their identities being disclosed. Employers may have employees take a survey or evaluate their managers anonymously to eliminate any fear of retaliation. Individuals may also anonymously report any complaint or ethics violation.

OPT-IN/OPT-OUT POLICIES

Opt-in and opt-out are both ways to gain consent for a particular policy. To **opt-in** requires a positive action to confirm consent, participation, or agreement. For example, an opt-in policy might require checking a box to acknowledge consent to a policy or procedure during digital onboarding. An **opt-out** policy requires an action to withdraw consent, participation, or agreement. An example of an opt-out policy is requiring employees to fill out a waiver when declining benefits coverage.

INTERNAL ETHICS CONTROLS
CODE OF CONDUCT

A **code of conduct** is a set of behavioral rules rooted in moral standards, laws, and best practices that a company develops, adopts, and communicates to employees. It outlines expected behavior as well as behavior that will not be tolerated. The document should also outline the disciplinary actions that employees could face if they violate the code of conduct.

Employee involvement in the development of a code of conduct leads to greater employee buy-in and adherence. The code should be written in ambiguous language that can be applied to specific situations as they arise. Once it is finalized, the code should be shared with all employees. Employees should then be required to sign a document acknowledging receipt and understanding of the new code.

PERSONAL INTEGRITY

A person who develops and sticks to an internal code of ethics that deems what is right and what is wrong is someone with **personal integrity**. Personal integrity is strengthened by choosing thoughts and actions that are based on moral principles and personal values. Some character traits of those with high personal integrity include honesty, trustworthiness, kindness, courageousness, respect, and loyalty. An example of personal integrity in action might be helping an elderly neighbor with yard work or home repairs, even when it might not be convenient. This type of behavior develops an individual's personal integrity and reputation. Those with high personal integrity are not generally motivated by popularity, nor are they compelled to seek ill-gotten gains. The stronger one's sense of personal integrity, the less likely one is to succumb to corruption.

PROFESSIONAL INTEGRITY

Choosing actions that adhere to moral principles and codes of ethics (both internal and organizationally imposed) while at work is known as **professional integrity**. It originates from an individual's personal integrity. Professional integrity avoids corruption or any potential conflicts of interest and develops professional credibility. An example of professional integrity in action might be telling the CEO that you made a major mistake, even though you will likely face sanctions. Professional integrity often leads to high professional standards, resulting in an increased quality of work. Moreover, leaders who demonstrate unyielding professional integrity frequently have a greater following of employees and customers.

PROTECTION OF EMPLOYEE CONFIDENTIALITY

The department of human resources (HR) keeps and is aware of a significant amount of **confidential information** about employees. To maintain confidentiality within the workplace, HR should complete occasional confidentiality training, which should be documented and updated as needed. Confidential employee information should be stored securely with limited access. For information stored physically, storage areas should be locked. For information stored digitally, restricted permissions should be set up with the information technology (IT) partner. Confidential information should be shared only on a need-to-know basis, at relevant levels. HR professionals should be able to communicate that when an individual comes to them with a concern or complaint, HR will keep that employee's information as confidential as possible. Disclosure of confidential information will only occur within the appropriate resolution process and should take place in the least invasive manner possible. HR practitioners should familiarize themselves with laws and regulations surrounding what information can be released and to whom. Because the role of HR involves balancing meeting the needs of the employee and protecting the organization, HR should be the ethical example throughout the organization.

STANDARDS FOR EMPLOYEE INVESTIGATIONS

Investigations into employee misconduct can have far-reaching consequences, and as such should be handled very carefully. Each HR department should have guidelines or a set process in place to handle **employee investigations** effectively to resolve the conflict and minimize damages. Investigations, when completed correctly, help protect both employees and the business by recognizing misconduct or misbehavior and allowing for unbiased and informed decision-making. Proper investigations can protect the employer from wrongful termination claims and other legal issues that can arise. The following guidelines can help HR conduct thorough and objective investigations:

- Begin an investigation as soon as the complaint or concern is brought to HR's attention. Timely action is key to collecting statements and evidence. In cases of harassment, acting quickly to separate the parties involved is critical. The level of separation needed depends on the severity of the claim.
- Select an individual to lead the investigation. This person should have some level of familiarity with investigations and should not be associated with either the person making the complaint or the person being complained about. The investigator should not be the same person who will determine the action that may result from the investigation. This helps ensure an objective and impartial resolution.
- The investigator should create a detailed plan for conducting the investigation. This should include a description of the issue, names of individuals who need to be interviewed, and steps to collect any additional evidence, like viewing surveillance camera footage or taking photographs. The investigator should also review company policies and procedures to determine which may have been violated. Part of the investigation plan must include telling the employee who is being investigated what is going on, why the investigation began, what the investigation will entail, and what the next steps may be.
- The investigator should begin each interview with specific and relevant questions that were prepared in advance. Important details to gather include what led up to the incident, when the incident occurred, how long the incident lasted, what physical proof exists of the incident, who else may have witnessed the incident, and a description of the incident.
- The investigator should fully document each step of the investigation. For all statements and interviews, he or she should list the date, time, and names of those present. Investigators can review the notes taken during the interview with the interviewee to ensure that information was recorded correctly. Witnesses who provide written statements should sign and date the documents.
- Once all of the interviews have been completed and evidence collected, the investigator should share all of the gathered information with the decision-maker and the individuals affected by the investigation. The investigator might provide applicable parties with a summary of the investigation that does not detail the statements from witnesses. This helps maintain confidentiality of those involved. From that point forward the decision-makers will determine the best course of action.
- After the investigation is complete, determine how to move forward. Organizational policy and past practice should be followed. Staff may need to be briefed on the general issues at hand and refreshed on related policies.

Communication following an investigation is critical, so that company expectations and potential consequences are clear going forward.

ETHICAL AGENTS

Ethics and compliance officers ensure that business is conducted in accordance with rules, legal regulations, and industry standards of practice. Additionally, an **ethical agent** makes moral judgments based on fundamental ethical principles that are rooted in his or her personal character, not a situation's potential gains. **Ethical dilemmas** occur when a corporation or individual is faced with a conflict of interest or actions that are blatantly wrong or deceptive or have uncertain consequences. Many ethical conflicts involve valuing profit over moral principles. Over the past few decades, ethics and business conduct have received increasing attention that has led to more stringent **compliance regulations**, like the Sarbanes-Oxley Act.

TRANSPARENCY FOR HUMAN RESOURCE PROGRAMS, PRACTICES, AND POLICIES

Not all audiences need to be completely informed about human resource (HR) initiatives, and not all information is of equal confidentiality. HR should be a transparent department—to a certain extent. In order to determine the correct level of **transparency** for various policies, programs, and practices, it is important to first assess the level of confidentiality involved. Reasons for termination, budgeting, and disciplinary actions may be more confidential and restricted than job opportunities or promotions. HR should work with senior management to determine how much of each initiative should be communicated out, as well as who should receive said communication. All employees should also know how to find open positions and what promotion opportunities are available. Policies on conduct such as harassment, discrimination, and whistleblowing should be highly shared, and all employees should understand and know how to report misconduct and what the process looks like. Individuals within an organization should also know what happens once a complaint is filed, or what happens during the raise process. HR should strive to be as transparent as possible, increasing accountability, improving trust, and building a stronger team, while respecting confidentiality and sensitive business issues.

CONFLICTS OF INTEREST AND ETHICAL RISKS

An understanding of business ethics and company policies can help individuals identify where possible **conflicts of interest** may exist. There should be a formal conflict-of-interest policy that outlines expectations and potential violations. The company should also have a reporting process for disclosing conflicts of interest. Once a potential conflict of interest has been reported or discovered, the policy needs to be reviewed to determine if the complaint is legitimate. If a complaint is verified, it should be escalated to the appropriate level(s) of the organization.

Ethical risks are the potential negative consequences stemming from unethical decisions and actions. An example of an ethical risk is an employee using the company credit card to make personal purchases. Companies should also have a detailed **code of ethics** with reporting guidelines. The same process should be followed if an ethical violation is reported as for a potential conflict of interest: investigate the accuracy of the complaint and then escalate accordingly. Conflict-of-interest and ethical violations can have serious repercussions, including loss of employment, so they need to be investigated and addressed thoroughly.

> **Review Video: <u>Ethical and Professional Standards</u>**
> Visit mometrix.com/academy and enter code: 391843

Diversity, Equity, and Inclusion

CHARACTERISTICS OF A DYNAMIC WORKFORCE

MULTIGENERATIONAL

A **multigenerational** workforce employs members that span a variety of generational cohorts, such as Baby Boomers, Gen X, Millennials, and Gen Z. Organizational teams that include members from different generations can benefit from differing workstyles and life experiences. Team members with more experience can help to share interpersonal wisdom, organizational knowledge, and consistency; team members who are newer to the workforce can help to share agile approaches, technology-based strategies, and collaborative feedback. However, this frame of thinking can also take away from team cohesion if one becomes too tied to the stereotypical characteristics that are often associated with different generations. When organization members make assumptions about other workers based on generational stereotypes, they can lose out on unrealized potential, create friction between team members, and possibly open themselves up to charges of discriminatory behavior in the workplace.

MULTICULTURAL

The diversity of thought that comes from a **multicultural** workforce can beget a diversity of solutions, innovation, creation, and desired business outcomes. This diversity of thought can aid in preventing **groupthink** and the risks associated with blind team compliance or agreement. Additionally, a multicultural workforce can be more effective when interacting with and attracting customers on a global scale and in an increasingly interconnected market. Diversity of thought that comes from a multicultural workforce is rooted in the constructive conflict of collaboration. This collaboration can be stifled if other team members exhibit narrow worldviews or resistance to change or opposing ideas. Different cultures can come with a variety of values, social norms, and business expectations that may lead to misunderstandings, disagreements, and hostility among team members from different backgrounds. Organizations can get ahead of these challenges through leadership commitment to diversity, effective communication, training programs, and policies and procedures adapted to support multicultural teams.

MULTILINGUAL

A **multilingual** workforce can be better equipped to communicate with a wide array of customers, business partners, and community members. In addition to reducing the costs associated with translation services, employing individuals who are able to speak languages other than English (especially Spanish, French, Korean, or Mandarin) can help to create higher-quality relationships with customers and partners whose native languages are not English. Multilingual employees can also help to bridge the gap not just between the languages themselves but between cultures as well. In addition to building improved relationships with both internal and external stakeholders, employees who speak more than one language may also bring enhanced creativity, problem-solving skills, and agility to the workforce.

MULTITALENTED

A **multitalented** workforce consists of individuals and teams who bring a variety of skills and abilities to the workplace instead of one specialized talent. For example, a graphic designer may also have a knack for spreadsheets and be highly skilled in communicating with unsatisfied customers. Also referred to as **multiskilled** or **multipurpose** employees, multitalented employees can help to improve the creativity, agility, and efficiency of an organization. In addition to recruiting multitalented teams and individuals, organizations can work to develop their current workforce through cross-departmental trainings, developmental opportunities with open enrollment or participation options, and the use of coaching leadership styles.

MULTIGENDERED

The effect of a **multigendered** workforce on an organization's performance can vary based on the organization's cultures and beliefs. The benefits associated with a multigendered workforce are more often found in organizations or industries where gender diversity is considered normal. Corporate cultures that value gender diversity are more likely to reap the benefits from it in terms of business performance and outcomes.

Diversity within the context of both multicultural and multigendered workforces can bring about diversity of thoughts, solutions, and positive outcomes, but individual beliefs and values regarding diversity must be taken into consideration before assuming that benefits will follow diversification efforts.

APPROACHES TO DEVELOPING AN INCLUSIVE WORKPLACE
EXECUTIVE SPONSORSHIP

A workforce that trusts its leaders and their commitment to creating an inclusive organization should develop an **executive sponsorship** program. As sponsors, executive team members can function in a multitude of roles: as mentors, advisors, strategic guides, networking connections, or loudspeakers. Additionally, it is critical for sponsors to understand the relationship between themselves and the team or individual seeking sponsorship, in order to most effectively support the diversity effort or project being championed. Executive sponsorship for diversity and inclusion initiatives can lend legitimacy, urgency, authority, visibility, and funds to the effort or project and improve its chances of success.

MENTORSHIP

A **mentorship** is an intentional relationship between two parties where the mentor, who is typically more experienced or skilled in some way, helps to advise, guide, and listen to a mentee, who is typically seeking to advance or develop in his or her professional or personal life. Within the context of **diversity, equity, and inclusion (DEI)**, mentorship can help to foster higher retention rates, job satisfaction, and job advancement among program participants who may not otherwise have had exposure to an individualized development experience. Mentoring can also help to open doors for mentees if they are connected with mentors who can help their mentees network and can advocate for their mentees as they grow within the organization. In addition to the traditional mentor-mentee construct, organizations can also support reverse mentoring and mentoring circles. In **reverse mentoring**, the mentor-mentee roles are reversed, so a more-senior employee learns from a newer or less-experienced team member; this mentoring relationship can help to push information regarding obstacles or challenges faced by entry-level employees up the chain. **Mentoring circles** help to promote learning, growth, and belonging and are composed of groups of individuals with comparable goals and experiences who work together to advance in their careers.

LEADERSHIP BUY-IN

Leaders can contribute to DEI in the workplace in a wide variety of ways. Executive sponsorship and mentorship can help to support and advance grassroots-driven DEI projects and efforts. Additionally, leaders play a critical role in designing an organization's guiding vision and the strategic plan that follows. **Leadership buy-in** to the importance of diversity to business outcomes leads to diversity being placed at the forefront of that vision. An organizational vision that celebrates diversity can cascade to strategy, goals, and rewards practices that advance DEI in the workplace. Leaders can also shoulder the responsibility of recognizing potential mistakes along the organization's history in an effort to promote transparency, humility, and honesty in business practices and workforce development.

Perhaps the most important responsibility of a leader seeking to advance diversity in the workforce is that of being a **role model**. Role modeling stretches across all other responsibilities in the way that a leader's actions align with their words; promoting education efforts, designing budgets to support DEI efforts, speaking out in support of underserved populations, asking questions, and listening with an open mind are all examples of ways that leaders can practice role modeling in the workplace.

ALLYSHIP

The intentional effort to support, celebrate, and promote internal or external stakeholders who identify as part of a group that has been historically discriminated against is known as **allyship**. Allyship is intended to be inclusive in nature, in order to advance society or an organization as a whole. In order to be effective, allyship intended as support must be recognized as such by those it supports. While leadership buy-in is more heavily anchored in the power dynamics that an individual at the head of an organization can contribute to diversity efforts, allyship transcends power dynamics and focuses more on the social dynamics of "people helping people." Acting as an ally can involve advocating for a peer, speaking out against **microaggressions** and other inappropriate behavior, showing up for DEI efforts and events, and active listening when others share their experiences.

EXPLICIT AND UNCONSCIOUS BIASES

A set of stereotypes, beliefs, and attitudes held about a person or group of people on a conscious level is called **explicit bias**. These attitudes and beliefs tend to be prejudicial or discriminatory in nature. An individual with explicit bias is aware of these attitudes and beliefs, and may express them with conscious thought. These behaviors and expressions can be regulated. **Unconscious bias,** or **implicit bias**, refers to stereotypes, attitudes, and beliefs held about a person or group of people without conscious awareness. These attitudes are learned and develop over time. Expression of these attitudes and beliefs can occur unintentionally or without awareness. In order to counter unconscious bias, the individual must be aware it exists, seek education on the area of bias, and actively change his or her behaviors and patterns to eliminate the bias.

UNCONSCIOUS-BIAS TRAINING

Implicit-bias training, or **unconscious-bias training**, requires careful planning and execution in order to elicit the intended results. Unconscious-bias training seeks to reduce the impact of these biases, with training goals ranging from raising awareness of unconscious bias to contributing to the elimination of bias in the workplace. This training should have clearly defined desired outcomes. These outcomes should not only be measurable, they should also be actively measured, tracked, and responded to. Key success factors for unconscious-bias training include avoiding training designed to merely "check the box" and avoiding the assumption that a training is a "one and done" fix for diversity in the workforce. Unconscious-bias training that is intended to stand on its own may run the risk of failing or backfiring. It is important that this training is implemented as one piece of a larger process that also includes actions such as policy review, mentorship, and auditing of compensation practices.

EMPLOYEE RESOURCES

Organizations can offer and support a number of **employee resources** in the workplace to help strengthen DEI efforts and outcomes. At the institutional level, organizational leadership can spearhead policy and procedure reviews and improvements to better serve their employees. These actions can include compensation audits, job description reviews, and flexible work options. From a training perspective, organizations can seek to provide comprehensive training and development opportunities for employees to not just learn about diversity but also to further develop the critical thinking, creativity, and communication skills that can benefit a diverse workforce. At an individual level, organizations can champion mentorship programs designed to help develop and advance individual employees regardless of where they came from or what their personal short- and long-term goals may include. At a social level, companies can support the creation of employee resource groups, which aim to acknowledge and address inclusion in an organization.

EMPLOYEE RESOURCE GROUPS

An **employee resource group (ERG)** is a voluntary association of employees within an organization who share a certain **diversity dimension**, such as women, people of color, Hispanic people, neurodiverse people, or LGBTQ+ people. These groups seek to advance inclusion efforts within their organization by harnessing the experiences and perspectives of their particular diversity dimension. An ERG seeks to create social connections for employees who may otherwise feel isolated or marginalized from the company workforce at large. These connections can be created through safe meeting spaces, volunteer opportunities, social gatherings, professional development opportunities, and ally-friendly environments. Several ERGs can come together to identify physical or procedural inequities in the workplace and advocate for solutions or changes to the status quo.

DIVERSITY METRICS

As a tangible means to demonstrate not just shifting practices but also improved business outcomes, **diversity metrics** can be an integral piece of DEI efforts and projects in the workplace. Metrics associated with DEI interventions can help to evaluate the impact of the interventions and demonstrate any tangible financial returns. Metrics can also be used to test an intervention's impact on a social or operational level. One way to test for **adverse impact** in a given process is to utilize the **four-fifths rule**. According to this rule, if the selection rate of a protected group is less than four-fifths of the selection rate of a nonprotected group for the same process (e.g., promotion), the disparity could have an adverse impact on the protected group. Examples of diversity metrics, some of which can be tested using the four-fifths rule, include:

- Demographic ratios at varying hierarchical levels
- Retention or turnover rates categorized by various diversity dimensions
- Recruiting ratios of different diversity dimensions compared to the corresponding community or candidate pool
- Compensation audit data across diversity dimensions
- Net promoter scores among employees across diversity dimensions

PSYCHOLOGICAL SAFETY

Workplace **psychological safety** is the sense of comfort an employee has (or does not have, if psychological safety is lacking) to offer new or different opinions, to make mistakes, to speak up and contribute in groups, to ask questions, or to take advantage of open door or whistleblower policies. High levels of psychological safety in the workplace can lead to improved collaboration efforts, more-creative solutions, improved learning outcomes, increased job satisfaction, and improved performance by both teams and individuals. The importance of psychological safety is greater for diverse teams, as diversity can create an uncertainty rooted in differences in values, experiences, communication styles, cultures, and behaviors. Human resource (HR) professionals can help employees develop a strong sense of psychological safety in a number of ways, many of which are rooted in communication tactics and strategies. In addition to the standard diversity trainings and general best practices, HR professionals can design and champion trainings for leadership to better understand how to frame the learning opportunities often attributed to diversity in the workplace. Leaders who can design meetings, evaluations, and group projects in a way that genuinely celebrates different opinions can help to create improved psychological safety. Additionally, performance reviews and evaluations with leaders can involve components where leaders are held accountable for "temperature checks" and can include strategies that leaders use to find out what their team members are really thinking. Leaders and key team members can also be coached regarding how to create "sharing moments" among team members that connect individuals' professional values, obstacles, and goals in order to find commonalities that transcend day-to-day behaviors and are rooted in the bigger picture.

PREFERRED GENDER PRONOUNS

Gender identity is a core component of an individual's sense of self. Recognizing individuals by their **preferred gender pronouns** acknowledges and respects that core component. Failing to recognize someone by his or her (or their) preferred gender or mistakenly referring to someone by the incorrect gender can create a sense of embarrassment, condescension, disrespect, or humiliation for both parties. In addition to being aware of whether an individual prefers the binary terms *he/him/his* or *she/her/hers*, it is also important to be aware if the individual uses more **gender-expansive** terms or pronouns and prefers nomenclature such as *they/them/theirs* or the honorific title of *Mx* instead of gendered honorifics such as *Ms* or *Mr*. There can be both social and legal challenges when individuals are incorrectly gendered.

Employees who come from more traditional or conservative backgrounds may feel uncomfortable using gender-expansive pronouns or resist changing the pronouns they use to refer to a coworker who has come out as transgender, and may intentionally use the incorrect pronouns. If the uncomfortable employee cites religious or cultural objections to using different gender pronouns, the organization must respond carefully, to ensure that all employees are treated with respect and without encroachment on their civil rights.

BARRIERS TO SUCCESS INVOLVING CONSCIOUS AND UNCONSCIOUS BIAS

GENDER-BASED DISCRIMINATION

Blatant acts of **gender-based discrimination** can include negative remarks or comments about women and what their role in the workplace should be, sexual harassment, or reactions to pregnancy or other announcements that may be seen as gender-related. Other forms of discrimination can be directly tied to workforce decisions and practices such as hiring or promoting one gender over the other (disregarding work experience or performance indicators), intentionally electing to compensate men and women at different rates, or holding employees of different genders to different standards. Subtler forms of gender-based discrimination can include excluding employees of a certain gender from meetings or decisions, inequalities in dress codes, or pervasive historical compensation practices. Whether blatant or subtle, gender-based discrimination can lead to an environment where employees feel a reduced sense of self-efficacy, collaboration and teamwork are negatively impacted, and a toxic environment can lead to poor work outcomes.

RACISM, INCLUDING SYSTEMIC RACISM

Pervasive policies, systems, beliefs, and practices that are built into everyday society and enable inequalities between races to endure across time and generations are forms of **systemic racism**. Fear and grief in response to race-related killings or incidents can impact an employee's performance. Minorities who grew up in poorer neighborhoods due to historical zoning or housing policies may have had reduced access to education that may be required for certain jobs. Minorities who have been through the justice system at disproportionate rates compared to their nonminority peers may have criminal records that prevent them from eligibility for certain jobs. Historical disparities in health and wellness resources may create a distrust in medical systems and can lead to poor health outcomes and subsequent absence challenges in the workplace. Human resource (HR) professionals can help to break down these barriers in a number of ways: reviewing job education and experience requirements to confirm relevance to the job in question; sponsoring employee resource groups, mentorships, and referral programs to create a more inclusive and welcoming environment for employees and candidates whose voices may not otherwise be heard; and celebrating and modeling a culture of safe spaces where employees feel comfortable sharing their experiences and viewpoints.

STEREOTYPING

When assumptions are made about a person's character, values, behaviors, or skills based on his or her appearance or a particular diversity dimension to which he or she belongs, that person is a victim of **stereotyping**. Women may be stereotyped as weak or emotional and therefore not up to certain tasks. Older workers may be stereotyped as backwards or not technologically savvy, and they may be spoken down to or passed over for certain opportunities. Asian workers may be assumed to be talented at math and technology but discounted for their actual strengths or talents in other realms. Hispanic workers may be assumed to be of a different nationality, and how they are treated may fluctuate based on their perceived origins. HR professionals and other leaders in the workplace can help reduce the impact of stereotyping by utilizing operating principles based on work performance and outcomes. This may mean trying to find common ground among employees, focusing and developing teams and individuals based on their strengths and interests, and screening written policies and job descriptions for stereotypical language used to describe desired work outcomes. Diversity training that is designed to highlight the differences among workers may also need to be reviewed to ensure that it is achieving desired outcomes as opposed to reinforcing existing stereotypes.

AGEISM

Financial uncertainty, shifting retirement and pension plan trends, and changes to Social Security have led to shifting workplace demographics with record-high levels of workers who are 65 years of age and older. With an aging workforce come the challenges of combating age-based stereotypes in the workforce as well as **ageism**, or discrimination based on age. From a branding and marketing perspective, organizations can review websites, flyers, and other published pieces to review for age diversity in the photos and language that are used. Phrases such as "high energy," "digital native," or "new blood" in job descriptions can shut out older candidates; additionally, these phrases in workplace operations and descriptions of advancement opportunities may create an exclusionary environment. Leaders can also assess other policies, such as asking for graduation dates during the recruiting process. This type of information is unlikely to be relevant to the job in question but can reveal a candidate's age. Other constructive approaches to addressing ageism in the workplace could include assessing current diversity, equity, and inclusion (DEI) efforts and projects for the inclusion of age as a diversity dimension in addition to dimensions like race and gender. Organizations can also consider the inclusion of employee resource groups designed to help support the professional and social needs of older workers in the company.

ABLEISM

The form of discrimination where groups or individuals are discriminated against based on their perceived or actual disabilities is called **ableism**. Some of the obvious forms of ableism in the workplace can take shapes similar to other modes of discrimination, such as stereotyping, offensive comments, harassment, and disparate treatment. Other apparent forms of discrimination specific to ableism can include exclusionary facility elements and setups such as a lack of ramps, narrow door frames, emergency systems that use only light or sound but not both, and excessive tripping hazards or obstacles in high-traffic walking areas. Forms of ableism in the workplace that are less obvious might include either a disregard for an employee's disability or the perception of a disability that does not exist or does not affect the employee within the context of work. This could include requiring an employee to work from an office instead of from home in a position that does not require an office presence; requiring office attendance can be discriminatory for employees who have physical or other disabilities that prevent them from commuting.

On the other end of the spectrum, an employer who selects an ambulatory employee for an out-of-town conference may believe that they are doing a favor for a team member who uses a wheelchair in "saving" him or her from the challenges associated with travel and crowds, when in actuality they are preventing the employee from career growth opportunities. Leaders and other workforce members may not be familiar with best practices regarding **ableist language** or the need to not define any individual based on a disability. For example, language such as "special needs" or "crippled" can be derogatory in nature, and defining an employee by their disability (e.g., "the blind sales rep") can be offensive, especially if the disability is irrelevant to the conversation.

INGROUP/OUTGROUP BIAS

An **ingroup bias** is the tendency for individuals to prefer those perceived to be from the same social group as their own and, inversely, rejecting others perceived to be from a different social group, or **outgroup**. Ingroup biases can lead to reduced communication and cooperation across teams and departments as well as reduced interactions within teams if there are perceived differences between individuals that make up the teams. This bias can be exacerbated by a scarcity of resources or other perceived threats in the workplace; additionally, the "us versus them" mentality of ingroup bias can also be found rooted in individuals' definitions of their own self-worth and self-esteem. Diversity without inclusion can create an environment prime for ingroup bias if employees who are part of the majority group treat those they perceive as "outsiders" as if they are less valuable or less capable.

AFFINITY BIAS

The tendency for individuals to connect more quickly and more often with those perceived to have similar beliefs, values, backgrounds, and characteristics is called **affinity bias**. Affinity bias can affect recruiting and hiring if the hiring managers make selections based on their perceived similarities with candidates rather than work-related skills and abilities. It is important that when searching for the "right culture fit" in the recruiting process that a company's culture is defined based on desired work outcomes as opposed to candidates who already get along or fit in to the current workforce. Affinity bias can also show up in the workplace when forming work teams, supporting peers, and advocating for (or disparaging) coworkers and other team members. Organizations can work to reduce affinity bias using processes and procedures that help to guide HR professionals and managers through workplace decisions based on performance outcomes instead of perceptions of or relationships with employees and candidates. Organizations can also combat affinity bias by utilizing diverse teams when making workforce decisions and acknowledging affinity biases and other biases before decisions and meetings, so all parties are better able to spot them and refocus to outcome-centered interactions and decisions.

GENDER IDENTITY BIAS

Implicit or explicit negative beliefs and actions of an individual toward transgender individuals constitute **gender identity bias**. Intentional gender identity bias can take the form of blatant harassment and discrimination based on gender identity, such as passing over transgender employees for promotion or hiring opportunities, or using derogatory language or statements to humiliate, embarrass, or harm transgender individuals. Unintentional gender identity bias may occur in the form of discriminatory restroom policies, accidentally **misgendering** transgender employees when speaking with or about them, or accidentally using a transgender employee's **deadname** instead of their correct name. Two of the main points of distinction between intentional and unintentional bias are genuine intent and frequency of occurrence. For example, if an employee purposefully misgenders a transgender coworker, then the bias is intentional; if an employee accidentally misgenders a transgender coworker multiple times and does not adjust their behavior despite corrections, then the bias that started as unintentional becomes intentional.

To address both intentional and unintentional gender identity bias in the workplace, organizations can design and communicate clear and public acceptance and celebration of gender identity diversity; respond quickly and decisively to intentional harassment as well as unintentional bias in order to prevent it from becoming intentional; create and follow clear company policies and procedures that both value work experience over personal identities and create avenues of success for individuals with complex employment backgrounds due to historical discrimination.

SEXUAL ORIENTATION BIAS

Discrimination based on sex is prohibited under **Title VII of the Civil Rights Act of 1964**. Discrimination based on an individual's sexual orientation falls within the category of sex discrimination because an individual's sex and their subsequent sexual preferences inform their sexual orientation. **Sexual orientation bias** encompasses implicit or explicit negative beliefs and actions of an individual toward sexual minorities such as those who identify as gay, lesbian, bisexual, pansexual, asexual, or any other orientation. Organizations are responsible for addressing sexual orientation bias in their hiring and workplace practices, team interactions, employee management, and other policies and procedures in order to remain compliant with sex discrimination laws and to ensure an equal and fair workplace for all employees.

SOCIAL COMPARISON BIAS

When individuals compare themselves, often negatively, to others who they believe are better off in some way (physically, intellectually, or socially), they are engaging in **social comparison bias**. The compounding effect of social comparison bias has been amplified in recent years due to the advent and growth of social media and other technology. Employees affected by social comparison bias may reject or avoid peers or candidates they feel may outshine them in some way in order to improve their own social or professional standing. Employees affected by social comparison bias may also experience lower levels of self-esteem, which may affect their willingness to share ideas, take chances, and seek new professional opportunities. Within a diverse workforce, employees struggling with social comparison bias may shift their comparisons and look down on those perceived to be different or to be outsiders in order to improve their own self-esteem. This negative perspective toward those perceived to be different can impact the effectiveness of teams, the sense of belonging for those deemed as outsiders, and the overall outcomes of building diverse teams.

EXTROVERT BIAS

The tendency to regard individuals in a positive light due to attributes typically associated with being extroverted, such as having an outgoing personality and being highly sociable, is called **extrovert bias**. Employees who are often heard from and seen can be inaccurately accredited as more intelligent, capable, and valuable than their more **introverted** peers. Extroverted employees can certainly contribute to workforce outcomes in their ability to network and present the company to others, but introverted employees also bring their own unique value to the organization. Introverted individuals are typically known for their mindfulness, concentration, listening skills, and more. These skills can help to build strong and well-thought-out products and services; when these skills are combined with the skills of extroverted coworkers, the stronger products and services can be better sold and marketed in an extroverted world. Combining the best abilities of extroverted and introverted individuals will help to produce higher-quality and longer-lasting workplace outcomes.

NEURODIVERSITY BIAS

The implicit or explicit negative beliefs and actions of an individual toward individuals who are (or are perceived to be) **neurodiverse**, such as those with attention deficit hyperactivity disorder (ADHD), autism spectrum disorder (ASD), Tourette's syndrome, dyslexia, or other conditions, is called **neurodiversity bias**. Neurodivergence in the workforce can add to workplace outcomes by adding new and different ways to think about and approach problems, challenges, and processes. The best way to support neurodivergent employees in the workplace is dependent on each employee's individual needs and duties. Accommodations can include altering the color of paper used for internal documents; making revision software available; increasing or reducing external stimuli as appropriate; providing voice-to-text and text-to-voice programs; showing tolerance for dissenting opinions, atypical manners, or grooming practices; and using communication tactics that help to map or track conversation topics and questions.

MICROAGGRESSIONS

Verbal or nonverbal interactions that express subtle or indirect discrimination against individuals of a certain diversity dimension are called **microaggressions**. In the workplace, microaggressions can take obvious forms, such as individuals of a specific diversity dimension being interrupted or having their ideas stolen in teamwork or meeting settings. Additionally, microaggressions can include disrespectful or ignorant comments or questions specific to a diversity dimension, like telling women to smile more, asking to touch someone's ethnically or culturally appropriately styled hair, complimenting non-Caucasian workers on their English language skills, or ordering food for a team meeting without taking religious dietary restrictions into consideration.

Organizational leaders can help to combat microaggressions by discussing these types of comments and actions as a team before they occur to help create an awareness of the harm they can cause. Additionally, team, line, and HR leaders can maintain open-door policies for individuals to share when they feel that they have been a victim of microaggressions. In the moment of the microaggression or in follow-up meetings, it can be helpful to ask the aggressor to explain his or her actions or intent behind the behavior in order to better understand where the behavior is coming from, and to help the aggressor verbalize the action and potentially realize why his or her action or comment was inappropriate.

PERSONAL BARRIERS SUCH AS IMPOSTER SYNDROME AND IDENTITY COVERING

The condition or state of mind in which an individual feels as if they do not belong in a certain position of power or importance due to incompetence or lacking the required skills or abilities is known as **imposter syndrome**. Imposter syndrome can negatively affect employees and prevent them from embracing their roles and responsibilities or accepting credit for their accomplishments or achievements. **Identity covering** is an individual's tendency to hide or downplay parts of his or her personality or personal life in order to better fit in with a company or group. Employees affected by identity covering may choose to style their hair in damaging ways to better fit in with popular beauty standards, avoid talking about their families to avoid being discriminated against for being caregivers, or choose to hide in the office when they need to pray to avoid being treated differently for their religion. Employees affected by imposter syndrome or identity covering may find their work performance impacted by these and other feelings of not belonging. Organizations can help to address personal barriers by providing the appropriate support for diversity in the workplace through employee resource groups, mentorship opportunities, and **global celebration calendars** designed to acknowledge a variety of diversity dimensions.

CULTURAL TAXATION

The burden or responsibility shouldered by individuals of specific diversity dimensions to speak for or represent all others of the same dimension in both formal and informal situations is called **cultural taxation**. DEI programs and initiatives can be negatively impacted if the cultural taxation burden adversely affects the work outputs of individuals asked to lead these initiatives. The additional work requirement to lead these programs may lead to burnout and disillusionment with the cause if the individuals feel that they are asked to split their time between work and DEI responsibilities. Cultural taxation of marginalized workers may also lead to the reduction of these employees from high-value, high-quality employees to representatives of their diversity dimension and take away from their individual contributions to the organization outside of DEI initiatives. In order to avoid the negative impacts of cultural taxation, organizations can consider compensation or time-off solutions to balance the additional work responsibilities involved with formal DEI activities. Organizations can also ensure that participation in DEI projects and initiatives are voluntary so that individuals do not feel pressed into service if they prefer to focus on their own work. On a more informal level, organizations can assess representation of diversity dimensions at all levels of hierarchy, so that if an individual starts to feel the burden of cultural taxation, he or she can go to and seek support from someone who may better understand the situation. Additionally, organizations can review performance evaluations for consistent assessment standards.

WORKSPACE SOLUTIONS

LACTATION ROOMS

Companies covered under the **Fair Labor Standards Act (FLSA)** are required to provide "reasonable break time" and space for new mothers to express milk within the first year after their child's birth. In addition to federal requirements for lactation spaces, organizations should also be aware of state and local requirements, which may affect accommodation and compensation regulations. Providing **lactation rooms** or the means with which to create a lactation space is important for supporting the health and well-being of new mothers in the workplace, along with the health and well-being of their families. A company may choose to designate a temporary or permanent lactation room for mothers; such a room must be somewhere other than a restroom and must provide reasonable privacy and functionality. Whether the space is permanent or temporary, companies may utilize a number of accommodations to meet these privacy and functionality requirements, such as installing locks on office doors, ensuring appropriate (or separate) refrigerator space, ensuring flat surfaces and electrical outlets for the required equipment, designating space near sinks, or providing mirrors and cleaning supplies.

MULTIPURPOSE PRIVATE ROOMS

When faced with limited physical space, companies may wish to provide employees with a **multipurpose private room** to serve multiple religious, health, and physical needs. A properly equipped and conscientiously scheduled multipurpose room can help to function as a lactation room, a **prayer room,** a **meditation room,** or another type of accommodation space. Communication with employees is key when balancing individual needs for private spaces. Employers can use collaborative technology such as scheduling programs or shared calendars for employees to request time in the rooms. To help with oversight to ensure that fair and equal time is allotted, a member of management or human resources (HR) may be an appropriate figure to manage the schedule and sign out keys for room access when appropriate. The room manager should be fully informed of individual accommodation rights and creative when proposing alternate ways to support employees if there are simultaneous requests for the room for valid yet separate reasons. In addition to scheduling the space itself, organizations can further support the employees using the room by ensuring that the space is properly equipped, such as with comfortable places to sit or kneel, flat surface areas or cubbies for storing personal belongings, or other comfort or productivity items such as soft lighting or sound machines.

BRAILLE AND SCREEN READERS

Individuals with visual impairments may use **screen readers,** computer programs that convey the content on the screen in nonvisual ways. These programs use audio cues and can also include **braille** input and output functions. Many employment-related activities occur on computers, including via recruiting websites, employee portals, workstations, or training videos. Website accessibility features such as color contrast, text size, and zoom capabilities can be critical for employees and candidates with visual impairments. It is important that websites are coded with screen readers in mind, to ensure website usability for employees who are visually impaired; conscientious coding helps in navigating tables, describing images, and describing video output. In addition to screen readers, traditional braille materials and innovative braille tools (such as braille keyboards or braille tablets) can give employees opportunities to work independently and efficiently.

CLOSED CAPTIONING

In many major teleconference and virtual meeting platforms, **closed captioning** is an easy-to-enable accommodation for employees with some form of hearing impairment or related disability. In these platforms, captioning can be enabled for virtual meetings and trainings. Closed captioning technologies can also be extended to provide live captioning for in-person events. Closed captioning can be beneficial even for employees who do not experience a hearing impairment; they can improve learning outcomes and improve information comprehension, and help extend flexibility for employees to attend meetings or trainings even when they are in an environment where it is difficult to hear or audio is not available. It is, however, important to note that closed captioning is not a replacement for an American Sign Language (ASL) interpreter, especially for individuals who have learned ASL as a first language, so managers and HR leaders should take care when determining the appropriate accommodations.

WHEELCHAIR RAMPS

All accommodations for physical disabilities must, at a minimum, meet the standards set by the **Americans with Disabilities Act (ADA)** as well as any additional state or local regulations. Examples of accommodations include providing the appropriate number of accessible parking spaces (in general, two out of every 50 spaces), building or providing **wheelchair ramps** that meet slope and handrail requirements, and providing motorized entrances and exits that are wide enough to accommodate wheelchairs. For employees with disabilities of the upper extremities, possible accommodations include doorways that can be operated with feet, one-handed keyboards, speakerphones, grip assists, and lifting aids. Regardless of the nature of the physical disability, offices, desks, and workspaces should be provided in such a way that they are functional for the users given their specific needs.

GENDER-NEUTRAL RESTROOMS

Transgender and nonbinary employees can feel a greater sense of psychological safety if the workplace has **gender-neutral restrooms**. When instated as part of a larger diversity, equity, and inclusion (DEI) effort, gender-neutral restrooms can help to build an employer's brand as an inclusive company. Gender-neutral restrooms can elevate the company from a diverse organization made up of different types of people to an inclusive organization that affirms and celebrates all types of people. However, companies must be mindful that asking transitioning employees to use a unisex restroom when the company also has gendered restrooms may invite a hostile situation if these employees feel singled out or are hurt that they are not permitted to use the restrooms that align with their gender identities.

Organizations should also keep in mind the religious rights of employees who view LGBTQ+ accommodations as conflicting with their sincerely held religious beliefs. The overlap between accommodating these respective rights may be interpreted differently from state to state, so companies must be mindful of individual needs and beliefs, federal civil rights standards, and local regulations when navigating these situations. In addition to social and legal obstacles, changing a building's footprint to provide gender-neutral restrooms can be costly and structurally prohibitive.

TECHNIQUES TO MEASURE AND INCREASE EQUITY
DIVERSITY OF EMPLOYEES AT ALL ORGANIZATIONAL LEVELS

The first step in acknowledging diversity within each organizational level is to measure the diversity across the organization's hierarchy. Human resource (HR) analytics and metrics are key tools in this step. Using gender as an example, if an organization is 50 percent women and 50 percent men at entry-level positions, 40 percent women and 60 percent men at frontline-level manager positions, and 20 percent women and 80 percent men at mid- and upper-level management positions, the organization needs to assess why women are no longer being promoted or participating at the same rate as their male counterparts.

When assessing diversity across organizational levels, it is important to remember that there is no one universal cause or reason for representation drop-off, and HR professionals must dive deeper into data and employee perspectives to better understand and address diversity across organizational levels. In the example of gender in the workplace, a drop-off may exist because of a lack of childcare options that fit the greater responsibilities of higher positions, so women are turning down promotions or leaving the workforce. Alternatively (or additionally), there may be historically based discrimination or microaggressions that emerge at a certain level of the organization so that women qualified for positions at higher levels choose to leave the organization for more-inclusive companies. Each of these possible reasons for drop-off requires a unique approach to address and correct it in order to improve diversity across an organization's hierarchy.

PAY AUDITS

A **pay audit** is a tool that can be used to promote a greater commitment to **pay equity** and fair compensation practices. Organizations use pay audits to assess current compensation practices. Pay audits can help to reveal discrepancies in pay practices across similar functions and positions and help to identify if and how discrimination may be causing these discrepancies. By identifying pay discrepancies, employers can get a head start in correcting discriminatory compensation practices, show initiative in offering back pay if appropriate, identify the factors or individuals responsible for the discriminatory decisions, and seek correction by means of education, discipline, or other actions.

PAY EQUITY REPORTS

When a company makes a commitment to pay equity, it is committing to compensation practices that reward similar work, knowledge, and experience at similar rates regardless of an individual employee's specific diversity dimensions. In addition to making a commitment to pay equity, an organization can support its words with actions by performing and publishing the results of pay audits, including providing **pay equity reports**, banning pay history inquiries, and practicing transparency in compensation practices. Pay equity practices can help to build an organizational culture based on trust, honesty, and fairness, and to build a culture that treats diversity as a valued means to improved work outcomes and not just a box to be checked.

PAY TRANSPARENCY

It is important that organizations be aware of and follow all legal **pay transparency** regulations, regardless of their internal pay equity policies and practices. During the recruiting phase, transparency laws may require the job to be posted with the minimum and maximum pay range; these requirements vary from state to state, so organizations should be aware of the compensation laws of their home state as well as any state they aim to hire or recruit from. When addressing pay transparency among active employees, organizations also need to take note that discussing pay rates and practices is generally considered a **concerted activity** protected by the **National Labor Relations Act (NLRA)**. Companies are not permitted to prohibit employees from comparing salaries or discussing the details of their pay or compensation.

EMPLOYEE SURVEYS

Performing employee surveys can be helpful for gauging employee support, opinions, and perceptions of an organization, including any diversity, equity, and inclusion (DEI) projects, stances, or events. **Employee satisfaction surveys** can help to gauge employee opinion and overall perception of the organization. These surveys are also referred to as "opinion surveys" or "climate surveys." **Employee culture surveys** seek to measure how employee perspectives line up with the organization's overarching mission and goals. **Employee engagement surveys** can be utilized to determine how committed employees feel to the organizational mission as well as how motivated and driven they feel in their day-to-day work. There are four key characteristics to consider when utilizing employee surveys: design, medium, frequency, and follow-up.

Surveys should have a clear design (measurable data, questions that have been proofread for grammar and effectiveness, etc.), be given in an appropriate format (in-person, online, etc.), be given at a reasonable frequency (quarterly, annually, etc.) for their goals, and have resources designated to address survey follow-up (acknowledging or announcing results, laying out and seeing through plans for change or improvement, etc.). Survey follow-up and results transparency are critical to enacting actual organizational change. Employees are more likely to participate in surveys if they feel their voices are being heard.

BENEFITS AND PROGRAMS THAT SUPPORT DIVERSITY, EQUITY, AND INCLUSION

CAREGIVER BENEFITS

Caregiver responsibilities extend beyond childcare and can also include caring for a disabled or elderly family member. **Caregiver benefits** can take a number of forms and support employees across multiple stages of their lives. Caregiver benefits can be monetary in nature and include child or adult care subsidies, onsite childcare, partnerships with emergency care providers in the event of school or daycare closure, or healthcare plans with affordable options for senior care or senior care planning. Non-monetary caregiver benefits can include flexible work options such as remote work capabilities, hybrid scheduling, or flex scheduling, which can allow employees to balance their family responsibilities with their work responsibilities. By providing a variety of caregiver benefits and options for employees, an organization can benefit from both the improved morale of employees who feel valued and improved work outcomes from employees who are given the financial assistance, scheduling flexibility, and professional respect to complete their job tasks and duties and contribute to organizational outcomes.

FLEXIBLE WORKPLACE POLICIES

With a diverse workforce can come diverse personal and professional needs; organizations that are able to offer **flexible benefits and workplace policies** are better equipped to care for all of their employees. Remote or hybrid work options can help employees reduce commuting costs (in both time and money), reduce their environmental footprints, and improve their abilities to balance home and work responsibilities. Remote work can be especially useful for jobs that are measured in outcomes rather than in time spent. Unconventional scheduling may be a valuable option for employees seeking to work compressed hours or alternative hours such as nights or weekends to help balance their work and home lives. **Job sharing** may be a viable option if there are employees seeking part-time work for positions that are traditionally full time. Some companies also benefit from unlimited vacation time policies, which encourage employees to take the time they want or need but put a premium on effective communication and work outcomes. Flexibility in workplace policies can add to an employer brand when attracting new talent. Flexibility in workplace policies can also reduce stress outside of work, so employees are better able to perform at work. When mindfully designed and executed, flexible workplace policies can shift the focus from transactional and administratively driven work interactions to transformational and business-impact-driven work interactions.

GLOBAL CELEBRATIONS CALENDARS

A calendar that includes global festivities and events helps an organization to recognize and celebrate holidays beyond traditional big-ticket events like Thanksgiving and Christmas. Other holidays and festivals that may be included in the calendar include Eid-al-Fitr, Yom Kippur, Lunar New Year, Ramadan, and Kwanzaa. By including global and "nontraditional" holidays, organizations can help employees from diverse walks of life and backgrounds feel not just acknowledged but celebrated. Many holidays are based on religious celebrations, so they are personal to employees and may even require accommodations for these employees as a protected class. A **global celebrations calendar** can add to an employer brand when recruiting for positions by appealing to a wide pool of candidates.

Additionally, a company that acknowledges a global array of celebrations and holiday events can appeal to a wider customer base, especially in a global economy. When designing the global calendar, it is important to collect input from staff teams to ensure that all important celebrations are taken into account. Additionally, when introducing or launching the calendar, companies should take care in how they communicate the purpose of the calendar so as not to create tension or the misperception that celebrating "traditional" holidays is no longer acceptable or welcome. Any in-person celebrations of holidays should be voluntary and should be mindfully designed, particularly with regard to food, beverages, and activities.

Chapter Quiz

Ready to see how well you retained what you just read? Scan the QR code to go directly to the chapter quiz interface for this study guide. If you're using a computer, simply visit the bonus page at **mometrix.com/bonus948/shrmcp** and click the Chapter Quizzes link.

Behavioral Competencies: Interpersonal

Relationship Management

BUILDING RELATIONSHIPS

Success in business requires establishing strong networks of customers, candidates, vendors, and business professionals. Key elements in **building relationships** include connecting with others to find shared interests or goals, fostering a sense of community, and supporting others to solve problems or achieve goals. To build a relationship, an individual should first understand his or her own personality, style, and motivation, then listen and try to understand the other person's style of communication and needs, being sure to value his or her time. Many people will choose to do business with an individual or company with whom they have a strong personal relationship, even if competitive data supports a different choice. The relationship may be based on a recommendation via word of mouth or an employee referral. Relationship-building is an absolute necessity when trying to connect with passive candidates or creating a pool of potential future candidates.

USING TECHNOLOGY TO BUILD AND MAINTAIN STRONG RELATIONSHIPS

One of the most critical parts of building and maintaining strong relationships with workers in other locations is establishing a solid line of communication. This should begin at onboarding. Employees should be given a **communication plan**. While email can be used frequently, that line of communication can also be impersonal and somewhat anonymous. When onboarding new team members, the team should have 15- to 30-minute individual introduction phone calls or video calls with new employees. Regularly recurring meetings should be scheduled with workers at other sites. This helps prevent feelings of disconnection. Setting up a team Slack channel for simple conversations and interactions can be a great way to foster more meaningful conversations. Virtual lunches or happy hours can be implemented to increase contact. Additionally, team-building exercises and activities should be scheduled at specific intervals to create and maintain a strong feeling of connection. These activities can include remote workers, employees who work at other sites, and those on a hybrid work schedule.

PROFESSIONAL NETWORKING

A powerful tool in today's business world, **professional networking** involves creating a large group of business contacts and staying active with regular, mutually beneficial, communications. It is vital to use network connections to help others and not just to seek help for yourself. Nurturing these relationships through communication is the lifeblood of networking and can be done by providing recommendations, referrals, or advice. Some essential principles of networking include the following:

- Creating an engaging elevator speech about oneself.
- Smiling and being positive.
- Differentiating oneself.
- Setting goals and achievement plans.
- Striving to share information and facilitate opportunities for others.
- Building up personal reputation and credibility.
- Following up on all meetings and referrals.

TEAMWORK

When a group of people work cooperatively toward a common goal, it is important that all members of the team be familiar with the plan for achieving goals and feel valued and respected. Each individual should feel important and as though their contributions to the **teamwork** are validated. Creativity, innovation, and differing viewpoints can be fostered for new ideas. Strong, unified teams are often more efficient and productive due to the fact that members support one another and work collaboratively. Moreover, successful teams distribute work evenly, and everyone shoulders the burden when roadblocks are encountered. This synergy encourages employee engagement and makes businesses more competitive.

TYPES OF CONFLICT
TASK CONFLICT VS. RELATIONSHIP CONFLICT

Task-related intergroup conflicts are cognitive in nature and are typically based on goal definition or how work should be performed. Low to moderate levels of **task conflict** with sufficient levels of trust and safety are functional and may stimulate healthy competition or creative ideas. High levels of task conflict can be harmful to productive work processes and diminish team cohesiveness.

Relationship-related intergroup conflicts are emotional in nature and based on discord within interpersonal relationships stemming from differences in personal values or style. These conflicts carry a perception of interpersonal incompatibility and often involve tension, animosity, and aggravation among team members. **Relationship conflicts** are almost always dysfunctional, volatile, and destructive. Left unchecked, they can put a big damper on both productivity and morale.

INTERGROUP CONFLICTS

Conflicts between two groups, such as union and management, often result in undesirable outcomes for the organization. Each group is driven to pursue their own goals, and often there is little regard for the other or the organization's success. Thus, an **intergroup intervention** should be sought before the **intergroup conflict** turns the parties into lasting enemies. Intervention strategies include the followings:

- **Finding a common enemy**. This strategy brings two groups together by finding an outside party that both groups dislike. The groups must coordinate efforts to fight the outsider and achieve success.
- **Joint activities**. This strategy forces members of each group to interact and communicate with one another to achieve a shared objective. As increased activities foster more positive attitudes and sentiments, ill feelings should dissipate.
- **Rotating membership**. Often useful in international relations, this strategy involves moving members from one group to the other. Group attitudes are strongly influenced by their members, and transferring people between groups may help build awareness and perspective.
- **Conflict resolution meetings**. This strategy begins with a meeting of group leaders to share feelings and gain commitment to establishing cooperation. Each group independently identifies their internal feelings and those they perceive from the other group. Then, the groups meet to share and discuss, allowing only for clarification inquiries and not drawn-out explanations. This step is repeated until hostility has been diffused.

CONFLICT MANAGEMENT METHODS

Managing conflicts properly can increase trust, cohesiveness, and engagement levels. Human resources (HR) and leadership should partner to ensure that functional conflict, which can result in better problem-solving and more innovation, has a place in the organization. However, they should work to minimize dysfunctional conflict resulting from personal differences, as it is always counterproductive.

All employees should take part in **conflict management** training so that everyone can do their part to keep the office productive and professional, regardless of personal beliefs. To ensure consistency in addressing conflict, HR practitioners should evaluate conflict trends within the organization and create a **resolution policy**. Finally, HR and leaders should model how conflict resolution should be handled by dealing with their own interpersonal issues diplomatically.

CONFLICT RESOLUTION STYLES
AVOIDANCE

In the **avoidance** style of conflict resolution, conflict goes ignored. Those who employ this method generally dislike confrontation. If the issue is not urgent, avoiding it will likely not have any noticeable ill effects. The situation may even resolve itself. However, if the matter is truly important, conflict avoidance can lead to the problem getting bigger. If it festers long enough, it may become unmanageable. It is critical to nip real issues in the bud whenever possible to prevent this from happening.

COMPETITION

In the **competition** style of conflict resolution, whoever has the most clout determines how the conflict is resolved. For example, a conflict over how to complete a task is likely going to be won by a supervisor over an employee because the supervisor holds a higher position of authority. This type of resolution can also occur when one voice within the conflict becomes more dominant than the other(s) even if he or she doesn't have a formal position of power. This resolution style can be effective when decisions need to be made quickly. Its drawback is that it can make people feel trampled on, which negatively affects morale.

ACCOMMODATION

When **accommodation** is employed, one party decides to give in to the other. Once the other party has what it wants, the conflict should be over. This technique can be useful when the accommodating party wants to preserve the relationship, end the conflict, or is not that personally invested in the outcome of the situation.

COOPERATION

Resolving a conflict through **cooperation** means that preserving the relationship is viewed as more important than being right. The conflict is resolved via accommodation or collaboration. This style can be effective when there is enough time to come to a consensus or when maintaining harmony is critical to organizational success.

CONCILIATION

In the **conciliation** style of conflict resolution, one party attempts to gain favor with the other. He or she may try to overcome differences of opinion and reestablish trust to persuade the other person to adopt his or her view. Those who resolve conflict with this style seek to get their way as in a competition, but they are less aggressive than those who favor the competition style.

TRUST-BUILDING TECHNIQUES
EMOTIONAL INTELLIGENCE

The ability to be sensitive to the feelings of others, to manage one's own emotions or impulses, and to use this knowledge to motivate others, is called **emotional intelligence**. The four main fundamentals of emotional intelligence are self-awareness, self-management, social awareness, and social skills or relationship management. Important social skills include empathy, compassion, and the ability to motivate. Emotional intelligence is used in the moment to make quick assessments and adjustments. For example, if Sam sees Bob frowning during a meeting, Sam can use his emotional intelligence to deduce that Bob is not pleased. Sam can either try to change the course of the meeting, ask Bob what's bothering him on the spot, or talk to Bob after the meeting.

RELATABILITY

When a person demonstrates **relatability**, others may find it easy to form a connection with that individual based on shared or similar experiences. Being relatable is important when building trust, because when others identify or sympathize with someone, it lends credibility and validation. It is easier to trust someone when there are feelings of likeness and common ground, building deeper attachments and respect. For example, if Sam speaks with Bob after the meeting and Bob mentions that he was displeased with a particular metric, Sam can display relatability by not only agreeing with Bob, but also detailing a similar experience and how it was resolved. Sam connects with Bob by sympathizing and revealing a shared struggle. Establishing this deeper connection makes Bob more inclined to trust in Sam's recommendation.

43

VULNERABILITY

Being open or exposed to the potential to be ridiculed, harmed, or criticized on an emotional or physical level is known as **vulnerability**. Those who display vulnerability put themselves out in the open and accept that they have little or no control over the outcome. The ability to be vulnerable around others demonstrates a level of trust, because opening oneself up displays a level of faith and confidence in those one is sharing with. This can, in turn, encourage others to open up and further build on the trust in the relationship or exchange.

TRANSPARENCY

The act of being honest, open, and up-front is one of **transparency**. Those who act with transparency share appropriate information (both bad and good) and encourage feedback from others. A key aspect of transparency is intentionality. There should be boundaries, and those boundaries should be clear. Many negative workplace behaviors can be disguised as being "open" or "honest." Sam cannot tell Bob that he is bad for morale and then chalk it up to being "honest." Transparency can help foster improved communication, stronger relationships, trust, and loyalty between individuals.

RECOGNIZING INDIVIDUAL STRENGTHS

Knowing where individuals excel and where they may struggle is key to building a strong and successful team. If Sam is a really strong recruiter, tracking and analyzing absenteeism may not be the best fit for Sam's skills. **Recognizing individual strengths** by understanding each employee's talents and areas of expertise is key to assigning them tasks where success is achievable. This will also keep the individual engaged and productive. An employee tasked to complete an item in an area where he or she struggles can lower morale and decrease that individual's output. It is not possible to for everyone to excel on every item they are tasked with, but having a developed understanding of areas of competence will help ensure that each employee is set up to be successful.

NEGOTIATION

A vital technique for every business professional, **negotiation** is only possible when all parties are open to compromise and finding solutions that are mutually satisfying. For example, new or expired contracts and changing behaviors require skillful negotiations. Human resource practitioners must know how to handle negotiations to successfully avoid conflicts, improve relations, secure pay rates, and evaluate contracts.

TACTICS, STRATEGIES, AND STYLES

- **Perspective-taking**. Perspective-taking involves deeply understanding the position of the other party. If the negotiator understands where the other party is coming from, he or she will be better able to offer a deal that works well for both parties.
- **Interest-based bargaining**. A **principled bargainer** views negotiations as fluid, exploratory conversations, guided by principles, to ultimately achieve mutually beneficial solutions. The parties begin the negotiation process by plainly stating their main interests. The process involves coming to an agreement that satisfies those interests while minimizing the pain of any concessions to be made. Rather than viewing the other party as an adversary or a negotiation as something to be won, a principled bargainer sees all parties involved as problem-solvers looking for the most efficient outcome for everyone.
- **Auctioning**. An auction can be a great bargaining strategy when a decision needs to be made quickly and will be based solely on price. However, if service and value are important to the parties involved and time permits, entering into a negotiation process may be a better solution. Negotiations can account for more nuances and can be handled discreetly.
- **Position-based bargaining**. A bargainer may employ position-based bargaining when he or she holds a fixed position or idea of what is wanted and argues for that fixed item alone, without considering other interests. This bargaining approach is more adversarial, and each side is forced to make concessions until an agreement can be reached, or no agreement is made at all. This approach is less effective and not as constructive as interest-based bargaining.

CONCESSIONS

When working through a negotiation, each side has a particular goal in mind. Each side may also have a wish list of items that would be nice to have, but will have already decided the minimum of what they are willing to accept. The party presenting the first proposal in the negotiation aims high. The first proposal includes the items from the wish list and details the ideal outcomes. The opposing side then responds with a counterproposal. That counterproposal is be reviewed and the presenting party then determines what **concessions** they are willing to make in order to reach an agreement that achieves the desired outcome. Concessions must stay within the financial and resource constraints that have already been identified; one party cannot agree to a dollar amount that exceeds what is available to negotiate. Concessions usually occur a little at a time, until a compromise is reached and both parties walk away from the deal with essential goals agreed upon.

NEGOTIATION-RELATED LAWS AND REGULATIONS

The relationships among most employees, unions, and private businesses are governed under the **National Labor Relations Act.** The NLRA grants employees the right to join and form unions and to either engage or refrain from engaging in activities to improve working conditions. It also covers the responsibilities of an employer with regard to bargaining, interfering with employee rights, and the election process.

The **Labor Management Relations Act**, also known as the Taft-Hartley Act, restricts certain activities and powers of labor unions. The **Labor Management Reporting and Disclosure Act**, also known as the Landrum Griffin Act, regulates the internal affairs of unions as well as relationships between union officials and employers. The **Norris-La Guardia Act** restricted court injunctions against strikes, boycotting, and picketing in labor disputes. It also outlawed "yellow-dog contracts," or pledges by workers to not join a union. **Weingarten Rights** allow employees the right to union representation during investigatory interviews.

NEGOTIATION PLANNING

An internal **plan** should be established prior to any negotiation. This plan should identify the desired outcome of the negotiation as well as what alternatives may be acceptable. For example, when negotiating a new collective bargaining agreement, it is critical to work with different functions within the organization, such as finance, to come up with the bottom-line amount of money the organization can dedicate to the agreement. The first proposal submitted for review should be below the bottom line, allowing the organization to make some financial concessions to obtain the goals or objectives that are truly desired. As an example, a manufacturing company would like to move away from having a paid lunch break. In the first proposal, the company removes the paid lunch and offers a small increase to salary levels to entice the opposing side to agree. The company has budgeted a larger increase, but starts off small to allow room for discussion because the main objective is to get rid of the paid lunch.

Each step of a negotiation should keep the outlined objectives in mind. The proposals and counterproposals should all move toward achieving those objectives. If progress stalls, suspending negotiations is an acceptable option to allow both sides to regroup and consider the information and options presented. Sticking firmly to the end-state objective is critical, as organizations will have constraints and hardlines regarding financial figures and the concessions the company is willing to make.

Communication

ELEMENTS OF COMMUNICATION

The practice of exchanging information, data, ideas, and opinions is known as **communication**. There are many models that depict complex communication processes. However, almost all communications will include some variety of these fundamentals: sender, encoding, message, channel, receiver, decoding, and feedback. The **sender**, or source, chooses, creates, and **encodes** the **message**. The **receiver** must **decode** and interpret the message. In between, the message must be transmitted through some communication **channel** or medium like phone, text, email, video, or broadcast. Communications often pass through **noise barriers** such as environmental sounds, people speaking, traffic, and construction. Removing these barriers can decrease instances of misunderstanding and confusion. **Feedback** allows the model to be interchangeable and for communication to flow both ways.

GENERAL COMMUNICATION TECHNIQUES

PLANNING COMMUNICATIONS

Delivering messages can be difficult, especially if the message is serious in nature. The message content should be tailored to fit the audience. This requires understanding the roles, expectations, and perspectives of recipients. First, focus on eliminating any **barriers** or vague wording that may interfere with interpreting the message. Once the proper channel for delivery is selected, it may be important to focus on **nonverbal signals** and ensure that they coincide with the mood of the message content. Messages should allow for **feedback** that will lead to follow-up discussions. If the message is complex in nature, such as a business change or new benefits offering, it may be critical to share repeated reminders and have open lines of communication to reduce confusion and ensure success.

ACTIVE LISTENING

An important component of communication that requires paying close attention to what is being said, **active listening** often involves making eye contact and appropriately nodding to show engagement. To gain a better understanding, an individual should try to understand things from the speaker's point of view or to visualize what he or she is saying. It is important to be considerate, avoid distractions or interruptions, and respond appropriately. Additionally, an individual should try to pick up on emotional cues beyond the literal words that are used. Even if the message differs from his or her own opinion, an individual should try to focus on accepting what the other person has to say rather than being critical, and make sure to fully hear what the other person is saying before formulating his or her own response. It has been noted that, when compared to passive listeners, active listeners are more connected and conscientious.

CHECKING FOR UNDERSTANDING

During any communication, **checking for understanding** is necessary to ensure that all parties involved in the exchange are on the same page. This technique can ensure that individuals understand directions, content, or material correctly. This task is critical in both retaining and recalling information. If an individual does not understand, adjustments can be made and questions can be asked to clear up any areas of concern. An effective way to check for understanding is to summarize the information or instruction presented by going over the main points and key items. This highlights and emphasizes the most important pasts of the discussion. Another method to check for understanding is asking the other individual to explain or demonstrate what was said. If the individual misses important points, does not explain the item correctly, or varies significantly in the demonstration, the information should be reviewed. A lack of understanding indicates a barrier of some kind in communication.

ASKING QUESTIONS

One of the best ways to obtain information from others is **asking questions**. Using this skill correctly can make individuals feel valued and build stronger relationships. Asking content-specific questions is a technique to check for audience understanding. For example, when explaining how to correct timecard errors, the presenter

may ask a member of the audience to state how he or she would address the problem in the timekeeping system. This quick follow-up helps to demonstrate the efficacy of the information presented. Asking targeted questions will also help reduce errors and mistakes. Asking open-ended questions is another tool that can be used to gather additional data, clarify information, and continue the conversation. Open-ended questions allow the responder to reply with a more detailed and in-depth statement. A fundamental characteristic of an effective and successful communicator is the ability to ask questions.

COMMUNICATION TECHNIQUES FOR SPECIALIZED SITUATIONS

GIVING FEEDBACK

Although the process can be emotional, it is important that **feedback** be constructive in nature, detailing the quality of someone's performance or conduct without judging on a personal level. Feedback can be written or verbal and should be based on factual data. Effective feedback should be delivered in a timely, consistent, and positively framed manner. If informal, feedback can be used to give advice or to provide clarity. If disciplinary, the feedback should also include improvements that must be made and potential consequences for not meeting standards. When receiving feedback, one must take the time to carefully consider the content and implement it as appropriate. The most important thing to remember about feedback is that it is given to facilitate an improvement.

FACILITATING FOCUS GROUPS

Used to investigate ideas, opinions, and concerns, **focus groups** can be beneficial for clarifying supplemental research because they are relatively timely and inexpensive. The topic and objectives of the group should be clearly defined before potential participants are identified. Participants should be notified that they will remain anonymous and that all information will be confidential. Once a **pool of participants** has been selected and separated into groups, a trained **facilitator** should be chosen, and a guide for forming discussion questions should be constructed. Most studies contain three to 10 focus groups, each with five to 12 voluntary participants, and a typical discussion lasts approximately 90 minutes. A private location is ideal. Afterward, all collected information should be analyzed and reported.

FACILITATING STAFF MEETINGS

There are three core elements to a successful **staff meeting**: 1) invite all attendees to share something, 2) focus on the group and any outcomes that might need adjustment or improvement, and 3) allow time for feedback in the decision-making process. Staff meetings are an excellent way to increase organizational communication and alignment, offering an open floor for staff to give feedback on recent messages or events. They are also a low-budget way to promote staff recognition, wellness programs, employee referral programs, and employee surveys. Moreover, staff meetings have a history of improving productivity, workplace conflicts, team synergy, and employee relations. It is important to consider religious holidays when scheduling staff meetings, seminars, or training events. For example, staff meetings scheduled on Ash Wednesday, Good Friday, Passover, Rosh Hashanah, or Yom Kippur might have low attendance.

USING STORYTELLING OR SKITS

Using creative methods for communication both internally and externally can be valuable. **Storytelling** and **skits** engage the listener in what the speaker is presenting in a meaningful way that other modes of communication do not. With stories and skits, the speaker can conjure emotions, call to action, or build investment in the topic at hand. When utilizing storytelling or skits, one should be authentic and honest. This sincerity builds trust. The problem and the resolution should be detailed: what was not working correctly and how was it addressed? Emotions add power to the story and make it more relatable. The story should be simple, and the problem, the path to the solution, and how it applies elsewhere should all be discussed. The content of the skit or story should be relatable. When the audience can relate to the story or the skit, it becomes more about them and thus more meaningful.

CREATING COMMUNICATION PLANS

A **communication plan** is a strategy used to outline objectives related to communication and how those objectives will be achieved. The plan should detail what specific information is being communicated, who is receiving that information, and when that information should be distributed. How will the communication be delivered (e.g., email, internal posting, social media, or mail), and how will that information be tracked?

A communication plan that clearly states the goals and objectives of the communication is more likely to be successful. This plan should help highlight who needs to know what and identify the best way to reach diverse audiences. It should also include a variety of methods to distribute the communication, and help single out the most effective ways to do so. Everyone involved needs to know what their contribution and expectations are. They should collaborate to find solutions and seek feedback to achieve the best results, and analyze the plan for strengths, weaknesses, obstacles, and threats. This will allow for course correction and to establish a more effective plan.

TRANSLATING TECHNICAL JARGON

Communication that is heavy on technical language can be difficult to understand and detract from the point. Know the audience being addressed and use language that they can understand. As often as possible, without diluting the meaning, try to use more common terms and language in place of **technical jargon**. If it is necessary to use a technical or specific term, the term and its meaning should be explained the first time it is used. Messages should be clear and concise. Long and drawn-out explanations do not hold attention and can prove problematic for recall. Acronyms can be very specific and confusing, so they should be avoided whenever possible. When the use of an acronym is necessary, it should be accompanied by a clear definition. It is also beneficial to determine if the information can be communicated by using an infographic or other visual medium.

FACILITATING COMMUNICATION FROM AN ANONYMOUS SOURCE

Organizations tend to receive **anonymous feedback** in one of two forms: feedback/survey programs and whistleblowing/complaint-reporting channels. Both options are constructive for the organization overall. When implementing and distributing a pulse survey or employee satisfaction survey, the promise of anonymity will likely lead to more detailed and authentic responses. The same is true for reporting or whistleblowing, as an individuals will be more likely to report an issue if his or her identity is private. It is possible to partner with external vendors to implement either program. The program can be detailed, and administration and monitoring can be completely offsite. This process can also be as simple as providing a central location for feedback submissions, such as a comments box.

INFORMAL COMMUNICATION

Free from the rules and policies of formal communication, **informal communication** is casual and is often built around social relationships that develop in the workplace outside of the normal organizational structure. There are advantages and disadvantages to communicating informally in the workplace. One disadvantage is that informal communication is not formal. This can lead to unofficial information or rumors spreading in the workplace. Advantages include employees having someone they can reach out to about various topics when in need of help or guidance. Informal communication can also be more enjoyable, increasing engagement and productivity among employees. This can be a very helpful and beneficial tool when used correctly.

COMMUNICATIONS MEDIA

Communication can be transmitted through a wide variety of **channels** or **media**, such as phone, email, face-to-face, reports, presentations, or social media. The chosen method should fit both the audience and the type of communication. **Information-rich communication channels** include phone, videoconferencing, and face-to-face meetings or presentations. **Information-lean channels** include email, fliers, newsletters, or reports. Attempts to sell a product or service might use a series of phone calls, face-to-face meetings, and presentations. This is because information-rich media are more interactive, which is more appropriate for complex messages that may need clarification. Information-rich and oral communications should be used when there is time urgency, immediate feedback is required, ideas can be simplified with explanations, or emotions may be affected. Information-lean and written communications should be used when the message is simply stating facts or presenting information that needs to be permanently recorded.

ELEMENTS OF NONVERBAL COMMUNICATION

EYE CONTACT

Nonverbal communication can play a critical role in conversation. In order to be an effective communicator, one must develop the skill of making frequent **eye contact**. The way that one person looks at another can convey many sentiments, like hostility, affection, and interest. Maintaining proper eye contact indicates that an individual is engaged and attentive to the communication exchange; it is a sign of active listening. It helps foster feelings of recognition and validation in a conversation and displays a level of respect. It is important for both the sender and receiver of a message to maintain good eye contact. A speaker who consistently makes eye contact with the audience appears more confident, assertive, and authoritative.

BODY LANGUAGE

A person could be giving one message with their verbal language but telling a very different story with their **body language,** another nonverbal form of communication that can convey more powerful messages than verbal communication. This element can help an individual to analyze the feelings and moods of others, demonstrate his or her own confidence, and reveal engagement in the conversation. There are many ways body language is displayed, such as **posture** (how an individual holds his or her body) and **body movement** (how an individual walks, sits, moves his or her head, or stands). There are two main categories of body language: **positive body language** can include an open and relaxed posture and smiling, while **negative body language** can include fidgeting or excessive movement or having one's arms crossed in front of the chest. Understanding the appropriate body language to display in a particular setting and being able to decipher the body language of others will strengthen communication skills overall.

PROXIMITY

Nonverbal messages can be sent by the speaker's **proximity** to the listener. Standing too close while having a conversation can create feelings of discomfort or fear. The field of proxemics (the study of how humans use space) has identified four types of distances based on the level of the relationship between the individuals or groups involved. **Public distance** is used by public speakers. The distance from the speaker to the audience calls for exaggerated gestures and body movements to emphasize the message. **Social distance** is the standard distance for social events or working in the same area. It is often used for formal relationships and tends to rely on eye contact and body position. **Personal distance** consists of interactions between friends and significant others. Touch is common in these interactions. **Intimate distance** is reserved for family, close friends, and romantic relationships. Facial expressions are subtle, and intimate touch (like hugging) can occur. Determining which of the four identified distances to use can increase comfort and understanding among those interacting and provide the right conversational set-up.

GESTURES

An integral part of communication, **gestures** are used to signal understanding, interest, support, approval, irritation, and disapproval. Pointing, giving a thumbs up, eye-rolling, and hand movements while speaking are commonly used to provide meaning and expression while communicating. Some gestures are used with intent (waving with a greeting), while others can be used unconsciously (annoyed eye-rolling). Using the right gesture for the context can improve communication and help ensure that the message is received clearly. It is important to be mindful of the audience when utilizing gestures. Gestures that are common and acceptable in one culture can be offensive in others. The gesture and the message should be matched to avoid miscommunication or misunderstanding.

DELIVERING MESSAGES
PRESENTING INFORMATION TO STAKEHOLDERS

Stakeholders have varied reporting requirements. A presenter should identify what specific information the stakeholder is looking for and how often updates are required. If a stakeholder requests monthly updates on key metrics, that information should be presented concisely. Graphs or tables can be used to track changes or patterns. A presentation for an initiative should begin with the main point, and the problem should be addressed using data and logic. The solution should be detailed and backed up with facts. The presentation should be visually appealing and highlight the key points. Context should be provided for content-specific areas, as many stakeholders have a high-level understanding of the material but may not be familiar with the details. Presentations to stakeholders should be direct and focus on the critical information.

CHOOSING THE CONTENT AND MEDIUM OF COMMUNICATION

Communication will vary significantly across different work groups. For example, a presentation about a new recognition platform for key stakeholders should differ considerably from a presentation of the same topic to non-supervisory employees. A key stakeholder presentation will have data, metrics, and cost analysis, and will build a business case. The presentation to standard employees should demonstrate the perks and benefits of such a platform, leaving out statistical information and costs. Office-based employees will be more likely to read an email or Slack announcement. Production-based employees may be more likely to read a quick post to Slack or another communication channel. The best method of communication depends on who the communication is meant for, what message is the most impactful, and what mode of delivery is the most convenient. The ability to tailor the content and format of messaging to various levels of employees is a critical skill.

EXCHANGING ORGANIZATIONAL INFORMATION
COMMUNICATING HUMAN RESOURCE PROGRAMS, PRACTICES, AND POLICIES TO EMPLOYEES

Human resources (HR) will not achieve much success in initiatives, policies, and programs if they are not properly communicated. Policies should be communicated throughout the onboarding process, whenever changes occur, and as often as the organization believes a revisit is necessary. Employees should be given access to updated copies of policies when changes are made. Compliance items or employment-contingent items should require a signature and be kept on file. HR programs should be advertised. This can be through Slack channels, on the organization's intranet, or even posted on a bulletin board. HR should send out regular communications on policy or program changes. Keeping employees informed about HR-driven material helps build an informed, engaged, and compliant workforce.

HELPING NON-HR MANAGERS COMMUNICATE HR ISSUES

There are certain issues and messages that should come directly from human resources (HR). However, non-HR supervisors, managers, and team leads can be guided through various HR-related conversations. HR should really drive personnel development, which includes training individuals on how to handle sensitive or HR-related issues. This can be accomplished by holding training meetings where different topics are discussed and the proper way to address (and document) these issues is reviewed. Companies can put together guides and instructions for topics like how to respond to an issue if HR is not present. Leadership can be coached on how to approach dress code violations or how to address progressive discipline up to a certain level. Understand the ultimate responsibility of HR in these circumstances, and coach and develop leadership to have responsibility in appropriate situations.

Global Mindset

CULTURAL NORMS, VALUES, AND DIMENSIONS
HALL MODEL OF ORGANIZATIONAL CULTURE

Edward T. Hall developed the **Hall model** to describe cultural relationships and separate them into two classes: high-contrast and low-contrast. **High-contrast relationships** tend to last longer and have more defined patterns of behavior or boundaries of entry; such relationships include families, religious congregations, and on-campus associates. In high-contrast environments, there may be more implicit communications, body language interpretation, shared values, and a great deal of commitment. **Low-contrast relationships** tend to be short-term and require more rules and structure; these include a cafeteria line or navigating a large international airport. In low-contrast environments, there may be more explicit communications, diverse beliefs, and limited commitment. It should be noted that every culture incorporates both high- and low-contrast interactions.

HOFSTEDE'S MODEL OF CROSS-CULTURAL DIFFERENCES

The following are the six values identified by Geert Hofstede's **model of cross-cultural differences**:

- **Power distance** is the social acceptability of power distinctions, such as rich versus poor. In *low power distance societies,* high power distance is regarded as undesirable, and inequalities are kept to a minimum. In *high power distance societies,* power differences or castes are generally accepted, and individuals of particular status receive privileges.
- **Uncertainty avoidance** is the acceptability of ambiguity and the unknown. Societies that practice *strong uncertainty avoidance* attempt to avoid risk and impose structure. Societies that practice *low uncertainty avoidance* view risk as unavoidable and are more tolerant of ambiguity.
- **Individualism vs. collectivism** is the relationship between society as a whole and the individual. *Individualistic cultures* believe in self-reliance and acting in the best interest of the individual. Power is more evenly distributed, and economic mobility is attainable. *Collective cultures* believe in cohesiveness and are loyal to the best interests of the entire group. Power is contained within the ingroup, and economic mobility is limited.
- **Masculinity vs. femininity** is the societal perception of the value of typical male and female traits. *Low masculinity societies* accept the blending of male and female roles and tend to favor traits like cooperation and modesty. *High masculinity societies* accept clearly defined gender roles, and traits like achievement, assertiveness, and competition are championed.
- **Long-term vs. short-term normative orientation** describes a society's propensity to remain traditional or change with the times. Low-scoring societies are skeptical of change and hold steadfast to their norms. High-scoring societies are likely to prepare for the future.
- **Indulgence vs. restraint** is whether a society values fun and gratification or regulation. Societies that favor indulgence allow members to give in to their desire for enjoyment. Those that favor restraint suppress these desires.

SCHEIN'S MODEL OF ORGANIZATIONAL CULTURE

Edgar Schein developed his well-known **model of organizational culture** in the 1980s. Many of Schein's studies indicated that culture is rooted with the CEO and developed over time. The model separates culture into three core layers: 1) artifacts, 2) values and beliefs, and 3) underlying assumptions. The first layer, **artifacts**, is the most visible. This includes the vision and mission, office dress codes, and generally accepted behaviors. Employee **values**, thought patterns, and organizational goals make up the second layer. The deepest layer is the **underlying assumptions**, ideologies, and perceptions of the organization. These cannot be easily measured but can greatly affect the organizational culture.

TROMPENAARS'S MODEL OF ORGANIZATIONAL CULTURE

Fons Trompenaars designed a **model of organizational culture** that divides people and cultures into seven dimensions:

- **Universalism vs. particularism.** What is more important (rules vs. relationships)?
- **Individualism vs. communitarianism.** Who comes first (me vs. community)?
- **Specific vs. diffuse.** How much separation (work/life balance vs. work/life blend)?
- **Neutral vs. affective.** What is appropriate (reason vs. emotion)?
- **Achievement vs. ascription.** Do we need to prove status or title (accomplishments vs. identity)?
- **Sequential time vs. synchronous time.** How do we work (focused vs. multitasking, punctual vs. flexible schedule)?
- **Internal direction vs. outer direction**. What is in control (autonomy vs. circumstance)?

TECHNIQUES FOR BRIDGING INDIVIDUAL DIFFERENCES AND PERCEPTIONS

EMPLOYEE RESOURCE GROUPS

Voluntary employee-led groups known as **employee resource groups (ERGs)** come together based on a shared interest or background. They also sometimes form at the request of an employer. ERGs typically focus on creating a diverse and inclusive workspace. ERGs can form around gender, disability, religion, or race. For example, an interfaith ERG might work to spread awareness of norms and practices of various faiths and cultures. This group might celebrate all religious holidays and seek to respect cultural and religious sensitivities. ERGs benefit both employees and the organization by creating diverse and inclusive environments with resources for support and development.

REVERSE MENTORSHIPS

In a **reverse mentorship**, a junior employee is paired with a more senior employee so that the junior employee can share advice, experience, and skills with the senior mentee. This practice can be especially helpful with new and emerging technologies and work practices. Senior employees may have more tenure within the organization or the workforce, but partnering with junior employees provides them with opportunities to pick up on new skills and perspectives. Senior employees may benefit by gaining more tangible skills, and junior employees gain leadership skills, confidence, and opportunities for continued growth and development. Reverse mentoring improves workplace relationships, increases employee engagement, and helps broaden skills and improve learning.

SENSITIVITY TRAINING

The goal of **sensitivity training** is to create a more open and collaborative working environment by helping individuals within an organization become aware of attitudes, behaviors, and biases that may impact others. This training can involve employees gathering to participate in group activities and discussions in order to develop greater acceptance within the group. Many trainings are directed toward diversity, while others focus on various forms of harassment. Sensitivity training can help workers to develop emotional intelligence, provide guidance on how to deal with difficult or opposing personalities, and review appropriate workplace conversations and interactions. Companies that implement strong sensitivity training programs can benefit because these programs can lead to a more respectful and accountable workforce.

FOCUS GROUPS

A great method to collect qualitative data on different workplace topics, in a **focus group** employee feedback is gathered to provide the employer with insight into the employees' ideas and opinions. A focus group is made up of several individuals who participate in a moderated discussion aimed at gathering information and data regarding a particular topic, issue, or initiative. The moderator asks open-ended questions to encourage conversation. Focus groups are beneficial because they provide the employer with important data while also empowering employees by allowing them a voice in decision-making processes. Focus groups can help identify both weaknesses and strengths within the organization. Holding focus groups and taking action on information discovered in this fashion also shows employees that their feedback is valued and the organization is committed to improvement.

BARRIER REMOVAL

Global and **cultural barriers** are increasing as businesses spread across oceans and countries. When two different cultures clash, gestures can be misinterpreted and communications can be misunderstood. For example, although Americans shake hands when meeting new people, other countries might bow, hug, or kiss. Similarly, making eye contact or expressing emotional sensitivity might be considered offensive in some cultures. As operations grow and the company turns to outsourcing or sending manufacturing overseas, language and other barriers can make finding the best resources difficult and delay communications. **Inclusive cultures** are key to removing these barriers because they welcome individuals regardless of culture, age, race, ethnicity, sexual orientation, religious belief, disability, or any other factor. Inclusive cultures foster understanding and ensure that appropriate accommodations are made in the workplace. Companies dedicated to fostering an inclusive culture also provide team members with regular training to underscore the value of cultural diversity and instill a sense of acceptance.

ASSIMILATION

During a job transition process, employees are separated from their previous roles and gradually initiated into their new roles. **Assimilation** is the final stage of the transition process, when the individual has overcome any initial shock and successfully integrates into the new role and company culture. During this stage, individuals become part of the group and begin to fit in while new expectations are formed. To ensure that the process is a success, new employees should be partnered with long-tenured staff who can show them the ins and outs of the organization. The new employee should be given ample time to ask questions, make and correct mistakes, and adapt to the new environment. They should also be immediately included in office events and meetings.

BEST PRACTICES FOR MANAGING GLOBALLY DIVERSE WORKFORCES
TRANSLATING POLICIES AND PROCEDURES INTO LOCAL LANGUAGES

Many organizations have locations across the globe. This diverse and widespread employee population can lead to issues with policies, procedures, and work rules. If the employer has a significant employee population whose primary language differs from that of other offices, the organization needs to work with an individual or service to **translate** necessary procedures into the other language(s). This ensures that all employees have equal access to policies, expectations, and legal documents. Working with a credible individual or organization for translations ensures that there are no communication or translation issues and the documents are correct and legible. Having these items translated helps prevent miscommunication and other problems, and demonstrates to the diverse workforce that the organization has a commitment to every employee.

ACCOUNTING FOR MULTIPLE TIME ZONES

Global organizations face unique challenges when it comes to scheduling calls or meetings. Mid-afternoon in one part of the world could be the middle of the night in another area. Having productive and beneficial meetings or calls is the goal, so learning how to schedule to account for time differences is key. Having multiple sessions can be helpful. Some sessions can be scheduled first thing in the morning, and others can be scheduled for later in the day to try to capture multiple time zones. Creating an alternating schedule for calls can also be useful. One person may host a meeting later in the evening one week, but then switch off to another person and time for the next meeting. If a meeting relates to an announcement or topic where little input is required, recording it may prove useful, provided that participants are given an avenue to ask questions and address concerns. There may not be one perfect answer, and several options may be required to arrive at the best solution.

OPERATING IN A CULTURALLY DIVERSE WORKPLACE
ADAPTING BEHAVIOR TO DIFFERENT CULTURAL CONDITIONS, SITUATIONS, AND PEOPLE

Adaptability and flexibility are necessary for success in various corporate environments. When traveling for work or collaborating with others from different backgrounds, take steps to learn about the professional preferences of that culture. **Hofstede's model of cross-cultural differences** is an excellent tool that can prepare an individual or organization to interact with **diverse cultures**. Hofstede's model defines six categories of values that can be used to assist with understanding cultural differences: power distance, uncertainty avoidance, individualism vs. collectivism, masculinity vs. femininity, long-term vs. short-term orientation, and indulgence vs. restraint. Using this tool can help individuals to identify proper attire, etiquette, and communication. Having a basic understanding or preview of cultural differences allows an individual to better tailor his or her behaviors in such settings.

DEMONSTRATING ACCEPTANCE OF COLLEAGUES FROM DIFFERENT CULTURES

Today, perhaps more than ever, organizations may have individual employees from all around the world. Demonstrating **acceptance** of colleagues from different cultures can be both exciting and challenging. Learning about the cultures that colleagues and team members come from can avoid a potential misstep, as well as show initiative and open-mindedness. Flexibility also demonstrates acceptance—other cultures may have differences in their workplace priorities, which can affect workflow. For example, different holidays may be recognized, and coworkers may take time off for those holidays. Being aware of these differences and getting to know coworkers from other cultures can help educate individuals on how to best support and embrace diverse backgrounds. Actively listening can prevent miscommunication while also revealing needs, ways of work, and cultural practices, allowing both parties to learn from one another. Individuals and the company as a whole should be respectful and be transparent. Openness, honesty, and kindness maintain accountability and build trust.

OPERATING IN A GLOBAL ENVIRONMENT
TAILORING HUMAN RESOURCE INITIATIVES TO LOCAL NEEDS

Encouraging or even incentivizing employee participation in employee resource groups or diversity, equity, inclusion, and belonging groups can help to educate and involve staff in bridging cultural differences. Having teams take the time regularly to learn about the different cultures and backgrounds represented on the team and in the locations where the organization does business can help build a more-informed workforce. Having the corporate calendar include holidays (religious, cultural, and civic) of the diverse working group is another way to tailor human resource (HR) initiatives to various local needs. HR should also ensure that they have truly equal employment opportunities, working to ensure that job postings and interview processes are open and free from potential prejudice or unconscious bias. Different countries and cultures require different amounts of vacation or working hours. Understanding of labor practices in other locations can help HR design more culturally inviting policies. Benefits programs should meet the needs of various cultural backgrounds. For example, having parental leave versus just maternity leave is very important for some cultures.

MANAGING CONTRADICTORY PRACTICES, POLICIES, AND CULTURAL NORMS

Different cultures have different ways of work, different expectations, and different business practices. When operating in a global environment, navigating these many differences can prove to be quite challenging. Not every location can have a totally different set of policies, procedures, and work rules. However, an employee handbook for a company location in the United States may look significantly different than the same company's handbook in China. Being able to create policies that incorporate and consider cultural differences is imperative to creating a strong and diverse working environment. Organizations must also be willing to make accommodations when specific practices or working rules potentially go against a religious or cultural practice. Providing time and a dedicated location for prayer in the workplace is not an undue burden on the organization and can help build a more integrative workplace.

Chapter Quiz

Ready to see how well you retained what you just read? Scan the QR code to go directly to the chapter quiz interface for this study guide. If you're using a computer, simply visit the bonus page at **mometrix.com/bonus948/shrmcp** and click the Chapter Quizzes link.

Behavioral Competencies: Business

Business Acumen

BUSINESS TERMS AND CONCEPTS
COMPETITIVE ADVANTAGE

An organization may seek to produce goods or provide services better than those of a similar organization, or to produce specialized goods or services to focus on a specific target market. **Competitive advantage** is what sets one organization above another in the eye of the consumer. Competitive advantage leads to higher profit margins and increased value for the organization and its shareholders. This advantage can originate in numerous ways, such as having access to developing technology or other resources not readily available to others, employing a highly skilled workforce, and leading in price points. There are four key areas for building competitive advantage:

- **Cost leadership** is the ability of an organization to offer the same quality product or service as the competition but at a lower price. Companies will often look for the best way to produce goods and services with minimal inefficiencies and well-developed production methods.
- **Differentiation leadership** is another key area to establishing competitive advantage. It entails marketing products and services that are significantly different than offerings from competing organizations. This method requires continuous improvement and investment in research and development.
- **Cost focus** is a strategy similar to cost leadership, but with emphasis on a specific market. It involves offering a quality product/service at a low price with a targeted market segment in mind. Using the cost focus strategy helps an organization establish brand awareness more readily in that market.
- **Differentiation focus** is a strategy like differentiation leadership, in that they both offer specific or custom products, but the differentiation focus strategy offers those specialized products/services to a narrow and targeted market.

REVENUE

For an organization, **revenue** is the total amount of money brought in, measured over a specific time period. The revenue of an organization is its gross income before subtracting any expenses. Revenue is calculated as the total of the company's earnings plus gained interest and increased equity over a specified period, such as a quarter or year. Calculation and analysis of revenue is critical to understanding the financial success of the organization.

PROFIT AND LOSS

The difference between revenue and expenses that determine if the company made or lost money is referred to as the **profit and loss**. Profit and loss can be simply explained as the money brought into an organization and the money going out of an organization, respectively. Net profit and loss can be calculated by finding the difference between gross profit/loss and the sum of indirect income/expenses of the organization. If the difference is positive, the company is making a profit. If the difference is negative, the company is experiencing a loss for the calculated period. There are many expenses that come out of the revenue of an organization, such as compensation, advertising/marketing, utilities, licensing, building fees (rent/mortgage), the cost of making a product or providing a service, and insurance. These expenditures are often tracked through a **profit and loss statement**, which helps the organization determine if the business is generating revenue or losing revenue.

FINANCIAL PROJECTIONS

Financial projections are a collection of financial statements used to forecast future expenses and revenue. These projections have numerous uses both internally and externally. Additional funding can be secured using financial projections. An organization can also analyze overall business performance and determine areas for improvement. Financial projections are used to demonstrate what an organization plans to do with its money, and what its growth expectations look like. Financial projections are made up of external and internal data. Internal data included in the projection should include an income statement, a cash flow statement, and a balance sheet. The **income statement** displays expenses, revenue, and profit for a set time period. The **cash flow statement** details incoming and outgoing cash. The **balance sheet** shows business assets, liabilities, and equity. External data included in the projection can include market growth rates, historical growth trends in the market, and consumer demand.

QUALITY

The **quality** of an organization plays a large role in the image, branding, and reputation of the organization to the public and consumers. It can have various definitions, depending on how the word is applied. For example, it can be defined as how well an organization meets the expectations and needs of its customers. This metric can be measured using customer satisfaction surveys, customer complaints, and other methods of feedback. Some business areas have specific ways to measure quality. In manufacturing, for example, there are set standards related to the reliability and safety of a product and customer satisfaction with the product. In a service business area, quality may be measured based on response time, how complaints are addressed and resolved, and levels of customer service.

SERVICE-LEVEL AGREEMENTS

A **service-level agreement (SLA)** is a contract between at least two parties, where one party (or group) provides a service to another party (or group). SLAs can be informal contracts, such as between departments, or they can be formal and legally binding contracts between one organization and another. There are three main types of **SLAs:** customer-based, service-based, and multilevel.

- A **customer-based** SLA exists between a vendor and a customer. It details the level of service that will be delivered to the customer. An agreement between a customer and a payroll service is an example of a customer-based SLA.
- An **internal** SLA can exist between departments to outline the roles and responsibilities of the teams so that there is a clear understanding of expectations. An SLA between the marketing and sales departments might detail lead requirements from marketing to sales in order to reach goals.
- A **multilevel** SLA is divided into different tiers or sections based on the level of access or service provided. For example, a software-as-a-service (SaaS) provider might offer basic email services to all individuals within an organization, and access to additional features or software such as word processing or storage options to those in specific departments.

FIXED AND VARIABLE COSTS

Organizations are responsible for both fixed and variable costs related to the operations of the business. **Fixed costs** do not change in relation to the activity of a business; they remain the same regardless of how much or how little a company produces. Property taxes, rent, licensing, and insurance are examples of common fixed costs. **Variable costs** do change based on business activity. These costs increase as production increases, and lower as production shrinks. Utilities, raw materials, and payroll are examples of common variable costs.

SUPPLY AND DEMAND

The term **supply and demand** refers to the economic relationship involving the cost of a product, product availability, and buyer demand for the product. **Supply** is the amount of the product that is being sold on the market by companies producing that item or service. When the price point is high, it is profitable for an organization to increase supply. Supply can be impacted by numerous factors, including cost of production and availability of raw material. **Demand** is how many goods buyers are willing to purchase at different prices. If the price point is higher, fewer items will be demanded. As the price point lowers, demand increases. Factors that can impact demand can include pricing, the buyer's expectation, and the buyer's budget.

NET INCOME

The amount of money that a business makes after deducting the costs of raw goods/materials, taxes, wages, and operating expenses is its **net income**. This measurement is concrete and, for a publicly traded organization, is used to help calculate the earnings per share. This calculation is also the "bottom line" on an income statement and is used to understand how profitable a business is.

KEY PERFORMANCE INDICATORS (KPIS)

Quantifiable metrics used to measure the long-term performance of particular areas, **key performance indicators (KPIs)** are used to gauge the efficiency of operational and strategic plans within an organization or department. These metrics help stakeholders and management to make data-based decisions that will improve performance and profitability. KPIs allow organizations to identify areas for improvement, assess actual performance against goals, and determine how to best allocate available resources. KPIs can be used in almost all business areas, including sales, customer service, production, human resources, and information technology. It is helpful to be familiar with and understand the following types of KPIs:

- **Leading KPIs** can be used to help project future outcomes based on the available data. The percentage of growth in a sales pipeline is a leading indicator for increased sales revenue.
- **Lagging KPIs** measure performance after the event has taken place and are used to support long-term trends. For example, an employee's sales average (percent of consultations that resulted in a closed deal) is a lagging indicator.
- **Functional unit KPIs** are used to measure specific functions or areas within an organization, providing information on whether that area is achieving its objectives and performing well. Customer service response time is a functional unit KPI.
- **Operational KPIs** measure performance over a short term (such as month over month) to give insight into efficiency and how operational objectives are being met. How quickly inventory is turned over is an example of an operational KPI.
- **Strategic KPIs** typically track big-picture and high-level goal progression. They really indicate how the organization is doing. Return on investment is a major strategic KPI.

ANALYZING AND INTERPRETING BUSINESS DOCUMENTS

STRATEGIC PLANS

A **strategic plan** defines and communicates the direction that an organization will take over the course of three to five years. The plan contains the company's mission and vision, organizational goals and objectives, and the actions that it plans to take to achieve those goals. A strategic plan differs from a business plan in that strategic plans are recommended for companies that are already established. There are three main elements in the strategic planning process:

- **Forming the strategy.** Assess the current situation using internal and external audits. These assessments gather data in areas such as relevant industry data, employee feedback, and **SWOT** (strengths, weaknesses, opportunities, and threats) analysis. This information helps stakeholders determine where to allocate company resources for maximum return, which markets should be pursued or abandoned, and how growth and expansion should occur.
- **Implementing the strategy.** Once the strategy is formed, the organization needs to establish objectives and targets related to achieving the desired strategy outcome. Key performance indicators (KPIs) should be used to map out the processes and help monitor progress. Communication about the plan and changes throughout its implementation is key to success. Communicating the desired results and updates will help garner "buy-in" from individuals, helping to ensure the success of the initiatives.

- **Evaluate and revise the strategy.** Internal and external factors affecting strategy implementation need to reviewed, as does the success of the objectives and targets. When necessary, corrective steps should be taken and revisions should be made to make the strategy most effective.

Each of these three elements need to occur throughout all levels of the business, so that each area is aligned with the others. Communication and feedback throughout the organization are critical to help the organization function more effectively as a team. Establishing strong strategic plans allows an organization to move from a reactive approach to a proactive approach, which means that the company may have the opportunity to influence a situation versus just responding to it.

CONTRACTS

Documents that define binding agreements between two or more individuals or groups, **contracts** are vital to the success of an organization. They help outline and define interactions between parties, which helps to eliminate ambiguity and friction. Contracts should include guidelines for how to handle issues and problems that may arise over time and outline expectations for vendors, employees, and partners. Contracts are also utilized to prevent proprietary information from being leaked or keep trade secrets internal. For a contract to be legally binding, it must contain several elements:

- **Offer.** The terms of the contract such as parties involved, length of service, value or price, and the scope of services.
- **Acceptance.** The involved parties agree on the offer.
- **Consideration.** The parties in the contract exchange something of value. If the buyer contracts for a recognition program, the buyer receives the program. The seller receives money based on the terms outlined in the offer.

When properly implemented and utilized, business contracts help manage business expectations and aid in avoiding unnecessary liability.

GRANTS

A business **grant** is money distributed to a company to be used for growth, hiring, development, or expansion. Grants are frequently bestowed on businesses that require research funding, are looking to expand, or that are starting up. There are two types of grants: grants from the government and private grants from other organizations or corporations. Grant programs have specific criteria and application requirements. In order to obtain a grant, a business needs to state the need for the grant money, that the grant money will be used for business purposes, and that there is a set purpose and goal outlined. Additionally, the business needs to follow the application process and provide any documentation or information requested. Grants are typically reserved for small businesses.

STANDARD OPERATING PROCEDURES

A **standard operating procedure (SOP)** is a collection of step-by-step instructions put together by an organization to help employees perform routine tasks and duties. **SOPs** aid in quality assurance, consistency, efficiency, and uniformity of output from employees. The use of this tool helps to minimize miscommunication and errors. Internal processes and procedures are clearly outlined to keep all employees and stakeholders on the same page. **SOPs** improve employee training and onboarding because key tasks are clearly defined with work instructions, eliminating guesswork and uncertainty. They also help maintain organizational knowledge as turnover and promotions occur. These instructions are documented so that there is no confusion or loss of understanding as people move in and out of a department or company.

BUSINESS PLANS

A **business plan** is a detailed outline and definition of an organization's objectives and how the organization plans to achieve its goals. Business plans are used to identify metrics and priorities within a company. This document can be used for both internal and external audiences. Internally, it can be used to drive the company toward achieving its objectives and goals. Externally, it can be used to obtain investments or lending opportunities. No two business plans are exactly alike, but many share common key parts:

- **Executive summary.** This section introduces the company, including the mission statement and detailed information about employees, location, leadership, and operations.
- **Products and services.** This section introduces the products/services the company offers, including information like pricing, benefit to the customer, and how long the product will last. Companies can also use this section to highlight research and development or trademarks/patents specific to the organization. Information about the manufacturing or production process can also be included.
- **Market analysis.** The company should detail its strengths and weaknesses here. Expected demand should be listed, as should opportunity to gain market share. The company may also detail its competition and how it fits into that particular market.
- **Market strategy.** Advertising and marketing campaigns should be outlined, including the channels that will be used to target audiences. The company should also detail how it intends to attract and keep its customer base.
- **Financial planning.** Balance sheets, revenue projections/estimates, and financial statements should be provided, along with a detailed analysis of each, to describe the current and projected financial state of the organization.
- **Budget.** This area of the business plan includes costing information related to development, marketing, production, staffing, and any other related business expenses.

The information in the business plan can serve as a guide for how the organization should run.

ORGANIZATIONAL CHARTS

Visual diagrams that detail and outline the reporting structure within a company, **organizational charts** depict the different departments in the company, displaying the relationships between individuals within the organization. Many organizational charts follow a **hierarchical** model, with the highest-ranking individuals at the top and lower-ranking individuals below them. **Matrix organizational charts** are slightly more complicated; they interconnect employees, teams, or departments with more than one manager based on projects and interactions. **Flat organizational charts** display individuals on the same level, reflecting more power equality than shown in hierarchical charts. **Divisional organizational charts** may display employees based on product type or region.

BUSINESS CONTINUITY PLANS

A **business continuity plan (BCP)** is a set of standards and guidelines that an organization uses to ensure proper risk management and to prevent and recover from potential company threats such as natural disasters or cyber threats. The BCP should protect both personnel and assets, . It should also guide the company on how to react quickly and continue to function when faced with a threat. The planning process for the BCP should contain the following steps:

- **Business impact analysis.** Functions and resources that are critical or time-sensitive should be identified.
- **Recovery.** Critical or time-sensitive business functions must have guidelines and implementation steps for recovery.
- **Plan development.** Framework plans should be developed and documented, and teams should be assigned to carry out required roles.
- **Training.** Teams assigned to required roles should complete exercises that review the plan and ensure that they are prepared to react.

Having a proper BCP in place will allow an organization to reduce company downtime and loss in the face of a threat or disaster.

ELEMENTS OF A BUSINESS CASE

A **business case** is a document produced to explore solutions to a business problem. Based on objective data, it facilitates decision-making for scenarios such as committing to large purchases, choosing vendors, or implementing new initiatives. A properly written business case clears up potential confusion or disagreements early on in the project timeline, helping the firm complete its objectives more effectively. Although the content requirements of a business case will vary based on leader preferences, there are common elements that should typically be included:

- **Problem statement.** The business case should begin with identifying the problem that needs to be fixed.
- **Background.** The problem background will help readers understand the cause(s) of the issue. It should also state the requirements to combat the issue in general terms.
- **Objectives.** The business case should state how solving the issue will help the firm.
- **Current status.** The business case needs to describe how the solution will affect current operations.
- **Requirements.** This section should clearly define the resources that the project will need to be successful, such as capital, staffing, time commitment, software, and so on.
- **Alternatives.** The business case should list, describe, compare, and contrast several alternatives to the proposed solution. This gives leadership options and demonstrates that human resources has done their due diligence in their research.
- **Additional considerations.** The business case must account for potential risks and anything else that may be affected by the project.
- **Action plan.** The action plan should spell out specific steps that will be taken both in the short (first three months) and long (beyond three months) term. Project milestones need to be established and measurements for success defined. It should also be clear who will oversee the project.
- **Executive summary.** This should be a high-level, one-page document showing how the information gathered culminates in a specific conclusion.

BUSINESS INTELLIGENCE TOOLS AND TECHNIQUES

Businesses are constantly generating data, and they need an effective way to utilize this data to become and stay competitive. Previously, businesses would simply construct reports with their data and use the reports for decision-making. Although that still happens every day, data is now also being used in more advanced ways.

ONLINE ANALYTICAL PROCESSING (OLAP)

An on-demand method of processing data that facilitates decision-making, **online analytical processing (OLAP)** is capable of reporting, what-if planning, and trend spotting, to name a few of its uses. OLAP also allows the user to view data from different perspectives, which provides a deeper understanding of the subject at hand.

BUSINESS INTELLIGENCE PORTALS

A **business intelligence portal** is a centrally stored collection of firm data that is accessible on demand across the organization. This type of portal has a user interface that allows employees to run a number of analytical processes. It shows the results of queries in a visual format, making it easier to spot trends and answer business questions.

ADVANCED ANALYTICS

Although **advanced analytics** includes reporting data, it goes way beyond that. By way of data mining, formulas, and algorithms, advanced analytics can be used for forecasting, detecting patterns, and revealing correlations. Advanced analytics is also a part of keeping up with technology, including machine learning and artificial intelligence. Although advanced analytics is a powerful business intelligence tool, there is a caveat. Using data for reporting produces straightforward, typically accurate results. Analyzing the data, however, requires interpretation. Those handling the task should be trained to do so and prepared to continuously refine their approach.

PREDICTIVE ANALYTICS

The use of statistics, historical data, and modeling techniques to make predictions about outcomes and performance in the future is called **predictive analytics**. This type of analysis looks at current and past data patterns to establish whether those patterns are likely to appear again. These techniques can help the organization determine what resources need to be adjusted to be best prepared for future events. Numerous industries rely on predictive analytics as one of many decision-making tools. Human resources uses predictive analytics to determine staffing needs, determine the causation behind high turnover, and for diversity and inclusion initiatives. Supply chain uses predictive analytics for managing inventory levels, downtime, and demand. Marketing uses predictive analytics for targeted campaigns, looking at content and strategies that appeal to specific demographics. The benefits of using this technique are plentiful and can help reduce risk to the organization and allow better positioning for future growth.

TREND ANALYSIS

Using a company's financial statements to identify and recognize patterns within the market and to forecast future performance, in an attempt to make the best decisions based on the results of the completed analysis, is called **trend analysis**. Trend analysis is performed by collecting data from records and plotting that information on a chart, with time on the horizontal axis, to define patterns from the information provided. There are three primary types of trends to understand:

- **Downtrends** indicate that the market is moving downward. The value of stocks and assets may decrease. The size of the economy may decrease. Businesses may need to seek new and innovative ways to stay competitive. Job loss and production decreases may occur. This may also indicate that the market is not favorable for further investment.
- **Uptrends** indicate that the market is moving upward. This can mean that the price of stock or the number of jobs available is increasing. This can also indicate a period of economic growth, that the economy is moving into a positive market, and that the investment cycle has begun.
- **Horizontal trends** indicate that the prices of shares and assets are staying relatively consistent and are not moving noticeably upward or downward. It can be difficult to determine the direction of this trend and whether it is a good time to invest. Forecasting may be challenging. The government will often attempt to push the economy toward an upward trend.

Trend analysis is used in sales patterns, budget forecasting, and expense reporting. When using this technique, the goal is to determine the change within the market from one period to another to make more informed business decisions.

SCENARIO PLANNING

Companies may use **scenario planning** to consider potential future events to develop relevant and long-term strategies. Scenario planning is different from forecasting in that it considers quantitative data and past occurrences in addition to qualitative data and trend analysis. Scenario planning encourages the company to think outside of the box, which can help to anticipate various and unexpected changes. This can assist with risk mitigation, impacts on costs, and successful allocation of materials and resources.

BALANCED SCORECARD

The **balanced scorecard (BSC)** is a strategic metric that is used to recognize and manage internal processes and their external outcomes to provide continuous improvement. This tool is used for planning and aligning day-to-day duties with company strategy. The BSC has four key areas used to develop goals, objectives, and to measure key performance indicators (KPIs):

- **Finance** details areas such as sales, costs, and income to get a clear picture of how the organization is performing financially.
- **Customer/stakeholder** covers the organizational performance from the customer or stakeholder point of view. This area relies on feedback from customers or stakeholders to determine satisfaction related to quality, availability, and service.
- **Internal process** relates to how smoothly the organization is running. This section targets reducing waste, improving delivery of products/services, and minimizing waste.
- **Learning and growth** considers the corporate culture, technology, training, and how efficiently those areas are leveraged to perform competitively.

FINANCIAL ANALYSIS TERMS AND METHODS TO ASSESS BUSINESS HEALTH
FINANCIAL RATIOS

There are several types of **financial ratios**, which can be broken down into categories for management, stakeholders, and auditors. **Profitability ratios** analyze a business's ability to generate earnings in comparison to expense costs. **Liquidity ratios** measure the business's available cash or ability to pay off short-term debts. **Operational efficiency and employee productivity ratios** measure the efficiency of employees and business resources to generate a profit. **Leverage or capital structure ratios** assess how the business uses debt to finance operations. Although being able to calculate financial ratios is important, being able to interpret financial ratios is more valuable.

BALANCE SHEETS

A **balance sheet** conveys a company's financial position and reports its assets, liabilities, and equity over a specified period of time. A balance sheet reflects the following equation:

$$Assets - Liabilities = Equity$$

An **asset** is any resource possessed by the company as a result of previous actions and from which future gains are expected. A **liability** is a current obligation as a result of previous actions expected to result in an outflow of resources. **Equity** is the residual interest and assets after deducting all liabilities.

BUDGETS

For many businesses, creating a **budget** involves collecting relevant or historical data and often stems directly from the organizational vision and the strategic plan. The **strategic plan** should ensure that resources are used to support the organizational objectives. Fixed costs, variable costs, and revenue estimates can be developed to establish the budget. **Budget performance** should be monitored on a monthly, quarterly, and annual basis. Any **budget variances** should be investigated to determine the cause; some variances may be caused by unforeseen situations, such as a change in compliance regulations or training requirements. Some businesses will provide individual departments with a budget. Factors to consider when constructing the budget for a human resources (HR) department might include the number of employees, benefit cost projections, training needs, and any anticipated legal expenses.

Budgeting helps to ensure that future financial costs are coordinated and controlled. There are two basic methods for creating budgets: a bottom-up approach and a top-down approach. **Bottom-up budgeting** requires department supervisors to forecast departmental expenses and payroll costs for the coming period. This method relies heavily on lower-level supervisors, with assistance from HR and final approval from top managers. **Top-down budgeting** involves estimating expenses and payroll costs for an entire organization and then allocating a set amount to each department manager, leaving them responsible for managing their funds.

CASH FLOW STATEMENTS

The amount of money taken in compared to the amount of money spent during a given period is known as **cash flow**. Profits, credits, and loans are each an **inflow** of cash, whereas expenses, purchases, and payments are each an **outflow** of cash. Most businesses prepare and rely heavily upon a **cash flow statement** to monitor business performance. One obvious key factor of cash flow is **profits**. An organization can sustain itself with additional funds or reserved savings in spite of a lack of profits, but not for long. The other obvious key factor is **expenditures**, which must be kept within budget and sustained. Many businesses will utilize cash flow **forecasting** and then compare forecasted figures to actual amounts. Businesses should always strive for positive cash flow. Negative cash flow can be an indication of poor company health. While debt in certain cases is necessary for growth, negative cash flow forces the business to take on debt just to operate.

PROFIT AND LOSS STATEMENTS

A **profit and loss statement** reports a company's income, expenses, and profits over a specified period of time. **Income**, or **profit**, increases in the form of inflows, expansion of assets, or reduction in liabilities, resulting in an increase in equity, not including contributions. **Expenses** include declines in the form of outflows, depletion of assets, or undertaking of liabilities, resulting in decreases in equity, not including distributions.

OVERHEAD

The costs required to run a business that cannot be directly tied to any specific product, service, or business activity are referred to as **overhead**. An organization's overhead can be fixed, variable, or a hybrid combination.

- **Fixed overhead** refers to costs that remain consistent over the long term and are not closely influenced by changes in the business. Fixed overhead variable examples include insurance premiums, licensing fees, and rent.
- **Variable overhead** refers to costs that fluctuate with changes in the business. Variable overhead is less consistent than fixed overhead. The slower the business activity, the lower the variable overhead. Variable overhead examples include marketing, shipping, and maintenance.
- **Semi-variable overhead** refers to a hybrid of fixed and variable overhead. With semi-variable overhead, some cost is generated regardless of the activity of the business, and these costs will likely increase as activity increases. Examples can include the cost of utilities and commission earnings.

CASH FLOW

The amount of money moving in and out of a business is its **cash flow**. Cash flow is typically separated into the categories of cash flow from operations, cash flow from investing, and cash flow from financing. A cash flow statement details the company's sources and uses of cash over a given time period. Cash flow that is negative for an extended amount of time could indicate trouble for the business. Tracking and analyzing the cash flow of an organization is important because it helps determine where the company stands.

CASH RESERVES

Funds that organizations set aside in case of an emergency, **cash reserves** can be critical for a company when there is an unexpected expense or decline in revenues. While cash reserves may limit investment opportunities, they can protect the company during an unexpected event.

RETURN ON INVESTMENT (ROI)

The **return on Investment (ROI)** is usually shown as a percentage that measures how beneficial a new tool or practice has been compared to its initial investment. The **ROI** can be calculated as:

$$\text{ROI} = \frac{\text{Net return on investment}}{\text{Cost of investment}} \times 100\%$$

HR professionals may be asked about ROI to determine the effectiveness of training programs, recently implemented software, or supplementations to the workforce. However, it is important to consider all associated costs. For example, the ROI of a harassment training seminar should include the travel costs to get employees to the seminar. Total costs associated with the seminar can then be compared to alternatives such as videos or webinars. Another strategy is to compare the firm's ROI with the ROI of other companies. If there is a competitive return, strategic plans should not be drastically changed. However, if the ROI is much lower than that of competitors, a new strategy is in order. It should also be noted that when making decisions among investments, an estimated ROI is used.

SALES PIPELINE

The **sales pipeline** is a model that tracks incoming potential leads/prospects for a business as they enter the sales process and move toward becoming customers. The model allows visibility into forecasted deals, as well as offering the data and analysis to improve upon lead generation and closing. With a sales pipeline, the number of deals that are expected to close in a given timeframe are visible, which helps determine if sales quotas will be met.

BUSINESS AND COMPETITIVE AWARENESS

It is important to have an understanding of the organization's operations, products, and services while considering the economic, social, and political environments in which the business may operate. **Business and competitive awareness** covers a broad range of areas, especially on a global scale. The organization must be knowledgeable of other practices in similar industries while keeping up with internal, external, and local factors. This can be done through **benchmarking** or by following news and trends. Moreover, organizations can ensure they are competitive by focusing on human development, the current labor market, financial policies, level of business sophistication, and overall quality of products, services, and work environment.

BUSINESS ANALYSIS

The methodology of **business analysis** works as a vehicle for introducing change into an organization, the product of which is often a series of proposed solutions that align stakeholder needs and business capabilities. Human resource practitioners might assist with business analysis in the form of identifying leadership goals , functioning as strategists, or acting as change agents. Business analysis comes in many forms, all of which involve collecting and analyzing data, then investigating any gaps. One popular method of business analysis is the **SWOT analysis**, which looks at the **strengths, weaknesses, opportunities, and threats** of the enterprise. Business analysis may be used to investigate business processes, management styles, team collaboration, employee engagement, information systems, or organizational communication and culture, to name a few.

STRATEGIC ALIGNMENT

Coordinating business resources and practices with the organizational mission and environment is called **strategic alignment**. Business partners should investigate potential challenges, both internal and industry-wide. The goal of strategic alignment is to optimize performance and competitiveness to meet strategic goals. Human resource practitioners might support strategic alignment by following these steps:

- Outline **departmental objectives** that support business success.
- Establish **departmental goals** such as reducing costs or increasing engagement and retention.
- Develop an **action plan** for meeting goals.
- **Collaborate** with others, and set the plan into motion.
- **Report** and **monitor** the results.

Consultation

ORGANIZATIONAL CHANGE MANAGEMENT THEORIES AND MODELS

DALTON'S THEORY OF LASTING CHANGE

Many change efforts struggle to produce **lasting and sustainable results**. Although initial goals may be met, the ability to stick to the efforts or behaviors needed to prolong success proves to be more difficult. Gene Dalton argued that change will not occur without a feeling of loss or pain to motivate it and that people will continue old patterns of behavior unless they feel a need for change. He also noted that individuals initiating and supporting organizational change should be those perceived as trustworthy facilitators.

LEWIN'S CHANGE MANAGEMENT MODEL

Kurt Lewin's theory of **change management** describes three stages for planning change: unfreezing, change, and refreezing. **Unfreezing** occurs when current values, attitudes, and behaviors are challenged, and people understand the need for change. **Change** happens during the action phase, whereby the situation is examined and a new equilibrium is created. People develop new values, attitudes, or patterns of behaviors. **Refreezing** is when the change is stabilized and new patterns are solidified. Refreezing requires that people experience positive consequences to strengthen their continuing commitment to the change process.

MCKINSEY 7-S MODEL

The **McKinsey 7-S model** is frequently used in strategic planning and change management. The model is founded on the principle that each company has seven **elements,** or key factors. The seven key elements of the McKinsey 7-S model are:

- **Strategy:** plan for competitive advantage and growth regarding business, products, and markets
- **Structure:** composition of reporting hierarchy
- **Systems**: everyday procedures and processes
- **Shared values**: core concepts and work ethic, organizational mission, and goals
- **Style**: leadership approach and operational culture
- **Staff**: employee development and empowerment
- **Skills**: competencies and capabilities

Strategy, structure, and systems are easily identified. Shared values, style, staff, and skills can be more difficult to describe and may be continuously changing. All of the elements are interconnected and each may affect any other.

KOTTER'S 8-STEP CHANGE MODEL

John Kotter's **8-step change model** describes eight steps for implementing effective change:

1. **Create a sense of urgency.** Examine the competitive market, identify threats or opportunities, articulate importance of speed, and make the case for change.
2. **Build a guiding coalition.** Establish support from executives, and construct a group with credibility and power to lead change efforts.
3. **Develop a shared vision and strategy.** Create a plan to direct change efforts, and develop success metrics.
4. **Communicate the change vision.** Readily and persistently communicate the new vision and strategy from the top down.
5. **Empower action.** Eliminate obstacles, systems, or structures that undermine the new idea, and reward creativity.
6. **Generate short-term wins.** Recognize and reward visible improvements in performance.
7. **Capitalize on momentum.** Take advantage of small wins, reinvite those who have resisted, and become reenergized.
8. **Make the change stick.** Continue to encourage new behaviors and leadership development.

KUBLER-ROSS CHANGE CURVE

The **Kubler-Ross Change Curve** (which is adapted from the Kubler-Ross model of five stages of grief) is a model of the emotional stages experienced when going through transition or change. The Change Curve can be used to help an organization identify potential barriers to change in various projects and initiatives, so that strategies can be developed to overcome such barriers. There are several different versions of the Kubler-Ross Change Curve, and it is important to keep in mind that each individual handles change differently based on experiences, personality, and adaptability. A common change model has the following markers:

1. **Shock:** surprise or astonishment about an event/initiative
2. **Denial:** skepticism or distrust, trying to disprove or escape the impending change
3. **Frustration:** beginning to see that things are different, may be anxious or angry at times
4. **Depression:** gloominess, lack of motivation, lowered levels of energy
5. **Experiment:** starting to engage or interact with the new situation or state of things
6. **Decision:** adapting to the new situation, feeling more positive or resolved toward the change
7. **Integration:** once the changes have been adopted, an improved outlook and refreshed perspective

The Change Curve can be utilized to help organizations and individuals understand and navigate the changing feelings and reactions to substantial loss or change.

> **Review Video: Organizational Change Management Theories**
> Visit mometrix.com/academy and enter code: 404217

ORGANIZATIONAL CHANGE PROCESSES

LEADERSHIP BUY-IN

Leadership **buy-in** is support or endorsement for something. In the case of change, leadership buy-in is critical. Often, leadership support is necessary to get the change movement started because leaders may need to approve the use of resources or major modifications to business operations. If the change requires endorsement from leaders but they will not give it, the change will be defeated before it can get started. Additionally, leadership buy-in is necessary to champion the change across the organization. If the leaders believe in the effort, they can communicate their enthusiasm for it and model the new desired behavior, making it easier for the change to take root.

BUILDING A CASE FOR CHANGE

One useful way to approach organizational change activities is the **action research model**. Once a problem has been identified, there are six basic steps that follow: data gathering, feedback of data to the target group, data discussions and diagnosis, action planning, action, and recycling. **Data gathering** involves collecting information about the problem from various sources, such as observations, interviews, surveys, and archived data. **Feedback of data to a target group** involves making the gathered data openly available and sharing it with a group through presentations. **Data discussions and diagnosis** involve a roundtable conversation and analysis by the target group to diagnose a root cause and to explore alternatives or viable solutions. **Action planning** involves creating a plan to implement solutions, which may require outside parties. **Action** involves the execution of new changes. Finally, **recycling** involves reviewing and repeating the processes to ensure that problems do not reoccur.

ENGAGING EMPLOYEES

For changes to be implemented successfully, employees need to embrace them, or at least understand them. This can be accomplished by engaging the employees in the change process and ensuring that they remain engaged overall. **Engaging employees** in the change process includes asking for and using their feedback, when possible, before, during, and after the change. Doing this shows that the organization values their opinions and places an importance on collaboration and transparency. When employees can help to shape a change, they are far more likely to go along with it. Additionally, when employees are truly engaged at work,

they will have an easier time adapting to change, even if unpleasant, because of their strong emotional commitment to the company.

COMMUNICATING CHANGE

It is important to provide **clear communication** to employees and all stakeholders as early as possible. Communications should be simple, with explanations of both the necessity and the timeline for the change. Employees should be fully informed as to what will be staying the same, any negative reactions that can be anticipated should be countered proactively. There should be opportunities for **two-way communications**. This provides employees with the chance to ask questions. Then communications should be repeated, with an explanation of how employees will be kept informed throughout the process so as to manage expectations. Finally, leadership should get involved to advocate for the change and lead by example to keep morale high.

REMOVING BARRIERS

Human resource practitioners must be cognizant of any **barriers** to organizational change. Change actions can be thwarted by barriers such as staff attitudes or behaviors that discourage implementing new ideas, insufficient skills or technologies, and distances or obstacles between formal structures. These barriers can be eliminated by regularly communicating the rationale and timeline of the change, implementing new training programs or technologies, involving employee advocates in decision-making processes, and welcoming feedback from all levels.

CONSULTING PROCESSES

DISCOVERY

The consultation process begins with **discovery**. During the discovery phase, the consultant should begin by gathering all relevant information through an audit process and reviewing the facts. In this phase, the consultant will learn the business and user requirements. This may be done through methods like content analysis and employee interviews. The consultant should start each potential project with an open mind and consider all perspectives to build trust.

ANALYSIS AND SOLUTIONS

After all the information has been gathered, **analysis** can begin. The consultant should conduct a SWOT (strength, weaknesses, opportunities, and threats) analysis as well as utilize any other methods that are appropriate for the situation. The consultant should investigate industry best practices and strive for solutions that fit the staff and customers. Once the organizational culture and any potential barriers have been considered, a diagnosis can be made, and **solutions** can be created. It is a good idea to engage stakeholders in the development of solutions when possible. This will lead to increased satisfaction with the consulting process and outcome.

RECOMMENDATION

Following the analysis, recommended actions and goals should be detailed in a **strategic project plan**. During this stage, it is important to clearly document how the solution will develop from the current state to the desired state and how the process will be managed.

IMPLEMENTATION

Once the strategic project plan has been accepted, successful **implementation** of the recommended solution is critical. Human resource consultants must manage all logistics to include staffing, scheduling, procuring needed supplies and equipment, and communicating the project status to stakeholders. Clear processes and procedures to support and utilize the solution should be established, and training opportunities should be available as needed. Throughout the implementation process, the consultant must maintain brand image, integrity, and a good working relationship with stakeholders. Once the solution has been implemented, the consultant should schedule follow-ups with affected stakeholders to ensure satisfaction and to make any necessary adjustments.

EFFECTIVE CONSULTING TECHNIQUES
UNDERSTANDING ORGANIZATIONAL CULTURE

The **organizational culture** is essentially how and why an organization operates. Consultants must understand and factor in the organizational culture as they craft their strategic plans. If the consultant tries to implement a change that doesn't fit the culture, the change will not take root. Knowing the culture will enable the consultant to see potential roadblocks to and opportunities for developing and facilitating new strategies.

UNDERSTANDING AREAS AND LIMITS OF ONE'S OWN EXPERTISE

Consultants must recognize the **areas and limits of their expertise**. Knowing this, they will be able to enjoy greater success because they can get involved with projects that play to their strengths. Ignoring this may lead consultants to get in over their heads and underperform, which damages their credibility and reputation. When the needs of the client fall outside the realm of the consultant's areas of expertise, the consultant should recommend other resources or consultants. This will help strengthen relationships with clients and build more meaningful networks with other consultants whose strengths might offset existing limitations.

SETTING REASONABLE EXPECTATIONS

Customer satisfaction and understanding **client expectations** are vitally important to a consultant's success. Managing client expectations and establishing needs, priorities, and timelines early in the relationship will save both the consultant and the client from future headaches. A consultant must be honest and avoid making any unrealistic promises. A consultant should explain what is realistic and why. Once both parties are in agreement, specific and measurable goals, objectives, and timetables should be outlined to establish credibility. Client expectations should be revisited with regular discussions to review how the project is advancing and the lines of communication should be kept open to include any necessary changes to the schedule. This will help to avoid inconsistencies and misunderstandings.

AVOIDING OVERPROMISING

Although everyone wants to guarantee the best service, consultants should **avoid overpromising** in an effort to gain a client or please everyone. Overpromising and underdelivering will likely lead to a lot of frustration and dissatisfaction. Setting reasonable expectations, while being transparent and honest with clients, can help avoid any difficulties or misunderstandings. It is far better to set goals and objectives that are attainable and overachieving.

KEY COMPONENTS OF SUCCESSFUL CLIENT INTERACTIONS

- **Listening.** The consultant should truly listen to stakeholders involved in the process. This will go a long way in terms of relationship-building and satisfactory outcomes.
- **Empathy.** The consultant should display empathy when working with stakeholders. The consultant needs to understand where the stakeholders are coming from when designing and implementing solutions. By being sensitive to stakeholder thoughts and feelings, the consultant can make stakeholders feel heard and valued. This positive working relationship will ensure a smoother overall process.
- **Communication.** The consultant should continuously communicate with stakeholders. Effective and consistent communication reduces confusion, frustration, and errors while promoting unity and positive project outcomes.
- **Follow-up.** The consultant should follow up after project completion to ensure satisfaction and to see how else they can be of service.

METHODS FOR DESIGN AND DELIVERY OF HUMAN RESOURCE FUNCTIONS AND PROCESSES
ISSUE TRACKING

There are many approaches to keeping track of problems, some more complex than others. In its simplest form, **issue tracking** is like pulling a ticket at the deli counter: there is a single channel that leads to a single point of service. In larger corporations, issue tracking may involve various channels and span across many service centers. For example, customer service or support centers may be an initial contact for issue tracking. Customers open cases or ticket requests through communication channels like phone, chat, and email. Once a case or ticket is created, it can be assigned to individual users or departments. More-complicated tickets may also be escalated through service level ranks, with relatively involved tasks assigned to senior-level staff and simpler tasks assigned to new or lower-level staff. Tickets may also be flagged by priority, such as low, medium, or high. Robust tracking systems show the status of each issue and include helpful notes regarding what has been discussed and done. This allows more than one person to easily be involved in the resolution. It also creates a historical record.

CLIENT SERVICE

Whether human resource (HR) professionals are working as outside consultants or as internal members of an organization, they should be **service-minded**. They are there to balance the needs of the organization with the needs of the employees, trying to keep them in alignment whenever possible. Although often tasked with duties that will make them unpopular, HR professionals strive to keep people satisfied if it is in their power to do so. Everything that HR does should be done with effective client service in mind.

Analytical Aptitude

SURVEY AND ASSESSMENT TOOLS

DEVELOPMENT

To perform a **survey or assessment**, human resources (HR) can either create a survey or assessment tool in-house or use a third-party solution. In either case, HR needs to have a clear understanding of the survey's purpose and what it is supposed to measure. If historical survey or assessment results exist, they should be reviewed, as they can provide context and potential survey items. Further, HR could elect to use employee **focus groups** to help clarify questions before the survey is administered.

HR should ensure that the survey is short (takes less than 30 minutes to complete) to encourage participation. To help keep the survey concise, only the most-relevant questions should be asked. The survey should ask clear questions about single topics to avoid skewing results. For example, the survey should contain separate items for compensation and benefits, as an employee could be satisfied with one but not the other. Additionally, closed questions often work better than open-ended questions because they make analysis and trend detection much easier. Finally, the survey must be written using neutral and balanced language to mitigate bias.

ADMINISTRATION

HR should communicate about a survey before, while, and after participants take it. Management and employees alike need to understand why the survey is happening, what the survey process looks like, and when results will be shared. HR should provide ample notice to any unions, if applicable, so they can determine what union participation will look like.

Although times of stress within the organization could provide useful results to HR, surveys should ideally be administered during slower periods of production. This allows employees to have enough time to participate. HR should avoid administering a survey around the time of a holiday, as staff absence will affect the participation rate. Survey participation should be completely anonymous and voluntary. This allows employees to provide their feedback freely because they know they can't be identified, which reduces the fear of retribution.

Electronic means of survey administration have several benefits. For one, it is often faster to click than to select an answer by hand. Additionally, electronic survey systems tabulate the results, saving HR from the task of manually counting them. However, because is it possible that not all employees use a computer, HR should ensure that a paper version is easily accessible.

Finally, HR needs to keep their promise and release the survey results by the announced date. They should also work closely with management to implement solutions for any problems uncovered in the survey. Additionally, HR can use employee focus groups to explore dominant themes brought up in the survey and solicit input for how to address concerns.

VALIDATION

If HR uses a third-party vendor for their employee surveys, they need to research the credibility of the vendor to ensure that the survey instrument is **valid**. Unfortunately, some companies will violate copyright laws by compiling bits and pieces of other surveys. Not only are their actions illegal, but the survey may not produce valid results. If HR creates the survey in-house, they should be prepared to discard questions with low response rates or that come across as poorly phrased.

SOURCES OF DATA

OBSERVATIONS

Sometimes the only way to answer certain research questions is to make **observations**. For example, the best method to assess a job redesign proposal is to observe a work group and determine if their efforts flow smoothly and cooperatively. The disadvantage of observations is that they are invasive, which could lead employees to behave differently. They can also be time-consuming.

SURVEYS

A very effective tool to collect data and determine satisfaction, **surveys** can be created internally or externally and can cover a huge variety of topics. Depending on the topic and specific questions of the survey, the respondent can answer anonymously or can be identified. There are many different types of surveys. Some compile **qualitative** data, such as feelings, opinions, and/or reflections to help gain an understanding of a particular subject or to help create a hypothesis. Other surveys compile **quantitative** data, which is information that can be given a numerical value, counted, or measured. Quantitative data can be used to measure satisfaction, engagement, and probability for retention. Some surveys use a combination of both methods. One of the most important things to remember when conducting a survey is that it should be analyzed, some results should be shared, and action must be taken for future surveys to be effective.

INTERVIEWS

Another effective way to understand employee perspectives and feelings about issues is by conducting **interviews**. The advantage to interviews is that they provide richer data than surveys. They also allow for follow-up questions. Interviews can be time-consuming, however, and human resources (HR) should note that not all employees will be comfortable sharing feedback in this way.

FOCUS GROUPS

One method for making interviews less time-consuming is by using **focus groups**, in which more than one person is interviewed at the same time by a single moderator. Although more perspectives can be captured in less time with this technique, HR should bear in mind that not all employees will feel comfortable discussing issues in front of their peers.

MARKETING DATA

Organizations can gather **marketing data** from various marketing materials. This data can reveal information about consumer engagement with the marketing materials, the number of closed sales for each customer exchange, and the demographics of the audience. Data can be collected through qualitative and quantitative methods as well as through intent data such as internet cookies. Analysis using marketing analytics, third-party information, and customer surveys are common ways to collect marketing data. Marketing data is used to determine the efficacy and success of various marketing initiatives. This allows for process revision and design improvements to reach a wider audience or see greater success from marketing initiatives.

ANALYTICAL REPORTS

An **analytical report** is a document that evaluates or details certain information about a company's performance, situation, or outlook. The information is usually either quantitative or qualitative and is used to analyze business strategies or initiatives. Analytical reports have many benefits, including increased adaptability; the information revealed in an analytical report can help teams develop, adjust, and implement changes depending on the market or collected data. Improved collaboration can be another benefit, as collaboration involves presenting data and opening the floor for productive conversations. Improvements to communication among teams and departments can be another positive effect of analytical reports, as team members can use the data to review possible solutions and enhancements.

BASIC CONCEPTS IN STATISTICS AND MEASUREMENT
DESCRIPTIVE STATISTICS

It is important to summarize any data that has been collected. **Descriptive statistics** can measure central tendency, dispersion, variability, frequency distribution, and proportions. The most common numerical descriptive statistic is the average, or **mean**. The **mode** is the value that occurs most frequently. Other descriptive statistics include frequency count, range, standard deviation, and correlation coefficient.

First, data is collected through primary methods such as surveys, observations, or experiments. Then, the data is analyzed or characterized by variable and presented using graphs or charts such as a histogram. As samples get larger, the sample distribution often begins to appear more like the population distribution, which is usually a bell-shaped curve.

CORRELATION

A **correlation** is the relationship between two variables. There can be a positive relationship or a negative relationship. The strength of this relationship, or the **correlation coefficient**, is reflected as a number from –1.0 to 0 for negative correlations and 0 to 1.0 for positive correlations. The numbers closer to 0 represent a weaker relationship, whereas the numbers closer to –1.0 or 1.0 represent a stronger relationship.

RELIABILITY

The consistency of a particular measure is its **reliability**. A research tool is said to be reliable if it produces consistent and repeatable measurements every time it is used. For example, measuring tapes and stopwatches provide consistent and reliable measurements. Surveys should be reliable if the questions are clear and straightforward, but ambiguous questions might return unreliable results.

VALIDITY

A research instrument should accurately measure what it is supposed to measure. The **validity** of a survey may be difficult to interpret. For example, can a survey accurately measure company commitment or employee satisfaction? For a research instrument to be deemed as valid, it needs to go through and pass rigorous statistical testing.

INTERPRETATION OF GRAPHS AND CHARTS

LINE GRAPHS

Line graphs have one or more lines of varying styles (solid or broken) to show the different values for a set of data. The individual data are represented as ordered pairs, much like on a Cartesian plane. In this case, the x- and y-axes are defined in terms of their units, such as dollars or time. The individual plotted points are joined by line segments to show whether the value of the data is increasing (line sloping upward), decreasing (line sloping downward), or staying the same (horizontal line). Multiple sets of data can be graphed on the same line graph to give an easy visual comparison. An example of this would be graphing achievement test scores for different groups of students over the same time period to see which group had the greatest increase or decrease in performance from year to year (as shown below).

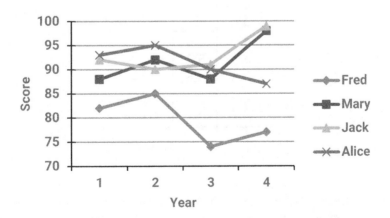

> ### Review Video: How to Create a Line Graph
> Visit mometrix.com/academy and enter code: 480147

73

BAR GRAPHS

A **bar graph** is one of the few graphs that can be drawn correctly in two different configurations – both horizontally and vertically. A bar graph is similar to a line plot in the way the data is organized on the graph. Both axes must have their categories defined for the graph to be useful. Rather than placing a single dot to mark the point of the data's value, a bar, or thick line, is drawn from zero to the exact value of the data, whether it is a number, percentage, or other numerical value. Longer bar lengths correspond to greater data values. To read a bar graph, read the labels for the axes to find the units being reported. Then, look where the bars end in relation to the scale given on the corresponding axis and determine the associated value.

The bar chart below represents the responses from our favorite-color survey.

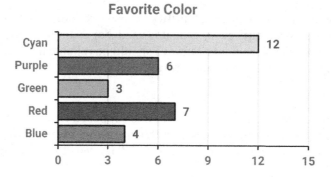

HISTOGRAMS

At first glance, a **histogram** looks like a vertical bar graph. The difference is that a bar graph has a separate bar for each piece of data and a histogram has one continuous bar for each *range* of data. For example, a histogram may have one bar for the range 0–9, one bar for 10–19, etc. While a bar graph has numerical values on one axis, a histogram has numerical values on both axes. Each range is of equal size, and they are ordered left to right from lowest to highest. The height of each column on a histogram represents the number of data values within that range. Like a stem and leaf plot, a histogram makes it easy to glance at the graph and quickly determine which range has the greatest quantity of values. A simple example of a histogram is below.

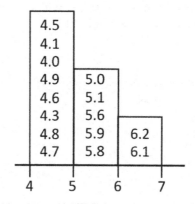

SCATTER PLOTS

Bivariate data is simply data from two different variables. (The prefix *bi-* means *two*.) In a **scatter plot**, each value in the set of data is plotted on a grid similar to a Cartesian plane, where each axis represents one of the two variables. By looking at the pattern formed by the points on the grid, you can often determine whether or not there is a relationship between the two variables, and what that relationship is, if it exists. The variables may be directly proportionate, inversely proportionate, or show no proportion at all. It may also be possible to

74

determine if the data is linear, and if so, to find an equation to relate the two variables. The following scatter plot shows the relationship between preference for brand "A" and the age of the consumers surveyed.

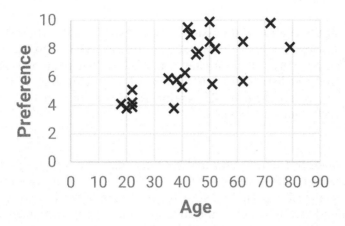

Scatter plots are also useful in determining the type of function represented by the data and finding the simple regression. Linear scatter plots may be positive or negative. Nonlinear scatter plots are generally exponential or quadratic.

USING DATA TO SUPPORT A BUSINESS CASE

When human resource (HR) professionals present a business case to senior leadership, they must show a compelling need for the resources that they are requesting. They can accomplish this by incorporating relevant data into their business case. For example, if HR wants to hire an additional maintenance technician on each shift, they should include things like the average machine downtime (and the resulting cost of lost productivity) and how long the average repair ticket stays open. Additionally, HR could add descriptive data in the form of complaints from production management and current maintenance staff, who are experiencing major disruptions in productivity or are feeling overworked, respectively.

INTERPRETATION OF DATA

Presenting a business case involves drawing conclusions from data sets with the goal of answering a question and spurring meaningful action. There are two categories of data, qualitative and quantitative. **Qualitative data** is descriptive and focuses on categorizing concepts based on making observations, conducting interviews, or reviewing documents. **Quantitative data**, on the other hand, involves a numerical, statistics-driven approach, in which data is derived from surveys and other quantifiable media.

Data **interpretation** refers to the process of reviewing data to draw meaningful conclusions from the material using a variety of analytical methods. Interpreting data aids researchers or presenters in categorizing and summarizing information to illustrate a point, trend, or need. Data interpretation can be used to answer critical questions and to help make solid business decisions. When used appropriately, data interpretation can help provide factual evidence for proposed initiatives or utilization of resources. Data interpretation is a critical component of presenting a business case, as it highlights statistical or numerical proof for a statement or problem.

GRAPHICAL REPRESENTATION

The use of graphs and/or charts to visually display numerical data, **graphical representation** helps with data analysis, interpretation, and clarification, and illustrating the relationship between data points. Data is entered and then a graph type, such as a bar graph, pie chart, scatter plot, or frequency table, is selected. Graphical representations allow viewers to quickly draw conclusions from data, like trends, relationships, and

75

correlations. When presenting a business case, graphical representation provides solid visual evidence, which is helpful when seeking buy-in from key stakeholders.

DATA VISUALIZATION

An extension of graphical representation, **data visualization** is when data is represented through visual elements such as infographics, and pictures. Visualization is an effective way to translate complex or detailed data into an image that is easier to process, understand, and follow. Visualization is an excellent aid in supporting a business case because listing statistics, numerical values, and data can cause the audience to become overwhelmed or lose sight of the overall intention. Displaying data in a visual format can add emphasis to the data without going too far into the weeds.

STORYTELLING

The art of **storytelling** involves translating data analysis into a narrative that helps illustrate the data and both influences and informs an audience. Storytelling can add significant value to a business case, as it highlights key points to the audience while adding a human touch. A recitation of hard data can be difficult to digest, but when a story is crafted around the information, the audience is more engaged and drawn into the presentation. Storytelling also allows the presenter to alter the presentation based on the audience, and can therefore reach a variety of listeners. Storytelling can also add value to the data by making it more relatable. Data visualization or graphical representation can be included in storytelling to create a compelling presentation. Using this method can help turn analysis into action.

DATA ADVOCATE
IDENTIFYING DECISION POINTS THAT CAN BE INFORMED BY DATA AND EVIDENCE

Every issue, opportunity, trend, or initiative has at least one **decision point**. Being able to accurately identify such decision points and then supporting those decision points with evidence and data is critical to moving forward with a solution or implementation. For example, if an organization is experiencing low morale or decreased employee engagement, there is likely a reason. Data resources such as satisfaction surveys, exit interviews, and employee interviews can be used to identify the cause, or the decision point. Once the cause has been identified, it can be backed up with evidence. A solution can be proposed. Understanding the culture and atmosphere of an organization will help leaders and stakeholders identify areas where improvement or changes may be needed.

DATA GATHERING
APPROPRIATE METHODS OF GATHERING DATA

Collecting data to assist in creating organizational solutions is a key business function. There is an abundance of data collection methods that can be utilized. When determining how to gather the data there is a lot to consider. The individual in charge of **gathering data** needs to determine if primary or secondary data collection will be used. **Primary data** comes directly from the source or through interacting with respondents. Primary data gathering can occur through surveys, interviews, observations, and focus groups. **Secondary data** comes from using data that was previously collected for a purpose other than its original intention; this data is analyzed with the new purpose in mind and relevant information is drawn out. Secondary data can come from online databases, previous research, public data, government records, and published materials. The correct method may depend on what information is being sought. When evaluating a policy change, a focus group or survey might be the best method. Using previous research studies would not provide relevant or accurate information, so it would be a poor choice at that stage. Before gathering data, it is also key to understand if qualitative, quantitative, or a combination of both types of data will be needed to meet the investigative goal.

SCANNING EXTERNAL SOURCES FOR DATA RELEVANT TO THE ORGANIZATION

Organizations can easily identify **internal factors** that may affect the business such as staffing, finances, and procedures. **External factors** that may affect the business, such as inflation, scarcity of resources, or changes to regulations, are a little more difficult to identify and analyze. A SWOT (strengths, weaknesses, opportunities, and threats) analysis can help identify some of those factors, particularly in the "threats" category, but that analysis is still largely focused internally. A highly successful environmental or external scan that can be used by organizations is the PESTLE (political, economic, social, technological, legal, and environmental) analysis. Conducting a PESTLE analysis can better prepare an organization to understand which external factors may impact business operations and success.

DATA ANALYSIS
STATISTICS AND MEASUREMENT CONCEPTS
IDENTIFYING POTENTIALLY MISLEADING OR FLAWED DATA

Misleading or flawed data contains faulty or inaccurate information from the data gathering, processing, or presentation. This fault or inaccuracy could be purposeful or unintentional. There are several ways that flawed or misleading data can be identified. In a visual representation, if the baseline is missing or begins with a specific number, this data could be skewed to show a favorable result. If the axes of a graph are manipulated (such as using different scales), the graph can be hard to read and interpret without getting into the raw data. Incomplete data is difficult to validate, and some visual representations will only illustrate some of the data to create a larger impact. Selecting data that only presents a favorable time period also causes issues, because the data for the full time period is incomplete. When reviewing and analyzing data, it is critical to check sources. Know who conducted the research and where the data was derived from. Data should be objective, but research funded by a vested party can often be subjective. The length of the study and the size of the sample being presented are also important to know, as is the framing of the research questions. Some research questions are misleading and manipulate respondents. If an individual is conducting his or her own research, the analysis should be done by a third party in order to limit potential bias.

IDENTIFYING DATA GAPS BASED ON ANALYSIS

It can be difficult to identify **data gaps**, particularly for the individuals collecting the data. However, missing data leads to an incomplete and inaccurate analysis. There are several areas researchers or analysts can examine when reviewing data to check for gaps. The first area to examine is time-related gaps: the time of year could impact data collection, weekends and holidays might cause missing data, or changing data collection methods could cause gaps during transition periods. Examining the data looking at these key points can help determine if time-related gaps exist. Another key area to examine is the aggregation of the data. Would the information look different if grouped using different methods such as by city, or is the data being sampled at a consistent interval that may miss oddball occurrences, or is the correct sampling method being used, such as groups of five versus ten? Examining if human bias has created a gap is important as well.

Once any gaps in the data have been identified, the individual analyzing the data needs to determine what to do next. There are several options. With statistical data, the missing data can be replaced using **imputation**, which is estimating value based on available data. Alternatively, the set of data with a gap can be deleted. This can shrink the sample size and impact the validity of the data, so this is not always the best solution. For other types of data analysis, similar research can be analyzed to provide additional insight into the missing data. If the missing data comes from internal content, data gathering can be resumed in order to pick up the missing data. Surveys, interviews, and questionnaires can be collected to address the gap.

Chapter Quiz

Ready to see how well you retained what you just read? Scan the QR code to go directly to the chapter quiz interface for this study guide. If you're using a computer, simply visit the bonus page at **mometrix.com/bonus948/shrmcp** and click the Chapter Quizzes link.

Human Resources Expertise: People

Human Resources Strategic Planning

APPROACHES TO PROJECT MANAGEMENT

The process of creating, implementing, and facilitating a plan that will lead to the completion of a particular task within defined constraints is called **project management**. It involves planning a project that meets quality standards, achieves predetermined milestones, and is completed within the time allowed and the established financial limitations. Project management ultimately makes it possible for a firm to prioritize a long list of large undertakings.

The three main factors project managers have traditionally been expected to control while completing a project are the cost of the project, the time spent on the project, and the scope of the project. The **cost of the project** is the total amount of money spent on the project, including raw materials, supplies, human capital, and other expenditures. The **time spent on the project** is the total amount of time spent by employees to complete the project tasks. The **scope of the project** refers to the requirements needed to complete the project in an appropriate fashion. In short, project managers must make sure that the project is completed within all of the parameters set and that the end result is of high quality and meets the organization's requirements.

Project managers may also be expected to control for risks associated with a project. Most projects carry some risk of failure, such as overspending, missing deadlines, putting out inferior work, or never being finished. It is essential for a project manager to find ways of minimizing these risks to avoid significant negative impacts to the organization.

While the project manager is in charge of overseeing and orchestrating the project, the tasks required to complete the project are carried out by the project team. Therefore, the project manager needs to ensure that the team has (or can develop) the right mix of skills, both technical and interpersonal, to get the job done effectively. The project manager must provide clear guidance to the project team and hold each member accountable for completing assigned work.

WATERFALL

The traditional approach to project management, often referred to as a **waterfall** approach, involves the establishment of a project management plan that clearly identifies all requirements, including scope, time, and cost, at the beginning of the project. All steps required to produce the product or services are identified, and each step is executed and concluded before the team moves to the next step in the sequence. The project manager is responsible for producing the product or service within the given time and cost constraints while meeting established quality standards. Changes in the requirements, the process, or any errors or quality standard failures that require rework are costly both in time and resources. A traditional waterfall approach and its stages are depicted in the following diagram:

78

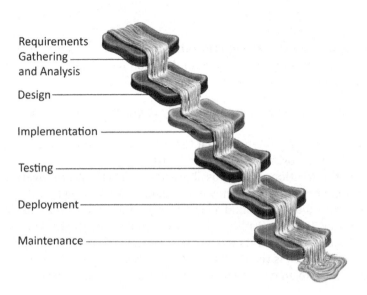

Requirements Gathering and Analysis
Design
Implementation
Testing
Deployment
Maintenance

LEAN SIX SIGMA

Most often used in manufacturing, **Lean Six Sigma** is a data-driven, results-oriented method for increasing speed and improving efficiency while solving problems, minimizing costs, and maximizing profits. Lean Six Sigma streamlines processes and eliminates activities identified as waste. There are eight types of waste: defects, overproduction, waiting, non-utilized talent, transportation, inventory, motion, and extra processing. This allows companies of all sizes to do more with fewer resources. There are **five basic phases** of Lean Six Sigma:

- Identify general problems with efficiency. For example, production line speed has decreased after a change to the product.
- Map and measure current steps in a given process to gather data. In this example, carefully observe the production line, and note how the people and equipment perform.
- Analyze the data, and identify specific issue(s). In this example, conclude that a better conveyor belt is needed to move the heavier product faster.
- Improve and standardize processes to solve the issue(s). In this example, purchase and install a new conveyor belt.
- Implement controls and procedures to maintain results. In this example, document the conveyor belt purchase so that it can be easily reordered as necessary.

AGILE

A method favored in tech, **Agile** is a software development methodology that is known for developing code in small chunks in a collaborative, team-oriented environment. Developers continually work in cross-functional teams to review and adjust their development process to meet the project needs. The team is held accountable for completing the project on time while meeting quality and functionality requirements. At the foundation of the project, there are development best practices that must be adhered to. Ultimately, the software solution must meet customer needs and align with company goals.

CRITICAL CHAIN

To reduce the likelihood of the project's completion being delayed, many projects are managed using a **critical chain** form of project management. The project is scheduled backward from the date the deliverables are due, and time buffers are added to protect the tasks that ultimately drive the duration of the project. These tasks are known as the critical chain. This form of project management is also known for identifying and mitigating bottlenecks, which helps expedite project completion.

DESIGN THINKING

Project managers utilize the technique of **design thinking** to innovatively solve business problems and add value to the design and delivery of solutions. Design thinking follows an iterative process that is focused on the user standpoint. The structured process is completed in five steps:

1. **Empathize.** Get to know the user comprehensively to ensure a thorough understanding of an ideal solution.
2. **Define.** Spell out the problem statement that the solution will solve. This step ensures a strong foundation and will drive workflow in the next steps.
3. **Ideate.** Brainstorm the solution and all possible options. This is the innovative step in the design thinking process. Foster creativity and novel idea generation during this step in the process.
4. **Prototype.** Take the best idea and build a prototype in the form of story boards, sketches, or a 3D model. During this step, it is imperative to keep the problem statement in mind.
5. **Test.** Determine if the solution meets the business need with the users. Assessments should be made to determine if the prototype is ready to be manufactured or created for release. Failures during this stage require going back to an earlier stage and reworking the solution.

KAIZEN

A substantial effort is involved in executing a project. The project team designs their own way to work, determining what processes, procedures, and protocols they will follow to accomplish the work. Given the uniqueness of every team, there is no universal set of best practices. Each team should strive to continually improve the way that they work together. **Kaizen** is a loop approach to changing (kai) team processes for the better (zen). The goal of Kaizen is to eliminate waste and work that is overly hard, thus improving the overall effectiveness of the team. Kaizen helps guide a set of experiments on team processes to see if the changes create a better way of working. Positive changes are incorporated into the team process, neutral or negative changes are discarded, and the loop is repeated to continually seek new and better processes.

PROJECT MANAGEMENT PROCESSES

Project management **process groups** are created when related processes and activities are assessed and sorted into logical groups that support specific objectives in the project. Although project phases follow a more time-based flow, process groups are not necessarily chronological and may draw from tasks at various points in the project. Processes can be classified into five major groups: monitoring, planning, executing, initiating, and closing.

- **Initiating:** grouped activities that define the charter, team, working rules, new phases, and project authorization
- **Planning:** activities that create the project scope, objectives, and project work breakdown and schedule
- **Executing:** activities that perform the planned work in the project
- **Monitoring:** processes that oversee the use of time, resources, quality, and change management
- **Closing:** processes used to complete individual phases or the project itself

SYSTEMS THINKING

A **system** is a group of interdependent, related parts that form a unified whole designed to carry out a specific purpose. The system must maintain stability by incorporating regular feedback. Because all parts of a system affect one another, the feedback occurs in a loop. **Systems thinking**, the opposite of linear thinking, is the discipline of seeing things as interrelated instead of looking at each in isolation.

The **input-process-output (IPO)** model involves putting information or resources into a process to achieve a result. In human resources, an example of this could be collecting resumes (input), screening them (process), and scheduling interviews (output).

PROJECT PLANNING, MONITORING, AND REPORTING METHODS AND TOOLS

GANTT CHARTS

A **Gantt chart** is a date- and time-based bar chart that is frequently used in project management. It depicts critical deadlines for planning, scheduling, and monitoring project timelines. It reflects all of the start and end dates of each element or task and measures the timeframes and relationships among tasks. Gantt charts have dates listed along the top and tasks listed along the left side. The anticipated time for completing each task or subtask is shown as a bar, with shading that conveys progress. The end result looks almost like a staircase. **Milestones** are frequently represented as diamonds, and small arrows indicate **dependencies**.

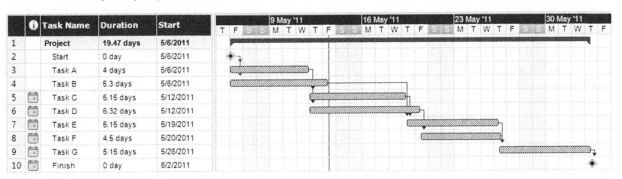

CRITICAL PATH ANALYSIS (CPA)

A project management scheduling and planning tool that allows project managers to track project goals and make course corrections as needed, **critical path analysis (CPA)** pinpoints which tasks must be finished on schedule for the project to meet its overall deadline. It also identifies which tasks can be deferred to catch up on the more-critical tasks as needed. CPA denotes which tasks are sequential (need to be completed in a certain order) and which are parallel (can be done at any point or after a certain milestone has been met). CPA shows project managers and stakeholders the minimum amount of time required to finish a project. CPA workflows are illustrated using circles (events in the project, like starting and finishing certain tasks) and arrows (actions and time required to finish tasks).

PROJECT EVALUATION AND REVIEW TECHNIQUE (PERT)

The **project evaluation and review technique (PERT)** is another method of determining how much time is required to complete a specific project. The PERT process consists of breaking the larger project into a series of smaller, separate tasks and then organizing each of these smaller tasks into a chart. Each task in the PERT chart is represented by a line or arrow drawn from a circle representing an event or goal (such as the beginning the project or completing a task and moving on to the next task) to a circle representing the next event or goal. Each event or goal circle is assigned a number, and the circles are arranged based on the order in which they are to be completed. The organization can then estimate the amount of time each task will take and note that estimate above the corresponding task line or arrow in the chart. PERT is a type of CPA. However, it assumes that tasks will take longer to complete.

OUTCOME MONITORING

For a project to be successful, the project manager must always remain informed of the project's status and monitor progress toward the desired outcome(s). If the project is not meeting preestablished **key performance indicators (KPIs)**, the project manager must decide whether to stay the course or make adjustments to the project plan. Rooted in systems thinking, **outcome monitoring** is a continuous cycle that spans the entire project's timeline.

VARIANCE ANALYSIS

Often, an organization's actual performance will be different than its projected performance. For example, an organization may sell fewer products, bring in less revenue, or spend more on labor than it had planned. When this occurs, it is important for leadership to try to explain why the variance exists. It could be that the firm lost a large customer due to service issues, or that a new product launch caused employees to work a significant amount of overtime. Gaining this knowledge through **variance analysis** will enable a company to make course corrections so that it can get back on track with its goals and make more accurate projections going forward.

PROJECT LEADERSHIP, GOVERNANCE, AND STRUCTURES
TEAM ROLES

Depending on the complexity, size, and time frame of a project, the number of **team roles** can vary significantly. However, there are a core set of roles that should be incorporated in all successful projects. These core roles include:

- The **Project sponsor** is a senior management member who serves as champion of the project and is responsible for vision and key decision-making.
- **Project stakeholders** are internal and external individuals with an interest in the product or service being produced. They are responsible for identifying constraints and risks and supplying feedback during the project.
- The **project manager** leads the team and is held responsible for ensuring that the project stays on time and within cost. Project managers are the primary communicators between the team, the stakeholders, and the project sponsor.
- **Team members** are all the people who work on the project. Team members include full and part time employees in both operational and administrative positions. Team members are responsible for completing their work on time and within budget.

The project manager must work with all of the team roles to keep the project on target while managing the output.

TEAM CHARTERS

The project manager is responsible for managing all of the resources of the project, including the team members. The project manager works with the project sponsor to establish the team, which can be through direct assignment or in a matrix configuration. Once the team is assembled, the project manager should work with the team to establish a **team charter**.

The team charter establishes the facts about the project on which the team forms consensus, and defines the values of the team, the basic rules of engagement, the decision-making process, and the conflict resolution and escalation process. The team charter also defines the roles and responsibilities of the team members, to eliminate confusion or duplicate roles. When conflict or issues arise, the team should refer to the team charter for clarification, and make changes to the charter as required during the project. Team performance is measured against the agreements laid out in the team charter. The project manager helps guide the team during the project to ensure successful completion of the work.

WORK BREAKDOWN STRUCTURE (WBS)

A **work breakdown structure (WBS)** is a method for breaking a project down into a series of separate, smaller tasks. The WBS method is based on the **100 percent rule**, which states that the smaller tasks must total 100 percent of the work necessary to complete the project. WBSs are usually depicted in a tree chart that starts off with the main project goal and then branches out to the smaller tasks. These smaller tasks are then broken down even further into subtasks. Each subtask is then assigned a percentage that denotes how much of the overall project is completed by doing that task.

SYSTEMS THINKING
SYSTEMS THEORY

The theory behind **systems thinking** is the understanding of a system in a holistic fashion and its connectivity to the world around it. It is a belief that a system is more than the sum of the individual parts. This holistic sum of the parts working together to bring more value can be described as **synergy**. The project manager and team members must consider that all of the parts of the project are both interrelated and interdependent—changes to one aspect of the project necessitates changes to other aspects.

A system has three components:

- **Elements:** the individual parts and pieces of a system
- **Interconnections:** the relationships that exist between the elements
- **Purpose** or **function:** the overarching goal or purpose of the system

For example, for a car to work, it needs an engine, a transmission, wheels, gas and brake pedals to control it, and a steering wheel to direct it. If changes are made to one part, such as switching to a supersized engine, without adapting others, such as the transmission or the size of the wheels, the car may be rendered undrivable. One change may dictate that other elements need to change as well.

SYSTEMS DIAGRAMS

While the goal of systems thinking is to think of the system on a whole, the execution of systems thinking requires that the team understand all of the parts and pieces of a system. A **systems diagram** is often used to clearly identify elements of the system. Whether it is a software system or a process, the diagram will assist in identifying all of the related parts. The diagram below considers the 'system' of a compensation plan and some of the related parts that would need to be considered if an organization was contemplating changing any part of the compensation plan.

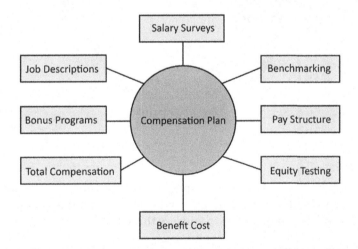

INTERDEPENDENCE

After the related parts have been identified, it is also necessary to identify the interdependencies between and among the elements of a system. In the example above, changing the benefits costs would impact the total compensation, which might require new equity testing. These elements are **interdependent** and changes in one will cause or require changes in another. Interdependence also considers the dependence of one system on other systems within the organization. The compensation plan has internal dependencies but may also have external interdependencies with the recruiting program and the performance evaluation program. A team must understand the relationships and connections and how each part is impacted by the rest of the system before changes are implemented

FEEDBACK LOOPS

Feedback in the design, development, or alteration of a system is one of the most critical elements. Because each part of a system has an interdependence and interrelationship with other parts, any introduced change must be monitored and observed across the entire system to gauge the impact and results. There are four steps to a single **feedback loop** and the team must perform as many loops as necessary to determine the impact of a change.

The steps to performing a feedback loop are:

1. **Selecting an action.** The team must choose a course of action based on the change required.
2. **Executing the action.** Once an action is selected and documented, it is executed within the system.
3. **Monitoring the reaction.** This critical step involves monitoring the entire system for both expected and unexpected consequences that may appear anywhere in the system.
4. **Measuring the reaction.** Once the intended and unintended reactions within the system are identified, the team must measure the impact on each part of the system and the amalgamation of the changes across the system.

Systems Thinking: Feedback Loops

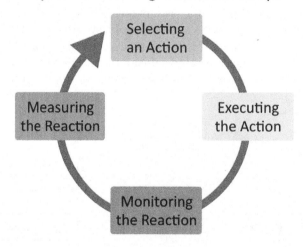

DIFFERENTIATION OF UNITS

Systems are made up of individual units. When developing a strategy, this **differentiation of units** is a critical element in clarifying both the individual unit strategies and ensuring that the strategies come together in a cohesive organizational strategy. It is imperative to address three levels of strategy:

1. **Organizational.** The organization is viewed as a single unit driven by vision, mission, and a set of long-term goals. All actions taken throughout the organization must contribute to the goals and mission of the organization.
2. **Business unit.** The strategies of each of the business elements, or units, can be very different, focused on different market segments, product development, or services provided. Each unit may have its own processes, procedures, and even culture. However, the core strategy should reflect the organizational vision, and the units should be interdependent and coordinated to achieve the organizational goals and mission.
3. **Operational.** The organization and business strategies must be translated into actions at the functional level. Functional strategies create changes, activities, and challenges at the lowest unit level and can have substantial impact across and upward through the business units and the organization.

In systems thinking, management must continually be aware of the work of each of the component pieces, or units within the organization, how each unit functions within its own strategy, and the role the unit plays in the overall strategy, and seek to continually evaluate how the units are impacting the organization and its mission.

STRATEGIC PLANNING ANALYSIS FRAMEWORKS

SWOT ANALYSIS PROCESS

Performing a **SWOT analysis** involves scanning both internal and external factors to identify potential sources of competitive advantage, or the organization's **strengths, weaknesses, opportunities, and threats**. There are six steps to the process:

1. Define the organization's **mission and objectives**.
2. Analyze the external environment for prospective **opportunities or threats**.
3. Analyze the organization's resources for **internal strengths or weaknesses**. Unique skills that set the firm apart from others and support a competitive edge are called **core competencies**.
4. Combine both the external and internal analysis and formulate a stable **strategy**.
5. Establish **trust** in leadership and encourage **involvement** from all levels of the organization to implement the new strategy.
6. **Evaluate and monitor** organizational results to preserve the competitive advantage.

PESTLE ANALYSIS

An extension of the SWOT analysis, a **PESTLE analysis** looks at how the following factors impact a business:

- **Political.** Changes made by the government can affect a business in the forms of tariffs, tax policy, and fiscal policy.
- **Economic.** Changes to inflation, interest rates, and foreign exchange rates can affect the firm's finances and operations.
- **Social.** Cultural trends affect consumer purchases, which affect an organization's revenue and profit.
- **Technological.** Technology used in a business can enhance or detract from a company's innovation level and competitive advantage.
- **Legal.** External laws and internal policies affect a firm's day-to-day operations.
- **Environmental.** Climate, weather, and geographic location all have impacts on a company's performance.

INDUSTRY ANALYSIS

A company can perform an **industry analysis** to figure out how it ranks among its competitors so that it can find a way to differentiate and therefore gain a competitive advantage. This examination should be completed in the context of the findings of a PESTLE analysis, described above, as those factors will likely affect the entire industry similarly. Companies should understand the potential for new entrants to the industry (more competition), substitute goods available (substitutes limit profits and promote competition based on price), the power of suppliers (having fewer suppliers puts pressure on firms), and the power of buyers (having fewer buyers puts pressure on firms).

LOCATION-SPECIFIC PLANNING

A **location-specific** framework for strategic planning relies on determining the needs of the location at which the project is being developed or implemented. Some requirements may be legislated, some may be local "norms" to which the community adheres. Planners must consider:

- **Local customs.** These could include language preferences, time allotments for meals, and holiday observations.
- **Wage Requirements.** Local communities may have legal requirements for wages, salaries, bonuses, and holiday pay.
- **Decision-making.** Circumstances of a particular location may require engagement of the local people as active participants in decisions that may impact the workforce or community.
- **Development constraints.** The locale may have restrictions or limitations on construction or may require green construction or environmental impact studies.

It is the responsibility of the project manager to review these and other **enterprise environmental factors** during project planning to ensure that all requirements, constraints, and local norms have been addressed.

SCENARIO PLANNING

A company performing **scenario planning** makes assumptions about what the future will look like, anticipates how the future will affect the company, and creates a strategic plan to address that impact. The four-step process begins by **forecasting** upcoming major societal, political, economic, and technological shifts. These are identified as **driving forces**. Next, the company must choose two of the most pertinent driving forces to work with. The company should create a conceivable range of potential situations it may face based on the selected driving forces. Finally, the potential **impacts** of those situations must be assessed, and the company must create a new business strategy that accounts for them. Although the subjective scenario planning process isn't meant to be a stand-alone strategic planning method, it provides another layer of information to be used in conjunction with other business analysis techniques.

GROWTH-SHARE MATRIX

The **growth-share matrix** is a long-term planning tool used to evaluate a company's products or services to determine whether the company should continue investing in them. The matrix is a graph labeled "market share" along the x-axis and "market growth" along the y-axis and divided into quadrants. Products can be classified as **stars** (top left quadrant: high market share, high growth), **question marks** (top right: low market share, high growth), **dogs** (lower right: low market share, low growth), or **cash cows** (lower left: high market share, low growth). Because dogs do not bring in a lot of money and do not have a lot of potential, the company may want to stop investing in them. Stars, on the other hand, are making money and have a lot of potential for further growth. The company will likely want to invest in them to try to turn them into cash cows. Cash cows are the most profitable products, but because that market is not growing, companies need to consider how much to invest in them. Finally, question marks have potential, but they could become either stars or dogs, so companies need to think carefully before investing a lot into them. The growth-share matrix has some limitations. For one, it is best suited for larger firms. Additionally, there are always exceptions to the rules, so companies should use other forms of analysis and their knowledge of their own firm to supplement what they learn from using the growth-share matrix.

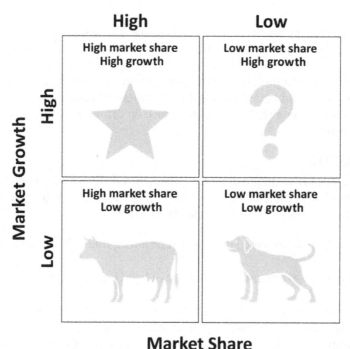

REAL-TIME STRATEGIC PLANNING

The **real-time strategic planning** framework is a dynamic approach to capturing, analyzing, and acting on the opportunities and challenges a company faces in achieving its mission. The process involves three steps to achieve a successful plan, as shown in the figure below:

1. **Organizational.** The organization should collect and analyze data on the trends, partnerships, competition, and market positions to establish the mission and vision for the organization. Rather than the traditional model of reviewing mission and vision yearly or every five years, this data should be collected on a day-to-day basis and factored into the vision and mission. This allows a company to be more proactive and stay ahead of the market.
2. **Programmatic.** Programs and activities that support the mission and vision are developed in the programmatic phase. These executable activities should achieve specific outcomes and support the target customer.
3. **Operational.** The policies, procedures, and systems of the organization in the areas of human resource, information technology, communications, marketing, and finance should be established and administered to support the programmatic activities and the mission and vision.

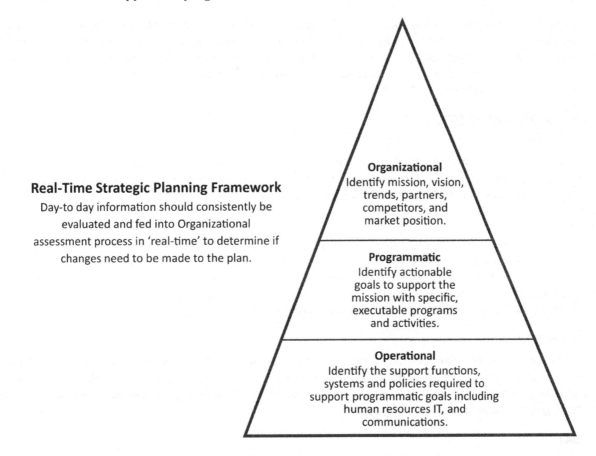

Real-Time Strategic Planning Framework

Day-to day information should consistently be evaluated and fed into Organizational assessment process in 'real-time' to determine if changes need to be made to the plan.

Organizational
Identify mission, vision, trends, partners, competitors, and market position.

Programmatic
Identify actionable goals to support the mission with specific, executable programs and activities.

Operational
Identify the support functions, systems and policies required to support programmatic goals including human resources IT, and communications.

BLUE OCEAN

The **blue ocean** approach to strategic planning focuses on innovation and reinvention. Most companies exist in the **red ocean** of over-developed, saturated markets figuratively fighting tooth and nail, drawing blood from their competitors. The blue ocean, in contrast, is where innovation and imagination take hold. The blue ocean is uncontested and growing. The blue ocean strategic planning model is based on four key points:

- It is **theoretical and beyond.** The blue ocean framework is based on proven data from a study that lasted more than 10 years.
- **Competition is immaterial.** Goals are not focused on the competitors. Rather, the aim is to reset the industry boundaries and create a new space within which to operate.
- It **values innovation.** This is the concept that there doesn't have to be a binary choice between value and affordability. If what the customer wants is known, the company needs to rethink how to provide it more affordably.
- It creates an **idea index.** The framework creates a process by which ideas can be refined and opportunities that have the most potential can be identified. This testing of commercially viable ideas can reduce the overall risk.

One example of a company that uses blue ocean ideas is Uber. This company took the industry standard for taxis and used it to develop innovative approaches to customer requirements, such as advanced payment options and location tracking, including a new mobility service. By having drivers use their own cars, Uber avoided having to buy a fleet of cars and therefore reduced its overall risk. The traditional taxi service competitors became irrelevant to the Uber strategy.

STRATEGIC PLANNING PROCESS

FORMULATION

To set the foundation for a strategic plan, the company must perform analyses such as SWOT, PESTLE, industry, and others as described above. Once the company understands its current position both internally and externally, it can move into the goal-setting phase of the process.

GOAL-SETTING

There are a variety of ways to ensure that specific **goals** are well-defined, valid, and useful. The most effective way is to use the acronym **SMART: specific, measurable, achievable, relevant, and time-bound**. Valid goals should be specific and well-defined, able to be accurately measured, feasible considering present resources and environment, and relevant to overall objectives. A valid goal should also have a specific deadline to ensure that it is completed efficiently and can be accurately compared to other goals.

IMPLEMENTATION

Once goals are established, the company must take action to **implement** changes that support those goals. Changes, or interventions, could include modifications to policies, workflows, or personnel, to name a few. The changes may be scheduled to occur all at once or at set intervals. All interventions need to remedy a concern or help the organization achieve its strategic goals.

EVALUATION

To see which changes help and which changes don't, the strategic plan needs to be **evaluated** regularly. The company should have methods of measurement available to gauge the effectiveness of the interventions. If the changes aren't working as intended, the plan should be modified so the company can get back on track.

Talent Acquisition

METHODS FOR CREATING AND MAINTAINING A POSITIVE EMPLOYER VALUE PROPOSITION AND EMPLOYMENT BRANDING

The act of marketing an image that makes people want to work for the organization is called **employment branding**. This image stems from the organization's **employer value proposition (EVP),** which is what they have to offer as compared to other firms. The EVP may include the work environment, internal opportunities, benefits, and compensation. Employers should consider **active branding** because it can increase the talent pool, firm productivity, and team morale while reducing the turnover rate.

An organization can showcase a positive EVP and brand in the following ways:

- Describing their benefits, perks, and culture on their website, in their job ads, and in other promotional materials
- Sharing current employee testimonials about how great it is to work there
- Doing charity work in the community and demonstrating a commitment to corporate social responsibility

CULTURE

As a part of employment branding within the EVP, it is imperative to help potential candidates get a feel for the **culture** of the organization. Organizational culture is the set of shared beliefs and values that embody the organization, drive employee behavior, and direct how employees do their jobs in the workplace. Values and beliefs are created, communicated, and reinforced by the leaders of the company in the formal and informal systems and norms that establish the working environment.

Culture underlies the standards set by the company leaders, is evident in the attitudes of the managers, and can impact the firm's reputation in the market. Potential employees should seek to identify an organization with a culture that fits well with their own beliefs and values systems. The reputation and culture of an organization are critical elements of the EVP and employment branding.

OPPORTUNITIES FOR GROWTH

When a company is recruiting, potential new employees evaluate the attractiveness of the organization and its EVP. The factors determining this attractiveness include the value of the work, the social environment of the organization, the salary and benefits package, and the perceived value of the **opportunities for personal and professional growth** and expansion. Candidates want to know that they can not only apply their current skills and knowledge, but also that they will be recognized for hard work and rewarded with career-enhancing opportunities.

In addition to being strong recruiting tools, career-pathing and advancement opportunities are often cited as strong employee retention elements. High-performance employees seek recognition and reward. A **learning organization** that is based on continual transformation, that embraces and integrates change in its culture, will use advancement and reward as components of its branding campaign.

An additional benefit of internal growth opportunities that adds value to the EVP is the satisfaction and goodwill gained by promoting from within. Organizations must constantly evaluate the requirements of vacant positions with the advantages and disadvantages of promoting internal candidates. Elevation of current employees boosts morale, motivation, and loyalty. These positive attributes assist in creating a stronger culture and attractiveness, which in turn allows an organization to recruit the best and brightest.

PURPOSE

One of the strongest drivers of employee retention and commitment is meaningful work. Employees believe that their work and efforts are meaningful if the work:

- Fulfills a life purpose
- Helps them achieve their personal goals
- Is in line with their personal values
- Allows them to do what they do best
- Helps them achieve their best self
- Adds value to the world
- Connects to the vision and mission of the organization

An employee is much more likely to be engaged and committed if there are intrinsic rewards such as recognition and involvement.

An employer can deepen the connection between the employees and their work by getting to know them, understanding what motivates them, what they are best at, and how they view themselves in the world. **Job assessments** can help to align the right people to the right jobs. Adapting or altering jobs to better fit the employee and the organization can increase job satisfaction. Clearly identifying the vision and mission of the organization will help employees to see how they fit with the overall purpose of the company.

VARIED WORK ASSIGNMENTS

One constant in a company and the world is change. Organizations change, missions change, and employees change. In every organization, there is undoubtedly a core group of employees who detest change, and the organization will spend a lot of time and energy on helping those employees cope with the reality of change. Alternatively, however, there are many employees who like to grow, learn, and diversify their abilities and contributions to the company. Affording employees the opportunities to learn new tasks, expand their knowledge, and develop new skills will create a learning organization and improve the morale and motivation of its team.

Varied work assignments can be permanent or temporary, lateral across the organization or up or down within an organization. Some employees will welcome an opportunity to take a step back or down in an organization if doing so gives them the opportunity to learn new skills and holds the promise of growth over time. Learning organizations are constantly assessing the environment and adapting to new technologies, new products, and new demands from customers. Evolving the skills and abilities of its employees allows the organization to stay on par with or ahead of the competition.

JOB ANALYSIS AND IDENTIFICATION OF JOB REQUIREMENTS

A **job analysis** is an essential part of any workforce planning process because it identifies specific skills, knowledge, and traits required to meet staffing goals and organizational objectives. It outlines what a worker needs to be successful in a given role and also establishes the relative importance of each role to the company.

The three main parts of a job analysis are job competencies, job specifications, and job descriptions. **Job competencies** are detailed lists of all broad skills and traits (such as leadership ability) needed for a particular position. **Job specifications** are detailed descriptions of all specific qualifications (such as experience or education) an individual must have to perform the role. A **job description** is a detailed written breakdown of all tasks that a worker in that role must complete, along with the job competencies and job specifications required for a worker to be qualified for that role. Equal Employment Opportunity Commission (EEOC) guidelines encourage employers to prepare written job descriptions listing the essential functions of each job.

Some of the major uses of job analysis include the following:

- **Human resource planning,** to develop job categories
- **Recruiting,** to describe and advertise job openings
- **Selection,** to identify skills and criteria for selecting candidates
- **Orientation,** to describe activities and expectations to employees
- **Evaluation,** to identify standards and performance objectives
- **Compensation,** to evaluate job worth and develop pay structures
- **Training,** to conduct needs assessments
- **Discipline,** to correct subpar performance
- **Safety,** to identify working procedures and ensure workers can safely perform activities
- **Job redesign,** to analyze job characteristics that periodically need updating
- **Legal protection,** to identify essential functions that must be performed to protect the organization against claims

JOB ANALYSIS METHODS

To determine what a job entails, human resources (HR) needs to do research using their existing workforce. HR can observe people perform work, ask employees to fill out questionnaires about their jobs, look at work logs kept by employees, or interview staff for deeper insights.

TASK INVENTORY ANALYSIS

One of the techniques used for determining the elements of a job and the kind of tasks an employee will perform is **task inventory analysis**. This job analysis process requires breaking down the job into duties and tasks. A **job duty** is a responsibility that the employee is obligated to complete. These are typically long-term assignments and may not have a specific time period attached. Each job can involve anywhere from five to twelve duties. A **task** is a step required to accomplish a duty. This is a specific assignment that should be accomplished within a defined, limited timeframe. Each job can involve anywhere from 20 to 100 tasks. Once the tasks have been identified, the analysis should expand to indicate the frequency, importance, and associated difficulty for each individual task.

Job Analysis Techniques: Task Inventory Analysis
Example: Accounting Manager

Internal Controls
- Establish annual control metrics in January.
- Audit internal controls monthly
- Provide audit reports weekly

Performance Management
- Establish staff performance goals annually.
- Meet with staff members weekly.
- Provide mid-year reviews in April.
- Provide year end reviews in September.

Quality Control
- Review business activity reports daily.
- Review forecast reports monthly.
- Review budget reports for eachy new project before initiation of project.

Reporting
- Submit Accounting ledger monthly.
- Submit Overdue report bi-weekly.
- Respond to audit department report weekly.

Tax Planning
- Completes annual tax returns annually.
- Files quarterly tax returns in January, April, July, October.

Compliance
- Review federal goverment requirements semi-annually.
- Review state requirements semi-annually.
- Updates company guidance monthly.
- Audits for compliance monthly.

Once all the duties are identified, the next step is to evaluate the frequency, importance, and difficulty of the required tasks. For example, for the reporting duty:

Reporting	Duty	Task	Frequency	Importance	Difficulty
• Submit Accounting ledger monthly.	Reporting	Accounting ledger	Monthly	Medium	Medium
• Submit Overdue report bi-weekly.	Reporting	Overdue report	Bi-Weekly	High	Low
• Respond to audit department report weekly.	Reporting	Audit report	Weekly	Low	High

CRITICAL INCIDENT TECHNIQUE

Another method of performing a job analysis is the **critical incident technique**. This relies on the assessor observing **critical incidents**, or behaviors, of the employee currently performing the job. These incidents can include performance that is effective in getting the work done, or performance that does not meet the requirements to get the task accomplished. There are three elements to a critical incident technique assessment:

- A basic description of the incident observed by the assessor that includes both the context around the incident and the circumstances leading up to the incident
- The behavior of the employee while performing the observed incident
- The consequences or results of the behavior while performing the task

These types of assessments are particularly effective in jobs that require physical work and may have health/safety elements or concerns. The technique can also be used for poor performance to do an in-depth analysis of how the employee is doing the work, which can allow for identifying process issues, behavior issues, or training requirements.

POSITION ANALYSIS QUESTIONNAIRE

The **position analysis questionnaire** is one of the most common techniques for **position analysis**. This technique involves sending a questionnaire to the employee to solicit input regarding the work being performed, which the assessor can utilize in creating or updating a position description. There are three basic types of questionnaires that are used most often:

- **Highly structured questionnaires** are developed by HR and are designed to determine the exact tasks being performed, the skills required to accomplish the tasks, the frequency of the tasks, and the relative importance of the tasks. This expands the critical incident technique discussed above, as it covers all of the tasks an employee performs. This does have the potential to be biased in favor of the employee's perception.
- **Open-ended questionnaires** are developed by HR and focus on the knowledge, skills, and abilities required for the position. They are completed by HR, not the employee. HR can observe or discuss the job elements with the employee, but it becomes a more objective analysis when completed by HR.
- **Interviews** are more time-intensive and consist of direct face-to-face conversations between HR and the employee performing the work. The HR representative should start with a set of standard questions about the knowledge, skills, and abilities required for the position, but the interview format also allows for a more in-depth discussion about elements and features of the job that are more nuanced. This technique is particularly effective for professional positions.

METHODS FOR EXTERNAL AND INTERNAL SOURCING AND RECRUITING

When a job opening has been identified, human resources (HR) must determine whether to recruit externally or internally. Often, unless HR is certain that the position will be filled internally, both methods will be used.

Recruiting **internal candidates** allows the employer to encourage loyalty and reward high performance; it is also less expensive. A **job posting** notifies employees of available positions. **Job bidding** allows qualified employees to apply for opportunities.

Recruiting **external candidates** can be accomplished through several avenues. **Referrals** are often touted for being relatively quick and inexpensive while returning high-quality candidates. **Online job posting** reaches the largest audience, but it can be time-consuming to review the high number of applications that this can produce. **Employment agencies** are viable resources for locating executives or other highly skilled candidates, fulfilling temporary needs, or evaluating performance prior to extending an employment offer through temp-to-perm opportunities. However, employers should consider that the average fee charged by employment agencies falls between 10 and 25 percent of an employee's annual salary. **College recruiting** can return a large pool of professional candidates, whereas vocational schools and associations are usually good sources for technical or trade skills. Other common external recruiting sources include job fairs, social media, state workforce websites, and the company's own applicant tracking system.

When common recruiting avenues do not provide an adequate number of candidates, more-unusual methods may be needed. Alternate methods include looking for individuals leaving vendors and suppliers who may make good employees, restructuring the position to accommodate remote workers if top talent is not local and does not want to relocate, and offering sign-on bonuses. Recruiters can also build **talent pipelines** by networking both on- and offline with professionals that possess critical skills. That way, when a job vacancy occurs, the recruiter already has a short list of people that they can contact regarding the position.

Methods for Selection Assessment

Selection methods and tools are essential parts of an organization's hiring process because the goal is to find a group of acceptable candidates and then choose the best candidate from that group. Eliminating unqualified candidates saves money and time and focuses resources on those individuals most suited for each position. The screening tools most commonly used include employment applications, resumes, and interviews. **Employment applications** include any form designed by an employer that requires an individual to give personal information, previous experience, education, and so on. **Resumes** are usually one to two pages long and list experience, education, and references that qualify an individual for a particular position. Resumes are not usually a premade form to be filled out, but rather a document designed and written by the individual seeking employment.

Even once an organization has located a suitable group of potential employees, it can be extremely difficult for an interviewer to separate the most qualified individual from the rest of the group based on applications and resumes alone. As a result, it is necessary to have a set of well-defined selection tools and methods that are both valid and reliable.

Selection Process

The **selection process** is sequential and includes a series of steps, each of which systematically screens out unsuccessful individuals who will not continue to the next round. The order of steps is often organized based on a cost/benefit analysis, with the most expensive steps at the end of the process. Steps of a selection process may include introductory screening, questionnaires, initial interviews, employment testing, final interviews, selection decisions, reference checks, drug testing, post-offer medical exams, and placement. The two basic **principles of selection** that influence the process of making an informed hiring decision are 1) past behaviors and 2) reliable and valid data. Past behavior is the best predictor of future behavior, so what was done in the past may be indicative of future actions. **Reliable data** is consistently repeated, whereas **valid data** measures performance.

Preemployment Tests

Two of the most common types of **preemployment tests** are aptitude tests and inbox tests. An **aptitude test** is an examination designed to determine whether an individual has the basic knowledge to perform the tasks associated with a particular position. For example, an aptitude test for a bank teller might consist of a series of basic math problems related to specific banking activities (e.g., determining an account balance after several deposits and withdrawals).

During an **inbox test**, also called an in-basket test, the individual must determine the appropriate way to handle particular problems. For example, an applicant for a position as head bank teller might be asked to describe the appropriate way to handle a check deposited into the wrong account.

The two main advantages associated with preemployment tests are that they allow the organization to have more control over the information gathered and they make it easier to gather information in a consistent way. Preemployment tests comprise premade questions that assess an individual's ability to use specific skills and areas of knowledge. The results will either support or refute the information gathered during the interview. Preemployment tests provide consistent results as long as each applicant takes the exam under the same conditions.

There are some disadvantages to using a preemployment test. First, it is easy to unintentionally cause a disparate impact to a protected class if questions are not relevant to the position for which the individual is applying. A series of poorly worded or irrelevant questions may make it more difficult for members of a particular group of people to get the job, which may make the organization legally liable. Second, preemployment tests do not allow for flexibility, because the same questions are asked of every applicant. An interviewer is able to ask questions specifically related to each individual applicant, whereas a preemployment test cannot.

ASSESSMENT CENTERS

An **assessment center** is a standardized system of tests designed to gauge candidates' knowledge, skills, abilities, and behaviors in relation to the position for which they are being considered. The assessment center may include interviews, psychological tests, simulations of scenarios typical to the role, and other forms of measurement. A firm employing this screening approach may use live raters. However, technological advances, such as objective computerized tests, have made it possible to rate candidates without human intervention, resulting in a more cost- and time-effective process.

INTERVIEWS

After making it through the resume and job application review rounds, and possibly a phone screening, the applicant advances to the **interview** phase of the selection process. Some reasons for conducting interviews are to obtain information about the applicant, to provide information about the company, and to build relationships.

There are many different types of interviews. A **structured, or patterned, interview** allows the interviewer to ask a series of prepared questions and may even contain a list of multiple-choice answers. In a **semi-structured interview**, the interviewer follows a guide of prepared questions, but can ask follow-up questions to evaluate the applicant's qualifications and characteristics. **Situational interviews** that gauge responses to hypothetical problems and **behavioral interviews** that question previous or anticipated behavior are frequently semi-structured in nature. An **unstructured, or nondirective, interview** is more conversational and allows more freedom so the applicant may determine the course of the discussion. To be successful, the interviewer should listen carefully without interruption. Sometimes interviews involve many parties. **Group interviews** involve multiple candidates, whereas **panel interviews** and **board interviews** involve multiple interviewers.

Thanks to technological advancements and the rise of telecommuting, the number of **virtual interviews** has increased. These may involve the candidate sitting in front of a webcam and answering recorded questions, or both the candidate and the interviewer speaking in real time from their respective locations. These interviews are often less expensive and more convenient than in-person interviews, and can include both personality and standardized evaluations.

There are two main disadvantages associated with a selection interview. First, it can be heavily affected by the interviewer's own biases. Regardless of how much experience or training an interviewer has, preconceived ideas of a particular candidate or a particular type of candidate can influence the evaluation. Second, even the best-planned interview can be rendered useless when intelligent applicants, wanting to cast themselves in the best possible light, control the interview. Further, when the interviewer does not ask the right questions, the applicant may appear to be a viable candidate even though he or she lacks the necessary skills or traits to do the job.

After successful interviews, candidates may be required to go through additional screening, such as preemployment testing, a physical examination, drug testing, a background investigation, academic achievement verification, and/or reference checking.

CONCERNS WITH USING BEHAVIORAL OR PERSONALITY ASSESSMENTS IN THE HIRING PROCESS

When evaluating the potential use of behavioral or personality assessments in the hiring process, human resource practitioners should focus on what they are trying to achieve, and research options carefully to ensure that they are not **unethical** or violate any employment regulations. If human resources decides to use such assessments, they must ensure that the assessments are designed specifically for making employment decisions and that they have undergone rigorous reliability and validity testing.

EMPLOYMENT CATEGORIES

EXEMPT AND NONEXEMPT EMPLOYEES

The **Fair Labor Standards Act (FLSA)** separates employees into two main categories: exempt and nonexempt. Nonexempt employees must be paid minimum wage and overtime rates that meet both state and federal regulations.

- **Exempt.** Generally, employees who are paid an annual wage are exempt from overtime provisions of the FLSA. Exempt workers include administrative or outside sales workers, information technology specialists, professionals, and executives. To be classified as exempt, employees must be paid at or above the threshold for exempt workers ($35,568 annually as of January 2020) as well as meet certain job duty requirements.
- **Nonexempt.** Those paid an hourly wage and covered by minimum wage and overtime provisions of the FLSA are considered nonexempt. Nonexempt workers include blue-collar workers, maintenance workers, technicians, laborers, and novice workers.

TEMPORARY OR CONTRACT WORKERS

Sometimes, employers may have a temporary need for contingent or contract workers. **Temporary worker** assignments are generally entry level and are often short in duration, such as a seasonal role at a retailer.

These workers are eligible for unemployment insurance and workers' compensation from their employer of record, often a staffing agency. Nonexempt temporary workers must be paid at least the federal minimum wage and are eligible for overtime provisions under the Fair Labor Standards Act.

INTERNS

Employing **interns** can be a win for all parties involved. A well-designed internship program allows interns to gain practical experience to reinforce their studies, learn new skills, prepare for their careers, and expand their networks. The firm benefits from inexpensive labor and a pool of potential hires for the entry-level roles. An effective internship program also fosters goodwill with local colleges and the community.

However, human resources must be careful that the internship program is compliant with labor laws. In most cases, interns must be paid at least minimum wage and are eligible for overtime pay. Nonprofit and public-sector organizations generally can offer unpaid internships. However, for a for-profit firm to do so, the intern must receive academic credit for the internship and be the primary beneficiary of the experience. This means that the firm cannot have the intern complete actual work. The intern can only be involved in training and purely educational exercises.

IMPORTANCE OF CORRECTLY CLASSIFYING WORKERS

Organizations must be diligent when classifying workers as **employees** versus **independent contractors**. Courts are more likely to favor employee classifications than independent contractor relationships to be sure that employers are not inappropriately avoiding income taxes, Social Security contribution matches, unemployment or workers' compensation protection, and healthcare costs. The difference between an employee and independent contractor is determined by the entire working relationship. The Internal Revenue Service (IRS) looks at several factors when evaluating a worker's classification: behavioral control, financial control, and type of relationship.

If the company directs the workers on how to act or perform their work, the court is likely to label them as employees. If, on the other hand, the company allows the worker to reach a mutually agreed-upon objective in the manner that they see fit, they're more likely to be classified as an independent contractor. In terms of financial control, if the firm provides the worker with the necessary equipment to perform the work, that worker is more likely to be an employee. Conversely, if the workers purchase their own tools and supplies, they are probably independent contractors. In terms of the relationship, if the company offers the worker benefits, that worker is an employee. However, if the firm does not provide any benefits, the worker may be an independent contractor. The IRS views the relationship between the parties holistically and weighs every detail before making a determination.

JOB OFFER CONTINGENCIES

Many employers will conduct **preemployment background checks** on candidates to ensure that employees have sound judgment and are unlikely to engage in improper conduct, and that they do not have criminal records. Human resource departments often order credit checks or criminal record searches through online service providers and then review the results. However, drug screening may either be administered by staff or conducted at a local or national site. The **Fair Credit Reporting Act**, like many legal regulations, requires not only that employers notify applicants that they administer background checks, but also that applicants sign a written release confirming consent that the employer may receive their personal information. Furthermore, when implementing a preemployment background check, employers must consider whether doing so may be discriminatory and, as such, must validate the business necessity. Many states have joined the **Ban the Box** movement, which prohibits employers from asking about an applicant's criminal history at the time of application. If an offense is found, employers should consider the severity of the offense, the amount of time elapsed since the offense, and if the offense is related to the nature of the job. Applicants must also have the opportunity to contest or explain adverse results before officially being turned down for employment. The prospective employer must furnish a copy of the report to the applicant. The Federal Trade Commission advises employers to give the applicant five days to respond before sending them an official letter of rejection.

PHYSICAL OR PSYCHOLOGICAL EVALUATIONS

Other pre-employment screens that employers can administer are physical or psychological evaluations, or, in some cases, both. The first critical element is establishing the requirement for such testing; its value to the organization; its connection to the knowledge, skills, and abilities required for the position; and the potential negative impacts of administering such tests.

There are three types of **physical tests** for positions that involve a substantial level of physical activity:

- **Isokinetic testing** to assess strength and muscular endurance, which focuses on the movement of joints such as knees, ankles, and shoulders, and can measure muscle strength in a stationary position.
- **Dynamic lift testing** assesses specific groups of muscles in motion. These tests are designed to cover such activities as lifting equipment, boxes, carts, and other items. These tests are often performed with simulators that use weights.

- **Aerobic testing** examines how much aerobic activity an individual can perform, how long this activity can be performed, and the level of oxygen consumption required to perform the activity. This testing method utilizes treadmills or bicycles.

Psychological tests can be administered via questionnaires or in interviews and are designed to assess the candidate's skills and knowledge and their personality traits, behaviors, and potential motivators.

JOB OFFER NEGOTIATIONS

Once a job offer is extended, there is a period of time when the candidate can request **negotiations** on aspects of the agreement. Although salary is the most common ask for candidates, human resources (HR) usually has the flexibility to create a total reward package that may involve more than direct payment and can be used to incentivize candidates to join the organization. Several of these elements that can be used in negotiation are discussed below.

SALARY

During the interview process, HR has the opportunity and responsibility to be up-front with **salary** discussions. A candidate may be reluctant to discuss salary immediately, but the recruiter or HR professional screening the candidate should be prepared to broach the subject and ensure that neither the candidate nor the company are on such different levels of expectation that the interview process will be a waste of time. HR can inquire about the candidate's expectations are for the new position. Asking about the candidate's current wage may be informative, but also may be prohibited under state or local laws.

Once the offer is made, if the candidate comes back for negotiations, there are several critical questions HR needs to ask. The first question: How badly does the organization need this particular candidate? If the organization has a critical requirement for this individual's skill set, perhaps more money is warranted.

Second, HR should ask: Has anything changed since the interview/offer was made? Both the company and the candidate may have had circumstances that changed their requirements. This is a starting place for a discussion.

Most importantly, HR needs to maintain control of the conversation. Asking questions, listening to the answers, and knowing what the parameters are will help guide the negotiations.

RELOCATION ASSISTANCE

Typically, the decision on whether a position is eligible for a **relocation** allowance should be made before the job is advertised. The decision should be based on the organization's strategic objectives, and should be included in the job offer. However, once an offer is extended to a candidate who lives outside of the geographic location of the position and that candidate comes back to negotiate the offer, HR can consider the possibility of offering a relocation package or improving a proposed relocation agreement. Relocation is complex and can involve moving expenses, housing and real estate issue support, family support, and legal support.

Relocation agreements must be executed formally, in writing, based on company policies. Company legal representatives should review the agreement and the candidate should be encouraged to have their own legal representative review the document. Oftentimes, relocation agreements will include a payback clause if an employee leaves the company before the allotted time frame has been reached.

TELECOMMUTING

Especially in today's world, the work environment is a very personal and complex situation. Some employees value the social comradery of the workplace, while others blossom working in a more-private home environment, where they can concentrate on their tasks without distraction. Offering options for employees to **telecommute**, or **telework,** fully or partially can be a big negotiating chip.

Before offering a telecommute option, HR should consider the following elements:

- **Job responsibilities.** The work to be done in a particular position must be compatible with a remote working arrangement. Some tasks require collaboration or partnership that cannot be attained working from disparate locations. However, organizations are getting more creative about how to bring employees together in collaborative environments.
- **Equipment requirements and workspace environments**. An assessment should be made to determine what physical equipment, information technology (IT) equipment, and IT support is required. Additionally, the employee should be able to attest that they have a suitable workspace at home that is conducive to productive work.
- **Legal and tax regulation**. Legal reviews should be carried out to ensure that both the organization and the employee understand the implications for taxes. Employees are fully responsible for any obligations with regard to taxes.
- **Employee suitability**. It is difficult to perform suitability assessments with a candidate; however, employers should do their best to assess the candidate's suitability, and to ensure that the candidate's supervisor is onboard to support the working arrangement.

Telecommuting agreements can include benefits such as equipment, IT support, and flexible work hours.

VARIABLE JOB SHARE

Like telecommuting, **job sharing** is an arrangement that creates flexibility for the employee and can allow the employer to improve employee retention. Job sharing involves two employees collectively performing the tasks of a single full-time position. Each employee works part-time, and the arrangement may involve one or both working flexible hours or telecommuting. The duo is jointly responsible for meeting the requirements of the position. Job share positions require that the two employees to be compatible, cooperative, collaborative, and very communicative. Managers must also be supportive and adaptable when introducing job sharing arrangements into the organization.

Employers can use job sharing as an incentive to capture highly desired skill sets while offering flexible work arrangements for the employees. In turn, this can lead to employee loyalty and job satisfaction.

APPROACHES TO EMPLOYEE ONBOARDING

There are many approaches to **onboarding** newly hired employees, from the interview, to orientation, through the 90-day review. However, all companies do things a bit differently, and the size of or engagement from the welcoming committee will vary. A majority of the responsibility will fall upon HR in most cases, but the hiring manager and information technology personnel often share some responsibilities as well. Here are a few steps that might appear on an onboarding checklist for new hires:

- **Phone interview:** brief 10- to 30-minute screening of applicants (HR)
- **Live interview**: more in-depth discussion, often lasting one to three hours (HR/hiring manager)
- **Offer letter:** formal written offer to finalist (HR)
- **Computer access:** workstation set up with email, phone, and systems access (information technology)
- **Keys, equipment, and business cards:** order/log equipment usage (operations)
- **Welcome email:** introductory email welcoming new hires with tips for success (HR)
- **Federal paperwork:** employment eligibility and tax forms (HR)
- **Company paperwork:** handbook, policies, nondisclosure agreements, and benefits acknowledgments (HR)
- **Orientation:** thorough company and policy overview and required training (HR/hiring manager)
- **Position overview and mentoring/training:** buddy assignment, job expectations, and process manual (hiring manager)

- **Introductions:** site tour, staff introductions, and icebreaker questionnaires or games (HR/hiring manager)
- **30-/60-/90-day reviews**: summary of how the new hire is assimilating into the new role (HR/hiring manager)

ORIENTATION

While all of the initial paperwork and equipment set-up is vital to ensuring success for the new employee, the new hire **orientation** is an opportunity for the organization to communicate its mission, vision, values, and objectives. The orientation is typically designed as a one-time event to bring newly hired employees together and share information that allows employees to quickly receive the information they need to start functioning within the organization.

Some of the core information shared at a new hire orientation should be organization charts, phone lists, performance review schedules, policies and procedures, and a calendar of critical company events.

Orientations create a connection to the organization and its goals. Employees should be able to see how they fit in and how their work adds value to the overall objectives. The meeting sets up communication channels for new employees to seek guidance and assistance.

Employees should be provided with a copy of their job description to ensure that they fully understand the requirements of the position. Available training opportunities can be shared to assist employees in any areas of weakness or development.

The orientation should establish a communication channel for the new employees to help them fit in and provide them with resources to go to for questions, concerns, ideas, and suggestions.

BUDDY SYSTEM

Starting a new job can be a very exciting period for the employee, but it can also be very stressful. A positive program that employers can implement is a **buddy system**. HR, or the manager for each new employee, identifies an experienced employee to partner with the new employee for some period of time. It is beneficial if the buddy is from the same work area as the new hire. Buddies can offer the new employee some of the following benefits:

- Help in navigating the organization, including how different business elements integrate.
- Guidance on identifying relevant stakeholders of the organization or project to which the new employee is assigned.
- Advice on assimilating into the corporate culture.
- Determining how his or her role fits within the team.
- Counsel for thinking strategically when approaching work issues.
- Offering an ear for questions, issues, or concerns, and advice from a trusted source.

A buddy system can significantly increase employee satisfaction for both the new employee and the buddy, which drives improved productivity and retention.

PERSONALIZATION

Onboarding that is done well can be an effective tool for setting up new employees for success, therefore adding great value to the organization. However, as diversity, equity, and inclusion programs expand and become more integrated in organizations, organizations will start to embrace changes in new hire orientation programs. Treating every new hire the same way, presenting information in the same manner, and assuming that everyone will benefit equally from it is missing the opportunity to **personalize** the new hire orientation in ways that reach individual employees more efficiently and effectively. Some of the approaches to personalizing new hire programs are:

- Use data tagging software to customize each employee's journey through the online onboarding process. Landing pages, training pages, and letters can be customized with the employee's name, job title, email address, and start date.
- Administer a personality assessment test as part of onboarding. This can help HR and managers understand some traits that may impact the willingness of a candidate to ask questions or push back if they don't understand the material.
- Group new hires by career paths or goals. Similar employees onboarding together, whether in face or remotely, can create a sense of comradery and bonding that will help the employees feel more welcome and give them a familiar face with which to interact.
- Personalize the onboarding process. Employees straight out of college may need more information, more background, and more support starting their first job. Late-career employees need less information about the job but may benefit from learning more details about the company culture and customers.

Taking the time to get to know the incoming employees and tailoring the onboarding process to be inclusive and personalized will help the employees integrate and settle into their positions more quickly and easily. This will benefit productivity and long-term retention.

TALENT ACQUISITION METRICS

Organizations of all shapes and sizes should regularly review their recruiting processes and try to make them more efficient. When evaluating recruitment efforts, it is important to consider two main metrics: the average cost per hire and the average time to fill.

$$\text{Cost per hire} = \frac{(\text{External costs } + \text{ Internal costs})}{\text{Number of hires}}$$

$$\text{Time to fill} = \frac{\text{Total days elapsed since job posted}}{\text{Number of hires}}$$

Human resource (HR) professionals should also ensure that their job ad spend is effective.

APPLICANT-TO-INTERVIEW-TO-OFFER METRICS

One of the most critical metrics used in the talent acquisition field is the calculation of both the time and cost of bringing a new employee on board. There are multiple components to that long, tedious path, which will be broken down below:

Time from vacancy identification to job posting. Identification of an opening or vacancy in the organization is the first step in hiring. Partnering between managers and HR is critical in anticipating when and where vacancies occur and determining the requirements to fill the position; this requires forecasting, planning, and aligning with the organizational strategy.

Time from posting to applicants. Once the vacancy is identified and the job description is properly updated, the job advertisement must be posted; then the organization waits for applicants from internal or external sources. The hurdles to this process can be driven by process, policy, and regulation. Submitted applications must be initially reviewed either by HR or the hiring manager. All applications should be acknowledged, typically with a return email. Non-qualified candidates should be eliminated and acknowledged. Qualified candidates may be ranked, rated, or otherwise assessed based on the match of their qualifications to the job description. HR or the manager can identify the candidates who will be offered interviews.

Time from application to interview. After identifying the candidates to be reviewed, interview offers should be extended and scheduled. Managers may use HR to screen candidates, interview candidates themselves, schedule panel interviews, or any combination of the above. Many times, especially in technical or management positions, multiple interviews are required.

Time from interview to offer. The interview process should narrow down the candidates to the top one or two. The top candidate may be offered a position verbally at first, but all final offers should be issued in writing. A negotiation period may require some time to go back and forth on the compensation package.

Time from offer to onboarding. Upon acceptance of a final offer package, the candidate will typically have to give notice at their current employer, and can establish a start date after that. For companies who have set new-hire orientations, the candidate's timeline must be coordinated with that schedule.

Time to fill. All of the steps above, from vacancy to onboarding, are then combined to calculate an offer metric of "time to fill." Some organizations may also have to include a security review process between offer and onboarding, which can add weeks, months, or even years to the process. Talent acquisition analysts will dissect all of the steps above to determine where bottlenecks exist and where process improvement or process automation can assist in getting past them.

Cost per hire. All of the steps above cost the organization time and money. Talent acquisition analysts will identify the most time-consuming parts of the process and the costliest elements of the process. They will partner with HR and management to work to achieve more efficient and effective processes.

The steps from position vacancy to a filled position has both time and money implications. However, the talent acquisition analyst will also look at how the process works in terms of the number of candidates in the pipeline. Each of the above steps is also reviewed to assess how effectively the organization is making decisions on the candidates in each step of the process. For example, if the organization starts with 200 applicants, it takes both HR and management time to review, qualify, and downselect the number of candidates who will ultimately be interviewed, which is the costliest part of the process, both in time and money.

With the end goal of getting the most qualified three to five candidates to the manager to interview, HR must have processes in place to move through the downselect process efficiently but effectively. The qualifications for the position must be clearly identified. A metric or rating system may be employed to move through the process in an objective manner; these systems can be automated.

CANDIDATE YIELD FROM PROACTIVE SOURCING

Not all positions are created equal, and not all candidates can or should be sourced the same way from the same segments of society. New efforts in diversity, inclusion, and equity demand creativity in actively sourcing candidates. There are several specific metrics that need to be considered when sourcing candidates:

Sources of applications. HR needs to consider how many sources they use to find applicants for a position. There should be a database of potential sources that the organization has used successfully and new channels that can be tried. Each channel should be tracked to capture the number of applicants, the quality of the applicants, and the cost per application based on how much the organization pays that source to post the vacancy.

Application per acquisition. Each vacancy must be assessed based on how critical the need is, how hard it is to find candidates for the position, and how much each source costs the organization. For example, if an organization needs to fill a senior technical position that is a unique position critical to the company strategy, and the need is immediate, HR may choose to post in eight to ten different sources, at a high cost, because of the seniority and criticality of the vacancy. However, HR may be able to post about a junior administrative vacancy in just one online source, at a relatively low price, and receive more than enough qualified applicants for consideration. The high number of applications for each position helps to ensure that the hiring manager will have an acceptable number of qualified candidates to review.

Referrals per employee. Organizations rely quite a bit on internal employee referrals. This path to finding new talent is considered less risky than open job postings because the candidates are referred by existing employees who understand the organizational culture, the strategy, and the work to be done. It makes sense that employees would only refer people who would fit in with the organization. This then creates less risk for the company. Organizations typically have a strong employee referral program, which offers money for each referral that is hired. However, for an organization that wants to actively expand their diversity, there is a consideration for expanding beyond its comfort zone to bring in new thoughts and ideas. Understanding the metrics associated with the employee referral program can help to bolster its effectiveness.

Diversity per hire. Hand in hand with the referral program, HR analysts must understand the diversity pool of their applicants and the diversity of their hires. Most organizations understand the need and benefits of diversity, but achieving diversity can be a challenge. If an organization is actively seeking to diversify, it is usually a better strategy to rely less on employee referral programs and more on diversity sourcing for posting vacancies. The number of diverse candidates should be tracked through the entire hiring process from posting to onboarding. If the organization spends the time and money to post in diverse sources, and then all the diverse candidates are removed from the process during the initial resume review, there is a problem with the process, and it needs to be addressed.

TALENT ACQUISITION TECHNOLOGIES
CHATBOTS

Companies try to anticipate the questions that candidates might ask when applying to an organization. Previously, these questions and their answers were posted in a Question and Answer (Q&A) section of the applicant website that candidates could browse to get information. However, this required candidates to search through categories of questions and a myriad of Q&A to get the information they sought.

As artificial intelligence (AI) has become more mainstream, companies have adapted these Q&A sections to use interactive **chatbots**. Chatbots harness the power of AI to allow candidates to ask their questions in a "live" environment and get answers immediately without having to weed through the Q&A. According to surveys and other assessments, AI chatbots can answer about 80% of standard questions, and a majority of candidates surveyed thought that they were talking to a live person rather than using a chatbot.

This improves the customer service experience for candidates and gives them a better impression of the organization. It is anticipated that chatbots will only keep improving over time.

ARTIFICIAL INTELLIGENCE RESUME SCREENING

Sifting through resumes is one of the most labor-intensive, time-consuming components of the hiring process. Recruiters can receive several hundred resumes for every position they post. Screening each resume and assessing for suitability for the position is exhausting. It is estimated that the average recruiter spends approximately six to seven seconds on a resume before deciding on suitability. This can do a tremendous disservice to both the organization and the candidate, but the reality is that there just isn't a more efficient way for a recruiter to process the high number of applications they receive.

Recent developments in AI are bringing a whole new life to the **resume screening** process, which allows the company to better assess candidates in a much more efficient and effective manner. AI can be utilized for resume screening in three areas:

- **Keywords**. The AI resume screening system is built to extract keywords, phrases, and text patterns from the resume based on the qualifications for the position.
- **Grammar**. The system is designed to seek out certain grammatical patterns, words, and phrases on the resume to aid in "understanding" the context of the text of the resume or cover letter.
- **Numbers.** The system is designed to analyze certain numbers and patterns of numbers to recognize addresses, phone numbers, and timelines.

Utilizing AI to screen resumes not only significantly reduces the time required for screening resumes, but also reduces subjectivity or unconscious bias that may occur in a recruiter's review, thus improving the quality of the candidate pool.

SOCIAL MEDIA TO IDENTIFY PASSIVE TALENT

While the standard method of searching for applicants includes posting vacant positions and waiting for applicants to apply, this only captures the active job candidates. **Active candidates** are those who are proactively seeking work. These candidates will search for positions, complete applications, and seek feedback. **Passive candidates** are those potential employees who are typically working in jobs that they are satisfied with and not actively seeking new jobs.

While passive employees may not be actively looking for new work, it may be possible that they can be enticed to consider a new position if employers can find and approach them. Finding and reaching passive talent is important when positions are hard to fill, competitive, or the job market is tightening and unemployed workers are hard to come by.

Social media has opened a new path to finding and attracting these passive candidates. Employers can approach passive candidates in several ways:

- Post vacancies on social media sites where the type of employee you are seeking is most likely to be present. This can include niche sites based on interests, hobbies, or professional associations. This approach may yield some passive employees who see your ad and are interested.
- Search social media sites based on skills or attributes required for the job, seeking to identify specific individuals that you believe have what you are looking for. Recruiters can send messages inviting the employee to chat with them or review the position description to see if there is mutual interest.
- Engage in networking by reaching out to individuals you know and seeking associations with passive candidates who may have the skillset you need. This can work a bit like referrals, in that the recruiter has a comfort level with the individual that gets them entrée to the passive candidates.

Some benefits of using social media to attract passive talent are:

- **Brand awareness.** Posting advertisements for your company and your positions on social media sites that your target audience uses frequently will raise your brand awareness with candidates who may not have previously been familiar with the company.
- **Increased visibility of job postings.** Many employees browse sites such as LinkedIn for networking and visibility. Posting position advertisements on these sites can catch the eye of users who may not have been looking for a new job but may find themselves interested in what you have to offer.
- **Filling jobs more quickly.** If you can target and approach a specific individual with the skillset required, the time spent reviewing large groups of applicants who may not be qualified can be avoided. This is both a time and cost savings.

There are several tools available to creative, resourceful recruiters:

- **LinkedIn**. Employers can post jobs, and also search on keywords that may be in profile descriptions, company names, education accomplishments, and other areas of the site, which may lead them to passive candidates.
- **Job search engines.** Some individuals will leave resumes attached to job search engines even after they have found employment. Recruiters can search on skillsets, educational accomplishments, etc., to identify potential qualified candidates and reach out to try to engage them.
- **Facebook/Instagram/Twitter/YouTube.** While LinkedIn is mostly professional in nature, these sources are more based in social interactions. However, they can be searched and sourced just as LinkedIn can to find skillsets and specific criteria.

METHODS FOR SUPPORTING A POSITIVE CANDIDATE EXPERIENCE

Organizations need to ensure that any candidate working his or her way through the hire process has a good experience. Candidates that make it all the way to hire will start their new position with an impression of the systems, people, and processes they encountered along the way. Candidates who do not make it through to hire, whether turned down by the company or self-selected out, will also walk away with impressions and emotions tied to their experience in the system. Those candidates will share their experiences with others, which can impact the ability of a company to recruit new employees. Organizations should work to ensure that all candidates walk away having had a positive experience with the company. There are several components to a positive experience for recruiters and managers to consider.

STREAMLINED APPLICATION PROCESS

The application process is typically the first interaction that a candidate will have with a company. New software that assists in gathering candidate data in a way that makes the backend easier for the recruiter can also be cumbersome for the candidate. It is important to remember that each candidate may be putting in many applications. Requiring the candidate to both submit a resume and build a resume in the online application system can be frustrating. Advances in software allow the system to "read" the candidate resume and prepopulate much of the online application. This can be helpful in alleviating the time requirement and frustration for the candidate while getting the organization the data it requires.

Systems should be designed to ask for all required information upfront. Having to go back to the applicant several times for resumes, cover letters, transcripts, references, and writing samples drags the application process out and creates work for everyone. Ensure that all required documentation is requested at the start.

LIMITED ROUNDS OF INTERVIEWS

Determine the most effective and efficient way to screen, qualify, and interview a candidate. Recruiters often do an initial screening, and should be trained to ask the proper questions to determine if an applicant is qualified for the position. If there are certain certifications, education, or years of experience requirements, these should be assessed by the recruiter to limit the number of candidates sent to the next stage by filtering out those who are not qualified.

Once candidates are screened, management evaluates the skill sets and qualities they seek at a deeper level. If there are multiple levels of management that must be involved in the hiring decision, consider a panel interview, which allows the candidate to meet with several people at once. This way all of the interviewers hear the same information and the candidate is not required to repeatedly return to the company to meet with each manager individually.

Interview time should be used wisely, with questions prepared beforehand to ensure that all of the necessary information is gathered during the interview. The candidate should be given time to ask his or her questions to prevent creating confusion or force additional rounds of back and forth for the candidate to feel comfortable about the job or the company.

FAIR CONSIDERATION OF APPLICANTS' TIME

The job hunt experience is typically long and emotional. Applicants are eager to join the company and take time and put forth effort to complete the application process. The first and sometimes most critical response from the company is an acknowledgement of the candidate's application. Organizations must make the effort to reply to the candidate and recognize receipt of the application. One of the biggest frustrations candidates reveal in surveys about their job hunt experiences is the disrespect they feel when they take their time to apply to a company and the company does not respond. The second biggest gap in the process is the time for recruiters to do the initial screening of the application and decide on whether the candidate will move forward or not. If an applicant is rejected, but the rejection is processed in a timely fashion and the decision is communicated respectfully, the applicant can accept the rejection and move on to the next job. Holding candidates in limbo for weeks and months at a time does a disservice to both the candidate and the company.

If an organization does decide to move forward with the candidate, the interview and offer phase should be executed in a reasonable timeframe. Scheduled appointments should be honored, and decisions should be made in a timely fashion. Candidates will develop a negative opinion of an organization that cannot make decisions in a reasonable timeframe.

FREQUENT COMMUNICATION

As with respecting the applicant's time, the communications employed by the organization can be a driving factor in whether a candidate's experience with the application process is positive. The initial acknowledgement of the application is critical, followed closely by the first decision on moving forward, or declining to move forward. This decision should be made quickly, and the communication of the decision should be done professionally.

Once candidates knows that they are moving forward in the hire process, the biggest enemy of the organization is silence. If candidates do not hear back from the recruiter for weeks or months at a time, they will develop a negative impression and most likely move on, even if they were very interested in the position.

Recruiters need to keep applicants in the loop, communicating when there is information or to let them know that things are still in process. This improves the candidate's experience and keeps them interested in the position and the company.

If at any time the organization decides that a candidate will not move forward to the next step of the process, this should be communicated in a timely and professional manner. The final offer and negotiations should also be done timely and positively. Candidates should always know where the process stands.

Employee Engagement and Retention

APPROACHES TO DEVELOPING AND MAINTAINING A POSITIVE ORGANIZATIONAL CULTURE

LEARNING STRATEGIES

Organizational culture should be a focal point beginning with new hire orientation. Introductory training materials should discuss the culture and provide examples of it in action within the firm. From there, managers should regularly coach and train staff so that the culture stays top of mind. Finally, leaders should live the company culture in all that they do. Employees may be influenced by their behavior.

COMMUNICATION STRATEGIES

Organizational culture should be communicated frequently, clearly, and consistently. If employees see inconsistencies in this communication, they may distrust leadership or be less engaged at work.

BUILDING VALUES

An organization's **values** are the foundation of its culture. Therefore, leadership must establish them early on. Human resources should hire candidates that embody the firm's values. Any new policies and procedures should reflect the same principles. Finally, discipline and rewards systems should be built upon these core values.

MAINTAINING ORGANIZATIONAL CULTURE

Culture encompasses every facet of an organization and comprises four **key elements:** norms, artifacts, values, and core assumptions. Shared **norms** are not always defined or obvious but often inferred from specific situations. For example, norms of punctuality and professionalism are demonstrated by leaders who practice them. Likewise, the collective beliefs, ideals, and feelings of the members of an organization construct its cultural **values**. Cultural **artifacts**, such as behaviors, language, and symbols, are tangible traits that portray core values. An organization's shared **core assumptions** reveal the basis of how its people think. This can be reflected by the extent of controls that management impose upon line staff. Organizational culture can be maintained through employee selection and disciplinary procedures, rewards systems, recognition ceremonies, stories, symbols, and leadership reactions to achievements and problems.

PERSONALIZED EMPLOYEE EXPERIENCE

The employee experience is the cumulative effect of every contact that an individual has with their employer throughout the course of the professional relationship. A **personalized employee experience** is the creation and development of a more-customizable work experience through avenues such as benefits, flexibility, and decision-making that tailor to the needs of each employee. For example, offering a hybrid work schedule for an employee who has a situation that requires him or her to work remotely for a portion of the week, or offering a low-deductible PPO for families with younger children while offering a high-deductible HSA for families with older children or healthier adults. A personalized work experience can include participative conversations about what each individual perceives as success, then working together to align that vision with the company vision, to ensure success for both parties. The personalized experience should begin with initial contact with a candidate, and continue through orientation, onboarding, and beyond.

INFLUENCE OF CULTURE ON ORGANIZATIONAL OUTCOMES

ORGANIZATIONAL PERFORMANCE

Studies have long demonstrated that organizational culture plays a significant role in **organizational performance**. How well a company is doing (based on how many tasks and objectives are successfully completed), heavily depends on the internal environment—the company culture. Organizations that prioritize engagement, training, and development are much more likely to see higher sales and customer satisfaction. The more invested an organization is in its employees, the more invested the employees will be in the organization, driving higher organizational performance.

ORGANIZATIONAL LEARNING

The process of how an organization acquires, retains, and transfers new skills, processes, and knowledge for continued growth and development, or **organizational learning**, is a key area for business success. The organizational culture heavily impacts organizational learning. A culture that promotes continuous learning and development will have a much stronger basis for organizational learning versus an organization where training and learning are not highly emphasized. Similarly, cultures that value the sharing and transferring of organizational knowledge will foster more collaboration and exchanging of ideas than a culture where certain areas and concepts are siloed. A culture of organizational learning helps to empower employees, retain employees, and keep individuals engaged while also simultaneously breeding innovation and strategic growth.

INNOVATION

A culture of **innovation** and the ability to think outside the box is required for organizations to remain competitive and attract new talent. The ways of working are always changing, so being able to innovate and stay on top of changes and trends deeply impacts the ability of a business to remain solvent. Organizations that develop a culture of challenging assumptions, experimentation, failure, learning, and acceptance of new ideas are likely to be innovative. Cultures where employees are expected to accept the way things are done, simply because that is the way they have always been done, are less likely to breed innovation and will be unable to keep up with the changing business landscape.

RISK-TAKING

Development and growth do not exist without risk. **Risk-taking**, or doing something with an uncertain outcome, is necessary for competition and progress. Organizations that foster a culture where failure and success are accepted, challenging the status quo is allowed, and thinking of less-conventional solutions is encouraged, are organizations that are open to at least some level of risk-taking. Having a risk-averse culture can stifle creativity, limit growth, and increase turnover. Employees who do not feel that they have a voice or say in one organization are more prone to leave for one where they feel they do.

WORKPLACE FLEXIBILITY PROGRAMS

There have been many benefits touted in favor of **workplace flexibility**, such as increased morale, better attendance, and higher productivity. Flexibility might involve either the **work location**, which is where work is performed, or the **work schedule**, which is when work is performed. However, the practice is gaining momentum slowly due to many employers embracing traditional viewpoints despite technological advances creating lower overhead costs for remote workers or greater employee engagement and satisfaction when they are allowed schedule flexibility to accommodate family or personal responsibilities. Workplace flexibility allows employees greater autonomy and empowerment as well. Flexibility can also be used to encourage brand recognition, attract talent, and support retention strategies.

TELECOMMUTING

Employees may be able to perform their jobs outside of a traditional company office by **telecommuting** using tools such as email, phone, remote in, and video/chat apps. Telecommuting can be done on a full-time, part-time, or intermittent basis. Telecommuting offers increased flexibility and work-life balance, allowing employees a little more freedom in scheduling. Negative aspects of telecommuting include loss of professional direction or face-to-face interaction. Strong organizational skills, scheduling, and autonomy are beneficial skills for individuals who telecommute.

ALTERNATIVE WORK SCHEDULES

Designed to provide an alternative to the "traditional" work week, **alternative work schedules** benefit individuals who need the flexibility that a standard schedule cannot offer. There are many options for alternative work schedules, such as a **compressed work schedule** of four 10-hour days or three 12-hour days. This allows the individual to work full-time hours in fewer days. **Flextime** is another type of alternative work schedule, where an employee is required work some of their hours during a specific designated time (for example from 9 a.m. to 12 p.m.) and their remaining hours on a flexible basis (for example, any time between 5 a.m. and 5 p.m.).

Job Sharing

Two (or more) employees each working in a position part-time to fill a role that may have been filled by a single person working full-time is known as **job sharing**. The employees filling the shared role work together to accomplish the assigned tasks and duties. Job sharing allows increased flexibility, as the two part-time employees can tailor their shifts, hours, and duties. Employees that are sharing a job may both work the same hours and focus on different areas. Alternately, they may split a shift, working different hours in the same day. A third scheduling option is splitting the work week, so one employee works one day, and the other employee works the next day. A combination of each of these schedules can also be used.

Methods of Assessing Employee Attitudes

Focus Groups

Companies may use **focus groups** to glean employee views and concerns or to assess a new benefit plan or organizational change. Most focus groups contain five to 12 voluntary **participants**, and a company may use three to 10 groups in total. Participants should be informed about the subject of the focus group and who will benefit from it, and that the information will be kept confidential. Participants may be selected at random or through the use of applicable filters. Focus group organizers should ensure that power differentials within the group are avoided. It is also important to involve participants from various levels of staff so they can fully represent the affected population. A neutral **facilitator** should be chosen to lead the discussion and ask open-ended, guided questions. Following the meeting, the data should be analyzed and reported.

Stay Interviews

A **stay interview** is a purposeful yet casual conversation between an employee and a company leader regarding the employee's propensity to leave the organization. The leader will ask the employee questions such as the following:

- What keeps you in your current role?
- What might cause you to leave the company?
- What is important to you professionally?
- What can I do to improve your overall work experience with the firm?

The objective is to increase the employee's engagement and prevent turnover.

Surveys

Employee **surveys** can be valuable when examining employee engagement levels and job satisfaction. These surveys, whether created externally or internally, may be completed on a number of websites and platforms. Employee participation should be voluntary and anonymous. Employees who want to participate should be provided with time during the workday to complete the survey. The survey should be available long enough to give all departments and shifts ample time to participate.

Many third-party vendors and national agencies conduct regular surveys and publish statistics about the results. Human resource practitioners should benchmark their own survey results against these statistics or those of similar organizations before presenting findings to the executive leadership team. Generalized survey results and plans to address concerns raised in surveys should be shared with the employees as soon as practically possible after the survey period ends. **Employee engagement** should be analyzed on a regular basis, and survey results should be kept on file for data comparison over time. Survey items should be measured against organizational **key performance indicators (KPIs)** like quality, productivity, and customer satisfaction.

JOB ATTITUDE THEORIES AND BASIC PRINCIPLES

ENGAGEMENT, SATISFACTION, AND COMMITMENT

Although there is no universally accepted definition for employee **engagement**, it can be viewed as the level of connection employees feel to their work and their employer. This connection affects the amount of effort that they will put into fulfilling their roles. **Satisfaction** is a measure of how happy employees are with their work and their employer. Satisfaction can also be viewed as an employee's level of gratification or fulfillment derived from their employment. **Commitment** is a measure of how dedicated employees are to their employer and their employer's goals. Commitment can also be viewed as an employee's sense of obligation to be loyal and perform at their best.

EQUITY THEORY

Employees can experience motivation problems and low levels of job satisfaction. According to **equity theory**, individuals tend to feel satisfied and report fair conditions when they perceive a state of equity. Attitudes toward pay can be influenced by the rate of pay, the work done to earn pay, and whether the ratio of pay to work appears to be fair in comparison to the pay-to-work ratio of others. Individuals ultimately evaluate whether what they get from a job is commensurate with what they put into the job. There are six methods that individuals may utilize to **reduce inequality**:

- Altering inputs, such as time effort, hard work, loyalty, commitment, and trust
- Altering outcomes, such as salary, benefits, recognition, and achievement
- Cognitively manipulating inputs or outcomes by rationalizing or self-justification
- Distorting the inputs or outcomes of others
- Changing objects of comparison
- Leaving the field

INTERVENTIONS FOR IMPROVING JOB ATTITUDES

There are several ways that a company can **improve the job attitudes** of their employees. First, it should conduct a survey to get a baseline reading and identify areas of concern. The company should make every effort to address any attitude issues revealed, as appearing to ignore them will further disgruntle staff. In general, doing the following can go a long way toward fostering positive employee attitudes:

- Make the work interesting and meaningful.
- Offer opportunities to learn and grow.
- Provide regular feedback on performance.
- Recognize a job well done and above-and-beyond effort.
- Communicate expectations, changes, and overall firm performance clearly and consistently.
- Be transparent whenever possible.
- Foster respect and fairness.
- Ensure that the compensation and benefits package is competitive and strategically designed.

JOB DESIGN PRINCIPLES AND TECHNIQUES

JOB ENRICHMENT

Many roles can be redesigned so that they have more meaning, are less monotonous, and are more challenging to employees. To achieve this **job enrichment**, employees may be asked to take on additional planning, decision-making, and controlling responsibilities. The goal of job enrichment is to provide employees with greater opportunities for autonomy, responsibility, recognition, achievement, and advancement. Ideally, job enrichment should create a greater sense of belonging to the organization as well as develop a multitalented workforce.

Job Enlargement

Depending on the employee's capabilities, employers may also consider **job enlargement**. Job enlargement consists of adding more duties are at the same level of difficulty as the employee's current tasks. Although employees are not able to exercise more discretion with job enlargement, they can learn new things and add variety to their workday, which may stave off boredom and increase engagement.

Work Simplification

Unlike job enlargement, **work simplification** is removing tasks from existing positions in order to make them more focused. This process is implemented to improve ways of working in order to maximize productivity while lowering costs. Complex tasks are broken down into smaller and more simple tasks in order to increase the productivity of the employee by reducing the amount of work that needs to be done. This breakdown leads to more repetitive work, increasing the individual's proficiency, which increases the individual's productivity.

Job Rotation

Some organizations find it beneficial to move employees to different jobs within the organization. These movements are usually lateral and are often temporary, with the employees moving back to their original roles after a set time period. **Job rotation** can provide many benefits, such as increased cross-training and skill development, which can be useful when a critical role is facing an extended absence. Employees are more engaged and interested because they have the opportunity to experience different roles. This also provides the organization with an improved talent pool for succession planning, as many employees will have training across various roles and key talent can be identified. The job rotation plan and schedule should be clearly laid out with expectations and timelines defined before rotations begin.

Employee Lifecycle Phases

The total timeline of the relationship between an employee and their employer can be divided into four **employee lifecycle phases**. **Recruitment** encompasses the process of finding and acquiring new talent, from creating job descriptions through onboarding a new hire. **Integration** is the subsequent phase of getting the recent hire fully acclimated and functioning well in his or her assigned role. The third phase, **development,** is when the employee grows as a professional via training programs, promotion opportunities, and so on. **Departure** is the last phase of the employment relationship. It is when the employee leaves the organization and human resources processes him or her out of company systems.

Employee Retention Concepts and Best Practices
Causes of Absenteeism and Turnover

Absenteeism is when employees miss work temporarily. **Turnover** is when employees leave permanently.

Poor morale, frustration, and conflict can lead to absenteeism and turnover. **Involuntary absenteeism and turnover** are caused by situations beyond the employee's control, such as illness, family concerns, relocation, layoffs, and terminations. **Voluntary absenteeism and turnover** occur when employees have a choice and intentionally miss work or resign. The reasons for absenteeism can be further categorized as planned absences, unplanned absences, intermittent absences, or extended absences. Employees may also permanently leave their jobs for higher-paying work, better benefits, a promotion, to start a business, or for other reasons.

Employee Retention Programs

An **employee retention program** is a set of policies, procedures, and practices designed to encourage employees to stay with the organization. This program can be an essential part of a staffing strategy because it decreases employee turnover, which is especially important for positions that are difficult and costly to replace. An employee retention program may offer extra benefits or compensation (such as vacation time and bonuses), which can help the organization retain key staff and function effectively.

REALISTIC JOB PREVIEWS

A **realistic job preview** to any activity that helps give applicants a clear idea of the specific day-to-day tasks and responsibilities that they will need to perform if hired. These activities can include watching videos about the organization, observing current employees, or looking at illustrations of the job being performed.

SUGGESTION MECHANISMS

Communication and collaboration are vital parts of employee retention. Organizations that offer a way for employees to contribute valuable feedback and suggestions will have more-engaged employees. **Suggestion mechanisms** such as an employee suggestion program are easy ways to obtain timely and relevant feedback from employees. Suggestion programs can encourage employees to identify possible improvements to work processes and the working environment, submit ideas for new products, or bring awareness to any potential issues and difficulties. These programs help establish a culture of continuous improvement, increased engagement, and higher levels of communication throughout the organization.

PREDICTIVE ATTRITION ANALYSIS

Attrition analysis focuses on turnover, particularly voluntary separations. Data is examined to determine the reasons behind departures, as well as what could have been done to retain the employee. This data is then used to help forecast the possibilities for future attrition. **Predictive attrition analysis** uses several factors to help identify potential attrition trends. Predicting such patterns requires looking into the past to answer key questions starting with *who*, *why*, and *when*. Employee surveys that were completed in the last year can be used to characterize employees who separated voluntarily. Analyzing this information will provide key details about turnover in specific positions, level of tenure, departments, and locations. This analysis can reveal where instances of turnover are higher. The next step is to review what employees had to say about the workplace. These answers can be found in satisfaction surveys and in exit interviews. Information about morale in the workplace, working relationships with peers, communication, and connection with the organization before leaving can reveal important aspects about company culture and the employee experience that may need improvement.

PERSONALIZED ONBOARDING

Every employee is different, so the onboarding experience for each should be different as well. **Personalized onboarding** is a technique in which the onboarding experience is customized and tailored to individual employees. This can be accomplished in different ways, but one of the first ways to facilitate this personalized experience is by creating individual tasks or programs based on department, role, and tasks to be completed. This exposes the employee to tools he or she is most likely to use. For example, sales will likely have different needs than human resources (HR), so providing each with a preview of the features and offerings that are most relevant to the role makes onboarding more informative and efficient. During the next step of the onboarding process, role-specific training and policies can be demonstrated, so that individuals are not working through generic and identical material. Finance could move into invoice management, vendor management, and accounting tools. HR might move into human resource information systems (HRIS), organization charts, and metrics. Some individuals may move through onboarding with relative ease on their own, with little external prompting or communication. Others may benefit more from check-ins or meetings. Personalized onboarding experiences offer both options.

KEY COMPONENTS AND BEST PRACTICES OF PERFORMANCE MANAGEMENT

An organization cannot thrive if individuals, teams, and departments are not effective in their roles. **Performance management** is the human resource (HR) function concerned with setting performance standards, evaluating employee effectiveness against those standards, identifying any problem areas, and implementing interventions to correct said problems.

Performance management systems, which can include specialized performance management software, vary from organization to organization, but most firms follow three basic steps:

1. Company leaders and HR professionals establish organizational goals through activities like goal setting, needs analysis, and the creation of a corporate value statement and code of conduct. They then identify the knowledge, skills, behaviors, and tasks required to achieve those goals and inform employees how to best work to meet the company's objectives.
2. The firm's management then monitors employee performance, documents any problems, and helps employees correct those problems, if possible.
3. At predetermined intervals (typically once a year), managers conduct in-depth performance appraisals for each employee. The appraisals measure performance during the period since the last appraisal. Often, the manager and employee will set goals for the employee to work toward in the new appraisal period.

DASHBOARD

A performance management **dashboard** is a virtual management and reporting tool that businesses utilize to determine the efficiency of specific metrics. These metrics can include items like customer satisfaction, employee performance, attendance, customer turnover rate, monthly sales per employee, hours of overtime, and many more key performance indicators (KPIs). Tracking performance in this manner allows organizations to monitor key tasks and operations. Dashboards are often customizable, so organizations can tailor them to display only the business aspects and metrics that are most relevant to them. Performance management dashboards place a great deal of focus on KPIs, which can be displayed in a way that allows trends to be easily identified and simple to understand. These dashboards help the organization gain a better understanding of real-time performance and the effectiveness of current operations. Adjustments can be made based on current and historical data tracked in the dashboard. The organization can also view what areas are the most successful, so those behaviors can be repeated in other areas.

CALIBRATION

A key component of a performance management system is performance **calibration**. Calibration occurs when supervisors, managers, and leaders responsible for facilitating employee reviews meet to discuss employee performance and ratings. The purpose of this discussion is to make sure that each employee receives a fair and objective appraisal, and that all individuals involved agree on a specific set of standards that will be applied to every employee during the review process. During this discussion, the individuals involved should go over current ratings, determine what each rating means, and justify the ratings assigned to each employee. Calibration ensures consistency of performance ratings so that, for example, employees are not poorly rated because they are not liked by the supervisor. Instead, they are rated without bias according to the objective rating scale. Calibration defines and clearly states the criteria that employees need to meet in order to qualify for a high rating, while also defining what behaviors lead to a lower rating. With the calibration process comes an understanding with both the organization and the employee as to what criteria are involved in the rating system. This makes the process fairer and more transparent. Calibration should be done prior to the annual appraisal process, so that each review period begins with a clear set of standards and equal application.

USER TRAINING

Everyone involved with the performance management system must be **trained** in the aspects of the system they interact with. For example, a leader who is responsible for conducting employee appraisals should be trained in how the performance management system functions. The leader should be familiar with the planning phase, which is when KPIs are identified and performance goals are listed. The leader should also have a detailed understanding of the employee assessment portion, starting with the criteria for each rating level. Leaders must measure how effectively the employee met the KPIs, how successful the employee was at achieving the stated goals, and how the individual's overall performance was rated. Familiarization with performance recognition is key to determining any wage or salary adjustment due. Finally, the leader should be able to identify career development opportunities for the employee, such as professional development seminars, certification or licensure, or other training. The leader should then determine what career-pathing options may exist for the employee in the future. An individual participating in an appraisal should be trained on the expectations for goal-setting, the criteria for ratings, what behaviors determine rating levels, and what future opportunities may exist, as well as how to work toward those potential opportunities. Everyone should be trained not only on the process, but also on the form. Neither leaders nor employees should be given a blank evaluation template and be expected to know how to fill it out—training should exist for that as well. Training is a critical component in the efficiency, accuracy, and meaningfulness of the review and appraisal process.

RECORDING GOALS

Organizations need a clear structure for setting and **recording goals** to ensure accountability and consistency. Recording the goals that have been established is critical in performance management, particularly in tracking progress and measuring achievement percentage, as well as in the review process. These goals should be reviewed regularly, to ensure that progress is being made or adjustments are made when needed. Employees should participate in this discussion, and have the chance to share their progress, any challenges that might have arisen, additional resources that might be needed, and feedback and support should be provided by the leader. Successes should be recognized and celebrated along the way, as this helps maintain engagement and motivation in the employee.

PRINCIPLES OF EFFECTIVE PERFORMANCE APPRAISAL

Performance appraisals serve four main organizational functions:

- **Guide human resource decisions.** Performance data is required for supporting and justifying promotion or termination decisions.
- **Reward and motivate employees.** Pay rate, status, and recognition should be based on performance.
- **Promote personal development.** Performance feedback will help employees identify strengths and improve weaknesses.
- **Identify training needs.** A well-designed appraisal process establishes necessary skills and abilities for each role and identifies individuals, areas, or departments that could benefit from additional training.

Each employee's **performance** appraisal should assess the following:

- Progress toward goals set at the last appraisal meeting
- Completion of normal job duties
- Organizational behaviors such as cooperation, innovation, motivation, and attitude
- Any notable achievements

SETTING GOALS

Performance goals consist of both short- and long-term targets that individual employees or teams are expected to achieve. These goals serve as guidelines for what employees should achieve and accomplish to help further the broader strategic goals of their department or of the organization. Goals also help employees concentrate their efforts on professional development, skills improvement, and personal development. Setting goals is very important in establishing a sense of direction in what employees are expected to achieve, as well as which behaviors and activities will help them toward that target. Goals can be set by HR, department heads, managers, supervisors, and the employees themselves. Goals should be clearly defined, specific, and realistic. Goals should also include an expected completion timeframe, to make tracking progress easier. Setting performance goals helps both the individual and the company. Employees are motivated to achieve goals, which drives performance and productivity. When there are group goals, employees collaborate to ensure that those goals are met by improving and promoting teamwork. Goal-setting helps to clearly state the expectations of the employees and the organization alike.

FREQUENT FEEDBACK

Feedback from leadership should not occur only during appraisal time. Employees should receive feedback from their supervisors and managers frequently throughout the year. Providing **frequent feedback** makes it clear whether an employee is meeting expectations, illustrates when an employee is doing something well, identifies an area that could use some improvement, discusses additional training opportunities, and demonstrates that leadership recognizes the employee and sees the work and development that the employee is putting in. Employees can ask their leaders for feedback, but feedback is something that leadership should provide on a regular basis even without being asked. This can be formal feedback such as a bi-weekly check-in, or informal such as through a simple affirmation about a certain item. Frequent feedback also ensures that employees and supervisors are aligned with one another, and there are no unexpected surprises during the annual appraisal process.

RETENTION AND TURNOVER METRICS

A company's **retention rate** is the percentage of employees that are employed at the company throughout an entire measurement period, such as a quarter or a year. A critical metric for tracking purposes, **turnover** provides good insight into the work culture, efficacy of hiring and onboarding policies/procedures, and management of employees. There are various ways to calculate turnover. The **turnover rate** is the number of employees who left the company during the measurement period compared to the average number of employees throughout the measurement period.

$$\text{Retention rate} = \frac{\text{Number of employees employed for entire measurement period}}{\text{Number of employees at start of measurement period}} \times 100\%$$

$$\text{Turnover rate} = \frac{\text{Number of employees who left during measurement period}}{\text{Average number of employees during measurement period}} \times 100\%$$

QUALITY OF HIRE

Quality of hire (QoH) is a metric that measures the value that a new hire brings to the organization. It is often found by gauging that employee's contribution to the long-term success and performance of the organization. QoH is a complex metric that includes several different indicators, some of which take time to measure. To calculate QoH, one must determine which indicators will be used in the metric; possible indicators include engagement, manager feedback, performance, and team feedback. Each indicator is then rated from 1 to 100, and the total of these ratings is divided by the total number of indicators to determine the QoH:

$$\frac{93 \text{ engagement} + 87 \text{ manager feedback} + 86 \text{ performance} + 71 \text{ team feedback}}{4} = 84.25 \text{ QoH}$$

When calculating the QoH for multiple recent hires, divide the total of each QoH by the number of hires.

$$84 \text{ Hire A} + 79 \text{ Hire B} + 96 \text{ Hire C} + 88 \text{ Hire D} = 347$$

$$\frac{347 \text{ QoH sum}}{4 \text{ New hires}} = 86.74 \text{ average QoH}$$

TURNOVER AT A SPECIFIC LOCATION OR LEVEL

Turnover can be calculated companywide, on a site-to-site basis, or even for a particular role or department. If an organization is seeing a lot of employees separating from the company at a specific site, human resources might want to calculate the turnover rate for that site. This calculation can be done by calculating the average number of employees at the site.

For example, on July 1st, a company had 47 employees at one site. On July 31st, the same site had 41 employees. During the month, 8 people at that location separated from the company.

Add the number of employees at the start of the month to the number of employees at the end of the month:

$$47 + 41 = 88$$

Divide by 2 to get the average number of employees for the month:

$$\frac{88}{2} = 44$$

Divide the number of employees who separated by average number of employees:

$$\frac{8}{44} = 0.181$$

Finally, multiply by 100% to find the turnover rate:

$$0.181 \times 100\% = 18.18\%$$

The monthly turnover rate for that location was 18%.

Measuring the yearly turnover for a particular location or role can be helpful in identifying trends and patterns. If the yearly turnover for either location or role shows an increasing trend, the organization should investigate the possible reasons for the higher turnover.

VACANCY RATE

The **vacancy rate** is the number of vacant positions compared to the total number of positions in the organization. The vacancy rate is also referred to as the job openings rate. It is calculated by dividing the number of open positions by the total number of positions and multiplying by 100.

$$\text{Vacancy rate} = \frac{\text{Number of open positions}}{\text{Total number of positions}} \times 100\%$$

TYPES OF ORGANIZATIONAL CULTURE

The system of beliefs and values established by a firm to guide the behavior of the individuals within it is its **organizational culture**. In essence, organizational culture is the work environment that the employees and managers of the organization have created, and continue to create as time passes. Companies typically attempt to control the culture to some degree, to make sure that employee motivation stays high and organizational objectives are met. However, the culture is usually heavily influenced by the specific experiences of its members and by external forces. As a result, it can sometimes be difficult for an organization to shape its culture, especially when prominent figures become unhappy or outside influences begin placing a great deal of stress on employees. Shared vision is the discipline of creating a culture that encourages employees to work toward a common goal.

AUTHORITARIAN

An **authoritarian culture** is extremely focused on efficiency and productivity. In this culture, employees produce out of fear of punishment or anticipation of reward. Characterized by micromanagement, this culture can be appropriate during times of uncertainty, when one strong leader takes the helm and makes all of the decisions. This culture can result in low morale because employees have zero input, autonomy, or ability to be creative.

MECHANISTIC

A **mechanistic culture** is characterized by organization, specialization, and strong guidance from leadership. Focused on productivity, employees in this culture operate like a well-oiled machine. This culture's decision-

115

making can be bogged down by an overly bureaucratic structure. In addition, this culture does not foster collaboration or creativity, which could result in low morale.

PARTICIPATIVE

A **participative culture** features open communication and shared power. In the spirit of democratic decision-making, employees may have the opportunity to voice opinions, give input, or take complete ownership of decisions. This culture is characterized by training, collaboration, empathy, and empowerment. Although morale may be high, it can be hard to get anything accomplished quickly.

LEARNING

A **learning culture** aims to use knowledge, abilities, and innovation to adapt to an ever-changing business environment. Characterized by creativity, initiative, experimentation, and collaboration, knowledge is shared freely. This culture earmarks a lot of resources for training and development. In a learning culture, failure is not feared, it is merely another learning experience. This culture encourages employees to solve problems and improve workflows whenever they see an opportunity to do so.

HIGH-PERFORMANCE

A **high-performance culture** promotes goal achievement by setting clear objectives, clearly spelling out employee responsibilities, encouraging continuous development, and fostering trust. This culture is characterized by innovation, collaboration, communication, leadership support, and accountability. To sustain high levels of productivity, this culture promotes employee wellness so that workers can continue to operate at their best.

APPROACHES TO RECOGNITION

Almost all employees have an innate desire to be **valued and appreciated** for their contributions. **Employee recognition programs** vary from firm to firm. However, they are most often used to motivate and reward achievements. The most common types of recognition include verbal praise, performance acknowledgements, employee of the month awards, length of service awards, or certificates for other achievements. **Rewards** may include thank-you notes, business paraphernalia, spot bonuses, gift cards, or extra time off. A combination of **tangible and intangible incentives** ensure that the program is valuable to all participants. Employee recognition programs can also be used to reinforce organizational expectations, attract and retain talent, increase productivity, improve quality and safety, and reduce absenteeism and turnover. Regardless of the methods chosen by an employer, a **formal written policy** should be published to describe the rewards that will be given, how they can be earned, and when they will be doled out. This policy will ensure fairness and consistency and increase the likelihood of desired behaviors being repeated.

PERFORMANCE OR SERVICE AWARDS

A common form of employee recognition comes in the form of a **service award**, which is a special kind of recognition given to an employee who has worked with an organization for a specific length of time. These pre-determined lengths of times are called **milestones**. Service awards are also called milestone awards, years of service awards, or service anniversary awards. The type of recognition that comes with the awards tends to increase as the employee becomes more tenured in the organization. For example, a first-year service award may be a certificate or a card. A 15-year service award might be a certificate with a $150 gift card. Some companies offer branded items as service awards instead of a gift card. There are many ways to structure a service award program. Service awards are a great way to recognize the organizational loyalty and commitment of an individual employee.

Another common form of employee recognition is a **performance award** based on productivity and efficiency in the workplace. This type of award takes the employee's overall performance into consideration. This can be done on a monthly, quarterly, or annual schedule, depending on how the program is set up. "Employee of the month" and "most improved performer" are common examples of performance awards. Performance awards can come in many different formats through gifts, certificates, paid time off, or company swag. Performance

awards are a great way to recognize individuals for their contributions to the organization and also a great way to create motivation for others to perform their best.

SPOT AWARDS

An employee can be given a **spot award** as a recognition or reward for his or her contribution as it happens. These awards are also called "on-the-spot" awards, because they happen immediately when an employee goes above and beyond or exceeds expectations in a particular area. Spot awards can be given as an immediate form of recognition for contributions by individuals or teams. These awards can come in the form of small bonuses or cash incentives, but may also have no cash value, like additional time off or experiential rewards. For example, Logan puts in additional hours to complete a presentation for an executive after a co-worker had to step away because of an emergency, so he is recognized by his manager with a gift card to a local coffee shop. Spot awards are a great form of recognition because they are totally customizable and can be tailored for the individual and the situation. The organization has considerable leeway when creating a spot recognition program because the options are almost limitless. Spot awards are an excellent form of immediate feedback and encouragement for employees. They boost morale and demonstrate to the employees that their efforts are recognized and appreciated.

POINTS-BASED SYSTEM

Another type of recognition that can be offered to employees is a points-based recognition system. A **points-based system** is one where employees decide which reward they really want. Employees are awarded points based on a variety of factors, which can include attendance, referrals, safety observations, performance, training, and many more. These points can then be cashed in to obtain a reward. Companies may offer gift cards, branded apparel, paid time off, charity donations, tickets to local events, and many more. A points-based system could be difficult to track and monitor without software, plus there are many factors to consider, such as who will be able to award points, whether recognition will be public, what rewards will be available, and what determines if a behavior is worthy of points. There are numerous companies that offer points-based platform implementation and administration. Points-based awards allow employees to choose a reward that is most meaningful to them, making the reward more impactful. Points-based systems increase engagement, boost morale, and decrease turnover.

PEER-TO-PEER RECOGNITION

When appreciation or commendation is expressed between two colleagues of equal status within an organization, the parties involved are on an equal footing, and one does not manage or supervise the other. This **peer-to-peer recognition**, or simply peer recognition, helps foster an environment of trust and support while also motivating high performance. Organizations with high levels of peer recognition will likely have increased levels of job satisfaction and strong teamwork. Peer recognition can occur formally (such as an announcement on a Slack channel or other platform) or informally (such as a verbal kudos or compliment). Both methods are effective, and peer recognition often grows organically.

PERSONALIZED REWARDS

Recognition matters more when it is meaningful. **Personalized rewards** are rewards given to employees that are tailored to their specific needs, interests, and motivations. With so many options for how to recognize and reward employees, it is easy to pick a wide variety of items that may never be used. Personalized rewards allow employees to choose things that hold value to them. Personalized rewards can be something as simple as a card with a handwritten note that recognizes an employee individually for a contribution he or she made. Employees feel valued when they are recognized on a personal level.

Learning and Development

NEEDS ANALYSIS

There are several reasons that it is important for an organization to perform a **needs analysis** before designing a training program. First, it is imperative for an organization to accurately identify problems. Second, even if a particular problem is known prior to the analysis, it can be difficult to identify the cause of that problem. Third, and most importantly, it is impossible to design an effective training program without first identifying the specific knowledge, skills, and abilities required to correct a problem or achieve other goals. A needs analysis can be an essential part of the training development process because it helps to identify and detail problems so that possible solutions can be found.

There are a variety of steps that might be taken during a needs analysis, but most begin by collecting data related to the performance of each part of the organization. This information is usually gathered from surveys, interviews, observations, skill assessments, performance appraisals, and so on. Once this information is collected, problems are identified within specific areas of the organization and solutions are proposed. Advantages and disadvantages of each solution are then identified and the plan that seems to provide the greatest benefit for the lowest cost is chosen.

PERSON

A **person needs analysis** is a type of needs analysis that determines several key items, such as how well an employee performs a task compared to expectations. Not all individuals within the organization will require training, so performing a person analysis establishes which specific employees need training or development. Once individuals are identified for training, the type of training can be selected.

ORGANIZATION

An **organization needs analysis** is conducted to ensure that training is aligned with the overall business strategy as well as making sure that there are adequate resources and support available for training.

TRAINING

A **training needs analysis** is completed to identify any gaps that may exist in the actual knowledge, skills, and abilities in a role versus the desired levels. The difference between the actual competency and the standard determines the training that may be required.

COST/BENEFIT ANALYSIS

Although training and development programs should be viewed as extremely valuable capital investments in themselves, they also provide measurable returns. Simple calculations can be used to measure the costs and benefits of training. **Costs** should include both direct costs (e.g., materials, facilities, etc.) and indirect costs (e.g., lost production time). The overall costs of training and development programs might contain staff hours, program materials, hardware or software, videos, and production losses such as training time and respective salaries. **Benefits** of training should be evaluated according to how well the training will increase productivity, advance product quality, reduce errors, improve safety, or reduce operating costs. One calculation for measuring training is the **cost per trainee**, in which the total cost of training is divided by the number of trainees. Regardless of this cost, the long-term benefits of training should outweigh the total costs, and this can be determined through a **cost/benefit analysis**. There are creative adjustments that can be used to reduce training costs. The size of training classes can be increased, and materials can be reused, as long as copyrights are not violated. Expenses can be further eliminated by making training available online or using videoconferencing.

SURVEYS

Learning and development surveys can help organizations determine which growth opportunities are desired by employees and which training method is preferred. They can also help organizations analyze how successful training and development programs are, and how satisfied employees are with current training and

118

development options. These surveys can also help identify if employees feel that there is access to learning opportunities, if management supports learning and development, if there is adequate time for training, and if the organization offers learning and development that will help the employee grow in his or her role as well as in his or her field.

Surveys can also gauge retention and recall of training and presentations, allowing the organization to determine the efficacy of a particular training. Surveys can be offered at various time intervals. For example, learning and development satisfaction questions can be included with an annual employee survey. Shorter **pulse surveys** targeted at determining training effectiveness can be offered soon after the training ends. Other surveys can be sent out when the organization is reviewing the learning and development budget or the budget of the organization overall.

OBSERVATIONS

Managers and leaders can track employee development over time using **observations**. This allows the manager or leader to identify areas where improvement may be needed. Observations may also be used to determine the efficacy of a particular training by watching whether employees display specific behaviors. The individual performing the observation identifies different scenarios that best demonstrate the skill or knowledge that either requires development or has recently been the subject of training. For example, if there was a training just conducted on handling customer complaints cordially and effectively, the observer could listen in to an employee addressing a customer complaint and determine where changes in the training program may be needed. Similarly, if data shows a concerning trend with how customer complaints are handled, individuals taking customer complaints can be observed, and methods or responses can be viewed and noted to highlight areas for improvement. One of the most important aspects of observation is the feedback that follows the observation period. When the observation is complete, the leader should provide feedback that will both empower the employee and address areas where he or she may be struggling or lagging.

INTERVIEWS

One use for a **learning and development interview** is to collect more-detailed information and feedback on the current learning and development opportunities within the organization. Leaders can meet with employees one-on-one to ask specific questions to solicit feedback on the learning and development that is currently offered, has been completed, or the employee would like to see. This allows the organization to determine if the current learning and development program and initiatives truly meet the needs of the organization and the employees.

An interview is more detailed and personal than a survey, and the in-depth feedback can assist in making any changes or adjustments to the programs. Learning and development interviews can also be used to create more-personalized development plans for each employee. This interview should be conducted by the employee's direct supervisor. The supervisor will discuss career goals, professional goals, motivation, strengths, areas of improvement, and positions of interest. This will allow for a more-tailored development plan, establishing a more-meaningful relationship between the employee and supervisor and a stronger level of commitment from the employee to the organization.

LEARNING AND DEVELOPMENT PROGRAM DESIGN AND IMPLEMENTATION
ADDIE MODEL OF TRAINING

The **ADDIE** model of training reflects the three primary phases of learning— assessment, training and development, and evaluation—in detail:

A	**Analysis.** Gather data and identify problems, needs, or discrepancies between current capacities and desired performance.
D	**Design.** Determine learning objectives and goals, decide course content or exercises, and plan delivery methods.
D	**Development.** Create training materials or purchase and modify existing training materials to meet objectives.
I	**Implementation.** Deliver the training program tools to the target audience and observe changes.
E	**Evaluation.** Compare training program results of knowledge and behavior to the course objectives.

SUCCESSIVE APPROXIMATION MODEL

Developed as a simplified version of the ADDIE model, the **Successive Approximation Model (SAM)** aims to create quick and cursory working models earlier in the training process, which also allows for earlier feedback and makes adjusting and altering the working model easier. There are three major parts to the SAM: the preparation phase, the iterative design phase, and the iterative development phase. The use of the key word *iterative* in the second and third phases highlights that each of those two steps are intended to be revisited and revised.

- **Preparation phase.** Similar to the analysis phase in the ADDIE model, this part of the SAM is all about gathering information about the project, such as identifying learning styles, what knowledge exists and what knowledge should be developed, current skills and desired skills, and learning outcome targets.
- **Iterative design phase.** This phase begins with a "Savvy Start," a session in which brainstorming, sketching, and early prototype development begins. Individuals involved with the Savvy Start can include subject-matter experts, learners, project managers, learning designers, and other key stakeholders. Once the Savvy Start is complete, an additional design period begins. During the additional design period, the best prototypes or drafts are further developed and refined to create a final design or product.
- **Iterative development phase.** During this phase, several possible and functioning solutions are developed, each one improving upon the last. The **alpha** version is the first fully complete and functional version of the proposed solution. The **beta** version is the product that results from corrections, edits, and additions to the alpha version. The **gold** version is the solution that does not need any editing or correction. Each of the three phases of iterative development can be subjected to evaluation and feedback from stakeholders and team members to create the best product possible. Once the iterative development phase is concluded, rollout and implementation are possible.

The SAM allows for constant evaluation and feedback of materials and proposed solutions. This method also allows for rapid development, with time to refine as it moves forward. Many out-of-the-box solutions can be developed because this model calls for several working prototypes. This model can lack consistency and cohesion due to the number of individuals involved in development. This model can also be a little chaotic and difficult to integrate with more-traditional technology.

ACTION MAPPING

With the **action mapping** method of instructional design, a performance issue is analyzed, potential training (and non-training) solutions are identified, and activities are created to challenge learners and assist them in practicing learned knowledge. An action map is a visual representation of the various steps required to complete a task or goal. A complex task is broken down into smaller, more achievable steps, which are organized visually using a flow chart or diagram. Separating out steps like this allows for the identification of skills or competencies that individuals must master in order to succeed in the task or process. An action map can be created by following some basic steps:

1. **Define the goal.** This can be done through a needs analysis or a meeting with key stakeholders. Once the goal has been clearly defined, the goal goes in the center of the action map. For example, if developing training for retail, a goal could be to grow sales by 10% before year end.
2. **Identify the actions needed to achieve the goal.** The purpose of the action map is to focus on what the learners need to *do* in order to be successful, not necessarily on what the learners need to know. In the example of retail sales growth, actions that the learners could take might include highlighting product benefits to customers by detailing how the products might meet current and future needs. Retail employees may need to ask probing questions to identify what a customer's needs are at that moment.
3. **Design practice activities.** This step is when the learners practice the activities identified in the previous step. These practice activities should train the learners in the desired actions. If retail employees attend in-person training, they could participate in role-playing scenarios that walk them through the steps needed to close a sale. If the training is done digitally, **branching scenarios** can help the learner uncover customer needs or provide the learner with the opportunity to overcome objections prior to closing the sale. These are practical exercises that reflect situations they will encounter in real-life exchanges.
4. **Identify need-to-know information.** Only essential information necessary to complete the task should be included on the map. Additional information can be distracting if it does not directly relate to identified training goals.

BLOOM'S TAXONOMY OF LEARNING

Learning occurs at several different levels. **Bloom's taxonomy of learning** is sometimes shown as a pyramid containing six **domain** levels. **Knowledge** forms the base of the pyramid. It is the stage at which learners can only recall previously learned facts. Learners then graduate to the **comprehension stage**, in which they are able to grasp the meaning of the material. The **application stage** comes next. In the application stage, learners can apply information to solve problems in new situations. Following application is the **analysis stage**, in which learners are capable of understanding the context and structure of material. The tip of the pyramid comprises synthesis and evaluation. During the **synthesis stage**, learners are capable of drawing from existing knowledge or sources and processing information to form conclusions. Finally, at the **evaluation stage**, learners are capable of judging the value of materials.

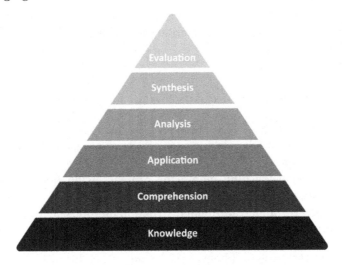

ADULT LEARNING THEORIES
LEARNING STYLES

A **learning style** is the way in which an individual learns most effectively. Because each person learns information differently, some teaching methods are more effective than others. The three main learning styles are auditory, tactile, and visual. Training programs need to be designed to take different learning styles into consideration so that participants can learn the material as efficiently as possible.

> **Review Video: Adult Learning Processes and Theories**
> Visit mometrix.com/academy and enter code: 638453

An **auditory learner** learns most effectively by hearing information rather than seeing it or using it. Auditory learners usually learn most effectively by hearing descriptions or instructions such as lectures, group discussions, demonstrations of a particular sound (such as an alarm that might indicate a problem with a piece of machinery) or by listening to themselves read aloud.

A **tactile learner** learns most effectively by touching or using something rather than hearing it or seeing it. Tactile learners usually learn most effectively by using a new tool or process, touching or moving an object, or physically applying the information in a controlled situation. They have difficulty learning through verbal instructions (e.g., lectures or explanations) and visual methods (e.g., reading a handout). Tactile learning activities include practicing techniques, role-playing, simulations, and other activities that allow the individual to learn through a hands-on approach.

A **visual learner** learns most effectively by seeing information rather than hearing or using it. Visual learners learn most effectively by seeing the information on a flashcard, chalkboard, handout, or book; seeing a representation in a picture or diagram; watching videos or presentations; or taking detailed notes and then rereading those notes. They have difficulty learning through verbal instruction (e.g., lectures and explanations) or by performing a task without written instructions or handouts.

LEARNING EVERYWHERE MODEL

The **learning everywhere model** provides the user with an opportunity to learn from anywhere at any time. Individuals can use laptops, tablets, smartphones, and desktop computers to access digital learning content. As long as there is a way to access the internet, learning can occur. This learning content can come in the form of interactive modules, quizzes, presentations, and even videos. Content can be self-paced or follow a prescribed timeline. Learning can be done autonomously or within a group. The learning everywhere model expanded significantly during the COVID-19 pandemic, when traditional learning methods were halted or altered due to lockdowns and limited social interaction.

70-20-10 MODEL

The **70-20-10 model** illustrates the ideal balance of three separate methods of learning and development. The balance is broken down as:

- **70% experience:** learning through working such as scenario-based on-the-job training, online simulations, and gamification.
- **20% social:** learning through coaching, mentoring, or peers using mediums such as webinars, online meetings, and face-to-face meetings.
- **10% education:** learning through traditional instruction methods such as textbooks, onboarding courses, recordings, and presentations.

This model can be used to design training that helps each learner reach his or her highest level of comprehension through varied content delivery. This model allows individuals to learn in the way that is most comfortable and effective for them. Having different training formats is also likely to increase engagement, because at least one aspect of the three approaches will appeal to each individual. This model can also help the organization create a stronger and more-comprehensive training and development program, by identifying the most effective programs that best support employee learning.

LEARNING AND DEVELOPMENT APPROACHES AND TECHNIQUES

ON-THE-JOB TRAINING METHODS

Companies frequently prefer to use **on-the-job training techniques** for employees due to the immediate production and lower cost compared to off-the-job trainings, which are designed more for education and long-term development.

Some on-the-job training techniques include the following:

- **Job-instruction training**, the most popular method of training, involves introductory explanation and demonstration or shadowing before the employee is given the opportunity to try performing the task alone.
- **E-learning** is generally on-demand training that can be taken anywhere with an internet connection, at a time that's convenient for the learner, although sometimes learners can log on live. E-learning modules can cover a range of topics such as company policies, job-related how-to topics, and more. E-learning is extremely cost-effective. The main drawback is that learners watching a recording cannot provide or receive any real-time feedback.
- **Apprenticeships** are the processes of working alongside and under the direction of a skilled professional. Apprenticeships are often used by employers in the trades, such as electricians, plumbers, and carpenters.
- **Internships, cooperative education, and assistantships** are similar to apprenticeships but are often paired with colleges or universities.
- **Job rotation and cross-training** involve a rotating series of job assignments in different departments for specified periods of time to expose individuals to a variety of skills and challenges.
- **Coaching and counseling** provide learners with an identifiable and virtuous model in setting goals, providing timely feedback, and providing reinforcement and encouragement.

OFF-THE-JOB TRAINING METHODS

A few **off-the-job techniques** include the following:

- **Independent study** is when people who are self-motivated to take individual responsibility toward learning attempt to train themselves by reading books, taking courses, or attending seminars.
- **Corporate universities** are where employees attend classes taught by corporate trainers, executives, and consultants.
- **Vestibule training** is similar to on-the-job training, but occurs in a separate training area identical to the actual production area.
- **Lectures** are an efficient way to transfer large amounts of information to a large audience.

JUST-IN-TIME LEARNING

Individuals can learn skills or knowledge when it is needed to solve a problem or to complete a specific task using **just-in-time learning**, which allows individuals to access relevant content right when it is needed. It is often on-demand, so users can get to the information quickly. Most just-in-time learning is self-directed, so users control their own learning and seek out information as they move through tasks. Just-in-time learning can be offered in small sections that can be completed quickly, allowing learners to absorb manageable amounts of information and then immediately apply it, which also helps the learners retain the information. These learning segments can be prepared for different positions, so key duties are taught through modules or sessions. This learning approach is budget-friendly as well, as it does not involve a workshop or face-to-face session, but rather is stored internally or on a learning management system that can be accessed any time.

MICROLEARNING

Obstacles to learning include the forgetting curve and short attention spans. **Microlearning** is an approach to training and education that seeks to overcome these obstacles. Microlearning is a training and education method that delivers short spurts of content that learners can study at their convenience. The content is presented in various formats such as images, text, videos, and games, and each piece of content lasts between two and five minutes. The use of multiple formats over that short time span helps to combat wandering attention. Microlearning content is easily accessible. Learners can access content on mobile devices and computers, allowing for both remote and onsite training. Microlearning requires a commitment from the learner, as information is presented in short segments and continued participation is key. Microlearning is not the best method to address complex or intricate subject matter, as the sessions are brief and may make such explanations confusing or difficult to follow. It is a useful tool for topics like compliance, soft skills, and professional skills. Microlearning is an excellent resource as it can be accessed easily, completed within a short time period, and promptly applied by the learner.

BLENDED LEARNING

A model that allows a more personalized and effective learning path for individuals, **blended learning** is a combination of both face-to-face learning and learning through online use of digital platforms and content. Using the blended learning approach, employees can learn from trainers in person, and if there is additional work or practice needed, they can access related online content anytime. One of the major benefits of blended learning is the flexibility. This approach provides employees with the opportunity to learn at their own pace. Not all content needs to be covered during face-to-face training, so there is less information overload. Not all employees will learn at the same pace, and the blended model allows more-individualized monitoring, so if an employee is struggling in a particular area, his or her struggles can be evaluated and addressed. Blended learning also benefits the organization, as having online sessions can make the training more accessible for individuals in other working areas, and cut down the cost of travel or organizing an offsite location for training. The organization can also conduct a more in-depth analysis of individual learning, and instead of the trainer attempting to ascertain whether each employee is on the same page, the online modules can help track progress and comprehension.

SELF-PACED LEARNING

The **self-paced learning** method allows individuals to create their own schedules and pace for studying new concepts, materials, and content. This type of learning caters to the preferences and learning styles of the individual. This particular type of learning requires an individual to practice effective time management, as deadlines are not laid out by an instructor and the learner is responsible for completing items and maintaining discipline. Self-paced learning can help learners balance education with other aspects of life and responsibilities without becoming overwhelmed. Self-paced learning also lowers pressure and anxiety related to learning, as items can be completed when the individual feels most confident and best prepared.

SELF-DIRECTED LEARNING

When an individual takes initiative and responsibility for his or her own learning, he or she is engaging in **self-directed learning**. This typically occurs through several steps:

1. **Assess readiness to learn.** Support, finances, commitments, study habits, and availability can all impact independent study and these factors should be identified before beginning the learning process.
2. **Establish learning goals.** What is the goal for each module, unit, or course? A timeline for completion should be set. Required resources for each goal should be outlined. Feedback should be reviewed, and goals evaluated accordingly. Applicable areas of improvement should be identified.

3. **Engage in the learning process.** The individual must understand that he or she will be the only one completing the work. Once this is understood, an approach to learning can be established. Some of the main forms of study include the **surface approach** (learning what is needed to pass the section and not much more), the **strategic approach** (getting the highest result possible), and the **deep approach** (understanding the content for yourself).
4. **Evaluate learning.** The learner should review his or her work and assess, without ego or bias, how well he or she is actually doing, including what has been learned and level of comprehension.

EXPERIENTIAL LEARNING

Learning through doing, or **experiential learning,** focuses on the premise that the best way to learn things is to have actual and meaningful hands-on experiences. These experiences stand out in memory and allow individuals to retain information and facts. This learning method is not just an experience, but also analysis of and reflection on the experience. Many organizations use experiential learning throughout the training process, such as when an individual shadows another or participates in role-playing exercises. Experiential learning can take place throughout an individual's career through mentorship, stretch assignments, and various trainings.

PEER-TO-PEER TRAINING

Coworkers teach other coworkers in **peer-to-peer training**, which typically occurs with employees in the same department or who work at the same level sharing what they know with one another. This can also occur when more-tenured employees share their knowledge with individuals who were hired more recently. Employees can hold a great deal of knowledge about their individual roles or have well-established best practices. The organization and employees all benefit when these methods are shared. Additionally, peer-to-peer training builds collaboration and helps establish cohesive teams. Peer-to-peer learning can take place in formal settings such as committees, focus groups, business meetings, or mentoring programs. It can also occur organically through conversation and interaction.

WEBINARS

A **webinar** is a seminar that takes place digitally. Webinars are often educational presentations that are live and allow attendees to submit questions or participate in a chat. Other webinars are recorded for on-demand access and do not provide opportunities for feedback or interaction. Webinars differ from online meetings as they typically have a set speaker (or group of speakers) with an agenda. Webinars are often used for training, professional development, and compliance purposes.

GAMIFICATION

Learning and development through **gamification** occurs when game-playing elements are added to traditionally non-game environments in order to motivate and engage individuals. This method can help foster competition, collaboration, and individual/group achievements. Gamification can use various incentives to help encourage participation and dedication. Examples of gamification include points-based quizzes or trivia during training, interactive points-based leaderboards, and reward-based simulations. Participation and performance can be measured and analyzed, providing insightful data on use and efficacy. Certain gamification implementations can place a heavy emphasis on rewards, which can focus more on the short term rather than on longer-term behavior changes. Certain offerings can also be complex and require a lot of resources, making the programs costly and difficult to implement. There are many different options, and there are ways to create gamification methods in house, so gamification can be a useful tool in training and development.

INFOGRAPHICS

An **infographic** is a tool that is used to communicate and demonstrate complex, detailed, key information in a format that is easy to follow and understand. Infographics use a combination of text, images, and data to grab attention and detail memorable information. Infographics are often used to explain complex processes, compare and contrast several options, detail a brief overview of a topic, display analysis or survey findings, or to raise awareness about a topic or issue. Infographics can be used in presentations, in white papers, on company sites, and sent through internal communications. They are a very effective communication tool, as they draw the reader in and keep the reader's attention. There are many different types of infographics, such as informational, comparison, timeline, process, geographic, list, and interactive. Infographics are visually appealing, easy to share, and easy to read, and they break down larger content into smaller snippets, which makes concepts easier to understand.

PODCASTS

Digital audio files in the form of **podcasts** can be an excellent addition to learning and development initiatives. Podcasts are on-demand, and they can be accessed anywhere and anytime. Unlike videos, podcasts do not require active watching. A listener can have a podcast on while completing work tasks, traveling, or even during downtime. Podcasts can be used to deliver lectures or presentations that do not require visual aids. They can present a variety of subjects in an efficient way that is convenient to the creator and listener alike. This content can be accessed on many devices and is easier to create and edit than video files. Podcasts can be used to introduce a training or development topic, train or educate on the topic, or follow up on a topic previously taught. Narration can engage the listener through compelling delivery.

ROTATIONAL PROGRAMS

Rotating through different business areas for a specific time period allows both existing and new employees the ability to gain experience and exposure throughout several departments and functions by holding actual responsibilities and temporary roles in various positions. **Rotational programs** are excellent for developing cross-training, identifying high-level talent, and providing employees with a preview into other roles for future development.

DEVELOPMENTAL ASSESSMENTS
360-DEGREE PERFORMANCE APPRAISALS

A **360-degree performance appraisal** is a developmental assessment technique that involves getting feedback from customers, coworkers, managers, and subordinates. It can be an effective tool because it involves broad and varied input, with the goal of painting a more holistic picture of employee performance. However, human resources must take note of the potential pitfalls of this method. For example, raters may not be adequately trained to provide effective feedback, and may not agree on what areas of performance to review. Further, office politics could get in the way of meaningful and fair input. For these reasons, human resources should be careful about making any employment decisions based on the results of a 360-degree assessment.

SIMULATIONS

With **simulations**, employees put their knowledge and skills to the test in life-like situations that mimic those they may encounter in their roles. Simulation assessments provide individuals with the opportunity to showcase their skills and professional competencies while demonstrating how they would handle a real-life situation. For example, if an individual had undergone training in how to cross-sell various banking products when opening a new account, a simulation of a new account opening would be designed. The employee would then demonstrate the skills and tools that he or she learned over the training and be assessed on how well the skills and tools were applied in that scenario. This assessment is very useful when analyzing the application of knowledge and skills, decision-making, and communication methods.

HIGH-POTENTIAL ASSESSMENTS

There are numerous assessments available to identify **high-potential employees**. High-potential employees and **high-performance employees** are not the same, though they are often confused with one another. High-potential employees are those that are best suited for promotion and advancement within the organization versus simply excelling in their current role. The High Potential Trait Indicator (HPTI) is an assessment method that functions on the assumption that there are certain personality traits considered "optimal" according to a given role's requirements. The HPTI measures adjustment, risk, curiosity, ambiguity, competitiveness, conscientiousness, acceptance, and approach. Not enough or too much of a particular trait will impact the results. Certain trait levels are considered indicative of a high potential for success, and others highlight characteristics that could affect that high potential in the individual. There are a wide variety of organizations that offer high-potential talent testing. High-potential assessments can also be done internally, through measuring characteristics such as engagement, drive, capability, sociability, morality, innovation, risk-taking, practicality, and desire for growth.

PERSONALITY ASSESSMENTS

Standardized assessments can be used to determine an individual's strengths and weaknesses, communication type and preferred communication method, sources of both motivation and stress, and problem-solving style. These **personality assessments** also determine how the individual interacts on a team and responds to conflicts, and how he or she may fit with the culture of the organization. These tests can help leadership form teams, delegate work, assign projects, and identify the employees that may have the best potential for growth. Common workplace personality assessments include the following:

- **Myers-Briggs Type Indicator**, or MBTI: measures the four dimensions of extroversion/introversion, sensing/intuition, thinking/feeling, and judging/perceiving
- **CliftonStrengths Assessment**: requires a taker to choose which statement in a pair best describes him- or herself
- **Big Five**: measures the five dimensions of openness to experience, conscientiousness, extroversion, agreeableness, and neuroticism
- **Enneagram**: divides people into nine numbered personality types
- **DiSC**: measures the four dimensions of dominance, influence, steadiness, and conscientiousness

SKILLS ASSESSMENTS

Candidates and employees can list out skills on resumes and describe them during interviews, but verbally detailing such skills does not necessarily demonstrate proficiency to an organization looking to hire or promote an employee. **Skills assessments** serve to do just that, evaluate the individual's ability to perform a specific skill or skillset. Typically, these skills assessments are directly related to the skills that will be needed to effectively carry out that specific role or duties assigned to the role. Skills assessments can be used in the hiring process, promotion process, learning and development, and to address any perceived talent gaps. Skills assessments can measure an individual's competency and growth and be used to create personalized development plans and to keep employees engaged through continued development. Skills assessments are widely available online and can even be offered through Employee Assistance Programs.

COMPETENCY ASSESSMENTS

A **competency assessment** or evaluation is used by an employer to review the current skill level of an employee against the requirements and duties of his or her role. These evaluations are performed to identify potential skills gaps, areas for improvement, and areas where additional training is required. Competency assessments can be used to evaluate the strengths and weaknesses of individual employees or teams. This information is critical when determining whether certain individuals in the group or the workforce can function and effectively perform in their roles. These results can help the organization create better training plans, reorganize teams, and create career paths for individuals within the organization.

GOAL-SETTING BEST PRACTICES
INDIVIDUAL DEVELOPMENT PLANS

An **individual development plan (IDP)** is a personalized plan of action that is targeted toward improving an employee's skills, abilities, knowledge, and competencies. The plan measures where the employee is currently performing against role expectations and requirements. An IDP helps the employee and the manager collaborate to build a plan for professional development, career growth, and advancement opportunity. IDPs can be created shortly after hire, or they can be created during performance appraisals. IDPs are excellent tools because they can help outline both long and short-term goals, along with a plan for how to achieve those goals.

IDPs detail strengths and weaknesses, so areas can be targeted for improvement. Skill gaps are also identified, so the employee can learn important skills to help with advancement. These plans also serve to improve engagement, because employees are empowered to develop confidence and invest in themselves.

SPECIFIC, MEASURABLE, ACHIEVABLE, RELEVANT, AND TIME-BOUND (SMART) GOALS

Clear and concise goals that help employees focus efforts and increase the likelihood of goal achievement, **SMART goals** are designed to be manageable and trackable, and can be adjusted as needed. SMART goals have the following attributes:

S	Specific: unambiguous, well defined, and clear, for effective planning
M	Measurable: contain specific criteria that measure progress toward goal completion
A	Achievable: attainable and can be accomplished in the given time frame.
R	Relevant: within reach and aligned with values and long-term objectives
T	Time-bound: ambitious but realistic end date, to help with prioritization and motivation

CAREER DEVELOPMENT

STAGES OF WORKING AND PROFESSIONAL CAREER DEVELOPMENT

Professional careers and trade careers both involve four stages of career development. For **professional careers**, the stages are internship, independent contributor, mentor, and sponsor. **Interns** are individuals who are continuing their learning under the supervision of experienced professionals. **Independent contributors** are autonomous workers whose success is based on how well they take initiative, meet objectives, and exceed expectations. **Mentors** have displayed their ability to perform, supervise, and coach others. **Sponsors** make strategic decisions while providing organizational guidance, influence, and accountability. For **trade or working careers**, the stages are exploration, establishment, maintenance, and decline. The **exploration stage** describes individuals who are just beginning their careers, often between the ages of 15 and 24. They are still working on trade programs or courses and may be prone to changing positions while trying to explore interests and abilities while meeting job demands. The **establishment stage** describes individuals, often between the ages of 25 and 44, who are striving to create a more stable position within their chosen occupation to establish work and build a reputation. The **maintenance stage** describes individuals, often between the ages of 45 and 64, who are concerned with job security and survival. The **decline stage** describes individuals, often older than 65, who are approaching the ends of their careers and entering retirement.

There are a variety of methods that a manager or supervisor can use to further an employee's career development. Some commonly used methods are **coaching**, **counseling**, **mentoring**, and **evaluating**. Employees can be coached to perform new tasks, handle certain problems outside of the scope of their current positions, and develop communication and leadership. Employees can also be offered counseling, advice, or emotional support. Managers or supervisors can act as mentors by helping employees apply for promotions, suggesting them for promotions, and offering guidance about other positions. Finally, managers or supervisors can help further an employee's career by candidly evaluating and discussing his or her strengths and weaknesses.

Similarly, individuals can use a variety of methods for their own career development. Some of the most important methods include attending training workshops, networking, and seeking additional education. Many organizations offer **training workshops** to help individuals seek management positions or positions in other departments, but most of these workshops are optional, so they will only help if an individual takes the time to attend the program and learn the material. **Networking** is essential because it is nearly impossible to progress in an organization if the individual is unwilling or unable to establish relationships with managers, supervisors, coworkers, and customers. Finally, when the knowledge or educational background required for a particular position is lacking, the best way to develop a career is to **seek additional education** from colleges, universities, or seminars.

CAREER PATHING

Creating a plan for employees to progress within the organization is called **career pathing** or **career mapping**. It involves that the employees perform a management-guided self-assessment of interests, motivations, knowledge, and skills. This can help to identify potential matching roles within the organization, whether a promotion or a lateral move. Plans to fill gaps in skills and knowledge needed for the potential roles can then be made. When the identified opportunities arise, employees will further explore and pursue them if ready.

CROSS-TRAINING

Employees are often trained on or taught to perform tasks from a different role or position than their own. **Cross-training** increases an employee's skill set, allows for higher flexibility within the organization, and provides a better overview of how the business operates at different levels. Cross-training also creates a great opportunity for hands-on learning. Identifying major tasks and duties of a certain role, then training employees in other roles to also carry out those duties ensures that multiple employees can step in and provide coverage when necessary. Cross-training opens opportunities for growth and advancement within the organization, by building on the employees' skills and talents. With a deeper understanding of the tasks required in a certain role, employees gain a deeper understanding of each other's contributions and can assist and communicate more efficiently.

APPRENTICESHIP

An **apprenticeship** is a program that prepares individuals for a trade or professional job by combining on-the-job training and classroom instruction. Apprentices are typically paired with a more-experienced mentor. The mentor guides the apprentice on how various tasks and processes work, which tools and resources are needed, and the best way to complete tasks. This hands-on training is paired with supplemental learning that often occurs in a classroom or instructional setting. Technical schools, trade schools, and community colleges can provide additional instructional content. Some companies design their own teaching material and instruct apprentices internally. Apprentices are usually compensated, either at an hourly wage or through a stipend of some kind. Accredited apprenticeships can be found through the US Department of Labor, which maintains a list of accredited programs across the nation.

KNOWLEDGE-SHARING TECHNIQUES AND FACILITATION

Knowledge management is a system of initiatives, practices, procedures, and processes used to ensure that each member knows or can access all of the information necessary to perform his or her responsibilities. Knowledge management can be important when there are many employees working in different departments at different times. It is designed to ensure that everyone has the same basic training and access to information from other departments to avoid performing the same task multiple times.

Knowledge retention is a collection of strategies designed to keep important information in-house so that a firm doesn't lose valuable insight or critical skills as employees leave the organization. It can be accomplished in several different ways, such as sharing information via mentoring programs and cross-departmental collaboration. Additionally, employees should be encouraged to reflect after each project completion and to document procedures and lessons learned for future reference. Companies should also make it easy to contact subject matter experts so that other employees know who to talk to when they need specialized information. This results in a more educated workforce over time.

KNOWLEDGE MAPS

A **knowledge map** is a visual display of where specific knowledge is held in an organization and how that knowledge moves across the organization. This helps stakeholders identify where any gaps exist or challenges may arise. To create a knowledge map, the organization needs to identify and categorize knowledge types, then locate these types within the organization. Then the map is created by linking it all together visually. Knowledge maps can demonstrate procedural, competency, or conceptual knowledge. These maps are very helpful when onboarding new employees, so the new hires know who to reach out to for specific information.

They can also be helpful during strategic planning sessions, so various areas can be consulted when developing ideas and proposals.

KNOWLEDGE CAFES

A **knowledge cafe** is a conversation or mini workshop that brings individuals together to share their experiences and knowledge about a particular topic. Knowledge cafes can be particularly useful for problem solving, as they allow multiples perspectives to be shared and explored. They can also be helpful at the start of a new project or initiative because people have varying levels of understanding and familiarity with a topic, and discussing this can make assigning roles and duties simpler. Knowledge cafes are also helpful for professional development because individuals in the same field can share best practices or processes to avoid.

MANAGEMENT AND LEADERSHIP DEVELOPMENT

Role-specific training and development is important for employees in management and leadership roles. **Management development** ensures that individuals have all the knowledge, skills, and abilities necessary to manage effectively. **Leadership development** ensures that individuals have all the knowledge, skills, and abilities necessary to lead effectively. Management development is designed to teach an individual how to ensure each function is carried out as expected, whereas leadership development is designed to teach an individual how to predict change within the business environment, identify how the organization needs to change to meet those needs, and encourage other individuals to meet the changing needs of the organization.

HIGH-POTENTIAL DEVELOPMENT PROGRAMS

Companies want to retain employees that demonstrate high-potential attributes. A **high-potential development program** is an internal talent pipeline that develops identified talent with exposure to more-challenging assignments, training in higher-level roles, the opportunity to engage with and learn from senior leaders, and identifying potential future assignments. These programs can be completely internal or can utilize external workshops, educational opportunities, and executive coaching.

STRETCH ASSIGNMENTS

A **stretch assignment** is a learning opportunity for an employee to work on a task or a project that exceeds that individual's current level of skill, knowledge, or experience. The stretch assignment helps demonstrate the employee's adaptability, flexibility, and problem-solving skills to management. Throughout the assignment, employees may be given a heightened level of responsibility, and be challenged to work in an unfamiliar area or with unfamiliar content. Stretch assignments can also provide the employee with a break from his or her norm, opening new opportunities and areas of interest. These assignments can be used by management to test an employee who may be ready for promotion or advancement. An example of a stretch assignment could be representing the company during an audit or organizing a meeting or company event.

APPROACHES TO COACHING AND MENTORING

COACHING

In business, **coaching** is a method of training in which an experienced individual provides an employee with advice to encourage his or her best possible performance and career. Having a strong coaching culture among strategic goals often leads to increased organizational performance and engagement. Coaching is a personal, one-on-one relationship that takes place over a specific period. Coaching is often used in performance management, but it can be applied to many business objectives as well. For example, coaching may be used to prepare individuals for new assignments, improve behavior, conquer obstacles, and adapt to change. Coaching might also be used to support diversity initiatives, such as generational differences, behavioral styles, or awareness and inclusion.

MENTORING

Similar to coaching, **mentoring** is a career development method in which a new or less-experienced employee is paired with an experienced leader for guidance. Formal mentoring programs need to be measurable and integrated into the culture without being seen as a rigid, forced system. These programs typically establish goals at the onset and track progress throughout. Like coaching, mentoring is a partnership relationship that takes place over a specific period, and both need a customized approach that fits the receiver. However, mentoring carries a history of recognition for having considerable impact with the power to positively transform a career trajectory. Successful mentors are able to support, encourage, promote, and challenge while developing deep connections with the mentee. Mentoring can also happen more informally, where the mentee looks up to and takes the advice of the mentor without defined goals or objectives. This happens naturally, and often the people involved do not even realize that the mentor–mentee relationship exists until later reflection.

EXECUTIVE COACHING

An **executive coaching** relationship is between an individual and a professional coach or consultant. The goal of this relationship is to help the individual develop key skills, improve motivation, gain self-awareness, and achieve development objectives. Executive coaches help the individual work with both strengths and weaknesses. The coaching or consulting is totally individualized, designed to meet the needs and skillset of the individual and his or her unique circumstances. Executive coaches challenge assumptions, provide resources, help identify and guide toward meeting and completing goals, and act as a sounding board for the individual. Individuals who receive executive coaching are often able to better support other leaders and employees while also honing their ability to successfully support business strategies and objectives.

ENCOURAGING A GROWTH MINDSET

Leaders who encourage a **growth mindset** foster an environment of collaboration where both efforts and successes are recognized. Team members are challenged to reach their highest levels of potential. Employees are encouraged to view challenges as opportunities, to entertain less-conventional approaches, become less risk-averse, and accept failure as a steppingstone to success. Employees are guided to persevere through setbacks and issues. A growth mindset develops skills, knowledge, and abilities through dedication and effort.

LEARNING AND DEVELOPMENT TECHNOLOGIES

LEARNING MANAGEMENT SYSTEMS

A **learning management system (LMS)** is a software system that handles the creation, management, distribution, and analytics of educational content. An LMS can be cloud-based and hosted by a vendor, or it can exist on the company server. With an LMS, administrators can upload content, deliver lessons and training, send out notifications and announcements, and share data with specific parties. There are many analytic features available to administrators, who can track how many individuals have completed training, which training leads to the best results, what offerings are popular, and how active employees are on the system. An LMS is used throughout multiple aspects of the employee life cycle, including onboarding, training, professional development, and compliance training. Specific training can be automated for certain times of the year to help establish a training calendar. An LMS allows for on-demand training options and easy access, and helps the organization create a culture of learning.

ARTIFICIAL INTELLIGENCE

As **artificial intelligence (AI)** becomes more readily available and evolved, it will have a tremendous impact on learning and development. Already, organizations can see how AI has impacted the learning and development landscape by helping to personalize learning pathways. AI can help training programs adapt to each employee. The learning process can be adjusted to meet the needs of the employee. AI can automate learning platforms, so all employee content is stored, delivered, and tracked. AI can also make training more accessible, as it is available around the clock without constraints. AI is also more cost-effective than physical in-person trainers.

VIRTUAL REALITY

Another technology experiencing rapid expansion and improvement is **virtual reality (VR)**. VR can offer many benefits to learning and development offerings. It allows the learner to become totally immersed in the

training, removed from external distractions and stimuli and focused purely on the content, which improves retention. VR also heavily relies on simulation, or experiential learning through doing, which is one of the most effective ways to present material for retention and comprehension. VR learning can also utilize gamification, which makes it more fun and interesting, motivating the learner to complete the module. Immediate feedback and analysis are available on VR training, which helps to track its efficacy. VR training is also on-demand and does not come with the expense of hosting on or off-site training.

CHATBOTS

An effective learning and development tool that can help personalize a user's learning experience, a **chatbot** can help walk the user through the learning process and help make the learning experience feel more one-on-one by creating a back-and-forth dialogue. This tool can be passive, simply waiting in the background until the user needs assistance. Alternatively, the tool can be programmed to prompt targeted topics at designated times, keeping the process moving. Chatbots are available around the clock and do not lose patience with the learner. Additionally, when a chatbot is faced with a question it cannot answer, it can try to redirect or refer the learner to other available resources. Chatbots help encourage engagement throughout the learning process by prompting the user on what to do and offering relevant feedback. Chatbots are a way to quickly access and deliver content and information at a cost that is greatly reduced compared to a live trainer.

Total Rewards

The concept of **total rewards** refers to all of the compensation and benefits received for performing tasks related to a job position, including both monetary and other forms of compensation. It is important to have an effective total rewards program for two main reasons. First, an effective program encourages employees to join and then stay with the organization. Second, there are legal concerns associated with the minimum compensation for a certain amount of work, making it essential to consider these concerns to avoid unnecessary fines or litigation.

A **total rewards strategy** is a plan used to design a total rewards program. It is based on the organization's total rewards philosophy and is primarily designed to establish the framework for the allocation of program resources. It refers to the ways resources are used to encourage individuals to work for the organization without exceeding limits.

There are a variety of factors to consider when designing an effective total rewards strategy. The four main factors are the competitive environment, the economic environment, the labor market, and the legal environment. The **competitive environment** is the effect of competition on the ability to allocate resources to the total rewards program. For example, if competitors are offering a specific product at a price that is far lower than its own, the organization may need to reduce the funds allocated to its total rewards program to compensate for a price reduction on the product. The **economic environment** refers to the effect of the economy on the cost of labor. For example, as the cost of living increases, the cost of labor will usually increase as well. The **labor market** is the availability of skilled employees, and the **legal environment** refers to taxes and regulations.

> **Review Video: Total Rewards and Compensation**
> Visit mometrix.com/academy and enter code: 502662

GATHERING COMPENSATION-RELATED MARKET AND COMPETITIVE INTELLIGENCE
REMUNERATION SURVEYS

A **remuneration survey**, also called a compensation or **salary survey**, collects and analyzes data on wages, salary, and benefits offered through a specific industry, position, or location. These surveys are used to measure the effectiveness of current compensation practices. These surveys can help ensure that employees are being paid at market rate or higher. If pay is lower than market rate, the organization has the option to make an adjustment. Salary surveys are very beneficial when performing benchmarking and creating compensation plans, helping the organization attract and retain the best talent. Analyzing the pay structure using salary surveys helps the organization remain competitive in the labor market while also ensuring regulations surrounding pay and wages are met.

LABOR MARKET TRENDS

Workforce trends, or **labor market trends**, are critical metrics that help employers with workforce-related decision-making that is necessary for continued success and competition. Key labor market trends include unemployment rates, demographic shifts, change in payrolls, job growth, and wage rates. These trends help employers determine whether to hire, what wage and salary adjustments to make, and what the future of the workforce looks like. Staying on top of various labor market trends will help a company with retention and recruiting as well as remaining profitable.

COMPENSATION DATA COLLECTION, INTERPRETATION, AND ANALYSIS
COMPARABLE WORTH

Also known as **pay equity**, **comparable worth** is the principle that all employees who perform work of the same or similar value should have the same or similar compensation. Employers should create compensation guidelines based on the skills and responsibilities of each role regardless of the demographics to which the employees belong.

BENCHMARKING

Salary or compensation **benchmarking** is a tool that is used to match internal job descriptions with similar external job descriptions to determine the market rate for each role. Benchmarking allows the organization to ensure that employees are receiving similar pay and benefits as those at other companies who have similar duties and responsibilities. This tool is critical when creating competitive compensation packages for employees. Benchmarking should be completed regularly, to ensure that the organization remains competitive in the market. Benchmarking also provides a realistic understanding of salary and benefit expectations for different roles, so that more-informed strategic decisions can be reached. To perform the benchmarking process, the organization must build a salary base, analyze compensation rates, and establish pay ranges for each role. When analyzing compensation rates, it is helpful to use more than one source to obtain external pay data information, to ensure that the most detailed salary and benefit picture can be created.

INTERNAL ALIGNMENT

The pay relationship between different jobs, responsibilities, and skills within an organization, or how much one job pays relative to another is called **internal alignment**. The pay structure should support the business strategy, be fair to employees, support workflow within the organization, and motivate or encourage employee behavior to meet objectives.

EXTERNAL COMPETITIVENESS

The pay offered by one organization compared to the pay offered by a competing organization is known as **external competitiveness**. It allows an organization to explore what pay can be offered to remain competitive while also attracting high-level talent. External competitiveness can decrease turnover within an organization, increase productivity, and result in more highly qualified candidates.

COMPENSATION PHILOSOPHIES

A **total rewards philosophy** clearly states reward goals and how those goals will be achieved. Identifying this philosophy is necessary to determine if the rewards reflect the values and goals of an organization or if they need to be modified.

The two types of total reward philosophies are entitlement philosophies and performance-based philosophies. An **entitlement philosophy** issues rewards based on the length of time a particular employee has been with the organization. It assumes that an individual is entitled to certain rewards because of seniority or length of time in a specific position. Entitlement philosophies encourage individuals to stay with the organization but do not necessarily encourage effective performance. A **performance-based philosophy**, on the other hand, issues rewards for good performance.

LEAD

A **lead** compensation philosophy is when an organization sets its pay structure ahead of the market for the entire year. This is done by ensuring that midpoints are targeted above the market throughout all 12 months. Even as the market tries to catch up, the organization stays ahead. Lead compensation targets are common when the talent pool is limited, the workforce is skilled, or the roles are very industry-specific, such as tech roles, which are usually highly competitive.

LAG

In a **lag** compensation philosophy, the organization chooses to stay behind the market trend for the year. Midpoints stay below market rate during all 12 months of the year. This compensation strategy occurs when the labor pool is saturated, the workforce is less skilled, or the industry is less specific, such as in retail.

LEAD-LAG

The **lead-lag** compensation philosophy occurs when the company's pay rates are above market for the first half of the year, then lag the market in the second half of the year. This occurs when the organization is not concerned about falling slightly behind for six months because the organization is in a healthy place labor-wise.

MATCH

A **match** compensation philosophy occurs when the organization pays according to the market. The organization meets the midpoint throughout the year. This allows the organization to be competitive without having labor costs rise considerably. Some employees within the organization will be paid more, and others will be paid less, but overall employees are paid right at the market rate.

PAY STRUCTURES

An organization's **pay structure** is the compensation system it uses to determine the appropriate base pay for positions by separating jobs into categories based on value to the organization. The pay structure is an essential part of any organization's total rewards program because it establishes a guide for appropriate hourly wages or salary. Specific base pay minimums and maximums for each category are well-defined and allow firms to avoid arbitrarily assigning pay.

Methods of creating a pay structure vary greatly, but most organizations begin the process by conducting a job evaluation for each position. Once all positions are evaluated and assigned a value, they are categorized based on their value to the organization. The organization will usually gather information from salary surveys to determine the market median for each category, or the midpoint of a similar pay category for another organization. Finally, using all of this information as a guide, a pay range is developed for each category.

COMPENSATION PLANS FOR COMMON AND SPECIAL WORKFORCE GROUPS

SALARY

A **salary** is an annual compensation amount, agreed upon by an organization and an employee, that is paid to the employee in scheduled increments. The salary payment can occur monthly, bi-weekly, or weekly. The annual salary is divided between pay periods so that the employee receives the same amount each pay period. Salary is based on the level of the role, the employee's education and experience, the location of the company, and other factors. Salary differs from wages in that wages are calculated based on the number of hours worked during a pay period and salary is not.

COST-OF-LIVING ADJUSTMENTS

A **cost-of-living adjustment (COLA)** is an increase in pay and/or benefits that is intended to counteract inflation. COLAs aim to keep the buying power of the employee the same, despite increases in the prices of goods and services or a move to a geographic area with a higher cost of living. COLAs are typically calculated once per year. COLAs can be a permanent adjustment to an employee's pay, or can be temporary if the employee is assigned to work in a more-expensive area for a short time period. When calculating a COLA, employers will often use the increase in the Consumer Price Index from the previous year. Providing a COLA is another compensation tool to attract new talent and retain individuals in the current workforce.

MERIT INCREASES

A **merit increase** is a compensation tool that offers an increase in pay based on the performance, achievement, or contribution of an individual employee. Merit increases can come in several forms. One of the most common types of merit increases occurs during the annual evaluation period, where the employee is reviewed on his or her performance over the year. High performers and those who have exceeded expectations are given a merit increase. Merit increases can also be awarded based on mastery or competence with a particular skill or subject. For example, if an employee is proficient in each outlined job requirement, he or she may receive a merit increase. Unlike COLAs, merit increases are awarded individually and can occur multiple times throughout the year. Merit increases positively impact retention, boost productivity, and improve morale.

Bonus Structures

A **bonus structure** is an incentive program that an organization can offer to all employees or a specific set of employees. Bonus structures are typically based on meeting set metrics or goals. Bonus structures can vary by department or work group. How a bonus structure is set up can depend on the size of the organization and the number of active employees. Certain organizations offer **referral bonuses** for individuals who refer new employees. Referral bonuses can be paid out based on completion of a set period or number of candidates referred. **Commission** is another type of bonus structure that is often offered to people in sales or lending. A lender may receive a percentage of commission on each closed deal, and sales employees may make commission once certain quotas are met. **Safety bonuses** can be offered when employees meet set safety goals on an individual or group level. **Annual bonuses** can be given out companywide or to specific work groups based on yearly performance. **Holiday bonuses** can be provided to all employees around the holiday season; these bonuses are not necessarily based on goals or metrics. **Profit-sharing** is an additional bonus structure where employees are given a percentage of the company's profits, based on company performance. Bonus structures enhance the total compensation package and provide both individual and group incentives for productivity and performance.

Domestic Worker Compensation Plans

Nannies, housecleaners, and other **domestic workers** are covered under minimum wage legislation. If the minimum wage in the state where the domestic worker is employed is higher than the federal minimum wage, the employer must pay at least the state minimum. In addition, domestic workers are covered under the Fair Labor Standards Act, and must be paid overtime (at a rate of time and a half) for all hours over 40 in the workweek.

Global and Expatriate Compensation Plans

Global employees may be provided additional income in the form of **expatriate allowances**, and these amounts may be as much as three or four times the employee's base salary. Their total compensation might include base salary, premiums for foreign service and hardship, and allowances for cost of living, housing, and storage. Tax considerations can make calculating these payments complicated. Some multinational organizations have begun the compensation practice of **localizing** or **mirroring** the local compensation package for employees on assignment in other countries. Most cultures will utilize similar factors to determine compensation and benefits structure or assign jobs to labor grades: skill, effort, and responsibility. Whereas wage levels and benefits may differ a great deal, individual wage decisions are frequently based on performance and seniority. For example, European remuneration packages consider benefits and perks to be a much larger part of the total compensation package than those in the United States, and American executives are excessively overpaid by international standards. Many firms pay a cost-of-living allowance to expatriates to equalize the costs of living in both the host and home countries. Housing allowances are often considered the single most expensive item in expatriate remuneration packages and must be frequently reviewed (as often as quarterly or even monthly) because of exchange rate fluctuations and inflation.

Executive Compensation Plans

Executives often receive compensation packages that include both monetary and nonmonetary rewards. **Executive compensation plans** may be influenced by many factors but are most often associated with revenue and responsibility. **Monetary rewards** might include salary, bonuses or commissions, stock options, director's fees, or multiple forms of deferred compensation. **Nonmonetary rewards** might include a company computer, parking, a company vehicle, first-class travel arrangements, car rentals, health club memberships, and more. **Executive bonuses** are frequently much higher than bonuses given to mid-level managers. CEOs might receive bonuses that are greater than 100 percent of their base pay, whereas upper-level managers more often receive bonuses that are closer to 50 percent of their base pay, and lower-level supervisors might receive bonuses between 10 and 35 percent. Moreover, executives often receive "golden parachutes," or extravagant bonuses, when they leave the office, whether they do well or are forced to resign. Stock options and deferred compensation plans can vary greatly from one organization to another. Human resource (HR) and compensation professionals should ensure that these plans are in compliance with the **Sarbanes-Oxley Act**.

SALES COMPENSATION PLANS

In a **sales compensation plan,** designed to incentivize top performers, salespeople will earn more if they meet or exceed predefined sales targets. These sales targets could be to hit a certain level of revenue, sales volume, profit margin, market share, or customer satisfaction, and should be tied to overall company goals. Typically, salespeople are compensated with a mix of salary and incentive pay, but a company could opt to offer straight salary or straight incentive pay. The incentive pay is usually a mix of commissions and bonuses but may include stock options or other prizes. When designing these plans, HR must determine the appropriate mix of compensation types based on the industry, product being sold, the salesperson's role, and other factors. They must also determine the territory that each salesperson is supposed to cover. Sales compensation plans must have detailed rules about what sales are counted, if salespeople can share credit, if there is a draw system, and more. Further, HR must ensure that the compensation plan is compliant with labor laws and that each type of pay is taxed properly. The compensation plan must be clearly communicated, and HR should make sure that the salespeople and management all understand it.

SHIFT WORKER COMPENSATION PLANS

Compensation plans may differ for individuals working less-desirable or nontraditional shifts. A common tool used to attract workers to these off-shifts is the **shift differential**. The shift differential means that individual employees are paid a higher wage for working specific hours or days. The amount of the differential can depend on the hours of the shift, the days worked, and the industry of the work. Shift differentials can be offered for second or third shift, weekend shifts, or holiday work. The differential for third shift is typically higher than that for second, because third-shift hours are even further outside "traditional" working hours. The amount of the differential is determined by the organization and is based on what will entice the most qualified individuals to fill the roles.

PART-TIME EMPLOYEE COMPENSATION PLANS

The compensation paid to a **part-time employee** can depend on the number of hours that the employee works. Part-time employees are most often paid an hourly rate. Under the Patient Protection and Affordable Care Act, employees who work at least 30 hours per week or 130 hours a month are considered full-time, so part-time employees must work less than this. The rate of pay for a part-time employee depends on the role and the employee's experience and education. Some part-time employees are offered health insurance and fringe benefits. Unemployment, workers' compensation, overtime, and retirement savings plans (once 1000 service hours have been reached) are required benefits for part-time employees. Offering more benefits to part-time employees can entice more-qualified candidates and can make an employer stand out from competitors.

LEAVE PLANS AND APPROACHES
PTO POLICIES

There are many different **paid time off (PTO)** policies across different businesses, industries, and geographic locations. Many of these all-encompassing PTO plans are available only to full-time employees. Whereas many companies recognize eight to 10 fixed holidays, some companies have implemented policies that provide employees with floating holidays. Trends have shown an increase in organizations of all sizes adopting a system in which vacation, personal, sick, and sometimes holiday days are kept in a **single pool** of PTO. Many employees and employers report that having flexibility in time-off plans leads to greater employee engagement and retention. However, as more states impose sick-time regulations, recent trends reflect a number of organizations moving back to traditional buckets of separate vacation and sick time. Additional consideration should be given to state regulations for **termination payouts**. Some states do not require employers to pay out accrued sick time, but many consider PTO pools equivalent to vacation during terminations, so employers must pay out any accrued balances. Companies must also determine whether employees will be gifted with a bank of time immediately upon hire or at a predetermined time versus **accrued** over time. Policies should provide details about **carryover** provisions and whether negative balances are allowed. Having an attractive and well-administered PTO policy can give employers an advantage against growing competition for talent, evolving legal regulations, and an increasingly diverse workforce.

Unpaid Leave

When employees have exhausted all of their PTO options and still need to take time away from work, the employer may allow them to take an **unpaid leave**. This leave may be classified as a personal leave or a work sabbatical. Criteria to qualify and rules that govern the leave will depend on individual firm policies. Policies will need to address items such as how to apply for the leave, the length of leave allowed, benefits continuance, the employee's right to return to the same role, the process to return from a leave, and more.

Open Leave

Some companies have adopted an **open leave** policy that does not assign a set number of paid days off, but rather allows employees to use leave whenever they need to, provided that it does not disrupt business. Open leave provides a great amount of flexibility, as there is no stated cap on time employees can take off. It may also make employees more efficient, knowing that the sooner they complete their work, the sooner they can take additional time off. Employees do not feel pressured or obligated to come into work when ill. There also is not a rush at the end of the year to use any remaining paid days out. However, without a clearly defined leave policy, employees may hesitate to take time off. Individuals may end up taking less time off. There is also a higher chance for abuse, as some employees may take time off without completing tasks first. This also puts additional work on employees who are covering for those taking time off. An open leave policy also prevents an individual from accruing any set days off during the year, losing a potential benefit during separation.

Vacation

In companies that do not use single-pool PTO or open-leave policies, **vacation** is a type of leave that employees use over the course of the year. Using a vacation day allows the employee not to work that day but still receive pay. Vacation differs from sick time in that it is usually planned and requested ahead of time. Vacation days can be accrued by pay period or by year. When vacation is accrued by pay period, a specific number of hours are added to the available balance each time payroll is processed. It is then available to use as the employee wishes throughout the year. Vacation can also be added in a lump sum at the beginning of the year, beginning of the quarter, or some other date. In this case, all of the vacation days granted are available at once for use throughout the year. Employers can determine whether vacation can be rolled over into a new year (and if so, what amount) or if vacation will be "use it or lose it." There are no federal requirements for vacation time.

Sick Leave

Employees that need to take time off of work to recover from an illness, manage a serious health condition, or look after an injury can use their allotted **sick leave**. Sick leave can be used for the employee's condition or for the condition of a family member. There is no federal law regarding paid sick leave benefits, though several states and cities have created their own legislation. Sick leave can either be paid or unpaid. Businesses covered by the ADA (Americans with Disabilities Act) and FMLA (Family and Medical Leave Act) must grant certain amounts of sick leave to eligible employees. Paid sick leave, when offered, typically follows an accrual-based approach. Sick leave can be a critical benefit within a total benefits package.

Holidays and Other Paid Time Off

Whereas the average number of **paid holidays** is around eight per year, most businesses will recognize at least the following six US holidays: New Year's Day, Memorial Day, Independence Day, Labor Day, Thanksgiving Day, and Christmas Day. Additionally, a majority of employers will pay a set number of days for **bereavement** and **jury duty** for eligible employees. However, employees may be required to provide documentation when taking days off for these reasons. Other instances in which employees might be paid for time not worked include reporting time guaranteed for minimal work, union activities, and time to vote.

RETIREMENT PLANNING AND BENEFITS

PENSIONS OR RETIREMENT PLANS

Pensions and **company retirement plans** can fund an individual's retirement by providing deferred payments for prior services. These accounts may be funded solely by the employer through a variety of means. Retirement benefits consist of the total amount contributed plus interest and market earnings. These **defined contribution benefit plans** are the traditional company-provided plans, such as 401(k)s, 403(b)s, Simplified Employee Pensions (SEPs), Savings Incentive Match Plans for Employees (SIMPLEs), and Individual Retirement Accounts (IRAs). A defined contribution benefit plan requires separate accounts for each employee participant, and funds are most often contributed by both the employee and the employer. Some employers will implement an auto-enroll policy, in which new employees are automatically enrolled and minimum contributions to the plan are withheld from payroll. The contribution rates may even automatically increase on an annual basis. However, the **Pension Protection Act of 2006** provides employees with a 90-day window to opt out of these plans and recover any funds contributed on their behalf.

OTHER BENEFITS

DISABILITY INSURANCE

If an employee is out of work due to an injury or illness, private **disability income insurance** can replace a portion of his or her wages. There are two categories of disability insurance: **short-term disability (STD)** and **long-term disability (LTD)**. Unlike workers' compensation, the injury or illness does not need to be work-related to qualify for STD or LTD. Many employers offer disability insurance benefits on a fully paid, partially paid, or ancillary basis. Employers should check state regulations to determine if they are required to provide partial wage replacement insurance coverage to eligible employees. STD typically runs for 90 to 180 days and provides employees with 60 to 75 percent wage replacement after a short waiting period. LTD kicks in after STD is exhausted. Depending on the plan, the LTD coverage may last 24-36 months, run until the employee can return to work (whether for the same company or a new one), or run until the employee is able to collect Social Security Disability benefits or becomes old enough to collect retirement benefits.

EMPLOYEE ASSISTANCE PROGRAMS

Employees with personal problems, such as a substance abuse problem or a marital separation, may receive help from an **employee assistance program (EAP)**, which may be able to provide counseling, referrals to experts such as recovery programs or divorce attorneys, or other services. An EAP may be categorized as a **welfare plan** and require reports to be filed with the US Department of Labor and IRS if it provides counseling for substance abuse, stress, anxiety, depression, or similar mental or physical health problems. These programs may be required to comply with reporting and disclosure requirements of the **Employee Retirement Income Security Act (ERISA)**. EAPs must adhere to strict guidelines to avoid legal risks regarding privacy, malpractice, or coercion.

FAMILY AND FLEX BENEFITS PROGRAMS

In recent years, employees have come to expect benefits that promote work–life balance and support their families. To that end, an increasing number of employers offer telecommuting, flex time, and compressed work week options to help workers juggle all of life's different demands. In addition, many workplaces now offer benefits like paid parental leave and designated lactation rooms to make it easier on new parents. Additionally, some employers have started offering paid caregiver leave, which allows workers to care for parents and other relatives without worrying about their paychecks.

EMPLOYEE WELLNESS PROGRAMS

Many companies have begun to implement **employee wellness programs** to encourage employees to take preventative measures to avoid illness and accidents. The details of employee wellness programs vary greatly. Some may include physical examinations to assess health and health education to teach nutrition or healthy habits, whereas others might assist with smoking cessation, but almost all employee wellness programs will include some element of weight management. Moreover, the Patient Protection and Affordable Care Act allows employers to **reward** employees for participating in wellness programs, such as covering a higher percentage of premiums for employees who comply with wellness program requirements like having annual physical examinations and attending trainings. However, rewards should be based only on participation and not on achieving health objectives.

LIFE COACHES

A **life coach** is a wellness professional that helps clients develop skills, set goals, identify strengths and weaknesses, and reach their full potential. Life coaches can be used at various stages in life, such as during a transition, when an individual is looking to break a particular habit, or when a person is undergoing a high amount of stress and/or anxiety. Life coaches meet with clients to determine what the individual's goals are and helps create a plan and path to meet those goals. Life coaches cannot treat mental health conditions, but can help people overcome obstacles that may stem from such conditions. Life coaches can help with a variety of goals such as improved financial security, good work/life balance, and deeper connections with friends and family.

EMPLOYEE STOCK PURCHASE PLANS

In an **employee stock purchase plan (ESPP)**, employees may purchase shares of stock in the company at a discounted rate, using their own funds. ESPPs are voluntary and are not considered a qualified defined-contribution retirement plan. ESPPs are voluntary purchases made with post-tax dollars. ESPP shares can be sold at any time, provided that there is no holding period. Many companies have a graded vesting schedule for employee exercise options. Shares sold are subject to applicable capital gains taxes. ESPPs have two categories: qualified and non-qualified plans. Qualified plans require the approval of company shareholders before implementation. Additional restrictions include a limit on the maximum allowed discount and the offering period for the ESPP (usually 3 years). Non-qualified plans do not have the same restrictions but also do not share the tax advantages offered by qualified plans.

HOUSING PARTNERSHIP

An **employer-assisted housing** program may provide employees with a grant or loan toward the purchase of a home. In some cases, the loan is forgiven after a graded schedule. For example, the employee receiving the loan might have to remain with the company for 5 years, and 20% of the loan would be forgiven each year. Employer-assisted housing may also include education and counseling for homebuyers, counseling to prevent foreclosure, and partnerships with realtors. The benefit for the employee is large, because the loan or grant can significantly help with the down payment and/or closing costs when purchasing a home. The benefit for the organization offering this program is also significant, as it can be used as a major perk when recruiting. Companies that offer employer-assisted housing may also see an increase in retention and a more productive workforce.

UNEMPLOYMENT INSURANCE

State-run **unemployment insurance** pays money weekly to qualified individuals who have lost their jobs. Unemployment insurance is funded through various employer taxes, including the Federal Unemployment Tax Act. Unemployment insurance requirements include meeting a state-mandated level for either wages earned or time worked during a given time period. Individuals who quit or are fired for cause do not qualify for unemployment insurance. Unemployment insurance benefits typically last up to 26 weeks, but this number can vary by state. An eligible individual who loses their position, through no fault of their own, can file an unemployment claim in the state where he or she worked. If a new role is not secured within 26 weeks, the individual may qualify for an extended benefits program.

OUTPLACEMENT SERVICES

Coaching programs called **outplacement services** help employees who have separated from an organization secure a new position quickly. Outplacement services can provide interview preparation, resume-writing assistance, career coaching, and general training to exiting employees. The employer pays for the service, which is free to the separated employee. Outplacement services are often included in severance packages, and benefit the outgoing employee by assisting with the job search and interviewing process. Outplacement services benefit the employer by lowering unemployment claims and helping to reduce legal risks.

WORKERS' COMPENSATION

Individuals who sustain work-related injuries are eligible for coverage of medical expenses and a continuation of income through the **workers' compensation** program. The program makes compensation and expenses the employer's responsibility without liability or fault to the employee, assuming that the employee has adhered to reasonable safety precautions. Each state administers its own workers' compensation program according to state and federal laws. There are three types of workers' compensation benefits awarded to employees: medical expenses, wage replacement payments, and death benefits. Wage replacement payments are often calculated based on an employee's average weekly wages and become available after a waiting period. Costs are determined by an experience rating based on an employer's claim history.

CAFETERIA PLANS

Section 125 of the IRS code defines a **cafeteria plan** as a defined employer plan that provides participants with the opportunity to receive certain benefits on a pretax basis. Funds allocated to these benefits are not included as wages for state or federal income tax purposes and are generally exempt from the Federal Insurance Contributions Act (FICA) and the Federal Unemployment Tax Act. Qualified benefits under these plans might include the following:

- **Medical healthcare coverage.** Plans may include some or all portions of physician services, office visits and exams, prescription drugs, hospital services, maternity services, mental health, physical therapy, and emergency services.
- **Dental coverage.** Plans may include some or all portions of routine exams, cleanings, x-rays, fluoride treatments, orthodontic services, fillings, crowns, and extractions.
- **Dependent care.** Plans may cover some or all portions of onsite childcare, allowances and flexible spending for childcare, day-care information, or flexible scheduling.
- **Short-term disability.** This provides partial income continuation to employees who are unable to work for a short period of time (three to six months) due to an accident or illness.
- **Long-term disability.** This provides partial income continuation to employees who are unable to work for long periods of time (greater than three to six months) due to an accident or illness.
- **Group-term life insurance** and **accidental death or dismemberment.** This provides financial assistance to an employee or his or her beneficiaries if the employee has an accident that results in the loss of limbs, loss of eyesight, or death. The cost of a group plan is frequently lower than that of individual plans, and payments are based on the employee's age and annual salary.

OTHER COMPENSATION

DEFERRED COMPENSATION

Compensation that is paid out at a specified future date or during retirement is likely a form of **deferred compensation**. These plans may be qualifying or nonqualifying pensions, retirement plan accounts, or employee stock option plans. **Qualifying plans** such as 401(k), 403(b), 503(c), Individual Retirement Accounts (IRAs), or Savings Incentive Match Plans for Employees (SIMPLE) plans must adhere to the **Employee Retirement Income Security Act** and IRS limits. **Nonqualifying plans** often involve funds that are withheld and may be invested to be paid out at a later time for tax advantages and potential capital gains. Companies might choose deferred compensation plans, such as top hat plans, restorative benefit plans, or supplemental executive retirement plans to attract and retain business officers. It is important to note that payments for nonqualifying deferred compensation plans must be scheduled for a specified future date, and funds may not be withheld in advance. Additionally, nonqualifying plans can carry concerns about company sustainability or what happens in the event of mergers and acquisitions or bankruptcy.

DIRECT AND INDIRECT COMPENSATION

The two main types of rewards used to compensate employees are monetary and nonmonetary. **Monetary compensation** is any tangible reward provided as payment for work, including salary and wages, paid sick days, paid vacation time, retirement plans, and stock options. **Nonmonetary compensation** is any intangible reward provided to encourage an individual to perform work, including better assignments, employee-of-the-month awards, flexible scheduling, and special privileges.

An organization can issue monetary compensation to employees through direct or indirect means. **Direct compensation** is any monetary compensation paid directly to the employee, including salary or wages, bonuses, overtime, or special pay. **Indirect compensation** is monetary compensation paid to a third party on the employee's behalf or paid without the employee having to perform work, including health insurance, paid sick days, paid vacation time, retirement plans, and stock options.

COMPANY-WIDE INCENTIVE PLANS

Profit-sharing and gainsharing programs reward employees based on the performance of the entire organization. In **profit-sharing plans**, employees receive a share of the company's profits in addition to their regular pay. These may be cash plans, in which payments are made after the close of a specified period, such as a quarter or year, or tax-advantaged deferred plans, in which funds are invested. If deferred, funds are a tax-deductible expense for the company for the year in which they are contributed, and employees are not taxed until their funds are received. In **gainsharing plans**, employees receive bonuses based on improved productivity as opposed to profits. Gainsharing plans often fall into three categories: Scanlon Plans, Rucker Plans, or Improshare Plans. **Scanlon plans** are most popular in union environments, and combine gainsharing with an employee recommendation system. These plans base payouts on a standard ratio of labor costs as a percentage of revenue. **Rucker plans** are similar, but the employee gains are based on production. These plans base payouts on the ratio of labor costs to the result of production minus the cost of materials. **Improshare Plans**, or improved productivity through sharing, provide bonuses to employees based on the amount of time saved compared to a baseline.

ESOPs

An **employee stock ownership plan (ESOP)** is created by establishing a trust into which the business makes tax-deductible contributions of cash or stock. Employees are then granted the ability to purchase this stock or allocate funds into individual employee accounts. The stock is held in an **employee stock ownership trust (ESOT)**, and the business can make regular contributions, typically up to 25 percent of its annual payroll. ESOPs became popular because it is believed that employees who have an ownership interest in the business will work more diligently and have a vested interest in the company's efficiency and profitability. Although this logic is debatable, many studies have shown that ESOPs actually do motivate employees and support business growth.

TUITION ASSISTANCE

Organizations may offer employer-sponsored **tuition assistance**, or **tuition reimbursement**, to employees. Tuition assistance helps employees pursue education, training, and skill development. There are several different forms of tuition assistance. Some companies will cover classes regardless of their content. Other companies will only cover courses that directly relate to the employee's current or next role in the organization. Most commonly, the employee pays for tuition, books, and lab fees (if applicable) up front, and the employer will reimburse the employee after receiving proof of a passing grade, typically a "C" or higher. In many cases, there is a cap on the amount that the employer will reimburse per year. Additionally, many organizations require employees to sign an agreement to return the reimbursement if the individual leaves employment before a certain amount of time passes.

PAY PRACTICES AND ISSUES

PAY INCREASES

The COVID-19 pandemic, inflation, and a highly competitive labor market have greatly impacted pay and **pay increases** for businesses across the board. An employee's wages and salary should not remain static, and there are many ways an organization can increase pay for an employee. Some of the most common are merit-based increases, promotions, and cost-of-living adjustments (COLA).

There are many factors that determine which types of increases are used and the total amount of the pay increases. Experience and performance can play a large role, with high performers typically garnering larger increases than mediocre or sub-par performers. Economic trajectory and health also play a large role in increase amounts. If there is a recession, increases are likely to be low and based on the performance (or anticipated performance) of the organization. The geographic location of an organization also plays a role in pay increases. A company headquartered out of the Midwest will likely have lower increases than a company based on the East Coast, due to significant differences in cost of living and other factors. The industry of the organization also has an impact, as does the growth rate of the company. For example, information technology companies are often high-growth and will have larger increases than those in education.

BASE PAY

Three of the most important factors involved in determining the appropriate **base pay** for a new employee are the value of the position, the education and experience of the individual, and the demand for individuals able to fill the position. The **value of the position** refers to the value identified during the job evaluation process, which is based on the importance of the position to the organization. **Education and experience** refers to the employee's knowledge, skills, and abilities beyond the minimum requirements necessary to perform the position. **Demand** for individuals able to fill the position refers to the employee's ability to seek employment with another organization and the ease or difficulty the organization would have in replacing the employee.

DIFFERENTIAL PAY

The Fair Labor Standards Act (FLSA) requires that employers pay **time and a half** for overtime hours in excess of a 40-hour workweek. Some regulations may impose additional overtime payments, such as overtime hours in excess of an eight-hour day. Companies may also provide an adjustment for employee transfers to locations with a higher cost of living or in compliance with localities that require a higher minimum wage. Many organizations use some form of **differential pay** for performing unpleasant or less-desirable work. For example, weekends or holidays might be paid at time and a half or even double time. FLSA requires that employers compensate on-call employees if their activities while on call are restricted, and premiums often compensate employees who are called back to work for emergency services due to the inconvenience. Likewise, those who work night shifts or put themselves in harm's way will often receive a shift differential or hazard pay.

INCENTIVE OR VARIABLE PAY

Many organizations use some form of **financial incentives** that are tied to productivity, as these pay-for-performance plans may increase worker output. One of the most popular methods is **merit pay increases**. Not to be confused with an annual cost-of-living increase, merit pay is an adjustment or one-time bonus awarded to top performers following an evaluation of clearly defined objectives. Some employers prefer to use **bonuses and commissions** to reward performance. Unlike merit increases that can increase annual pay levels, bonuses and commissions must be earned each period. Moreover, bonus payments do not need to be tied to individual performance. Sometimes, they are awarded at management's discretion or based on company performance. Employers may also choose to pay employees on a **production or piece rate plan**. One example of this plan that also ties in an additional incentive is the Halsey Premium Plan. Under this plan, production standards are determined by past performance, and employees receive a guaranteed hourly rate plus a percentage of the rate for any time saved compared to this standard.

Other common variable pay programs include gainsharing programs and profit-sharing programs. A **gainsharing** program encourages the achievement of certain financial goals by offering a percentage of the money the organization earns or saves from achieving that goal. A **profit-sharing** program encourages the achievement of certain goals by offering a percentage of the profit when goals are met.

PAY LEVELS AND PAY BANDS

Some compensation structures break out pay grades or ranges into separate **levels** or **bands** so the company can maintain pay equity and stay within budget. This is done by conducting a job analysis and grouping job titles into families. For example, jobs that fall into the first pay grade may have a pay band of $20,000 to $35,000, the second pay grade may have a band of $30,000 to $50,000, and the third pay grade may have a band of $50,000 to $100,000. Jobs may also be evaluated and ranked based on overall responsibilities and worth to the organization. Although pay bands are broken out based on job duty and skill level, they are also affected by whether the company tends to lead, lag, or match current market rates. Matching or leading the market is best for recruitment and retention. The magnitude of the pay bands tend to grow as employees move up the managerial ladder, with executives having the highest pay levels.

BROADBANDING

A variation on pay bands, **broadbanding** is a pay structure design in which all jobs are separated into a small number of broadly defined pay grades, such as general staff, management, and executives. Organizations usually choose to use a broadbanding approach to encourage teamwork and eliminate problems arising from perceived differences in status between different pay grades. The focus is on performance rather than activities related to achieving promotions.

WAGE COMPRESSION

Wage compression occurs when an employee is hired at the same or higher wage than existing employees with more experience already in that position. It can also occur when line-level employees earn almost as much as management. It is important to avoid wage compression because it leads to employees becoming dissatisfied and unmotivated because of the perceived arbitrary nature of pay decisions. Wage compression can happen in several ways, such as external hires expecting more of a pay bump to change jobs than a normal, internal annual increase (typically less than 4 percent), and companies being willing to offer inflated salaries in a tight labor market. To combat wage compression, human resources can use strategies such as reviewing existing staff salaries prior to hiring a new employee (and making adjustments if necessary) and promoting from within whenever possible, which should result in a lower salary than hiring externally.

PAY EQUITY

The principle of **pay equity** refers to the belief that employees performing equal or similar job functions are entitled to equal pay regardless of gender, age, race, religion, ethnicity, or other non-job-related statuses. This initiative is particularly important because for quite some time, some employees received lower paychecks than peers for discriminatory reasons. Pay equity is important to businesses because it can help prevent discrimination lawsuits, ensure compliance with pay equity regulations, attract new talent while also retaining current talent, and improve morale and organizational loyalty. There are many factors that can assist with pay equity, including pay equity studies, pay transparency, and banning inquiries into salary history.

PAY TRANSPARENCY

The practice of an organization disclosing information about compensation standards to others is known as **pay transparency**. This disclosure can occur internally and externally. There are many local and state laws surrounding pay transparency and what information can be requested or disclosed. For example, some regulations prohibit an employer from asking a candidate about previous salaries. Additionally, certain regulations require that a wage range is provided for open positions in job postings and advertisements. Other regulations require organizations to file annual reports that detail salary and wage compensation within the company. Pay transparency is a tool that can help reduce wage discrimination and can help foster pay equity.

ACCOUNTING AND FINANCIAL KNOWLEDGE FOR MANAGING PAYROLL
DIRECT AND INDIRECT COMPENSATION

Compensation provided to an employee by an organization comes in two main formats: direct and indirect compensation.

Direct compensation is monetary payment provided to an employee for hours worked or work-related achievements. Examples of direct compensation include:

- Salary/Wages
- Bonuses
- Commission
- Overtime

Indirect compensation is not directly received in cash from, but still holds financial value. Indirect compensation is also commonly known as the **benefits** or **perks** of a job. Indirect compensation can have monetary value, but that is not necessarily the case. Examples of indirect compensation include:

- Insurance (medical, dental, vision, life, etc.)
- Tuition reimbursement
- Paid leave (PTO, vacation, holiday, sick, etc.)
- 401(k) contributions or stock option plans
- Meals
- Childcare
- Phones, tablets, laptops, or other equipment

The direct and indirect compensation items combined make up an employee's **total compensation**. Total compensation can and does vary based on benefits and rewards offered to different positions and levels within the organization.

TOTAL COMPENSATION STATEMENTS

Employees can be shown the overall value of their compensation and benefits packages in a **total compensation statement**. In general, the more benefits included in the statement, the better. However, human resources should ensure that the following are highlighted: year-to-date pay, paid time off, retirement, and insurance. The point of issuing the statement is to demonstrate that the employee gets much more than his or her base salary and that the employer is making a significant investment in the employee's well-being.

TOTAL REWARDS METRICS AND BENCHMARKS

$$\text{Compensation as a percentage of operating expense} = \frac{\text{Total compensation}}{\text{Total operating expense}} \times 100$$

$$\text{Benefits as a percentage of operating expense} = \frac{\text{Total benefits cost}}{\text{Total operating expense}} \times 100$$

Employee burden: total cost to employ someone, taking into consideration pay, benefits, and taxes

Utilization review: an audit to ensure the accuracy of the healthcare provider's billing

INSURANCE PARTICIPATION RATES

Insurance plans typically require a **participation rate** of at least 70% for an employer to obtain coverage for the employer/employee group under group health insurance or employer-sponsored health insurance. This percentage can differ from state to state and by insurer, but 70% is most common. As an example, a small business has 40 employees who are eligible for the insurance plan. To meet the 70% participation rate to obtain coverage, 28 of those employees must enroll in the plan. However, if 19 of the 40 eligible employees already have coverage under another plan (e.g., through a spouse or parent), there are 21 only benefit-eligible employees. To meet the 70% participation rate threshold, 15 of the 21 eligible employees must enroll in coverage.

Compa-Ratio

The **compa-ratio** is a mathematical formula used to compare a specific employee's pay with the pay at the middle of the pay range. The compa-ratio is expressed as a percentage and can be determined by dividing the employee's base salary by the midpoint salary for the employee's pay range:

$$\text{Compa-ratio} = \frac{\text{Base salary}}{\text{Midpoint salary}}$$

For example, if an individual is in a pay grade that ranges from $25,000 to $45,000 a year and the individual receives $30,000 a year, the midpoint of the range is ($25,000 + $45,000) ÷ 2 = $35,000, and the compa-ratio is $30,000 ÷ $35,000 = 0.857, which is equal to 85.7%. Compa-ratios are primarily used to compare an employee's current pay with the pay of other employees in similar positions to determine whether the individual is receiving a fair amount considering seniority, performance, and so on.

Benchmarking

When organizations and compensation professionals need to make pay decisions or determine whether internal rates are competitive with the industry, most will rely on **benchmarking** of both internal and external peer groups. Benchmarking is a tool for measuring and comparing current practices or processes against the **competition** so that any gaps may be addressed. For example, making changes to incentive plans may be a tough sell. If your business practice does not involve providing employees with a bonus plan, benchmarking data might support new initiatives by showing that many in your industry do provide bonus incentives. Thus, not providing this incentive could jeopardize performance or risk losing top performers. However, it is important to consider organizational structure, size, location, industry, and other factors. Compensation rates in San Francisco will differ greatly from rates in Omaha, and smaller companies often pay less than large, national entities.

Remuneration Surveys

Competitive compensation structures are equitable and motivating, and they should also be legal, be cost-effective, and provide security. The most readily available **remuneration surveys** are those conducted by government agencies such as the Bureau of Labor Statistics (BLS) and wage surveys conducted by private organizations. These surveys frequently consider varying components of compensation, such as base pay, incentives, and benefits. Government surveys may include local, state, or federal data. BLS regularly publishes reliable findings on occupational earnings and benefits of blue- and white-collar jobs. Professional organizations, journals, and associations may perform sophisticated surveys to obtain remuneration data for top managers, supervisors, and entry-level workers. Some popular publications are the CEO compensation report published by *Forbes* and reports compiled by wage survey companies like PayScale or Towers Watson. However, the US Justice Department has stated that human resource professionals cannot conduct salary surveys on their own. Doing so violates Antitrust Safety Zone guidelines.

Chapter Quiz

Ready to see how well you retained what you just read? Scan the QR code to go directly to the chapter quiz interface for this study guide. If you're using a computer, simply visit the bonus page at **mometrix.com/bonus948/shrmcp** and click the Chapter Quizzes link.

Human Resources Expertise: Organization

Structure of the Human Resources Function

HUMAN RESOURCE MODELS
CENTRALIZED AND DECENTRALIZED DECISION-MAKING

While both centralization and decentralization guide how authority is distributed throughout an organization, they differ greatly in practice and functionality. **Highly centralized firms** are narrow, and prefer to control the decision-making process at the top executive levels. **Decentralized firms** are wide, providing more autonomy and responsibility to staff at the middle and lower levels of hierarchy, which allows for more active involvement from an increased number of employees. The amount of authority delegated will vary greatly between highly centralized and highly decentralized organizations. Many companies practice some level of decentralization and might impose internal operating procedures or standards for integration and control.

Centralized human resources (HR) is often known as **corporate HR**. In this model, the HR function resides at the corporate level, where department members set consistent policies and standards for the entire firm. The main drawback of centralized HR is that it can be too rigid and not account for the nuances of individual company locations. **Decentralized HR**, on the other hand, is when the HR function is housed at the local level. Because each site will be able to create policies and standards that work best for them, there will be little consistency among locations. This can be problematic for employees who transfer from one part of the firm to another. In addition, having multiple sets of rules and procedures is inefficient for the company as a whole. The main benefit to decentralized HR is that each site can quickly be responsive to its own needs. Many large organizations use a blend of these two approaches, where there is an overarching corporate HR group that sets some universal standards, and local HR departments have some latitude when providing service to their employee groups.

CENTER OF EXCELLENCE (CoE)

A **center of excellence (CoE) HR model** features internal groups of consultants that have expertise in different HR functional areas, such as payroll and benefits. Their main role is to provide each company location with guidance driven by best practices and assistance with problem-solving. Generally, business units must utilize this in-house resource before seeking external help.

SHARED SERVICES

Some larger organizations have begun to centralize certain business functions into **shared service centers**, such as finance, information technology, or HR. Shared services are essentially the merging and streamlining of business operations that are used by multiple units of the same organization. This helps business units retain more control and identifies ways to work more efficiently, improving service quality and the credibility of each function. For example, an HR shared services center may process all employment-related changes for an entire enterprise within the company's human resource information system (HRIS) at the request of HR staff at each location.

GLOBAL HUMAN RESOURCES

A company that has locations around the world needs a worldwide HR department. **Global HR** is a structure in which the HR department is involved with the workforce in more than one country or continent. Global HR is responsible for the acquisition, support, management, analysis, and engagement of employees in various cultures and locations. Standardized processes and policies should be developed by HR with the customs, legislation, and cultures of diverse localities in mind. Working hours and salaries may vary considerably from one country to the next. Holidays are also likely to look different. Some countries have offer letters of employment, while others have contracts. The global HR structure requires familiarity with local and global employment laws, regulations, and practices.

BUSINESS PARTNERS

A **business partner** HR model features a strategic relationship between HR and higher-level management. HR works closely with management to plan and elevate business goals and strategies. HR does not merely perform payroll, benefits, and administrative tasks, but also takes on a additional role in planning future workforce acquisition and development. HR business partners also determine how the functions of the HR department are run and executed. With this model, HR develops managers to deploy various levels of people management, empowering them to develop and coach employees instead of relying on the HR department to be the people manager for the entire organization.

MATRIX

Organizations where employees have multiple responsibilities often use a **matrix** HR model. An employee may report to one manager for day-to-day tasks and operations and a different manager for special projects or initiatives. For example, a recruiting manager might report to the director of the region for onsite tasks and roles while simultaneously reporting to the VP of People Management for an HRIS implementation project. The structure of the matrix organization is more flexible than a hierarchical design and allows for more collaboration and cross-training in various areas.

KEY ELEMENTS OF HUMAN RESOURCES

There are many elements to the **HR business function**. Key elements include the following:

- **Recruiting:** sourcing, interviewing, hiring, and onboarding new employees
- **Organizational culture:** collection of values, norms, and attitudes that support the vision
- **Employee relations:** evaluations, performance management, and grievances
- **Compensation and payroll**: wage earnings, tax withholdings, benefits deductions, and direct deposit processing
- **Benefits:** enrollment and education for medical, dental, vision, life, 401(k), and so on
- **Policy creation, communication, and distribution:** researching, drafting, disseminating, discussing, and enforcing employment-related policies such as cell phone use and attendance
- **Legal compliance:** maintaining records for employment eligibility, taxes, safety, and licensure
- **Training and development:** providing necessary information or continuing education
- **Health and safety:** reviewing practices, reporting incidents, and posting logs
- **Change management:** planning, communicating, and stabilizing changes within the company

HUMAN RESOURCE STAFF ROLES OR TITLES

The following are some of the major HR staff roles or titles and their levels of responsibility. Of course, the scope of each title varies from company to company, usually based on the size of the firm.

- **HR specialist/administrator/coordinator**: members of a department in the earlier stages of their careers who specialize in a particular HR function, such as talent acquisition, compensation, benefits administration, employee relations, or HR systems
- **HR generalist/manager**: leaders of a department who are experienced, knowledgeable, and required to understand all of the major HR functions
- **HR business partner/director**: divisional managers who take on a strategic partnership with leadership and corporate officers to align HR functions with company goals

OUTSOURCING

In the context of HR, **outsourcing** is the process of contracting with outside specialists to perform selected HR functions. Businesses may outsource some or all of their HR functions, such as payroll, benefits, or recruiting. The specialists who conduct HR functions in this relationship are not employees of the business but instead most likely employees of the company providing the outsourcing service. The value of outsourcing is that it allows managers to focus on more core business matters and decisions, whereas the legal reporting and responsibilities often fall to the company performing the tasks. However, outsourcing can be expensive to implement.

HUMAN RESOURCE FUNCTION METRICS

HUMAN RESOURCE STAFF PER FULL TIME EMPLOYEE

To calculate the ratio of human resource (HR) staff per full time employee (FTE), use the following equation:

$$\textbf{HR staff per FTE} = \frac{\text{Number of HR FTEs}}{\text{Total number of FTEs}} \times 100\%$$

This ratio allows for comparison of staffing levels among firms. In general, larger organizations employ more HR professionals to meet the needs of employees and to build an HR infrastructure that supports business goals while mitigating risk.

HR SERVICE MINDSET

The HR function is one of service. Every day, HR professionals must assist both job candidates and employees with a variety of issues. To do this effectively, they must internalize a **service mindset**, view each person that they interact with as a customer, and ensure that each interaction is respectful and helpful. To determine the satisfaction level of their customers and find areas for improvement, HR should periodically solicit feedback about the service that they render.

KEY PERFORMANCE INDICATORS

HR **key performance indicators (KPIs)** measure specific HR activities that contribute to the efficiency and effectiveness of a company. KPIs provide a company with quantitative measurements that can be used to examine qualities and actions that contribute to long-term success. KPIs and other HR metrics are evaluated and interpreted by leading and lagging indicators. **Leading indicators** anticipate, precede, and predict future performance. For example, a leading indicator could be foreseeing the amount of time to fill key role vacancies to ensure a qualified and efficient workforce. **Lagging indicators** measure the result of a process or change and often garner more consideration because they analyze revenues that executives use to measure success. HR scorecards and dashboards present metrics and KPIs to executives in a simplified, useful format. Many are designed to reflect four main perspectives: **strategic**, to measure initiative progress or achievement; **operational**, to measure process effectiveness; **financial**, to measure contributions and sustainability; and **stakeholder**, to measure internal and external customers.

BALANCED SCORECARDS

The expectations of all stockholders, customers, and employees must be satisfied for a company to be sustainable and profitable. A **balanced scorecard** reflects the vision and strategy for this success from the financial outlook, customer perspectives, and internal business processes. Understanding how vision and strategy lead to measurable goals and objectives is especially important for startup businesses seeking investment opportunities. If a scorecard reports that one of these stakeholders is not being satisfied, the company must attempt to realign expectations and correct behaviors to bring stakeholders back on board. HR should be included in the design of the balanced scorecard and should help choose what metrics are covered. Common HR metrics on a balanced scorecard pertain to staffing and training. They may include turnover rate, time to fill, training completion percentage, and so on.

Organizational Effectiveness and Development

INTRAGROUP DYNAMICS

GROUP FORMATION THEORIES

There are a few group formation theories, including **propinquity or proximity theory** (based on geography), **exchange or benefit theory** (based on rewards), **balance theory** (based on similar attitudes or interests), and **activity theory** (based on occupational task). **Formal groups** come in three main forms: **command groups** (like the departments on an organizational chart), **task groups** (working collaboratively toward a common task), and **functional groups** (created to accomplish specific goals and objectives for an unspecified period of time). Groups are often formed to achieve a particular task or goal. During the group-forming phase of group development, the group learns about group members and the group task. Members may choose to join a group for a sense of stability or to develop self-esteem. Groups can also foster feelings of power, status, or affiliation.

GROUP DEVELOPMENT STAGES

The five stages of group development developed by Bruce Tuckman are as follows:

1. **Forming** entails superficial introductions and determining boundaries of acceptable behavior.
2. **Storming** is the most difficult stage. The team must work through conflicts related to authority, vision and values, personality, and cultural differences. The amount of work often seems overwhelming at this point, and team members struggle to listen to the opinions and experiences of others. If quality-improvement processes are implemented and there is good communication, however, these barriers can become beneficial later on.
3. **Norming** entails greater cooperation and more cohesion as the team establishes norms for assignment completion, decision-making, and conflict resolution. There are three parts to norming: reducing conflicts as the team becomes more relaxed; developing a routine through scheduled events, such as meetings; and facilitating cooperation through team-building events.
4. **Performing** involves effective and unified team performance as the team addresses its objectives. Conflicts are mostly resolved, and the team has a clear purpose and structure.
5. **Adjourning** is the process of ending the group. Group members say goodbye to each other. Good closure is important.

GROUP COHESION

Cohesion may be influenced by similar traits or interests, attraction, shared commitment, and ability to trust. **Task cohesion** defines how well a group works together to accomplish goals, whereas **social cohesion** defines the sense of belonging held by members of the group. Establishing an organizational culture that promotes cohesion allows members of the group to work collaboratively and collectively as one while promoting positive feelings about activities. There can be advantages and disadvantages of cohesion. Advantages might include better quality and quantity of work, increased effectiveness, and increased engagement. Disadvantages might include greater likelihood of groupthink, ignoring ideas that deviate from group norms, and the chance of counterproductive ideas spreading.

INTERGROUP DYNAMICS

Intergroup conflict refers to a clash between two or more teams, groups, or departments. This occurs when there are expressions of hostility or intentional interference with an opposing group's activities. Some causes of intergroup conflict might include competition for resources, opposing viewpoints, lack of adaptation to environmental change, or task interdependence regarding the coordination of work. Intergroup conflict is often classified as either functional or dysfunctional. **Functional conflicts** may produce enhanced organizational performance as a result of alternative solutions. **Dysfunctional conflicts** often have a negative impact on organizational performance. Due to the disruptive nature of dysfunctional conflicts, management must address and eliminate them when reported or observed. Mediation techniques of communication and

150

channeling energies, expertise, or resources of the conflicting groups may help to negotiate solutions and attain organizational goals.

ORGANIZATIONAL STRUCTURES

CUSTOMER SERVICE ORGANIZATIONAL STRUCTURE

Often seen in healthcare, a **customer service organizational structure** is utilized by firms that provide a service. The structure organizes departments to provide specialized solutions to different customer segments. Although this structure can provide exemplary customer care, it can pose problems for the organization. Each customer division will have its own rules and processes that can lead to duplication of efforts or conflicting systems.

FUNCTIONAL ORGANIZATIONAL STRUCTURE

A **functional organizational structure** organizes firm departments based on their function or what they do for the company. Manufacturing, customer service, and human resources (HR) are just a few of the functional departments that may be in this common organizational structure. This vertical structure works best when decision-making power is centralized. This structure promotes the development of experts in their fields, ensures employees work in their areas of expertise, and is easy to understand. However, there is little in the way of cross-department collaboration, and enacting change may be difficult.

DIVISIONAL ORGANIZATIONAL STRUCTURE

A **divisional organizational structure** organizes a business based on the firm's different product lines, services, brands, or markets. This structure is vertical, and, like a functional structure, promotes specialization and expertise. However, there is some collaboration within each division, making the structure less siloed. This structure also features faster decision-making, as each division has a leadership team. Although there is coordination within divisions, each division stands alone and is concerned chiefly with its own operations. This leads to duplication of efforts across the firm, hoarding of resources by each division, and potential competition for customers among divisions. In addition, because each division orders its own supplies, the firm could miss out on the better pricing other companies may get for purchasing for the whole organization.

MATRIX ORGANIZATIONAL STRUCTURE

Many organizations facing uncertain environments find that combining functional and product departmentalization increases coordination and reporting relationships. A **matrix organizational structure** is best for uncertain environments that deal with constantly changing products and/or a strong focus on the customer experience. This dual, two-dimensional organizational structure supports the organization in achieving goals by dividing focus to gain simultaneous advantages. Matrix organizations support functional and divisional partnership, focusing on work and minimizing costs. Employees or departments report to both product and functional managers that are responsible for performance. One manager may be more administrative or focused on a core business unit such as HR, information technology (IT), or finance, whereas the other is typically involved with product, service, customer, or location. For example, a systems developer might report to a project manager as well as an IT manager, or a payroll integration specialist might report to a project manager and finance manager. Technical expertise is paired with marketplace responsiveness. However, reporting relationships may cause confusion, resulting in increased stress and lower performance levels. Functional leaders and product leaders must cooperate to determine priorities and standards.

GEOGRAPHIC AND PROGRAM ORGANIZATIONAL STRUCTURES

In a **geographic organizational structure**, a type of divisional structure, the firm organizes its business functions or departments based on their geographic locations. A project organizational structure, or **program organizational structure** is used to outline the hierarchy and levels of authority of individuals assigned to a specific program or project. The reporting structure details the function, workflow and the reporting process of each individual in relation to others during the time assigned to the program or project.

Workforce Management

WORKFORCE PLANNING APPROACHES, TECHNIQUES AND ANALYSES

STAGES OF HUMAN RESOURCE WORKFORCE PLANNING

Human resource (HR) planning systems should support an organization's business plans. Businesses must have a precise blend of knowledge, skills, and abilities among employees. **Human resource planning** can be separated into three forecasting periods: short range (less than one year), middle range (one to five years), and long range (five to 10 years). **Short-range planning** involves projecting workforce staffing requirements. **Middle-range planning** involves a mix of both short- and long-term forecasting. **Long-range planning** requires more strategic analysis and environmental scanning. The supreme test of an HR planning system is whether it provides the right number of qualified employees at the right time.

FORECASTING

Workforce planning requires understanding the current workforce, knowing where the future lies, and **forecasting** how to move the organization from the present to the future. Forecasting in workforce planning requires gathering and analyzing data, understanding supply and demand, executing a gap analysis, and planning the strategic moves to position the organization to capture the workforce necessary to be successful. There are several forecasting strategies that can be utilized, as discussed below.

LONG-TERM FORECASTING TECHNIQUES FOR PLANNING EMPLOYMENT NEEDS

Forecasting often covers a time frame of up to 10 years and is reviewed on an annual basis for adjustment. There are many techniques for such **long-term forecasting,** such as unit demand, probabilistic models and simulations, or trend projections and regression analysis. One example of **probabilistic forecasting** is a **Markov analysis**, which tracks the movement of employees across different job classifications to forecast movement among departments, operating units, salary levels, or from one category to another. **Expert opinions** may also be considered. The **Delphi technique** consists of having experts provide their best estimates of future needs based on questionnaires and interviews. An intermediary collects results and provide a summary or report to the experts. If one expert's opinion differs from the findings of the group, he or she is asked to justify his or her views so the intermediary can revise and redistribute the report.

BUILD, BUY, BORROW, AND BRIDGE STRATEGIES

Once employers understand the type and number of employees that will be needed to meet the future business objectives of the organization, they can pursue any of these four strategies:

- **Build.** An organization can utilize its current staff and training, offer development opportunities to raise the skill level of the staff, or introduce new skills to the employees. Investing in its own employees has several advantages from a morale and employee-satisfaction perspective. However, the company must have staff capable of learning.
- **Buy.** If the organization cannot build its own staff, it can look to the market and buy the talent that it needs. This is costly, but it will ensure that the organization has the skills and competencies required for the future. An organization that buys strategically can disadvantage its competitors by securing the top talent.
- **Borrow.** If an organization cannot build its own talent and cannot afford to buy the talent it requires, it can look to borrow talent from other sources. This strategy can include gig workers, contract or temporary workers, freelancers, or part-time workers. This does not build a permanent talent pool for the company, but it can help cultivate the skills required for the business.
- **Bridge.** This final strategy requires creative repositioning of current employees into new positions, or bringing outside workers into the organization in strategic positions that allow the company to take advantage of a critical sector of employees to mentor, teach, and coach the current staff to move the organization to where it needs to be.

ATTRITION

While all of the above strategies require employers to invest in their workforce to allow the company to meet business objectives, **attrition** is one area where employers can reduce or transfer expenditures and mold the workforce toward the target. Companies should analyze their attrition rates and the skill sets of departing employees and determine where they need attrition to increase. Typically, employers seek to reduce turnover and lower attrition rates. However, when organizations need to develop employees with new skills and competencies, it can be beneficial to increase attrition in the skillsets that are not part of the future plan. Attrition can be categorized in one of four ways:

- Voluntary:
  - o Resignation
  - o Retirement
- Involuntary:
  - o Termination
  - o Death

ANALYTICAL STEPS FOR EVALUATING LABOR SUPPLY AND DEMAND

HR practitioners must understand and follow the ever-changing labor market and talent supply, which can be influenced by the state of the economy, competitors, technology, new regulations, and other factors. Strategic **workforce planning** evaluates an organization's ability to sustain future needs so the organization can function accordingly. There are four analytical steps in workforce planning:

1. **Supply model analysis** reviews an organization's current labor supply
2. **Demand model analysis** estimates future business plans and objectives
3. **Gap analysis** compares the variances in the supply and demand models to identify skill surpluses and deficiencies
4. **Solution analysis** focuses on how to tackle gaps in current and future staffing needs through recruiting, training and development, contingent staffing, or outsourcing

SUPPLY ANALYSIS

A **supply analysis** focuses on examining the current workforce and how the organization anticipates the workforce will change over time due to turnover trends or changing business strategies.

The organization begins the supply analysis by defining how the current workforce aligns with the company business strategy, including how the staff is organized and distributed throughout the company. Then, the analysis seeks to forecast changes to the workforce over time due to events like attrition and retirement. Highlights of the analysis should include the impacts of key employee departures.

After analyzing the current data and future trends, the organization examines strategies for preparing for the future. The company may consider changing skill mixes, the current distribution of employees, or the way the workforce is arranged. HR should identify the hard-to-fill positions and the anticipated risks for upcoming departures, then establish recruitment strategies to be proactive in maintaining required staffing.

DEMAND ANALYSIS

A **demand analysis** focuses on understanding the current and future workforce requirements of an organization. In a demand analysis, the organization should be able to articulate how the current workforce requirements align with the business strategies and how the workforce is structured throughout the organization. Key questions are based on examining how many employees are required to deliver services and how many full-time equivalent (FTE) employees are required for the work to be done.

Once the current workforce requirements have been identified, the organization looks to the future to understand what the company anticipates it will require to meet future business needs. If the future trend of the organization changes any of the key requirements, such as the number of FTEs or the workload by service or product, HR must identify what changes need to be made to accommodate where the organization is going.

The organization should examine whether changes to strategies, technology, policies, or regulations will impact the workforce requirement demands and develop a workforce strategy to prepare for anticipated changes.

GAP ANALYSIS

A **gap analysis** requires an organization to collect data on its requirements for workforce skills and capabilities and compare those requirements to the workforce supply that exists in the market. The difference between the two, what the organization needs versus what is available, is the **workforce gap**.

A gap analysis requires the organization to do an in-depth analysis of what competencies and skills are required to execute the business effectively. This analysis should be conducted in line with the corporate strategy and business demands. HR should look at diversity planning strategies and workforce retention programs, such as retirement plans, that could influence the organization's ability to retain employees.

This data should be analyzed in light of the labor market to assess the availability of labor with the required competencies. Positions may be labeled as hard-to-fill if the skill set is in high demand or if the geographic location of the position limits available talent.

Once the gap has been clearly identified, the organization can consider adjusting recruitment and retention strategies to attract and retain the skill sets required.

SOLUTION ANALYSIS

The goal of a **solution analysis** is to incorporate any data, metrics, or conclusions reached in any of the workforce analyses that have been done, and identify interventions, plans, and activities that will proactively prepare the organization to close any workforce gaps and be best positioned to meet the supply and demand changes it anticipates the future will hold.

Key elements of a solution incorporate information from short- and long-term organizational goals, plans to acquire or build the talent required, communication plans for messaging to both management and employees, and establishing metrics to monitor the implementation of the solution.

HR and management must identify what the goals are for the future workforce and develop a plan to accomplish the goals. Changes to management strategies should be incorporated into the solution to ensure that the employees and organizational culture move along in a positive direction. The benefit of workforce planning is that it equips the organization to know what is coming and how to best position itself to embrace the future.

WORKFORCE ANALYSIS

A **workforce analysis** is required in most affirmative action plans. This analysis results in a **workforce profile** that conveys the talent, knowledge, and skills of the current workforce. The first step of a workforce analysis is conducting an examination of the **demographics** in the current workforce. Then, a **gap and risk analysis** can be performed to determine any vulnerability. Anticipated changes to how work is performed and the effects of advances in technology are documented. Finally, future talent needs can be forecasted. Workforce profile data can be obtained voluntarily or through publicly reported statistics and census results. Workforce profiles calculate employee traits such as age, experience level, and average education in the field, as well as status changes such as active, full time, part time, or temporary. These might be reported per department, per salary band, or as a whole.

WORKFORCE PROFILE

A **workforce profile** maps the composition of an organization's workforce. It can be created based on historic and current information, then used to create a forecast of the future. Data gathered every five to ten years can be very helpful in showing progress in diversity and adaptation to changing workforce requirements.

Key elements of a workforce profile include tracking the workforce by:

- Demographics, including race, gender, and disability
- Employee classifications
- Employee grades
- Staffing levels
- Competency levels
- Tenure (with special tracking of key staff)
- Retirement rates (with special tracking of critical skills)
- Performance levels (analyzed by grade, skill, and department)

A workforce profile can be an excellent source of data for management to see the staff holistically. Workforce profiles should be maintained and updated on a regular basis. If the workforce profile and analysis indicate that the workforce is not balanced properly for current work, or not positioned for future work, there are a number of actions that an organization can take proactively to better align itself for the future.

UPSKILLING AND RESKILLING EMPLOYEES

One of the options for re-tooling the current employees to better fit the organization's requirements for future work is to upskill or reskill the existing employees.

Upskilling is an approach that offers employees an opportunity to build knowledge and develop new competencies that relate to their current positions. Employees can be sent to classes, employers can offer in-house group courses, or employees can be paired with employees who are already skilled. After the training, the employee will retain the same position in the same part of the organization but will be better equipped to do the job. An example might be teaching programmers a new programming language to better equip them and the company to code in a new language. The employee will still be a programmer but will be able to meet future demand for a new programming language.

Reskilling is working with employees to have them learn a new skill that will allow them to move to a different position or part of the organization. Employees can be sent to classes, employers can bring in a trainer for a larger group, or employees can be paired with experienced individuals in other departments. An example of reskilling employees is offering a current administrative assistant the opportunity to learn accounts payable. Once done with training, the employee can move from the administrative pool to the accounting department.

Upskilling and reskilling allows a company to recognize and retain current employees but position them to be a better fit for future requirements.

REDESIGNING JOBS

Another approach to retooling the workforce for the future or even to better meet current needs is to **redesign** current jobs to meet demand. There was a lot of redesigning during the COVID-19 pandemic as organizations struggled to adapt to instant changes in workplace environments and employee needs.

Redesigning a job can enhance existing jobs or create new jobs. It requires reimaging how jobs get done. Four key factors to take into consideration are:

- **Organizational strategy.** A new strategy may require new teams or a new structure for the workforce. In turn, those changes may demand new core capabilities.
- **Processes and tasks.** Processes require streamlining to improve productivity or effectiveness. Automation may be a part of the new processes.
- **Technology.** New technology is constantly incorporated into business, and the interface between technology and people often requires redesign of current positions.
- **People.** Creating better jobs and more opportunities for current and future staff can be a large factor in redesigning jobs, including allowing for remote work, and finding ways to add value to job roles and attract new staff.

Reshaping and reimaging jobs should be part of an organization's long-term strategy for staying competitive and attractive to the labor market.

ROBOTICS

While there is a lot of angst that robots will replace people in the workforce, the reality is that there are many ways that **robotics** can complement the existing workforce and better prepare organizations for the future. Some of the ways robotics can enhance a workforce are:

- Robotics can be used to handle dangerous tasks, work in extreme environments, and handle hazardous materials.
- Robotics can allow an organization to work 24/7 to improve productivity on tedious, repetitive work.
- Robotics can enhance human capabilities, such as using drones to see and access locations in a non-invasive manner (e.g., using a drone to monitor the greens on a golf course)
- Robotics can make employees more efficient and effective by using machine learning technology to monitor and improve productivity.
- Robotics can speed up processes far beyond human capability in areas such as computing, machine learning, artificial intelligence, and data processing.

One of the key elements of introducing robotics to a work environment is to provide change management and clear communications so that employees understand the intent and the impact of the changes and are not left on their own to assume and conjecture.

IDENTIFYING HIGH-POTENTIAL EMPLOYEES

As part of any workforce analysis, HR and management must pay special attention to key positions and high-performance and high-potential employees. A **high-potential employee** is an employee who demonstrates the traits and qualities that the organization values. These can be an understanding of the business environment, special customer insight, excellent business values, leadership skills, strong ethics, or outstanding communication skills.

These high-potential employees may not be the top producers, as they may still be learning and working their way up in the organization, but they are clearly aligned with the future direction of the organization and align with the company culture.

HR should have a process whereby they work with management to identify these high-potential employees and involve them in mentoring, succession planning, and retention plans.

IDENTIFYING HIGH-PERFORMANCE EMPLOYEES

As with high-potential employees, **high-performance employees** have all the attributes and skills that the organization values, but high-performance employees have also demonstrated job performance. Four characteristics of high-performance employees are that they:

- Consistently accomplish established goals and frequently seek out additional assignments.
- Constantly work to improve their knowledge and skills.
- Actively seek feedback to improve job performance.
- Adhere to a very high standard of quality work at all times.

High-performance employees are an asset to the organization and should be identified and included in succession planning, promotion opportunities, and retention plans.

HIGH-POTENTIAL DEVELOPMENT PROGRAMS

Firms may offer targeted training and other enrichment opportunities to their best and brightest employees. These **high-potential development programs** should serve as career road maps, cultivating leadership skills and allowing employees to take on meaningful work so that they can see their impact. Some components of this program may include challenging assignments to promote professional growth, opportunities to mentor others, access to on-demand learning modules, and invitations to networking events both within and outside of the firm. To ensure the program's success, participating employees must receive regular and detailed feedback about their performance. Done well, a high-potential development program enables firms to get the best ROI from their staff while keeping them engaged and attracting new waves of high-potential employees for the future.

KNOWLEDGE MANAGEMENT, RETENTION, AND TRANSFER

An organization should make every effort to identify high-performance and high-potential employees to try to ensure that they reward, promote, and retain those employees. However, reality dictates that eventually some of these employees will disclose that they are leaving the organization. When this happens, the company has several options to try to retain employees. If retention fails, the organization has an obligation to work with these employees to transfer their institutional knowledge to others. **Knowledge management** is the process, policy, and procedure

RETENTION

Keeping high-value employees from leaving the organization can be critical to the business goals and objectives. There are several strategies for employee **retention**:

- Provide learning and development opportunities. High-performance employees are constantly seeking to learn new skills. Offering these opportunities can help meet those requirements.
- Seek out whether there are positions within the organization into which the high-performance employees can be promoted.
- Work with the employee to identify their motivators and how the company may be able to support them.
- Respect the employee's work/life balance. Consider accommodations for remote work or flexible schedules.
- Seek opportunities for pairing the high-performers with senior leaders to provide mentoring and build relationships.

TRANSFER

When an organization is at risk of losing a high-performance employee, the first step is to talk to the employee and listen carefully to the employee's ideas, concerns, and thoughts about his or her career and future. There are times when a high-performer is not unhappy with the organization overall but is dissatisfied with his or her current position. Understanding what motivates the employee may offer the organization an opportunity to **transfer** the employee to new position within the company that with both benefit the organization and meet the employee's desires. The new position can be combined with learning and development opportunities to further incentivize the employee to stay with the organization and continue to build his or her own skills and add value to the team.

BENCHMARKING

If retention or transfer fail, the company needs to make every effort to capture and transfer the employee's institutional knowledge to others. A **knowledge management system** can be used to assist in that effort. When organizations set up a knowledge management system for the first time, or realign their system later, **benchmarking** is a highly effective way to ensure that the company is handling knowledge management as effectively as possible. Benchmarking involves performing an initial high-level assessment of the organization's practices in managing information and knowledge, then comparing those practices against those of organizations that are known to be leaders in their operations and knowledge management. Benchmarking is important to help leaders identify gaps between their standards and the best standards. Those gaps can help prioritize the required improvements.

THOUGHT LEADERSHIP

Another approach to knowledge transfer, **thought leadership** is authentic, real information that utilizes the employee's expertise and experience in conversations to help others gain the knowledge that they must share. Thought leaders create relationships, build knowledge within the organization, and create value for the company. Thought leaders provide guidance and wisdom. They inspire innovation and influence others to achieve more.

ORGANIZATIONAL GAP ANALYSIS

When organizations set business goals, it is imperative to ensure that the company has the resources, capabilities, and human capital to achieve those goals. One technique for assessing whether the company can attain its goals is to execute an **organizational gap analysis**. This analysis defines an ideal state, compares it to the current state, and seeks to identify where gaps may lie. The gap analysis may utilize any, or all, of the techniques discussed below.

EXAMINATION OF HUMAN RESOURCES RECORDS

One of the most critical elements of an organizational gap analysis is identifying the skills and capabilities required to execute the business goals. When the ideal state has been identified and human resources (HR) understands what competencies are required, it is then possible to assess the current state of competencies to compare and identify gaps between the current and ideal states.

Reviewing HR records of current employees can give the organization several critical pieces of information:

- **Organization charts** to understand the current structure
- **Performance reviews** to identify high-performers, skill sets, and competencies
- **Job applicants** to assess the available talent pool
- **Exit interviews** to look for consistent themes around why employees leave the organization
- **Policies, procedures, and training programs** to assess whether the administrative structure supports the future direction

INTERVIEWS

Another step in the gap analysis process is to **interview** the current employees. HR should identify the key stakeholders in the organization and seek to solicit input from them to:

- Identify key areas of opportunities for the organization
- Review thoughts on future goals
- Discuss concerns about current staffing and future requirements
- Establish learning and development opportunities
- Identify positions that could use contractors or temporary staff

Questions for each interview should be established beforehand by the interviewer. The questions can be shared in advance to allow the key stakeholder to be better prepared for the conversation. Individual interviews are time consuming and should be targeted at key stakeholders only, but it can be worth the effort to gather vital information. The technique allows for follow-up and clarifying questions to ensure a full understanding of the information.

FOCUS GROUPS

A larger group of employees can be utilized to gather data similar to that discussed in interviews with key stakeholders. These **focus groups** can be organized in several different formats:

- By department: employees in a single department know one another, and thus may be more comfortable speaking out. They also have specialized information about recruiting and learning and development needs for their area of expertise. HR can have a focus group for each department.
- By employee level: HR can bring together managers in a single focus group, or create focus groups of team leaders or line workers. This approach allows for more frank conversation and unique insights from various levels of the organization.
- By topic: HR can organize focus groups based on a specific subject, such as staffing requirements, goal alignment, or learning and development. This will allow for more in-depth discussions on specific areas of concern.

The key to effective focus groups is to understand the objectives of the focus group, make sure the right people are in the room, establish thought-provoking questions in advance of the meeting, and create strong follow-up questions to elicit as much information as possible.

SURVEYS

Interviews and focus groups are excellent ways to gather data and allow for discussion and conversation about issues the organization wishes to understand in more detail. However, they are both time consuming and, therefore, expensive. Another technique for gathering information from a large team of employees is to utilize **surveys**. Gap analysis surveys can include any or all the discussion points above. Surveys can be organized as:

- **Quantitative** surveys, which take one of two formats:
  - **Dichotomous** survey questions have two options such as yes/no or positive/negative
  - **Scale response** survey questions have responses that run on a scale from one extreme to the other, such as five choices from "unsatisfied" to "very satisfied," with choices along a scale between those two ends.
- **Qualitative** survey answers are gathered in an open-ended narrative format that allows the respondent to write their response.
- **Mixed** surveys can ask quantitative questions and then allow the respondent to provide more insight in a narrative form.

Quantitative survey data collection is straightforward and easy to analyze; however, qualitative survey data can offer stronger insights.

EXIT INTERVIEWS

HR departments should execute **exit interviews** with all departing employees. The information gathered from an employee who has decided to depart can be very revealing. Interviewers should not just ask about why the employee is leaving but should also address larger issues about his or her experience while employed. Best practices for exit interviews include:

- Meeting **face-to-face** whenever possible. Remember the Mehrabian formula for communications: 55% of communication is nonverbal. There is a lot to be learned from an employee's demeanor and expressions if the interview takes place live.
- Ensure that the employee understands that the exit interview is an **information-gathering** session to help the employer improve their organization. Provide questions in advance of the meeting if possible.
- Ask the **same questions** for all departing employees. This ensures thoroughness and guards against biases.
- Ensure that the employee understands that he or she is free to decline to answer any uncomfortable questions.
- If any alleged issues of harassment or discrimination are raised, ensure that they are forwarded to the proper leaders for investigation. The organization has an obligation to pursue the investigation even though the employee is departing.

When executing a gap analysis for the organization, reviewing the data gathered from exit interviews is critical to seeking vulnerabilities or weaknesses that could be addressed in the future state of the organization.

DIGITAL SKILLS ASSESSMENTS

While reviewing performance reports in the HR records will help create a foundation for the current skills and performance level of the organization, a **digital skills assessment** will give the organization a much deeper understanding of the literacy level of the organization on such things as digital files, navigating the internet, online security, communication practices, creation of online documentation, and the availability of services, support, and products online.

Digital security is often a key element of annual training requirements and a skills assessment can help identify areas of weakness in understanding the application of organizational policies that govern online work.

NONTRADITIONAL STAFFING METHODS

As traditional staff positions change due to new remote opportunities and work/life balance issues, organizations must also adapt how they recruit and fill positions in their companies. Traditional staff are full-time, onsite, one person/one position, long-term employees who are paid either a salary or by the hour. In the current world, and looking to the future, non-traditional workers are, and will become, a larger percentage of the workforce. Some types of non-traditional workers are discussed below.

GIG WORKERS

Typically independent contractors or freelancers, **gig workers** are those people who are not considered employees of a company. The jobs they fill are considered temporary. As freelancers, gig workers are given a deliverable to submit and can set their own working hours and environment, as long as they deliver per the contract. Most gig workers have multiple clients and are responsible for balancing their commitments. Employers are required to give gig workers clear requirements, deadlines, expectations, and pay provisions.

REMOTE WORKERS

A **remote worker** is typically a traditional employee from a pay and position perspective, but one who does the work from a position that is not in the corporate offices. Remote workers can work from home, from a co-working or shared space, or anywhere else, as long as they have the equipment and materials needed to get the job done. Organizations should establish policies that govern how remote work is done, the equipment to be used, network security, and of course, what the performance expectations will be for the position. Remote workers typically do not have the same flexibility as gig workers in creating their own hours, as they can be required to participate in meetings, video calls, and correspondence during regular company hours.

SEASONAL WORKERS

A **seasonal worker** is a temporary worker who fills a position only during a specific time of the year. These workers fill a need for businesses who either only operate seasonally or increase sales considerably during certain months. These can be anything from farms that reap crops during harvest season, or businesses that pop up kiosks or special stores just for certain holidays. These organizations do not need the same number of staff for the entire year, but just to cover these bursts of activities. Typically, seasonal employees work six months or less in a year.

CONTRACT WORKERS

A **contract worker**, or **contractor**, is an independent worker. Like gig workers, contract workers typically have more autonomy and flexibility than regular employees, and do not receive benefits such as health insurance, retirement plans, and paid time off. Contract workers can save organizations money. However, there are risks and limits to what you can ask and expect of contract workers. Organizations hire contract workers for specific tasks and specific time periods, and contract workers are expected to have all the skills required to do the work when they are hired, unlike regular employees who can expect training and opportunities for growth. Organizations must ensure that contract workers are classified appropriately and always treated as contract workers. Mis-classifying a regular employee as a contract employee to save money and deny benefits can be very costly if the company is challenged and found to have misclassified regular workers as contract workers.

INTERNS

An **internship** is typically a short-term professional training experience offered to students, recent graduates, or inexperienced workers to allow them to learn the field, the specialty, or the organization. Classifications of internships include:

- Paid internships
- Unpaid internships
- Work research or graduate research internships
- Virtual internships

SUCCESSION PLANNING

A company should perform **succession planning** to determine how management and executive vacancies will be filled so that there are has highly trained replacements available to fill vacancies when they occur. First, the requirements for key positions should be determined and profiles that outline the responsibilities of these positions created. The experience, education, career progress, and future career interests of managerial candidates should also be reviewed. Then, the performance of prospective managers should be assessed to determine whether they are promotable and to identify developmental objectives to prepare for advancement opportunities. Performance should be evaluated based on traditional goals and standards. Developmental objectives might include seminars, training programs, special projects, or temporary assignments.

MENTORSHIP

Once an organization identifies the skills that will be required to meet future business objectives, it needs to identify internal talent and make plans to develop those employees to reach the levels that will take the company forward. One of the techniques that may help to achieve that goal is **mentoring**. Mentoring is the proactive development of a career path, the transference of knowledge, and the investment in internal employees. Employees that are mentored are given exposure to senior staff, are engaged in the company, and understand that they are part of the corporate succession plan. Mentored employees develop enhanced leadership skills.

CROSS-TRAINING

Employees identified in the succession plan should be proactively engaged in **cross-training** opportunities that the organization has identified as future required competencies. Cross-training is a very effective tool for investing in employees and the future of the organization. To effectively cross-train an employee, there are eight essential steps:

1. Identify the goals of the succession plan for skill and competency requirements. This should include long- and short-term goals and the expectations that will be required of the employees involved.
2. Instill motivation for the employees to participate in the cross-training opportunities. Employees should understand what the cross-training is designed to do and the benefits it will have for themselves and the organization.
3. Assess and analyze the current skill sets of employees and match them to new training requirements. Employees who are interested and knowledgeable about the new topic will be more engaged and successful.
4. Identify specific job categories that will be involved in the cross-training. Cross-training should be in a related knowledge area or skillset. Asking employees to learn something new that is completely removed from their daily work can be de-motivating or stressful.
5. Ensure that any training the company offers is professional. Experienced trainers and high-quality programs are essential. The company is investing in its employees and the quality of the program offered is a highly visible reflection of that investment.
6. Evaluate the programs that the organization offers. Administer evaluation tests to assess the quality of the programs to ensure that the company is investing adequately.
7. Utilize checklists to track which employees have been invited to cross-train, what they trained in, when they completed training, and how successful they were. This will enable organizations to react quickly to move trained employees into open positions.
8. Seek and record feedback. Employees and management involved in the cross-training should be invited to share thoughts, ideas, and levels of satisfaction with the programs.

9-BOX GRID

The **9-box grid** is a tool used in succession planning or general workforce planning. It is a visual representation of employee performance and potential. The employee's performance and potential are laid out on separate axes to form a grid with nine possible combinations. Management then identifies which box the employee falls into. This technique can be used for the organization to identify high-performers, identify organizational learning and development needs, and inform succession planning

162

APPROACHES TO RESTRUCTURING
RESTRUCTURING DURING MERGERS AND ACQUISITIONS

Human resource (HR) and change management professionals are often called on for consultation during **mergers and acquisitions**. This involvement should start at the beginning of the process and carry through to full integration. HR experts ordinarily investigate factors like employee benefit plans, compensation programs, employment contracts, and organizational culture. Experience and many studies have shown that issues with people and culture are the most frequent cause of failure in most mergers and acquisitions. HR departments must play an active role in these transitions, and there should be a unified purpose and message from each of the previous units. These steps have been established for joining two companies:

1. Develop a workforce integration project plan.
2. Conduct an HR due diligence review.
3. Compare benefits programs.
4. Compare compensation structures.
5. Develop a compensation and benefits strategy for integrating the workforce. Any reduction in pay or benefits must be explained and justified relative to the strategy or economic conditions. It is best to minimize changes and act quickly.
6. Determine leadership assignments.
7. Eliminate redundant functions. The best people should be retained, and the remainder should be laid off, with careful consideration given to avoid adverse impact and Worker Adjustment and Retraining Notification (WARN) Act violations.

RESTRUCTURING THROUGH DOWNSIZING

A firm may need to reduce the number of layers of management to increase efficiency or respond to changes in corporate strategy. This **restructuring through downsizing** can occur via layoffs or early retirement agreements.

CONDUCTING A LAYOFF OR REDUCTION IN FORCE

The following are the steps for conducting a **layoff or reduction in force**:

- Select employees for layoff using seniority, performance, job classification, location, or skill.
- Ensure that selected employees do not represent a protected class, to avoid adverse or disparate impact.
- Review compliance with federal and state WARN Act regulations, which require employers to provide 60 days' notice to affected employees while specifying whether the reduction in force is permanent or for a set amount of time.
- Review compliance with the Older Workers Benefit Protection Act, which provides workers over the age of 40 with an opportunity to review any severance agreements that require their waiver of discrimination claims. The act allows a consideration period of 21 days if only one older worker is being separated, or 45 days when two or more older workers are being separated. The affected workers also must receive a revocation period of seven days after signing the agreement. Additionally, they must be informed of the positions and ages of the other employees affected by the layoffs so that they can assess whether or not they feel age discrimination has taken place.
- Determine if severance packages, including salary continuation, vacation pay, employer-paid Consolidated Omnibus Budget Reconciliation Act (COBRA) insurance premiums, outplacement services, or counseling might be available to affected employees.
- Be empathetic, have tissues, ensure that all required documentation is available, and review all information in detail when conducting meetings with employees.
- Inform the current workforce by communicating sustainability concerns, methods used to determine who has been selected for the reduction in force, and commitment to meeting company goals and objectives to maintain morale and productivity.

RISKS AND ALTERNATIVES TO A LAYOFF OR REDUCTION IN FORCE

It is of utmost importance to remember that it could be considered illegal retaliation to consider any past grievances, complaints, claims, or leave requests in the selection process if a reduction in force is necessary. To ensure fairness and avoid risk exposure, **selection criteria** should include measurable data such as seniority, merit or skill set, full- or part-time status, location, job category, or prior disciplinary actions. Reductions in force are commonly due to financial strains on the organization. Thus, the goal is to reduce human capital costs by a percentage or specified dollar amount. Some measures that can be introduced as an **alternative to a reduction in force** include eliminating overtime, freezing or reducing compensation, reducing work hours, cutting perks, increasing employees' share of benefit costs, and imposing a hiring freeze.

FURLOUGHS

If an organization is restructuring and identified temporary constraints within the organization, **furloughs** can be used to temporarily reduce the size of the company while it completes the restructuring. Furloughed employees are typically put on unpaid leave on a temporary basis. In most cases, they will continue to receive benefits such as healthcare, but an organization can save the cost of salaries while they take the time to address the financial crisis. This reduces the company costs while keeping employees in their jobs.

However, this does not guarantee that employees will be available when the company is ready to bring them back. Unpaid employees will usually seek work elsewhere if they are uncomfortable with the stability of the organization. Therefore, furloughs should be used sparingly.

Employee and Labor Relations

EMPLOYMENT RIGHTS, STANDARDS, AND CONCEPTS

LABOR RIGHTS

Before **labor rights** can be discussed, terminology must be defined clearly, as the understanding and application of legal definitions can drive how decisions are made:

- **Employees** are persons who exchange work for wages.
- **Employers** are the entities that are responsible for the health and welfare of employees.

The relationship between the employer and the employee regarding terms and conditions of employment is defined by the rights of the employee and the employer. Labor rights are driven by the **Fair Labor Standards Act (FLSA)**, which was designed to protect workers against unfair employment practices. The FLSA has three main components:

- Minimum wage and overtime, with qualifications of exempt and non-exempt, which drive eligibility for overtime pay
- Accurate recordkeeping, consisting of hours worked and wages earned and paid
- Youth employment standards, including child labor laws to protect underage employees from harsh or damaging work conditions

Employers are bound to ensure that all applicable laws and regulations are implemented, documented, and adhered to.

THE INTERNATIONAL LABOUR ORGANIZATION

The **International Labour Organization (ILO)** was founded in 1919 to address global working conditions. A part of the United Nations, the ILO is made up of 187 member states. Its mission is to promote decent working conditions, including eliminating child labor, ending unlawful discrimination, protecting human rights, and supporting worker rights to organize. The ILO extensively researches compensation practices and advocates for a living wage for all. A living wage is pay that can cover a decent standard of living for the worker's household. Going a step further, the ILO also pushes for a fair wage, which uses the living wage as the foundation but is adjusted for a given country's pay laws (such as overtime), any collective bargaining involved, and an individual worker's skills and performance. The ILO has also championed the standard eight-hour workday, recognizing that overworked employees can experience negative health and safety outcomes. Although not every country adopts every ILO standard and practice, research from the ILO sets the tone for the discussion and aims to keep advancing working conditions for the world's employees.

THE NATIONAL LABOR RELATIONS BOARD

Unfair labor practices are actions taken by either the union or management that are prohibited by law or **National Labor Relations Board (NLRB)** rulings. Charges of unfair labor practices must be filed with the NLRB within six months of the alleged practice, and can be submitted in person or via mail. Then, a preliminary NLRB investigation will be assigned to a field examiner or attorney through a regional office. After the investigation, a formal complaint may be issued to the general counsel, or the case may be disposed of through withdrawal, settlement, or dismissal. A complaint issued to the general counsel may be either dismissed or moved forward to a formal hearing. After the NLRB issues a decision, dissatisfied parties may appeal; however, this process can be lengthy and take many years.

MINIMUM WAGE, LIVING WAGE, AND FAIR WAGE CONCEPTS

The **minimum wage** is the minimum amount that employers in the United States are required by federal regulation to pay employees; many states have higher minimum wages. The federal minimum wage is currently $7.25/hour. Poverty guidelines indicate that an individual needs to earn $14,580 to be at poverty level, which would be $7.00 per hour for a full-time employee. All employers that have annual gross sales or business of at least $500,000 must pay at least minimum wage, other than some specific categories that have been exempted, including:

- Farm workers and other seasonal workers
- Tipped employees
- Minors and young workers
- Full-time and vocational students
- Employees with disabilities
- Employees of organizations exempt from minimum wage requirements (some colleges, universities, and non-profits)

A **living wage** is the amount an individual needs to be paid to afford a decent standard of living including food and water, basic nonfood items (housing, education, healthcare, transportation, clothing, etc.), and other discretionary expenditures.

A **fair wage** is defined as a wage that is fairly and reasonably commensurate with the value of the services or class of services rendered. Components that can influence a determination of fair pay include:

- The market rate for a particular position
- Employee experience level, skill, and location
- Pay transparency and anti-discrimination laws

Organizations must comply with minimum wage requirements and should consider fair pay requirements when recruiting for positions and candidates.

STANDARD WORKDAY

A **standard workday** is defined as an eight-hour day for a full-time employee who is normally scheduled to work eight or more hours a day, 5 days a week, for a total of 40 hours a week. Standard hours are typically considered to be 9:00 a.m. to 5:00 p.m. A standard workday for employees who are scheduled for less than eight hours a day is defined as the average number of hours per workday in the preceding month.

Standard workdays of 9-to-5 were established in the 1800s through efforts by the National Labor Union to protect workers' rights. With manufacturing jobs predominant at the time, the average worker could be expected to work up to 100 hours a week. In the 1920s, Henry Ford introduced the 40-hour workweek at his Ford Motor Company.

The standard workday has been strongly affected by the adoption of electronic methods of communication that allow for instant access at all times of the day and night, and flexible, remote working options that blur the lines of a standard workday.

COMPLIANCE AND ETHICS PROGRAMS

Companies should design **compliance and ethics programs** to prevent and detect illegal and unethical conduct within an organization. Programs developed for training and development should be designed and implemented by professionals trained in the subject matter. The features below should all be addressed when planning programs for compliance and ethics training.

DESIGN

Programs to address compliance and ethics are more than just training. While training the employees is a critical element, the overall program must be more comprehensive. A strong compliance and ethics program should include the following elements:

- **Written standards of conduct.** The organization must publish standards for employee actions and behaviors. Without these, the company cannot ask its employees to adhere to ethical conduct.

- **Training on the standards of conduct.** Having written standards is good but not enough. The company must actively train employees, and document the training, to ensure that employees know and understand the standards and see the company's commitment to upholding the standards.
- **Company resources for advice on ethics issues.** Most organizations provide hotlines or other methods for employees to anonymously ask sensitive questions or report concerns or issues. These resources should be publicized so that all employees know where to go if they have a concern.
- **A process to report potential violations confidentially or anonymously.** Not only should there be a vehicle for employees to ask for advice or report issues, but there must also be a process by which an employee can appropriately escalate issues. **Whistleblower** programs can guide an employee through specific steps to receive legal whistleblower protections.
- **Performance evaluation requirements for ethical conduct.** If ethics are critical to an organization and an essential component of the culture and behavior, then employees should be evaluated on their commitment to ethical behavior. There should be a measurable goal for ethical conduct on every employee performance evaluation.
- **A system for disciplining violations.** If ethical conduct is evaluated, there must be consequences or ramifications for not meeting the organizational standards.

IMPLEMENTATION

A training plan must be **implemented** to be effective. Training is typically part of a new hire orientation program to ensure that all new hires are fully versed in the standards of conduct, the process and system for reporting issues or concerns, and the ramifications for failing to live up to the company conduct standards. Depending on the size and complexity of the organization, new hire orientation may be done in person or online, but each employee should be required to sign a document to verify that they have received the training.

Training should be repeated on an annual basis to remind employees of the content or update them on changes to the program. Again, dependent on the size and complexity of the organization, this can be done in-person or online, with a record of compliance with the training. The employee should walk away from the training with a full understanding of the company's commitment to compliance and ethics.

REQUIRED POSTERS

The US Department of Labor requires workplaces to post certain information in an area that is open and visible to employees There are both federal and state requirements, and it is the responsibility of the organization to know and comply with the posting requirements. Some of the **required posters** are:

- Job Safety and Health
- Employee Rights and Responsibilities under the Family and Medical Leave Act
- Know Your Rights
- Pay Transparency Nondiscrimination Provision
- Employee Rights Under the Fair Labor Standards Act

MEASURES OF PERFORMANCE

As with training, a compliance program is only as good as its enforcement, which includes **measures of performance**. Measuring performance in compliance is straightforward: organizations must comply with federal, state, and local requirements. These requirements can be itemized and reviewed for compliance. For example, human resources (HR) must post certain workplace posters, and a quick physical review can assess if they have complied.

Ethics is a more difficult area in which to measure performance and rate compliance. One of the most effective ways to do this is to have ethics as a stated goal on performance reviews. There should be a statement that lays out what compliance with the ethics program looks like, and managers should observe and assess compliance. Additionally, HR can provide input if employees have been confidentially coached or counseled about an ethics-related situation. It is critical to keep ethics concerns or complaints against specific employees confidential.

Organizations must have a dedicated department or, at a minimum, compliance and ethics performance officials whose responsibility it is to measure and report compliance.

ALTERNATIVE DISPUTE RESOLUTION
MEDIATION

When two parties, such as a union and company management, cannot resolve a dispute on their own, they may turn to **mediation**. Mediation involves bringing a third party into negotiations to hear both sides, assess the areas of conflict, clarify differences, suggest compromises, and identify similarities for further negotiations. Mediators usually enter a dispute when either the union or management requests their assistance. Mediation tends to receive less criticism and be more successful if it is requested by both parties. It is important to note that mediation is not **binding**. As such, a resolution may not be reached. There are three main styles of mediation:

- **Facilitative mediation** focuses on helping parties find a solution through a series of inquiries.
- **Evaluative mediation** is a formal procedure focused on protecting rights more than the interests of the parties; the mediators are often legal professionals.
- **Transformative mediation** is an attempt to resolve conflicts by validating both parties' worth and feelings.

ARBITRATION

The process of resolving a labor dispute with the assistance of an impartial third party who examines information from both sides and renders a binding decision is called **arbitration**. The parties agree beforehand to accept the decision of the impartial judge, or **arbitrator**. The decisions of arbitrators are generally more informed and unbiased than the decisions that are made by a jury of peers. Arbitration procedures, issues requiring arbitration, how to select an arbitrator, and limitations on the authority of the arbitrator are often described within a labor agreement. Arbitration is generally used more often for settling **grievances** than for settling labor disputes because most employers and labor union leaders will not let an arbitrator bind them to a contract.

After an arbitrator has been selected, an arbitration hearing is held, and a submission agreement statement is prepared to outline issues and grant final authority to the arbitrator. Written testimonies, statements, and affidavits are often prepared by parties prior to the hearing, so hearings rarely last more than a single day. The actual hearing may be formal or informal, and the burden of proof will often fall upon whichever party filed the initial complaint. Arbitrators will provide a written review and final award to both parties within 30 days. Arbitration is seen as a useful tool because it can resolve grievances without the expense of going to court and without the operational disruption of a strike. However, because arbitration is binding, both parties have no right to appeal and will have to live with the outcome.

RETALIATION PREVENTION

Companies should set up processes and policies for employees to bring concerns and issues to management. Compliance and ethics policies may require a formal notification process, and human resources (HR) should also have a process for reporting such issues as harassment, discrimination, hostile workplace environments, and Occupational Safety and Health Administration (OSHA) concerns.

Retaliation is any negative action taken by a company leader or manager against an employee who files a formal complaint. Retaliation can take the form of significant changes to the employee's regular work, changes to normal working conditions, and adverse personnel actions. Whatever the reporting process, it is critical for the company to have a non-retaliation policy in place and published for all employees to see. Strong antiretaliation statements should be part of the company documentation. Some practices that can help prevent retaliation can be found below.

OPEN-DOOR POLICY

One of the most effective ways to help encourage employees to have open, active conversations with their management and organizational leaders is to have an **open-door policy**. This policy encourages employees to bring up issues before they become intractable. It promotes an unintimidating workplace and encourages issues to be worked out quickly and judiciously before they escalate.

An open-door policy does not mean that a manager must drop everything at a moment's notice if an employee shows up at their door. However, the manager should acknowledge the employee's request to talk, and if an immediate conversation is not possible, they should schedule a time in the very near future to sit down with the employee. This follow-up is a critical element of an open-door policy.

OPEN COMMUNICATION

In line with an open-door policy, the most effective tool to prevent retaliation, or other problems in general, is training for managers and supervisors on the value of **open communication**. The skills of listening, hearing with empathy, and understanding the most effective responses are critical to improving communication and allowing employees to express their concerns and issues before they escalate. Once a claim has been filed, the managers and supervisors must continue to have open communication about any other changes to jobs, performance issues, or changes to work conditions to prevent misunderstandings or misconceptions about the actions or why they are occurring. A lack of communication is often the basis of a retaliation claim.

NON-RETALIATION POLICY

A formal **non-retaliation policy** should be part of the organization's policies and procedures. Managers should be fully trained on the policy on a regular basis; yearly training is quite common. Non-retaliation policies should cover all employees who are involved in reporting an issue and any employee who participates in an investigation of reports.

Leadership must be firm that retaliatory actions will not be allowed. The policy gives the company documentation to demonstrate their commitment to non-retaliation.

WHISTLEBLOWER PROTECTION

Several laws protect employees who file complaints about unsafe conditions or other compliance or ethical issues in the workplace. While OSHA protections were initially designed to protect employees who reported safety or health issues, protecting employees who reported their employers for compliance, ethics, and financial issues also became necessary.

The **Sarbanes-Oxley Act of 2002** provided significant protections for **whistleblowers** who report financial concerns, including fraud. The Sarbanes-Oxley Act provides protection for disclosing information that could impact investors. It is illegal to fire, harass, or discriminate against a whistleblower or a potential whistleblower because of his or her complaint. If a manager is aware that an employee is about to report an issue, that manager is prohibited from taking any illegal action against that employee.

DOCUMENTATION

When a whistleblower comes forward, the onus of investigating of the complaint and protecting the whistleblower falls on management and HR. The employee who makes the complaint is not responsible for the investigation, nor should they be involved in it unless they had a specific role in the situation. To ensure that the whistleblower does not become a victim of retaliation, HR must work with the employee's management and leadership to ensure that no adverse action is taken against the employee. The whistleblower's identity must be protected to the best of the organization's ability. Therefore, HR must monitor and **document** any issues that might involve the whistleblower and his or her work responsibilities.

Any action proposed by a manager must be scrutinized and documented. The manager may or may not know about the whistleblower's protection, therefore HR must be very judicious in their review and response. Any legitimate personnel decisions made against the whistleblower must be carefully documented to protect the organization.

TECHNIQUES FOR WORKPLACE INVESTIGATIONS

When an employee files a complaint, or when a manager has concerns about an employee, the human resources (HR) team should take immediate steps to begin an **investigation**, protect the parties involved, and address any conflict. These prompt investigations can help the organization identify internal issues, resolve conflict, and demonstrate its commitment to both the employees and the corporate goals and values.

CONSISTENCY

As soon as an investigation is initiated, a plan must be established to guarantee that all subsequent actions are effective and compliant with the organization's process for investigations. It is critical that the organization have a documented process for investigations to ensure that all steps are taken, properly documented, handled by the correct company representative, and, most critically, are **consistent** for all investigations. Using a **checklist** can be very effective in ensuring consistency. This will allow all investigations to be through and objective. HR should be able to demonstrate objectivity and unbiased actions in all investigations. Modifying the process, skipping steps, or otherwise adapting the process for any individual investigation could lead to complaints of biased behavior, which could taint the investigation.

INTERVIEW PLAN

The investigation interview process should be captured in an **interview plan**. The plan should include:

- **Questions.** Interview questions should be designed in advance of the session. Questions must be relevant to the issue and should be open-ended to elicit information. New questions may arise as new information is gathered during the process. These additional questions should be documented and added to the plan.
- **Confidentiality.** Confidentiality is of utmost importance to protect the rights of the employees involved. Interviewers and interviewees must be assured of confidentiality in the process.
- **Objectivity**. The interviewer must be impartial, gather data objectively, and be careful to not lead the interviewee. Results of the interviews should be captured per the plan and reported back to the lead investigator without the interviewer's opinions or viewpoints.

Creating and documenting a plan creates objectivity. Abiding by the plan adds credibility to the process.

EMPLOYEE MISCONDUCT INVESTIGATIONS

An **employee misconduct investigation** usually begins when a complaint is received or there is other reasonable cause to investigate an employee's conduct. The organization should identify exactly what is being investigated, what sort of evidence is needed to prove or disprove the misconduct, who should be interviewed during the investigation, and which questions need to be asked to gather the necessary evidence. Next, the organization needs to interview the person making the complaint, the individual the complaint is against, and any other employees who may have relevant information. Finally, the organization should come to a decision and take the appropriate action.

WEINGARTEN RIGHTS

In *NLRB v. Weingarten*, the Supreme Court established the right of employees to have **union representation** at investigatory interviews in which the employee must defend conduct or behavior. If an employee believes that discipline or other consequences might follow, he or she has the right to request union representation. However, management does not need to inform an employee of their **Weingarten rights**. It is the employee's own responsibility to know and request representation. When an employee requests representation, management can a) stop questioning until a representative arrives, b) terminate the interview, or c) ask the

employee to voluntarily relinquish his or her rights to representation. The company does need to inform the representative of the subject of the interview, and the representative does have the right to counsel the employee in private and advise him or her on what to say.

SUMMARY REPORT

When the investigation is completed, the investigator should prepare a final **summary report**, including an executive summary to capture the findings. A summary report should identify the following:

- The incident or event, including relevant dates, times, and locations
- The names, titles, and contact information of the employees or outside parties involved, if the investigation extended beyond the company
- The key facts and findings that were deemed credible and relevant to the investigation, with sources identified where appropriate
- Any company policies or procedures that were applicable to the situation
- The conclusions of the lead investigator, with objective language
- The names, titles, and contact information for the corporate leadership who were the final decision-makers on the outcome of the investigation
- If the situation was not resolved, the reasons for the lack of resolution
- Any actions taken by the employer that resolved the situation, held an employee accountable, or otherwise disciplined an employee

Ultimately, any documentation could potentially be referenced in any court proceeding that might occur because of the investigation. Investigators should present their findings in the report in an objective manner.

PROGRESSIVE DISCIPLINARY PROCEDURES AND APPROACHES

Disciplinary procedures often consist of several consequences, including training, correction, evaluation, punishment, and termination. The objective of a disciplinary action is to remedy a problem, with the goal of helping employees achieve success. **Maintaining order** can be accomplished with an appropriate accepted standard of conduct, fair evaluation procedures, and an order of progressively severe consequences for violators. Many organizations have adopted a **series of consequences** that begins with a verbal warning, which is followed by a written warning that future violations may carry penalties up to and including termination. Strong disciplinary systems protect employee rights and preserve the interests of the organization. It is important that employees are provided with enough time and opportunities to correct their behavior if they desire but also rigorous enough to discharge previously warned yet unresponsive and problematic employees.

Choosing the correct vehicle with which to begin progressive disciplinary procedure depends on the severity of the infraction, the employee's existing record of behavior, the longevity of the employee's service, and the established practice within the company for dealing with similar issues. Consistency is very important to avoid claims of discriminatory, retaliatory, or otherwise unfair practices.

CORRECTIVE ACTIONS

While all managers and human resource (HR) employees would love for 100% of their employees to be productive, well-behaved, and happy, the reality is that there will be issues. Effective managers deal with issues promptly, fairly, and consistently. **Corrective actions** are any steps that an organization employs to improve behavior or performance and prevent reoccurrence of poor behavior. Organizations should have documented policies and procedures in place that identify the standard steps of corrective action, while reserving the right to combine or skip steps, if necessary, based on the nature of the infraction. Below are some of the types of corrective actions that an organization may incorporate in its progressive discipline policy.

COUNSELING

Talking to an employee to address a small problem or concern is always a good first approach. This **counseling** can be an informal session before any formal discipline procedures begin. This can often fix small problems right away, without escalating the issue. This gives the employee and the manager or HR representative an opportunity to speak more informally about the situation and can help improve mutual understanding. The manager should clearly inform the employee of the behavior in question and the expected conduct. The consequences of future infractions should be clearly articulated. Counseling is different from a verbal warning in that counseling is appropriate when the infraction is not severe and the behavior can be remediated before it becomes a serious problem. If the informal counseling session does not produce the desired effect, it should be followed by a written letter to clarify the discussion.

VERBAL WARNING

The second stage in a progressive approach to discipline is a **verbal warning**. This can be the first step in the process if the offense is more serious and requires something more official than an informal counseling session. When issuing a verbal warning, the manager must clearly articulate the infraction, the required remedy, and the consequences of failure to comply. A written record of the verbal warning should be maintained but does not need be given to the employee. The manager may need documented proof that the verbal warning occurred if the problem persists. While a conversation can occur in this setting, this should be regarded as more straightforward and direct than a counseling session. The manager should leave no doubt in the employee's mind as to the nature of the offense and the expected behavior going forward.

WRITTEN WARNING

The next step in progressive discipline is a **written warning**. This is appropriate if the situation is escalating or if the first offense was serious enough to warrant going straight to documented discipline. The written warning can be appropriate for a continuation of previously addressed behavior, or if new unacceptable behavior occurs. As with counseling and verbal warnings, the manager should state the offense clearly, articulate the expected remedy, and outline the consequences of repeating the behavior. Dependent on the infraction, it may be necessary to give an employee time to remedy the situation. For example, if the infraction is tardiness because the employee's home day care provider is consistently late, it may take time for the employee to hire a new provider. If this is part of the discussion, management may state that the employee has a pre-determined amount of time to improve the situation and therefore the behavior. However, if the infraction is abuse of others or inappropriate language in the workplace, immediate change may be required. The written warning is documentation that should be placed in the employee's file. Management may require or request that the employee sign a copy of the warning. This can help the employee understand the seriousness of the infraction. A refusal to sign does not alter the memo or the inclusion of the memo in the employee's file. In some circumstances, a manager may choose to issue a second written warning if they see improvement but the behavior is still not at an acceptable level.

PERFORMANCE IMPROVEMENT PLAN

When issues with an employee impact the quality of his or her work or the dynamics of the workplace, and counseling, verbal, or written warnings have not remedied the situation, the manager needs to consider implementing a **performance improvement plan**. Managers can address two issues with performance with a performance improvement plan:

- **Quality of work.** If the employee is failing to achieve the individual goals and objectives in his or her performance plan, this is a quality-of-work issue. Management should work with the employee to ascertain whether the employee has the right training, tools, and support to do the job effectively. If all of these elements have been provided and the employee still fails to achieve, a performance improvement plan may be the next step.

- **Behavioral issues impacting the work environment.** If the employee's behavior is causing workplace issues with team members, management, vendors, or others, management can incorporate these concerns in a performance evaluation, making clear that failure to improve performance may result in a performance improvement plan. As always, management should ensure that negative information in a performance evaluation is not the first time that the employee becomes aware of the issue. Feedback, counseling sessions, and verbal and written warnings should have already taken place.

A performance improvement plan should be viewed as an opportunity to give an employee a chance to succeed. While it is typically part of a progressive discipline system, a well-developed performance improvement plan can facilitate improvement by providing clarity on deficiencies and creating opportunities for the employees to succeed. However, the plan should be carefully crafted and reviewed, as it may also serve as documentation of failure to perform and a step toward termination proceedings.

DEMOTION

Depending on the nature of the concerns, **demotion** is a step that is reserved for situations where other forms of disciplinary action have failed to achieve the desired results. There are two primary reasons to demote an employee:

- **Correct fit.** If an employee's behavior is egregious, demotion does not serve the organization well. The employee should be terminated to protect the company. However, in some situations, an employee may have been moved into a management position or a similarly situated leadership position where he or she simply does not have the skills to do the job well. This can be evident with excellent individual performers who are promoted to leadership positions but fail to rise to the occasion. Demoting an employee back to a non-supervisory position may serve both the organization and the employee well by allowing the employee to succeed in a position he or she is qualified for.
- **Failure to perform.** This type of demotion might be appropriate if a manager has an employee who is not performing at an acceptable level in his or her current position. The manager should first try counseling, training, mentoring, or a performance improvement plan to give the employee an opportunity to succeed. If the employee cannot be successful but has skills that are valuable to the organization and otherwise fits well in the company, a demotion to a position with fewer responsibilities or a skill requirement that better matches the employee may be the right answer.

If handled correctly by the organization and with the employee involved agrees, demotion can benefit the company culture by demonstrating management's commitment to the employees and to the element of fairness.

TERMINATION

Voluntary terminations may be due to a variety of reasons, such as new job opportunity, relocation, or personal obligations. **Involuntary terminations** most often occur as a result of employment problems, such as poor performance, excessive absenteeism, insubordination, or theft. Employers should have controls that require all terminations to be **reviewed** in advance to avoid the risk of legal or contract violations. The review should determine whether there are valid, job-related reasons for the termination. If the termination is due to a particular incident, the review should show that a proper investigation has been performed and documented. Additional documentation should show that the employee was made aware of performance problems and had an opportunity to correct behaviors. Terminations should also be consistent with prior treatment of other employees. Finally, it is imperative to ensure that the employee is not a victim of retaliation or violations of any civil rights.

TECHNIQUES FOR GRIEVANCE AND COMPLAINT RESOLUTION

INVESTIGATION

The goal of an **investigation** in the workplace is to help the organization identify and resolve problems in the company before they become widespread. The data must be collected, analyzed, and disseminated in a non-biased manner, and confidentiality must always be maintained. In cases of **harassment or abuse**, the first action taken must be to provide protection for the alleged victim. This must be done quickly but with careful planning. Moving an employee out of a bad situation should not be viewed as punitive or lead to complaints of retaliation. Actions should be determined in concert with the employee. Seeking legal advice before taking a major action, such as moving an employee to a different location or schedule or placing him or her on leave, is always advised.

Once the alleged victim is in a safe spot, the organization, typically human resources (HR), must take the following steps to complete a thorough investigation and report:

1. Choose an investigator who is unbiased, not associated with either party in question, and skilled at interviewing for investigations.
2. Create an investigation plan that ensures that all elements will be assessed, all participants have been identified, sources of information such as policies have been gathered, and a guide for how the investigation will proceed has been created.
3. Develop interview questions that will get the investigator started, are created to elicit facts, and are open-ended to get as much information as possible. More questions can be added after the investigator has begun, if necessary.
4. Conduct interviews, or have interviews conducted by the chosen investigator. The interviews should be conducted in quick succession to eliminate any talking, gossiping, or interference along the way. The investigator should ask the predetermined questions, take notes, and assess credibility. These interviews should not be treated as interrogations or be demeaning or accusatory in any way. The interviewer should be soliciting facts.
5. Analyze the information received from all of the sources and the interviewer, the policies in question, and any other relevant information. Follow-up interviews may be conducted if additional information is required.
6. Make a decision based on the facts and information gathered. The HR employee leading the investigation may need to document the proposed decision and brief senior executives and the legal department before taking any action.
7. Take action and provide any applicable documentation to the employee and for the official files.
8. Close the investigation with both the accused and the accuser to let them know that the organization took the complaint seriously, investigated it, and took any appropriate actions. Confidentiality should be reiterated at this stage.

APPEAL

While a perfect investigation would hopefully resolve any issues, there is always a chance that one or more involved parties will be unhappy with the results. When a disciplinary action is taken with an employee, he or she should be told at that time, in writing, what the **appeal** process consists of. Employees who wish to appeal decisions made by the organization as a result of a disciplinary action should submit a request in writing within a reasonable time frame, usually 10 days. The appeal should state the reasons for the appeal. HR and the management employee with the authority to uphold, rescind, or modify any decision should hold an informal discussion to discuss the action being appealed. The management employee with decision-making authority should make a final ruling. All decisions should be documented.

GRIEVANCES

A **grievance** is a work-related complaint or formal dispute that is brought to the attention of management. In union environments, grievances usually involve a breach of the labor agreement between the company and the union. In nonunion environments, grievances may encompass any discontent or sense of injustice. **Grievance**

procedures provide an orderly and methodical process for hearing and evaluating employee complaints. They tend to be more developed in union companies than in nonunion companies as a result of labor agreement specifications. These procedures protect employee rights and eliminate the need for strikes or slowdowns every time there is a disagreement.

Disagreements may be unavoidable in situations where the labor contract is open to interpretation because negotiators cannot anticipate all potential conflicts. **Formal grievance procedures** increase upward communication in organizations and make top management decisions more sensitive to employee emotions. The first step to resolving grievances is for a complaint to be submitted to the supervisor or written and submitted to the union steward.

If these parties cannot find a resolution at this point, the complaint may be heard by the superintendent or plant manager and the industrial relations manager. If the union is still unsatisfied, the grievance can be appealed to the next step, which may be arbitration if the company is small. Large corporations may have grievance committees, corporate officers, and/or international union representatives who will meet and hear grievances. However, the final step of an unresolved dispute will be **binding arbitration** by an outside third party, where the opposing parties come to an acceptable agreement.

PREVENTING RETALIATION CLAIMS

To **prevent retaliation**, employees must believe that a) complaints can be easily presented without a lot of hassle, embarrassment, or paperwork; b) complaints will be assessed by a fair and impartial third party; and c) they will not be mistreated or terminated for submitting complaints or pressing for resolution. The final protection is necessary for the success of both union and nonunion **grievance procedures**, although union employees typically have more protections than nonunion employees because their labor agreement is written and enforceable by collective action. However, federal regulations such as the Sarbanes-Oxley Act and Whistleblower Protection Act include safeguards for employees who have witnessed or stumbled on illegal or immoral actions and made the information known to the public. Employers can also follow a number of best practices to avoid retaliation, such as these:

- Treat all complaints seriously and similarly.
- Allow the employee a chance to be heard, investigate the claim, collect evidence or witness statements, and treat all cases as though they might result in arbitration.
- Review the labor agreement carefully, and follow any required procedures.
- Examine all information prior to making a final determination.
- Avoid any unnecessary delays and clearly communicate the outcome.
- Correct the problem if the company is in the wrong.

STRIKES, LOCKOUTS, AND BOYCOTTS

Strikes, lockouts, and boycotts are tools that employees and employers may utilize, if legally allowed, to force changes in wages, benefits, or working conditions. It is important to understand the terminology and differences between the three actions.

A **strike** is an action taken by employees that consists of a refusal to work or creating an obstruction to work in an effort to pressure the organization to resolve a labor dispute with the employees, usually represented by a union. In some situations, a strike may be illegal.

A **lockout** is a management tactic to pressure the union by temporarily shutting down the workplace, refusing to let employees work. A lockout is not a legal economic weapon if its use is intended to discourage union membership. Lockouts may be used for one of two defensive reasons:

- A lockout may be instigated to prevent unusual economic hardship created by slowdowns, destructiveness, or uncertainty about a work stoppage.
- A lockout may occur when employers in a multi-employer bargaining unit see a union trying to use a "successive strikes" strategy against members of the bargaining unit, often starting with the most profitable.

A **boycott** is a group refusal to deal with another group, such as an employer. Employees, through the union, may simply walk away from the bargaining table and refuse to continue to deal with the company representatives in the labor negotiations.

CAUSES OF STRIKES

When normal labor relations negotiations fail, and employees and employers end up at an impasse, employees, through their union representatives, may vote to initiate a strike or boycott to pressure the company into better negotiations. In turn, the company may, if legal, lock employees out of the facility to pressure the union to come back to the bargaining table.

Most negotiations fail over terms regarding wages, working conditions, benefits, schedules, hiring practices, work processes, or disciplinary proceedings. Strikes generally fall into one of two categories: unfair labor practices or economic grievances.

UNFAIR LABOR PRACTICES

One of the elements of labor relations that can lead to strikes is the union making a claim of **unfair labor practices** against an employer. Unfair labor practices are when an employer has violated a labor relations law. There are five categories of unfair labor practices that are prohibited by the National Labor Relations Act (NLRA), which is enforced by the National Labor Relations Board (NLRB). The NLRA prohibits:

- **Refusal to bargain.** The company must enter into labor relations discussions with the union.
- **Discrimination on the basis of labor activity.** Specifically, the company cannot take actions against employees for membership in a union or participation in union activities.
- **Interference, restraint, or coercion.** Employers cannot interfere with employees' participation in union activities.
- **Employer domination or support of a labor union.** The employer cannot interfere with the administration of a labor organization, nor can the employer financially or otherwise support the union.
- **Discriminating in retaliation for an employee contacting the NLRB.** If an employee contacts the NLRB to file a complaint or otherwise communicate concerns, the employer is forbidden to discriminate or retaliate against that employee.

ECONOMIC GRIEVANCES

There are typically four types of grievances raised by employees in the workplace:

- Working conditions
- Pay or benefits disputes, known as economic grievances
- Workload complaints
- Harassment, discrimination, or other treatment-related issues

Economic grievances are issues that relate to financial incentives that employees receive, including wages, overtime, and bonuses. They can also include the policies that drive those programs such as benefits programs, compensation plans, wage fixation and wage revision, and retirement policies.

METHODS FOR PREVENTING AND ADDRESSING STRIKES

There are several positive practices that employers can engage in to attempt to avoid the types of issues that cause employees to want to unionize or strike:

- Establish and implement policies and practices that are fair and consistent.
- Have an open-door management practice so that employees feel welcome to address their concerns before they become issues.
- Implement competitive pay and benefits practices. Employers who consistently pay below market and offer substandard benefits programs are open to continual unrest from the employees.
- Create a working environment that values trust and employee recognition. Not all benefits that a company offers need to be financial. Employee satisfaction can be significantly enhanced by an open and honest environment.

However, sometime, despite all efforts, employees, through their union, demand changes that the company is unable or unwilling to concede and a strike can occur.

STRIKE RESPONSE PLAN

If negotiations fail and a strike is imminent, employers should be prepared to engage properly with the union or employees. The key element to keep in mind is Section 7 of the National Labor Relations Act (NLRA), which protects employees' activities:

> "Employees shall have the right ... to engage in other concerted activities for the purpose of collective bargaining or other mutual aid or protection."

Strikes are included under the protected activities of the NLRA. In addition, Section 13 of the NLRA states:

> "Nothing in this act, except as specifically provided for herein, shall be construed so as either to interfere with or impede or diminish in any way the right to strike, or to affect the limitations or qualification on that right."

However, not all strikes are legal, and it is incumbent upon management to know and understand the basis of the strike (economic grievances or unfair labor practices), and whether the strike is lawful or unlawful under the terms and conditions of employment or the union agreement that may be in place.

If a strike does occur, there are a few items for human resource (HR) professionals to consider in response beyond continuing negotiations:

- **Supply chain issues.** If a strike looks imminent, proactive plans should be put in place to deal with disruptions to ordering, receiving, and running production.
- **Regulatory compliance.** The company is required to have and maintain certain documentation regarding the strike, actions taken, and decisions made.
- **HR planning for staffing.** The company may make a decision to hire temporary workers, or may need to be prepared to protect those workers who choose not to strike. Additionally, HR may reassign management to act as line workers if necessary. HR may want or need to provide safe transportation for temporary workers to get to and from the plant safely.

The key is for HR to be prepared, have a plan, have contingency plans, and ensure all actions are lawful.

HIRING TEMPORARY WORKERS

The company does have a right to **hire temporary workers** to protect the business and continue operations. However, the right of striking workers to retain their jobs depends on the reason for the strike, and any applicable rules or regulations that the company or union might have in place.

If the strike is based on an unfair labor practice, temporary workers must be relieved at the end of the strike, and any union employee who wants to resume work must be allowed to retain the position.

If the strike is due to economic grievances, there are fewer protections for the striking workers. A company is allowed to retain temporary employees, making them permanent, and the striking employees can be put on a recall list. When their original position or an equivalent position becomes vacant, the striking employee can be offered the opportunity to return. HR should identify the most critical positions to fill, and employment agreements with temporary workers must be clear that the position will end when the striking workers return. Care must be taken to ensure that temporary workers are fully qualified for the work that needs to be done, and all safety and health precautions need to be met to keep the workers and company from undue risk.

PROTECTION OF NON-STRIKING EMPLOYEES

If a strike occurs, it may not involve all of an organization's employees. The employees who are members of the affected union will be involved, but management, employees that are not covered by the union, employees who choose to cross the picket line, and temporary workers may still be reporting to work. It is the responsibility of the company to ensure the safety and well-being of these employees. The employees must be protected against physical and emotional damage and harassment to the best of the company's ability.

Companies can provide transportation between the plant and parking lots, escorts after hours, protected areas of the plant for mealtimes, and many other options.

SUPPLY CHAIN CONTINGENCY PLANS

An organization should have **supply chain contingency plans** for all kinds of risks to the supply chain. When a strike seems imminent, organizations should proactively review their supply chain contingency plan. The company's goal during a strike should be to try to maintain as normal a production and delivery schedule as possible, although there will be disruptions to account for.

There are four elements to a supply chain contingency plan:

- **Business impact analysis.** The goal of this analysis is to determine the impact of a supply chain disruption or failure, complete with assumptions, risks, and scope for both internal and external threats.
- **Incident response plan.** This plan should be a set of steps that the organization has identified as appropriate for dealing with a disrupted supply chain. The plan should cover scope; roles and responsibilities; processes for identifying, assessing, and responding to incidents; and procedures for communications both internally and externally.
- **Disaster recovery plan.** This plan should include the names of a disaster recovery team; procedures for identifying disaster risks and assessing the potential impact; documentation of critical applications, resources, and documents necessary for reconstituting the business; and the backup and off-site storage plans for all critical information.
- **Business continuity plan.** This plan should address assessment of impacts, preparedness for all kinds of impacts, the appropriate responses to incidents, and how to recover appropriate materials, information, processes required for business operations.

Technology Management

HUMAN RESOURCE SOFTWARE AND TECHNOLOGY

HUMAN RESOURCE INFORMATION SYSTEMS

A **human resource information system (HRIS)** is a computer system designed to help human resource (HR) professionals carry out the day-to-day HR functions necessary for an organization to continue functioning normally. Most HRIS are designed to collect and store data related to the use of employee benefits, hiring, placement, employee training and evaluations, payroll, and information about the work performed by the employee during a given period of time. An HRIS is designed to help an HR professional carry out all primary functions associated with HR needs, which include benefits administration, payroll, time and labor management, and HR management. An HRIS not only aids the HR department, it also helps the entire organization function effectively.

APPLICANT TRACKING SYSTEMS

An **applicant tracking system (ATS)** can be particularly useful for organizations that perform high-volume recruiting on a consistent basis, but they can be valuable to businesses of all sizes. Despite the initial cost, most medium to large businesses use an ATS due to the time it can save by scanning thousands of resumes or automating new-hire paperwork. New, cloud-based systems may integrate with social media or popular job boards and receive automatic updates that eliminate the need for pricy servers and onsite specialists. Additionally, an ATS is a positive first impression for applicants because it can make the process easier and save time on their end.

In addition, an ATS can allow you to do the following:

- Brand your company with a career page
- Modify or set up standard templates
- Save forms for compliance or reporting
- Push employee information to a payroll or HR module
- Collect data and metrics for reporting and strategic review

> **Review Video: Applicant Tracking System**
> Visit mometrix.com/academy and enter code: 532324

PERFORMANCE MANAGEMENT SYSTEMS

Just as a learning management system can deliver, monitor, and track learning and development content, a **performance management system (PMS)** is a software system that can track and monitor employee performance in a consistent and measurable way. A PMS allows collaboration between the employee and the supervisor or manager to identify expectations, set goals, recognize achievement, provide regular feedback, and discuss performance reviews. A PMS allows clear expectations to be established and communicated across the workforce while emphasizing individual accountability for meeting goals and objectives. PMSs can be administered in-house, through a cloud-based provider, or a hybrid of the two. It is important that a well-developed and properly implemented PMS includes information about previous performance (achievements, reviews, and discipline), a way to provide feedback, a score or rating for performance, and a way to detail future development plans for the employee. Performance should be both tracked and reviewed on a consistent and ongoing basis.

BIG DATA ANALYTICS SOFTWARE

Companies can use **big data analytics software** to examine and analyze large data sets to reveal information such as correlations, customer preferences, and various market trends. This is used to help make data-driven decisions in areas such as marketing campaigns, increased operational efficiencies, and increased personalization for individual customers.

In HR, big data analytics software is more often used to analyze people. Big data analytics can be used to refine the hiring process, helping an organization avoid making bad hires. Big data analytics can also be used to examine and map out retention and potential turnover. Big data analytics software can determine the efficacy of current training programs, and identify areas where improvements can be made. Big data analytics software can include programs such as Microsoft Excel for forecasting, and projections can be made using existing data. Big data analytics can also be compiled using various HRIS, as many offer numerous types of data analysis. Big data analytics software, when implemented and utilized correctly, can save the organization time, resources, and efficiency throughout any department or opening.

COLLABORATION SOFTWARE

The design and intent of **collaboration software** is to provide a central location where employees can share data, documents, and files; work on projects; share knowledge; and complete tasks together. Collaboration software allows users in various locations to work on the same project, page, or document at the same time. This particular type of software is especially helpful for organizations that have employees in different locations or employees who work remotely. Productivity is increased because the content can be accessed anywhere at any time. One person does not need to save and close the software for their work to be recorded and allow others to open it and add content. Collaboration software also includes internal messaging channels, audio and video calling, and presentation or screensharing aids. With collaboration software, information can flow openly from one employee to another and from one work site to another, eliminating siloed communication.

BLOCKCHAIN

A **blockchain** is a type of technology or software that allows information to be shared securely. Information is stored on a type of database called a **digital ledger**, and is transferred transparently and securely. Blockchain technology relies on decentralized computer networks to store, verify, and transmit data. Every transaction is forever recorded and linked to all other transactions before and after, creating an unbreakable chain. In HR, a blockchain database could be used for payroll processing, increasing efficiency and security. Blockchain technology could also be used to verify employment data, track performance, or even automate hiring and onboarding processes. Blockchain technology can also be used to create "smart" contracts, or contracts that automatically release payment after completion of certain tasks or time periods. Blockchain technology is still relatively new, so the full range of its uses in HR are still largely undiscovered.

ARTIFICIAL INTELLIGENCE

In addition to its important role in learning and development, **artificial intelligence (AI)** can be used in customer service and help lines: AI can be programmed to answer initial inquiries and then direct and escalate questions to the appropriate parties. This technology can be highly beneficial for an organization.

MACHINE LEARNING

A branch of AI, **machine learning** allows systems to improve based on experience even without being programmed to do so. The machine can "learn" and behave in a more human-like manner. Data and information are input and then algorithms are used to help create training models for the data. The better the data, the more efficient the learning. There are three main categories of machine learning: supervised, unsupervised, and reinforcement. In **supervised machine learning**, training models are labeled with data sets, which allows the learning to become more accurate over time. This is the most common type. In **unsupervised machine learning**, training models are not labeled, and the machine will learn to identify patterns or trends that were not explicitly stated. **Reinforcement machine learning** uses trial and error to determine what actions should be taken.

Machine learning can be used by businesses to tailor product recommendations or suggestions to clients or for AI helplines such as chatbots. Machine learning can also be used to help detect fraud by identifying suspicious transactions or attempts to log in. As this technology continues to evolve, it will become more evident in numerous aspects of business.

DATA AND INFORMATION MANAGEMENT

DATA INTEGRITY

Maintaining and protecting data content to ensure that it is complete, accurate, and reliable is vitally important. The design, implementation, and usage throughout the **data life cycle** is critical to any system that stores or processes data. Individual users, management, culture, training, controls, and audits can all affect **data integrity**. Poor configuration and inaccurate data entry can corrupt data. Therefore, thorough testing and safeguarding of data is required to avoid spending many hours debugging and reconciling information. Moreover, policies and training on what to do in the event of a breach can help mitigate risk by increasing staff awareness and ability to fight off breaches.

CONFIDENTIALITY DISCLOSURES

It is important to ensure that only the proper individuals have access to the information needed to perform their jobs. **Confidentiality disclosures** are used to keep private or secure information available only to those who are authorized to access it. Confidentiality disclosures should include definitions and exclusions of confidential information while outlining individual responsibilities. Moreover, legislation mandates **due diligence** to protect confidential employee and customer information. **Technology breaches** in confidentiality could happen via phone, fax, computer, email, and electronic records. For this reason, some businesses might utilize encryption software, limit the communications that can be sent via email, and include a statement to inform users about what to do if their information is inadvertently sent to the wrong person.

IMPORTANCE OF INFORMATION TECHNOLOGY SECURITY

As the world becomes more and more reliant on technology, **information technology (IT) security** is rapidly gaining more attention. It is important for HR practitioners to be conscientious of controls to mitigate organizational exposure and risk. Some companies may have IT security policies and acknowledgements in place to reduce liability and to identify and document compliance and security controls. Multiple layers of corporate IT security might include data file encryption, firewalls, access controls or logins, systems monitoring, detection processes, antivirus software, cyber insurance, and more. Implementing stronger IT security can provide companies with benefits such as mitigating lost revenue, protecting brand reputation, and supporting mobilization.

BACKUPS

Computer failures and malfunctions happen occasionally and, from a business perspective, such a malfunction could be incredibly damaging as it could lead to a complete loss of data. Having **backups**, which are digital or physical copies of files/databases saved to alternate locations, can prevent the data from being lost. Many organizations have routine backups for all information stored on a server. If an individual accidentally deletes an important file or experiences a malfunction, the backup can be restored and the data recovered. Similarly, if there is corruption or a defect on the company server, previous backups can prevent a complete information loss. Backups can save an organization money and a considerable amount of time and should be updated frequently.

CLOUD-BASED SOFTWARE

Any application, program, or software that is managed, stored, or available online is known as **cloud-based software**. Accessing the cloud requires an internet connection. This kind of software relies on data centers that have large servers that store data and make that data available online. There is usually one main server that is linked to additional storage servers. Individuals or organizations can access their data from anywhere at any time simply by signing in. The host of the cloud service also provides data security, so there is reduced fear of data loss or corruption. The amount of space available on the cloud server can be adjusted as needed, so if the organization is growing it can purchase additional cloud space, which can help to eliminate slow access during high-use times. Cloud systems can be public, private, or a combination of the two, depending on the requirements of the business. Cloud-based software provides a great opportunity for organizations, and there

are numerous providers for this particular service. This allows the organization to select the option that best meets its needs.

CYBERSECURITY

One downside of storing information digitally, whether onsite or in the cloud, is the risk of malicious digital attacks. **Cybersecurity** is the act of protecting devices, data, programs, systems, and networks from these attacks. Poor cybersecurity can lead to information leaks, unauthorized file changes, and individuals impersonating other individuals or organizations to attack or gain information from others for fraudulent purposes. To maintain proper cybersecurity, software should be kept up-to-date, passwords should be strong and contain a combination of letters, numbers, and symbols. Antivirus software should be installed and kept up-to-date. Installing a strong firewall is another good way to boost cybersecurity. Multi-factor authentication can be utilized to improve security, particularly if there are individuals who access the network remotely. The organization should have a cybersecurity policy, and employees should receive training on it as well as how to spot phishing or scam attempts via email.

DATA RETENTION

Businesses need to hold on to data for many reasons. **Data retention** is the act of recording, storing, and managing data. Data retention can assist with financial record maintenance and ensure compliance with laws, regulations, and other requirements. Stored data can also be used to help a business with analytics and forecasting as well as other information it needs to operate. Many organizations have detailed data retention policies that list what kind of data needs to be retained, where it is to be stored, and how long it needs to be maintained. Some data may be physically stored offsite by a third-party vendor. Other information can be stored onsite. It is becoming more common to have data retained digitally on a company server or a cloud-based network. Having a thorough data retention plan can help ensure that data and other information are secure and also ensures that records necessary for auditing, litigation, compliance, or review are available as needed.

ELECTRONIC SELF-SERVICE FOR HUMAN RESOURCE AND PEOPLE MANAGEMENT FUNCTIONS
EMPLOYEE SELF-SERVICE

Many human resource information systems (HRIS) and payroll software systems now provide employees with an **employee self-service module** that allows employees to create a login and review or edit their personal information. These modules give employees access to pay statements and might provide them with ways to update their addresses, phone numbers, bank information, and tax withholdings; enroll in benefits; or request time off. These systems ease the burden and workload of payroll professionals by reducing the volume of administrative requests and data entry that needs to be processed on a regular basis. If the software comes with a welcome portal, this also gives human resource (HR) professionals a place to streamline communications, build cultural branding, and post employee handbooks or benefit summaries.

SCHEDULING TIME OFF

Self-service portals allow employees to go in and request **time off** or enter sick, vacation, or other paid time off (PTO) hours or days. The employee can see his or her time off balance displayed and can request time off according to company policy. Typically, such time off is then approved by a supervisor or manager based on the needs of the business. Some organizations have requirements for when employees are required to enter time off. For example, a business may request that employees put in time off requests for the entire year in the first quarter, or require employees to take a specific amount of consecutive time off for auditing purposes, and the employees are able to enter these requests as required.

TIMEKEEPING

With changes and advancements in technology, employees who are required to "clock in" now have a variety of ways to do so. **Timekeeping** systems have options for remote clocking in, so it can be done from home or wherever the workstation is located. Other timekeeping systems have physical stations where employees can clock in using a badge, code, or biometric scanning option. Employees are responsible for accurately recording their time. When there are timekeeping issues, those should be reported to the lead or supervisor for verification purposes. Organizations also should create policies around falsification of timekeeping records for compliance and legal purposes. For example, in most cases, employees are prohibited from clocking in or out for anyone other than themselves. Written policies and procedures should be established so that there is no ambiguity about timekeeping expectations and requirements.

CONTACT INFORMATION UPDATES

Many organizations have adopted policies that require employees to be responsible for maintaining updated **contact information** in the company's HRIS. Employees are required to use self-service to update mailing addresses, phone numbers, preferred methods of contact, and name/dependent changes. With name or dependent changes, additional information may be requested for benefit-reporting purposes. Employees can also be required to update information regarding direct deposit or W2 delivery information. Again, some employers may require a form of verification for direct deposit changes to ensure that payroll is not disrupted.

BENEFITS ENROLLMENT

Numerous HRIS have options for self-service **benefits enrollment** during the **open enrollment period** or after a **qualifying event**. Employees can sign in to the HRIS and select benefits plans, enter information for any qualified dependents, and make any applicable changes or updates. Certain benefits providers require proof of a qualifying event, so employees should be informed when that is necessary. Additionally, some organizations may require employees to inform HR when any benefits changes are made, to ensure that the changes are accurately reflected in all appropriate systems because not all software is connected. For example, a change in a benefits portal may not automatically feed over to payroll deduction. A clear flow of communication is required to ensure that the employer and employee are both paying the correct amount for the correct benefits.

TECHNOLOGY USE POLICIES

Human resources should ensure that employees sign off on **technology use policies** when they are hired and as the policies change over time. These policies help to maintain productivity and minimize risk. At a minimum, they should include the following:

- The company reserves the right to monitor what employees are doing on the company network or while using information technology (IT) equipment owned by the company.
- The company network and IT equipment are intended primarily for business use. Minimal personal use is allowable.
- While using the company's network or IT equipment, employees must not create, access, view, download, or send any content that is illegal or vulgar, constitutes discrimination or harassment, or is otherwise inappropriate. Employees must also refrain from spamming others even when the subject matter may be permissible.
- Employees are expected to refrain from excessive personal cell phone use while at work. If employees are issued a company phone, they must use it for business reasons, protect it from damage or theft, and be ready to return it when they leave the company or upon request. Using a cell phone while driving on company time is prohibited. Employees must pull over or use a hands-free device.
- Employees may use their own personal devices for work with prior approval from management and the IT department. The IT department will install antivirus and other software designed to keep company information safe. Employees must refrain from backing up company data to the cloud other than the company server or accessing unsecure websites. Even though the employee owns the device, the company still reserves the right to monitor activity while on the company network.
- Employees should not use any device to record the goings-on of the company unless they have clear permission to do so.
- If employees violate the policy, they may be subject to disciplinary action up to and including termination.

BRING-YOUR-OWN-DEVICE POLICY

With a **bring-your-own-device policy**, an organization makes a determination to either require or allow an employee to use a personal technology device for activities related to work. Such technology devices can include work email or other productivity apps on personal phones, or the use of personal laptops, tablets, or computers for work activities and tasks. The policy should detail what security measures will be in place prior to using personal devices, such as tokens, remote-in processes, or two-factor authentication. Expectations for antivirus software, internet speed, and malware protection should also be stated. Acceptable use for personal technology should be included in the policy. All individuals using such devices should be familiar with the policy and acknowledge their consent to abide by the terms listed in the policy prior to any work-related use. A bring-your-own-device policy comes with benefits and risks, which the company and the employee should both understand before implementing or using such a policy.

OFFSITE NETWORK ACCESS POLICY

An **offsite network access policy**, or a remote work policy, is a policy that details the guidelines for connection to a company's network from any location outside of the office. Such policies are important as they help create guidelines and safeguards for corporate networks and data. IT and management should work together to create the policy, which should state user expectations, how to establish a secure connection, what actions constitute violations, how violations will be addressed, and how the organization will provide cybersecurity for offsite network use. The policy should be reviewed regularly to ensure that it is up-to-date and accurate. All employees should be trained in the offsite network access policy and cybersecurity on an ongoing, frequent basis.

INTERNET BROWSING

Internet use policies or acceptable use policies will often cover browsing the internet. Many organizations have restricted access to various websites, such as social media platforms, on work devices. There are several reasons an organization would discourage employees from freely visiting any website. First, allowing free use of **internet browsing** may decrease productivity because the employee is not focused on a work task. Second, many websites can have dangerous cookies or malware that can put the organization's network at risk. An employee policy that clearly states what website activity is permissible is important for data security purposes.

COMPUTERS FOR PERSONAL ACTIVITY

Determining the use of company computers for **personal activity** is a decision that varies by organization, and one that requires thought. A policy that defines acceptable use should be created, then applied equitably and consistently for all employees. For example, accessing non-work-related websites on company time causes a drop in productivity while also opening the network to potential viruses and threats. An organization can therefore strictly prohibit employees from visiting sites that are not work-related and can even set up blocks to prevent such access. On the other hand, an organization may decide that it is acceptable for an employee attending school to work on classwork during breaks and lunches. The level of access can vary, but the policy must be applied fairly and consistently across all levels of the organization in order to make it fair and enforceable.

INTERNET MESSAGING

Policies regarding **internet messaging** may vary from one organization to the next. The policy should cover both the technology owned by the organization and the technology used in the workplace. Some organizations have a high level of security, confidentiality, and sensitive information, and thus require a more stringent policy. The policy should also address what types of communication are permissible and when they can be used. For example, an employee may be prohibited from using a messaging app on his or her phone during working hours, but allowed to use such an app while on break or at lunch. There are three main types of internet messaging policies: a ban on all messaging apps, restricted use of only approved messaging apps, and incorporating software that monitors and stores information in messaging apps. The policy should detail what acceptable communication looks like as well as the consequences for communications deemed to violate the guidelines.

CORPORATE AND PERSONAL E-MAIL

Rules surrounding **corporate email** can differ from workplace to workplace. Most rules will serve to protect the company brand and help reduce the chance of data breaches or leaks. Policies surrounding corporate email should make it clear that business emails are meant for business use. Personal business should not be conducted using corporate email. Additionally, employees should understand that company email is the property of the company. Any email that is created, sent, received, or hosted in the organization's network can be viewed at any time. The policy should also establish guidelines for what use of **personal email** is permissible on company equipment, if any.

PROCUREMENT OF TECHNOLOGY

Human resources must ensure that management and staff follow the proper policies and procedures for **procuring new technology**. The IT department and senior leadership should establish policies and procedures that discuss technology upgrade timelines, budgets, potential compatibility issues with existing systems, potential risks for adopting new technologies, and other related topics. The IT department must be consulted prior to downloading new software to ensure that there are no viruses, malware, or other risks associated with it.

SOCIAL MEDIA MANAGEMENT
INTERNAL SOCIAL MEDIA PLATFORMS

Some companies find that **internal social media platforms** can be excellent tools for increasing engagement and communication among employees across an organization. Many platforms come with team or group messaging, collaboration tools, and project management tools. Creating a policy that outlines the boundaries and rules for internal social media platforms is a good way to protect the organization. Communication that is offensive or constitutes harassment should be explicitly prohibited, to prevent a toxic or adverse working environment. Guidelines about what kind of information can be shared over the platform should also be clear, so as to protect proprietary or brand information from leaking or being hacked. Employees also need to be informed about possible repercussions for inappropriate or unacceptable behavior on the platform.

SOCIAL MEDIA POLICIES

Many companies have a technology and **social media policy** to protect employers from the potential risks and litigation that may arise if an employee accidentally discloses confidential information or says something negative while online. Employees who actively use social media at work may fall victim to phishing scams or threaten system security and open the network to potential hackers. Employers are at even more risk if an employee solicits or distributes offensive material, uses social media as a platform to write negative remarks about the organization, or even shares proprietary information. However, the National Labor Relations Board (NLRB) has played an influential role in how social media law is developed and often protects employees who make comments about working conditions. Organizations should include human resources, legal or public affairs, and marketing when developing a social media policy. These policies should identify corporate leaders who are responsible for social media communications and explain how improper posts will be handled.

BRANDING

Social media **branding** is a great marketing tool that can be used to engage, entice, and expand an organization's target market and demographic. With this practice, social media promotion and marketing are used together to establish a consistent message and experience across various platforms. Successful branding sets an organization apart from its competitors on any given platform. Regular posting and interaction will increase hits and results. The brand is the lifeblood of the organization, so clear instructions and policies should be established regarding what content is posted, how audience engagement occurs, and what partnerships can be established. Choosing to partner with an individual or organization with a questionable reputation can damage the organization, so due diligence should be completed before such a thing occurs.

Chapter Quiz

Ready to see how well you retained what you just read? Scan the QR code to go directly to the chapter quiz interface for this study guide. If you're using a computer, simply visit the bonus page at **mometrix.com/bonus948/shrmcp** and click the Chapter Quizzes link.

Human Resources Expertise: Workplace

Managing a Global Workforce

HUMAN RESOURCE STRUCTURES THAT SUPPORT GLOBAL WORK

There are three **human resource (HR) structures** that work effectively for a global workforce. Multinational organizations can have an HR structure that is:

- **Centralized.** All administration and administrative decisions are made in a single location. Policies and procedures are designed to manage effectively across all geographic locations. There are tremendous benefits to having a consistent, single approach to HR management.
- **Decentralized.** This design allows HR professionals to make decisions within their own local areas. Each geographic location may have its own policies and procedures. The benefits to this approach are that it takes into consideration local laws and customs and allows the organization to tailor to the geographic area.
- **Hybrid.** This design delegates HR management to the local offices, but still has a corporate staff that can be relied upon for support and guidance.

Whichever structure that is chosen must be clearly communicated and documented so that the entire team understands the approach and knows who is responsible for decision-making.

IMMIGRATION AND MOBILITY SPECIALISTS

In a global organization, employees are always moving around the world. An **immigration and mobility specialist** is an individual or team who are experts on topics such as immigration, taxation, and local HR laws and regulations. Specialists manage long- and short-term assignments and collaborate with local vendors to ensure timely, cost efficient, and outstanding customer service for individuals moving into or out of a region.

Mobility specialists serve as a single point of contact for the employee, the employee's family, corporate HR, and the local vendors to ensure that moves are orchestrated and carried out with minimal issues.

Immigration specialists can serve as the go-between for employees and immigration officials to guarantee compliance with all regulations and laws and to keep ahead of issues or concerns.

GEOGRAPHIC CENTERS OF EXCELLENCE

An HR **Center of Excellence (CoE)** is a group of HR functions focused on developing best practices and capabilities to ensure alignment with organizational goals and priorities. Groups of functions can include such activities as learning and development, talent acquisition, HR data analysis, and compensation. The CoEs are staffed with experts in their respective fields, who work in partnership with corporate HR to create knowledge and expertise for guidance and for developing policies and procedures in their area of specialty.

Geographic CoEs are organized by regions of the world. Compensation and other HR functions may require different policies in Asia than in the United States. It is the responsibility of the members of the CoE to know and understand the regional requirements and regulations and to ensure that policy and procedure align not only with the organizational priorities but are in compliance with local rules.

GLOBAL JOB CLASSIFICATIONS

A **job classification structure** is a system that includes jobs, job families, pay structure, pay grades, and salary ranges. Classification systems help organizations to determine and document the jobs that are required to meet the goals of the organization. The job classification system helps to differentiate between job types.

The **International Standard for Classification of Occupations (ISCO)** falls under the responsibility of the International Labour Organization. The ISCO defines sets of groups of positions based on tasks and responsibilities that the individual is responsible for.

The benefits of using a **global job classification system** include consistency and clarity across parts of an organization and across geographic areas. It makes internal employee movement smoother and provides stability for the development of programs such as training, pay, and promotion. A global job classification system also helps management compile relevant statistics on performance because the organization can be confident that the same job title across the company has the same definition for execution.

INTERNATIONAL BUSINESS TRAVEL POLICIES

A set of **international business travel policies** provides a framework for who, what, where, when, and why employees are allowed to travel and to be reimbursed for that travel. International travel policies should cover such items as:

- Airfare, lodging, and other transportation (e.g., rental cars, taxis, or Uber)
- Allowable spending for meals, entertainment, and incidentals
- Security of persons and corporate material
- Appropriate approval processes required before or during travel should emergencies arise
- How expenses that arise during travel should be handled
- Rules regarding gifts that may be received or given to other parties involved in the travel

The goal of all policies is transparency, to ensure that the employee knows exactly what is expected of them. A global travel policy that provides that clarity and deals with any specific issues in particular areas of the world is strongly advised.

IMMIGRATION AND MOBILITY
LAWS

The **laws** that regulate immigration and the movement of employees across countries and continents are complex and fluid. Human resources (HR) may write policies and procedures on how these issues will be handled internally, but legal experts must be utilized to ensure full and ongoing compliance with all applicable laws and regulations.

In the United States, the **Immigration and Nationality Act** prohibits employers from discrimination based on national origin for activities such as hiring, terminating, or recruiting. Employers are responsible for verifying the identity and employment eligibility of all employees.

The **Immigration Reform and Control Act of 1986** established criminal penalties for knowingly hiring or recruiting unauthorized immigrants. It also established penalties for individuals using fraudulent work documents.

Mobility laws regulate the impact of employees who live and work in different locations, remotely, or virtually. Organizations need to be cognizant of the implications of worker mobility on workplace accommodations, tax implications, and potential discrimination.

VISA PROCESSES AND REQUIREMENTS

There are two main categories of **visas** that can be required to live and work in the United States.

Temporary Nonimmigrant Visas are established for people seeking employment in the United States for a fixed period. There are several types of non-immigrant visas, including H-1B, H-2A, and H-3, and specialized visas known as I, L, O, P, R, or TN NAFTA visas. Under each category, both the employer and the employee have certain obligations and requirements to meet the program specifications.

There are a limited number of employment-based Green Card visas that made available each year to **Permanent Immigrant Workers** in the United States. A majority of these visas require an offer of employment from an employer that has appropriate certifications with the US Department of Labor. There are five types of employment-based visas, EB -1 through EB -5, which cover workers with extraordinary skills, professionals with advanced degrees whose employment is in the national interest of the US, professionals with bachelor's degrees, and skilled and unskilled laborers with an offer of employment. In addition, these visas may be granted to certain categories of workers, such as religious workers, employees of US Foreign Service posts, retired international organization employees, and noncitizen minor children who are wards of the courts in the US.

In addition to understanding the rules and restrictions for working visas for foreign workers in the United States, a global corporation must know and understand the rules and regulations of any other country that it operates in to ensure full compliance.

SPONSORSHIP EXPENSES

It is not inexpensive or easy to **sponsor** a work visa in the United States. The requirements are strict and there are significant **expenses** involved. For a US employer to sponsor an individual, it must produce a written job offer and contract to the candidate and may be required to obtain a Department of Labor certification.

Expenses can run the employer anywhere from $4,000 to $9,000, which is dependent on the size of the employer because some of the fees are based on the number of employees and percentage of employees who are foreign nationals. The fees include attorney fees and filing fees. The employer must also demonstrate an ability to pay the employee's salary for a "reasonable amount of time."

BEST PRACTICES FOR INTERNATIONAL ASSIGNMENTS

In a global company, American employees may be assigned to work in another country for some period of time. Many of these **international assignments** end in failure. In addition, they can be both costly and difficult to manage. There is a plethora of factors that influence the success of an international assignment. Several critical considerations must be carefully planned to minimize risk. These include selecting people who fit both the culture and assignment, arranging their travel and transition, assisting their families with the transition, evaluating their performance remotely, and repatriating them after the assignment. Human resources (HR) should examine each step of the process, and be diligent to encourage open, inclusive communication throughout the assignment. If a employee's loved ones have a difficult time adjusting, he or she could decide to return early, resulting in an incomplete assignment. Therefore, it is important to also think about spouses or children who may be relocating as well. Organizations that have many employees involved in international assignments may choose to **outsource** global expertise and administrative responsibilities such as employment law, payroll, or taxes.

PERFORMANCE EXPECTATIONS AND EVALUATIONS

A majority of international assignments are temporary, typically only a few years. It is therefore critical to ensure that the goals and expectations for international employees are clearly identified and that performance is evaluated on a regular basis. The goal of an international performance plan is to clearly define performance expectations. Expectations should follow the **SMART guidelines**: goals should be **Specific**, **Measurable**, **Achievable**, **Realistic**, and **Time-bound**. Before job performance begins, the method of performance assessment should be established and documented.

Over the course of the performance period, international employees must be encouraged, barriers to success must be removed, and care must be exercised for the employee's physical living and work spaces during the assignment.

While domestic performance management can be very structured and consistent, international agreements are most effective when they are personalized and unique to the person and position. Some elements to consider are:

- Cultural adaptation to the environment
- Environmental concerns
- Time zones and geographic distance from the home office
- Economic considerations in the country of performance

Performance evaluation for international employees requires proactive, forward-leaning action from the corporate team.

ASSESSING EMPLOYEE AND FAMILY READINESS

Ensuring that an employee is mentally prepared and professionally ready to take on an international assignment is critical to success. There is work to be done by both the company and the employee in assessing whether the employee and his or her family are ready for the assignment. While finding an employee with the right skill set is important, many times skills alone are not enough for an employee to be successful in a foreign environment.

Corporate assessment. The company needs to consider some of the following elements when assessing candidates for international work:

- Technical expertise in area of concern
- Motivation level
- Flexibility
- Ability to handle uncertainty
- Sense of humor
- Level of emotional intelligence
- Level of familiarity with the host country
- Ability and willingness to learn
- Openness to new experiences and ideas
- Training required to ensure the employee is ready

Self-assessment. To reduce the risk of failure, employees considering an international assignment should assess their own readiness and that of their family members to adapt to the new assignment, especially if the family members will be travelling as well. The following are some of the elements that these employees must consider:

- Tolerance for stress
- Cultural adaptability
- Awareness of unconscious bias
- Strength of family relationships
- Maturity of emotional intelligence
- Ability to handle ambiguity

There are many self-assessment tools available, and corporations should offer counseling and tax and legal advice for employees and their families considering an international assignment.

TRAINING ON CULTURE AND RESOURCES

The goal of training an employee before and during an international move is to ensure a successful assignment. Training programs must be rigorous and formal, planned, and tailored to the host country. Cultural training is most effective when families are integrated into the program. There are several components that can be utilized to guarantee an effective training program.

Documentary training takes place in a classroom and utilizes textbooks and reading about cultural differences, expectations, norms, and customs. Employees are given access to ongoing resources for the duration of the assignment.

Cultural simulation training allows employees to practice interactions with foreign employees during simulated exercises, including role-playing and practicing exchanges. The goal of cultural simulation is to duplicate the host situation as closely as possible. Employees are paired with locals to give them access to resources for the duration of the assignment.

Field simulation training takes place after cultural simulation training and in the host country. When the trainer and the employee feel that the employee is comfortable with the host country's culture, he or she can venture out into neighborhoods that are ethnically representative of the host country. Employees practice language, interact with locals, learn to navigate transportation, and move into temporary housing.

LANGUAGE TRAINING

Corporations intending to send employees to a foreign country must invest in **language training**, even if the employee has some language skills. Training should begin as far in advance of the move as possible and should continue with an in-country host and resources while the employee is on assignment.

Language training should include both specialized training for the technical business area and for integrating into the social network of the geographic area that the employee and his or her family will be a part of. If an employee or family fail to thrive and become part of their community, they will be isolated and unhappy. This is a recipe for failure. If a family fails, the employee will not be able to achieve success. Language training is a critical component of transitioning and a successful assignment.

EDUCATION TRAVEL GRANTS

The US State Department issues **education travel grants** in conjunction with the US Department of Education; these grants are sponsored by individual organizations. The grants are designed to allow teachers or other educators to experience new cultures, explore new instructional methods, and interact with educators in other countries to expand their worldview. The travel is short-term and includes work in a local school. There is often a capstone project to complete the requirements for the grant.

RENTAL SUBSIDIES

It is usually not feasible or sensible for employees to purchase a home in the host country. **Rental subsides** are established to create equity across accommodations for employees moving to foreign countries. Companies can provide rental subsidies to assist employees in obtaining reasonable housing for themselves and their families. There are several considerations that an organization must take into account when defining rental subsidy policies:

- Rental subsidy policies must be administered consistently for all employees in the same situation. These policies should be documented, and must be cleared by through a legal review.
- The policies must make clear that the subsidy is temporary and provides assistance with rental properties only. Corporations should not provide assistance for housing purchases.
- Rental subsidy policies should clearly state that the employee who takes on the purchase of a home accepts all liability for host country real estate market fluctuations, tax implications, fees, commissions, etc.

TRANSITION PLANS

Companies and their employees who are moving to a host country should be fully prepared. **Transition plans** should include processes, activities, and standard operating procedures for the entire international assignment program. Some of the elements that need to be considered are:

- **Communication plan.** Create channels for communication with the home country, management, support systems, in-country support, etc. Technology systems should be established to aid in communication.
- **Duties and responsibilities.** The tasks for which the employee is responsible should be clearly laid out and documented to provide the greatest chance of success.
- **Key contacts.** Each employee must be armed with a thorough list of contact information for all individuals involved in the work and position. This should include names, email addresses, phone numbers, and locations. Each employee should receive all log-in information, usernames, etc. that are needed in his or her position.
- **List of resources.** The employee should be provided with a list of key resources that may be indirectly linked to the project, such as office supplies, transportation resources, etc.
- **Change management plan.** A change management plan should be designed to incorporate all of the individuals involved in the transition of the employee from one country to another. The relocating employee will need to break from his or her current position and have support to transition into the new position. Employees and support services on each end must be prepared for the transition.

CRITERIA FOR SELECTING INDIVIDUALS FOR INTERNATIONAL ASSIGNMENTS

Careful consideration must be given when selecting individuals for **international assignments**. Frequently used **criteria** for selection might consist of demonstrated performance, professional or technical expertise, specific knowledge, overall perceptiveness, leadership abilities, administrative skills, willingness, reputation, successful completion of prior international assignments, ability to adapt, and desire to learn a new culture. **Orientation and pre-assignment training** such as language classes are essential for achieving strategic and tactical goals. Moreover, the level of success of an expatriate depends on the entire family's ability to **adjust** to new cultures. Some factors that may help expedite the family's adjustment overseas include the spouse's ability to work or maintain career advancement, and the availability and quality of family living accommodations, education for children, and health and dental care.

EXPATRIATE TRAINING AND SOCIALIZATION

Many large international enterprise companies have implemented some form of **expatriate training** for managers and their families prior to international assignments. These may provide cross-cultural training or address problems with adjustment. Making the adjustment to foreign assignments, especially those in less-industrialized nations, tends to be difficult for expatriate families. Family members may need to learn a new language, find acceptance with new friends in new schools, and pursue different careers. To prepare managers for foreign assignments, preparations and training sessions should include language and cultural awareness studies with thorough coverage of local customs and religions. One method involves the use of a **culturegram**, or culture assimilator, which instructs managers on best practices and helps them acquire and practice new cultural practices. Subjects vary from social introductions, time orientations, and standard dress to customary diet and dining etiquette.

COMPENSATION ADJUSTMENTS FOR EXPATRIATES

An international assignment must be aligned with a **global compensation system** in which compensation adjustments are made for each assignment. That said, the arrangement must take into consideration cost controls while providing sufficient motivation and rewards for the expatriate employee. Multinational organizations must create global compensation plans that are consistent with global mobility and business strategy. Additional consideration should be given to housing, expenses, and taxes. There are four methods for calculating global compensation adjustments for international assignments:

- The **home-country-based approach** is based on the employee's standard of living in his or her home country
- The **host-country-based approach** is based on local national rates
- The **headquarters-based approach** is based on the home country of the organization
- The **balance sheet approach** calculates compensation based on home country rates, with all allowances, deductions, and reimbursements, before converting it into the host country's currency

HEALTH AND SAFETY CONSIDERATIONS FOR EXPATRIATES

Employers have a responsibility to ensure the **health and safety** of their employees while they are performing work for the company. To promote expatriate safety, HR and senior leadership should create an emergency plan in advance of the expatriate's deployment. The emergency plan should include what to do in the case of accident, injury, illness, disease outbreak, extreme political unrest, and other situations that could endanger the expatriate and his or her family. An evacuation strategy is also a critical component of the emergency plan, and should detail how the expatriate and his or her family can get to a safe region quickly. To promote good health, the expatriate and his or her family need access to high-quality medical care. HR should ensure that the provided medical insurance is region-specific, as each country has a different infrastructure for care. Some nations provide care to anyone living there, whereas others require private insurance to pay for treatment. HR should also make sure that the insurance is provided by a licensed carrier and that it offers a solid network of quality providers.

EMPLOYEE REPATRIATION

Research has revealed that approximately 30 percent of expatriates leave their employers upon return to their home country, often citing external competitiveness or saying that no appropriate job was available to them. It is important to **plan for the employee's return** well in advance, before the assignment has even begun, and to have career development discussions to identify suitable positions that utilize global skills. **Employee repatriation** is taking care of employees after an international assignment when they have returned to their home country. **Communication** is also a key element. Staying connected through email, newsletters, a mentor or buddy system, and home visits can ensure that the employee remains in the loop. The company should recognize the employee's return with a reception, and possibly ask him or her to provide a speech or presentation about the company's international operations. Additional services might include retraining courses, counseling for reverse culture shock, and outplacement services for the employee's spouse.

METHODS FOR MOVING WORK
OFF-SHORING

In addition to or instead of moving employees, a company may decide to move the work itself. **Off-shoring** is the act of moving work to another country to be performed by local employees, when it was previously done in-house by domestic employees. Although there are often benefits such as lower cost, better availability of certain skills, and the ability to get work done more quickly, **off-shoring** frequently receives criticism for transferring jobs, encountering language and cultural barriers, and encountering intellectual property or geopolitical risks. However, business reasons for off-shoring are sometimes strategic, such as reaching new markets or talent pools not available domestically. Some countries that receive allocated work from the US include India, China, Russia, Mexico, Philippines, Brazil, and Hungary, due to the apparent or actual lower cost of labor in these areas. The rush of outsourcing information technology, human resources, and other white-collar jobs is likely to continue, but companies will need to consider pros and cons, including training and knowledge transfer, as well as cultural traditions, to make their operations successful. Otherwise, the quality of products and services may decline, cultural challenges may arise, and consumer backlash could affect company image. There are several options or alternatives to off-shoring, such as:

- **Near-shoring**. A form of off-shoring, near-shoring is the process of moving business operations to a nearby or bordering nation, where the company can benefit from both reasonable proximity and lower labor costs.
- **On-shoring**. The opposite of off-shoring, on-shoring consists of a business moving to its home country to reduce costs.
- **Co-sourcing**. Co-sourcing occurs when a firm uses a blend of company employees and external resources to render services to customers.

REMOTE WORK

Companies need to consider many implications before making a decision to move employees from office-based to **remote work**:

- **The impact to recruiting and retention.** While many employees want to work remotely, there are those who do not embrace that arrangement. Employers should carefully assess the type of work required, the corporate culture, the support of management, and the geographical location of the job to understand how current and future employees will react to moving jobs remotely.
- **Corporate culture.** It can be very difficult to establish a strong corporate culture when employees are located remotely. There must be practices and procedures intentionally instilled that will support remote workers. Management must be fully on board.
- **Results over time worked.** In a remote environment, employees perform successfully when they are given a task and a deadline, and then are allowed to get the job done without constant oversight. If it is not absolutely essential to dictate the hours worked, employees should be given flexibility to achieve their tasks.

Employees who work remotely can be highly effective, but management needs to be trained on supervision approaches, employee support, and performance management.

Risk Management

Risk management is the process of identifying, analyzing, and prioritizing **risks or potential uncertainties** while developing strategies to protect the financial interests of a company. Risks or potential uncertainties may include workplace safety, workers' compensation insurance, unemployment insurance, security, loss prevention, health and wellness, data management, privacy protection, project failures, and contingency planning. Depending on the size of the company or severity of the threat, some or all of these areas might be assigned to human resources. The underlying goal of risk management is to mitigate the costs of these uncertainties as much as possible.

RISK SOURCES AND TYPES

RISK SOURCES

There are four primary **sources of risk** that organizations should focus on when executing an enterprise risk assessment:

- **People.** The people of the organization create an inherent risk based on the quality of their decision-making. Pricing a product too high, going to market too soon, and poor design choices, among other actions, all create a source of risk.
- **Processes.** The myriad of processes that the organization executes can range from supply chain processes to workflows, which can all be a source of risk.
- **Technology.** The complexity and sophistication of a firm's technology is a very large source of risk for failures, hacking, and power loss.
- **Facility.** Hybrid workplaces are growing in popularity and can mitigate some of the large facility risks, but they can also create their own sources of risk.

There are two specific sources of risk, however, that must be addressed in an enterprise risk assessment and both are preventable if management has the right focus: insufficient resources and project failures.

Insufficient resources are most frequently due to poor planning. The organization must know not only what their resource requirements are, but where their current resources are at. Management must ensure that the right resources and the right level of resources are matched against the requirements. Gaps should be identified, and a strategy implemented to address those gaps.

Project failures are the second preventable source of risk. A methodology for project management should be adopted before any project begins, and it should be reviewed on a regular basis over the life of the project to ensure compliance and successful completion. Project risks can include elements such as scope creep, high costs, lack of a vision, and so on.

RISK TYPES

- **Hazard risk** involves potential liability or loss of property and is generally mitigated by insurance. Workplace accidents, fires, and natural disasters are examples of risk that fall into this category.
- **Financial risk** involves potential negative impacts to a firm's cash flow. A major customer not paying invoices on time is an example of this type of risk.
- **Operational risk** involves an impact to a firm's ability to function effectively, and may include technology failures, process breakdowns, and human error.
- **Strategic risk** involves a firm's plans becoming outdated due to shifts in the economy, politics, customer demographics, or the overall competitive landscape.

ENTERPRISE RISK MANAGEMENT PROCESSES AND BEST PRACTICES

The process of **enterprise risk management** consists of assessing the uncertainty in a business and proactively preparing for disruptions to ensure that the organization can make informed decisions about its future.

UNDERSTANDING CONTEXT

Organizations undertake enterprise risk assessments and create management processes and systems in order to identify risks and put them in the **contexts** of:

- Resources: the ability to prioritize limited resources
- Decision-making: enabling timely decisions
- Strategy development: aligning objectives with reality
- Governance: building processes and systems to reduce or mitigate risk
- Investor confidence: assurance to stakeholders of a proactive management strategy
- Protection of the brand, the employees, and profit
- Regulations and laws: staying on top of and ahead of changing rules and regulations

Employees must be involved in the process to ensure that risk management is done fully and to the best ability of the organization. Employees must be trained, given the proper tools, and supported by management to achieve their goals.

The proper methodology and processes must be identified and incorporated into the project. It should include surveys, interviews, data collection and analysis to assess impact and likelihood of any given risk, and a framework for aggregating and prioritizing risks.

IDENTIFYING RISKS

The identification of **risks** is the first, and notably the most important, phase of risk management because it is impossible to analyze or plan for a risk that has not been identified. In the risk identification phase, the key element is data collection. The team assigned to collect data must have available tools and access to the organization to reach out and tap into all of the possible resources to ensure a thorough collection effort.

Data can be collected through:

- **Surveys.** Surveys can gather a large amount of data very quickly. However, it does not allow for clarification of input, follow-up questions, or deep dives.
- **Interviews.** One-on-one interviews with key personnel gather a set of data that can be much richer and more detailed than that gathered through surveys, and the process allows for clarification and digging deeper into a subject. Interactions between the interviewer and the interviewee can raise points that may have been missed otherwise. However, interviews are time-consuming and therefore expensive. The data collected is more complex and harder to quantify to incorporate into data analysis.
- **Data mining**. Required data from corporate systems should be identified, extracted from the appropriate applications, and compiled in a single repository for full analysis. Data from the following systems could be applicable and critical to analyzing company risk:
  - Financial data
  - Human resources data
  - Corporate manuals
  - Policies and procedures
  - Operational data
  - Compliance data
  - Marketing data

RISK ANALYSIS

Once all the data has been collected and compiled in some reasonable format, the hard work of **risk analysis** begins. There are three elements that can be used in assessing risk: probability, impact, and preparedness. **Probability** is the likelihood of this risk occurring. Probability levels are most often defined as low, medium, and high. **Impact** is the extent to which a given risk might affect the organization. Impact levels are most often defined as low, medium, and high. **Preparedness** is the level of organizational knowledge and capacity to react to and handle the risk should it occur. Preparedness levels are most often defined as not prepared, prepared, and very prepared. In all three cases, there can be additional levels to improve fidelity. These levels can be assigned numbers for calculations.

Once probability, impact, and preparedness are identified, there are four assessment methodologies that can be adopted to analyze the risks:

- Probability × Impact. The most common method involves taking the rating for probability of occurrence and multiplying it by the level of impact to the organization.
- Probability + Impact. This adds rather than multiplies the probability and the impact.
- Probability + Impact – Preparedness. This method adds probability and impact and then subtracts the level of preparedness of the organization.
- Forced ranking. This methodology uses no dimensions (probability, impact, or preparedness) but instead forces the team to subjectively rank the risks from highest to lowest. This is relatively uncommon because it does not use a definable method to compare the risks to one another.

PRIORITIZING RISKS

Once the risks have been identified and assessed, the team must determine how to prioritize the order in which the organization should react to them. It is unrealistic to believe that the organization can or should react in the same manner to every risk. A **risk matrix** that incorporates the probability and the impact is commonly used as a tool for visualizing risks.

Risk Matrix

The risks should all be placed in the applicable categories and ranked by the numbers assigned to them in the analysis phase. Prioritizing risks allows the organization to determine where to focus resources to avoid failures. The matrix should be reviewed with management and key stakeholders, revised as necessary, and communicated to all appropriate personnel to ensure consistency and collaboration.

RISK TREATMENTS

A business has several options when a risk has been identified: accept the risk, retain the risk, avoid the risk, diminish or mitigate the risk, or transfer the risk. If the risk can be easily handled and does not pose a large threat to the organization, it may be wise to **accept** it. Preparing for it in advance could be a waste of time and resources. A firm might choose **risk retention**, or keeping the risk in-house, if doing so is financially prudent. Although not all situations allow for this, it may be wise to try to avoid larger risks. For example, if a firm believes that a feature in its product is not going to be functional for the product launch, it could decide to introduce the feature as an upgrade later or omit it entirely. If neither accepting nor avoiding the risk is possible, the company could decide to **mitigate** or diminish it. For example, if human resources thinks that workers will miss important changes to their benefits during the open enrollment period, they could offer training sessions and extra office hours to help employees understand their options. Finally, firms may be able to **transfer**, or share, some risks. When a business purchases an insurance policy of any kind, it is transferring risk to the insurer. A company could also transfer risk to suppliers by using specific contract clauses.

APPROACHES TO QUALITATIVE AND QUANTITATIVE RISK ASSESSMENT

Risk assessments are critical elements of risk management. A **quantitative risk assessment** allows the business to assign actual dollar amounts to each risk based on value, exposure, single loss expectancy, annualized rate of occurrence, and annualized loss expectancy. **Single loss expectancy** is measured when a value is placed on each asset, and the percentage of loss is determined for each acknowledged threat. The **annualized loss expectancy** can be calculated by multiplying the single loss occurrence and the annualized rate of occurrence. In these calculations, potential loss amounts are used to consider whether implementing a security measure is necessary. A **qualitative risk assessment**, on the other hand, does not assign a defined monetary value to the risk. It uses descriptive statements to describe the potential impact of a risk, which can include a general reference to financial loss. For example, a major system breach would result in customer data being compromised, severe damage to the firm's reputation, and a significant financial blow to the organization due to handling the crisis, shoring up the system to prevent further issues, and possibly responding to lawsuits by those affected.

LEGAL AND REGULATORY COMPLIANCE AUDITING AND INVESTIGATION TECHNIQUES
AUDIT OR INVESTIGATION PLAN

A **compliance audit** ensures that an organization is meeting guidelines established by the company, the government, or a regulatory agency. The audit checks the organization's current state against all applicable bylaws, controls, or policies. Audit reports cover such functions as:

- Security
- Production
- Finances
- Human resources
- Risk management
- Compliance
- Processes and controls
- Health and safety

A finalized audit report assesses performance against a base standard, identifies gaps, and provides recommendations for resolving outstanding issues.

An audit or **investigative plan** includes a list of what risks will be assessed, results from previous audits to check compliance or resolutions, and any significant changes in the organization over the audit period. The plan includes a list of the team members who will perform the audit, assignments of duties, and outlines for interviews with key stakeholders, as well as a timeline for completion.

CORRECTIVE ACTIONS

An audit will identify failures to comply, gaps in compliance, weaknesses in processes, and any other non-conformity in the elements assessed. When an issue is recognized, the audit should also recommend a **corrective action** to bring the area into compliance. Corrective actions should clearly identify the **five Ws**:

- **Who:** the party responsible for taking the corrective action
- **What:** the exact failure or non-conformity that has been identified
- **Where:** the location of the failure, whether geographic or digital, to be corrected
- **When:** the timeframe within which the corrective action must be taken
- **Why:** the reason for the corrective action and the reason that compliance is required

Clearly identifying the specifics required to correct the failure will ensure that the right issue is being addressed and that the team is fully informed on the issue.

MEASURING QUALITY ASSURANCE

Quality assurance can be tracked and measured utilizing **total quality management** to reduce errors and improve service. Total quality management is a strategy to maintain the highest level of quality possible for the output of each specific task carried out by the organization. In most organizations, total quality management is implemented by using a series of procedures that are designed to establish a quality-oriented organizational culture and a system for monitoring and controlling the quality of each task performed.

Many total quality management programs share common elements, such as customer focus, strategic planning, or continuous improvement. Most of these programs include the following steps:

1. Planning performance to identify goals and desired behaviors
2. Setting and communicating performance standards using customer-centric products and services
3. Measuring results using statistical control methods and providing feedback
4. Implementing performance improvement strategies
5. Evaluating results and benchmarking

AFTER-ACTION ANALYSIS

Upon completion of a quality assurance assessment, the organization can review how the quality assurance assessment was executed to ensure that learning takes place, processes are improved, and corrective actions have been identified and assigned. An **after-action analysis** should include the following key questions:

- What was the plan for the quality assurance assessment?
- What actually took place during the assessment?
- What went well during the assessment?
- What did not go well during the assessment?
- What needs to be changed or modified for the next assessment?

Quality assurance assessments test how well the organization is performing against standards, and the after-action report should assess how well the audit performed against its plan.

INDUSTRY-SPECIFIC STANDARDS

Quality assurance programs are used to measure performance against **standards**. The standards, therefore, must be established as part of the quality assurance program. Quality assurance standards can be established one of three ways:

- **Establish standards from scratch.** This can be very challenging to do without significant background and experience in the industry and market.
- **Use regulatory standards.** Organizations such as the International Organization for Standards (ISO), a worldwide federation of bodies that set industry standards, create rules for quality, safety, and efficiency that organizations agree to abide by. This is a very common approach, and organizations can be certified based on compliance with the established ISO standards.
- **Industry-specific standards.** While ISO covers a very large breadth of industries, companies can create quality assurance standards based on the common and best practices within its specific industry. These frameworks provide standards to ensure that processes, inputs, services, and products meet specific requirements.

Whichever approach an organization takes to establish its quality assurance standards, it is critical to document, publish, and communicate the standards throughout the organization.

BUSINESS CONTINUITY PLANNING AND RECOVERY

There are a large number of emergencies that an organization can face, any of which could affect the ability of the organization to continue functioning normally. **Business continuity planning** is a process in which an organization attempts to ensure that the organization will be able to continue functioning even after an emergency. Organizations use business continuity planning to create a plan, or group of plans, that will help the organization return to normal after a natural disaster or similar emergency occurs. The process of business continuity planning usually begins with an organization conducting a threat assessment such as a SWOT (strengths, weaknesses, opportunities, and threats) analysis. Once the organization has identified the threats that exist, the organization can rank those threats based on the risk associated with each threat. Finally, the organization can create a plan or set of plans that establish a system that the organization can use to recover from emergencies. The organization can continually update these plans as threats to the organization change.

> **Review Video: <u>Emergency Response, Business Continuity, and Disaster Planning</u>**
> Visit mometrix.com/academy and enter code: 678024

EVACUATION PROCEDURES AND SIMULATIONS

Emergency **evacuation procedures** are designed and developed according to the requirements of the organization to protect the business and the people of the company. Evacuation procedures must be comprehensive and complete. The procedures should cover preparations, plans to leave the building, and plans to take care of any persons who are vulnerable or in danger. There should be maps of the building exits and meeting spots.

An **emergency simulation** is a critical element of the evacuation plan that is a step more advanced than the traditional fire drills or evacuation practices. The simulation has a specific plan that is modeled on a unique potential scenario to which the team must respond. The response is measured and scored to validate the response plan, procedures, and systems and to improve the plans. Simulations should be developed for many different scenarios to test each response plan.

PREPARING FOR EMERGENCIES AND NATURAL DISASTERS

Because it is an employer's obligation to provide a safe and healthy work environment, many companies have begun to create **emergency and disaster plans** for handling situations such as fires, explosions, earthquakes, chemical spills, communicable disease outbreaks, and acts of terrorism. These plans should include the following actions:

- Clarify the **chain of command**, and inform staff who to contact and who has authority.
- Choose someone to be responsible for **accounting** for all employees when an emergency strikes.
- Set up a **command center** to coordinate communications.
- Train employees trained annually on what to do if an emergency strikes.
- Ensure that **first-aid kits** and **basic medical supplies** are available. This includes water fountains and eye wash stations in areas where spills may occur.
- Name an **emergency team of employees** and train them to:
  o Organize evacuation procedures
  o Initiate shutdown procedures
  o Use fire extinguishers
  o Use oxygen and respirators
  o Search for disabled or missing employees
  o Assess when it is safe to reenter the building

COMMUNICABLE DISEASES

When there is an emergency or natural disaster that involves destruction of facilities and infrastructure, a primary concern is the development and spread of **communicable diseases**. Communicable diseases fall into four categories:

- **Waterborne diseases.** Drinking water and flood water contaminated with waste can spread illnesses such as *E. coli* infection, cholera, hepatitis, and diarrhea.
- **Airborne illnesses.** Crowded emergency shelters can lead to the spread of acute respiratory infections, including meningitis and measles.
- **Vector-borne diseases.** Flooding that results in contaminated water can create environments favorable to organisms that can spread malaria, rabies, and parasitic diseases.
- **Injury infections.** Wounds that are exposed to dirt, contaminated water, and bacteria can develop staphylococcal, tetanus, and streptococcal infections.

Company disaster plans should include responses for each of the four categories, complete with measures for prevention and treatment should such diseases occur. Management and employees should be informed in advance of their roles in the plan and how to access resources, if required. Prevention plans should include:

- Identification of risk factors
- Coordination with public health organizations
- Development and training of emergency response plans
- Acquisition of equipment, materials, and supplies for diagnosis and treatment of illnesses and injuries.

NATURAL DISASTERS

Preparing for a **natural disaster** is a mandatory exercise for a responsible organization to ensure business continuity, employee safety, and security of facilities and materials. An emergency response plan for natural disasters should include the elements below, based on the location of workers.

- Workers in a corporate work facility:
    - Create evacuation plans to vacate the building.
    - Designate meeting places outside the buildings to account for all employees.
    - Assign a lead for each area or department to be responsible for accounting for the employees.
    - Communicate plans to all employees.
    - Have periodic drills to practice emergency procedures.
- Workers in remote or home environments:
    - Establish, document, and disseminate emergency plans for employees to use in their remote location.
    - Invest in technology to increase the ability to connect with remote employees.
    - Create a contact list to be used during an emergency.

Ensure that support plans are created to assist employees who may be injured, homeless, or in emotional distress.

SEVERE WEATHER

Extreme weather conditions are becoming more frequent and intense in many areas of the country, which requires organizations to be proactive about protecting employees and company property during an emergency. The following steps are critical for preparing adequately for **severe weather**:

- **Be informed.** Organizations must be aware of weather conditions to ensure that they are not taken by surprise. Weather reports should be reviewed on a daily basis, and management should be aware of the locations of flood zones, tornado-prone areas, and earthquake lines.

- **Assess infrastructure**. Take a full inventory of both physical and digital equipment and data. Ensure that data is stored in multiple places for resiliency. Install protection for facilities, such as storm shutters, insulated pipes, earthquake quality building materials.
- **Develop communication plans.** Ensure that employees know beforehand what the responses should be and how to access resources. Communication plans should also be developed for customers to keep them informed.
- **Plan for disruptions in service.** Identify thresholds for suspension or limitation of services.
- **Automate.** Create computer programs and other systems that can run as many processes and procedures as possible to remove the requirement for humans to perform essential duties.
- **Drill, drill, drill.** Create plans for reaction to and recovery from any disruption, and practice regularly.

TERRORISM

A real threat to the workplace that has grown in the last decade, **terrorism** can be either physical or cyber-based, and organizations must be prepared to prevent and react to both types of terrorism.

Physical terrorism. Attacks such as shootings, bombings, chemical or biological agents in the mail, kidnapping, and assassinations are some of the forms of physical terrorism that can occur in the workplace. The goal of terrorism is to create fear, gain publicity for causes, or promote the concept that the government or corporation is unable to protect its people. Organizations should take the following measures to prevent or deter such attacks:

- Inspect suspicious packages being delivered to the company.
- Install strong air filtration systems in buildings.
- Identify shelter locations.
- Develop educational materials for management and employees.
- Prepare and train staff for events such as shooters.
- Maintain a proactive visitor control center.
- Provide mental health counseling for employees, especially during times such as layoffs or terminations.

Cyber terrorism. Cyber-attacks on organizations are becoming far more frequent. These attackers target company data for exploitation or ransom. Cyber-attacks happen quickly, so the response must be coordinated and all employees responsible for the response should be well-informed as to their role in responding. Some ways that organizations can prevent or deter such attacks are:

- Develop a cyber-attack plan and practice it on a regular basis using drills similar to fire drills.
- Invest in cybersecurity. Hardened and resilient systems are one of the best defenses to cyber terrorism, but they must be updated frequently and should include firewalls.
- Conduct a cyber security audit to identify weaknesses in the system.
- Include cyber security in the onboarding process for new employees and in annual training for all employees.
- Maintain all updates, patches, and fixes to company devices and hardware.
- Back up all documents and data on a regular basis.

Terrorism can be devastating to an organization, and companies must be aware and proactive about prevention and preparation.

MAN-MADE DISASTERS

Events that involve an element of human intervention either through purposeful intent, negligence, or an error in a man-made system are known as **man-made disasters**. Examples of man-made disasters are arson, crime, disorder, chemical or biological attacks, cyber-attacks, and release of hazardous materials. There are several approaches that employers can take to plan to prevent or deter such disasters:

- Establish safety practices and protocols, monitoring and auditing the protocols and ensuring employee adherence.
- Identify and map hazardous materials.
- Provide protection for power sources.
- Develop strong security plans for internal areas of vulnerability, such as air ventilation systems.
- Create a disaster recovery plan.

COMMUNICATION MECHANISMS

The systems and protocols put in place to transmit messages from person to person or place to place, **communication mechanisms** can include oral transmission, mail, email, telephone, radio, computers, and data sets. An organization's emergency plans must include who, what, where, when, why, and how for communicating information in a time of crisis:

- **Who.** Companies may create distribution lists that are tailored for crisis situations. Messages may be tailored for management, security, human resources, all employees, or remote employees.
- **What.** Determine what information is critical for each team to receive based on the crisis and the need to know.
- **Where.** Establish where information will be sent, and have backup plans if an email system is down or the phone lines are not working. Keep lists of personal email or phone numbers for employees where they can be reached if the company systems are not viable.
- **When.** Time is critical in an emergency, but delivering a crisis message too early, when information may not be verified, can also create a crisis of its own. Have a plan for timing messages to each of the identified groups.
- **Why.** The information that is shared should be essential to meet the business or humanitarian needs of the people and the organization. Share only the data that needs to be shared. For instance, in the case of a shooting, sharing the name of a deceased employee would not be necessary for other employees to find safety, and could be detrimental to focusing on the response at hand.
- **How.** Establish the mechanism for sharing information. Buildings have fire alarms and loudspeakers, auto-generated emails can be sent, and phone trees can be set up.

Every organization should have a plan and have a backup plan, and a backup for the backup, and practice these plans on a regular basis.

EVACUATION PLANS

As with all emergency preparedness plans, organizations must prepare **evacuation plans** designed to protect employees. Evacuation plans should include the following:

- An **overall strategy** for evacuation including procedures, protocols for notifying authorities, communication plans, employee training, testing of equipment and drills, and a list of emergency contacts.
- **Alarms and systems** to provide alerts, including fire alarms, loudspeakers, computer pop-up alerts, or phone notifications. Systems should be tested on a regular basis.
- **Evacuation routes** that all employees should be aware of and practice to be able to safely evacuate their workspace, as well as where they should meet to be accounted for once in a safe location.
- **Signage** to ensure that evacuation routes and meeting areas are visible, properly marked, and consistently maintained.
- **Equipment** such as properly chosen and maintained fire extinguishers should be kept in appropriate, visible areas. Employees should be trained on their use.

- **Trained personnel** to ensure evacuation accountability. Responsible employees should be designated as "fire wardens," leads, or emergency specialists and trained on how to safely evacuate employees, how to accommodate employees who use wheelchairs or have mobility issues, and other special needs accommodations. These trained employees should also be accountable for verifying employee rosters.
- Formal **training** should be implemented and practiced on a regular basis.

SAFETY AND HEALTH MANAGEMENT PLANS

According to the Occupational Safety and Health Administration (OSHA), there are four characteristics a **safety and health management plan** should have to be considered effective. First, an effective plan should establish a specific system to identify hazards in the workplace. Second, the plan should establish a training program that teaches employees to avoid hazards and to perform tasks in the safest way possible. Third, an effective safety and health management plan should include specific procedures and programs designed to eliminate hazards or at least minimize the risk that a hazard will injure or kill an employee or cause an employee to become ill. Finally, it should allow employees at all levels of the organization to be involved in the identification, prevention, and elimination of hazards in the workplace.

EMERGENCY ACTION PLANS

There is certain information that should be included in every organization's **emergency action plan**. All emergency action plans should explain the alarm system that will be used to inform employees and other individuals at the worksite that they need to evacuate, include in-depth exit route plans that describe which routes employees should take to escape the building, and include in-depth plans that describe what actions employees should take before evacuating, such as shutting down equipment, closing doors, and so on. All emergency action plans should also include detailed systems for handling different types of emergencies and a system that can be used to verify that all employees have escaped the worksite.

FIRE PREVENTION PLANS

There is a wide variety of information that might be included in a **fire prevention plan**, and the specific information included in a fire prevention plan will vary from organization to organization. However, certain information should be included in every organization's fire prevention plan. All fire prevention plans should provide detailed descriptions of the specific areas where employees can find fire extinguishers and other fire prevention equipment, detailed descriptions of the types of fire hazards present in the workplace, and detailed descriptions of the appropriate procedures to avoid these fire hazards. Fire prevention plans should also provide detailed descriptions of any hazardous waste that may be a fire hazard and the appropriate way to dispose of or store this hazardous waste to avoid a fire.

EMERGENCY RESPONSE PLANS

All **emergency response plans** should identify the records and resources essential to the organization, identify the individuals responsible for protecting those records and resources, and describe the procedures that individuals should follow to safeguard the records and resources essential for the organization to continue functioning. Emergency response plans must also establish a system that the organization can use to continue communicating with vendors and the public during and after an emergency.

DISASTER RECOVERY PLANS

There is specific information that should be included in every organization's **disaster recovery plan**. Equipment and locations that can be utilized temporarily in the event of an emergency should be identified. Agencies and personnel that may be able to help the organization continue functioning immediately after an emergency should also be identified. It is wise to establish a set of procedures that the organization can use to bring the personnel and equipment together after an emergency. Disaster recovery plans should also identify alternative sources that the organization can use to receive supplies or products if the emergency disables the organization's normal supply chain.

SECURITY CONCERNS AND PREVENTION
WORKPLACE VIOLENCE

Due to the growing number of workplace assaults and homicides, it is suggested that human resource managers be prepared and implement policies such as the following:

- **Zero tolerance:** prohibit any act of violence in the workplace, including verbal threats
- **Prevention:** present strategies and training to help managers recognize danger signs
- **Crisis management:** create plans for responding to threats or acts of violence
- **Recovery:** provide support and counseling for victims and survivors that may suffer lasting trauma

To reduce the likelihood that a troubled employee might become violent, managers should be encouraged to practice the following:

- Discipline employees one-on-one as a private matter as opposed to in public.
- Provide employees with an opportunity to explain or tell their side of the story.
- Ensure that managers refrain from disciplining employees when the manager is angry. Even if the employee's behavior may warrant immediate action, the employee should be removed from the scene, and disciplinary action should be discussed and decided at a later meeting.
- Try to calm angry workers or have a friend accompany them when leaving.

FRAUD AND THEFT

A serious concern for all companies is illegal or dishonest behavior, such as theft, embezzlement, falsifying records, or misuse of company property. Committing **fraud** often involves at least one of three main forces: situational pressure, opportunity to commit fraud, or personal integrity. When employees are suspected of stealing, the company must decide whether to conduct an investigation or prosecute. Investigations and prosecutions can be costly; however, most cases should be investigated. Some investigations will result in termination, whereas others may result in prosecution.

Organizations may also adopt **anti-fraud programs** to increase early detection and decrease opportunities. These programs often contain the elements of reporting, oversight, prudence, communication, compliance, enforcement, prevention, and advocating personal integrity. Companies prone to theft and dishonest behavior, such as retail corporations, often have **loss prevention departments** dedicated to protecting assets and cash while minimizing and detecting inventory shrinkage.

CORPORATE ESPIONAGE

When employees give corporate trade secrets to another organization, they are committing **corporate espionage**. They give the receiving firm a competitive advantage and may cause the first company to lose customers, sales, human capital, market share, or all of the above. Firms can protect themselves from corporate espionage by requiring employees to sign nondisclosure or noncompete agreements. These agreements outline what information is protected and what happens when an employee (or former employee) violates the agreement. Companies should also restrict their most important classified information to a small group of personnel that need it to do their jobs.

SABOTAGE

Workplace **sabotage** is the act of destroying or disrupting business operations. It can be overt, through behaviors such as erasing important files, intentionally failing to complete certain key tasks, or spreading rumors. It can also be much more subtle, and occur through behaviors such as taking a meeting off topic, practicing perfectionism, or being totally unwilling to bend the rules for overall gain or greater good. To combat deliberate sabotage efforts, firms should have a code of conduct in place that forbids such behavior and spells out what happens when an employee violates the code. To address the less-direct forms of sabotage, leaders should be trained to detect the behaviors at an early stage and firmly take charge to nip them in the bud.

KIDNAPPING AND RANSOM

When employees are kidnapped and ransomed, it is a terrifying ordeal for them, their families, and the organization. However, the firm can take several steps to both prevent a **kidnapping** from occurring and handle it effectively should it happen. First and foremost, the company should address the threat of kidnapping in a given area. It should also create a clear plan for how it would negotiate in a hostage situation. If an area is high-risk, the firm should consider whether it is worth having personnel there at all. If employees are sent to or are located in that area, the firm should teach them how to detect threats and be mindful of their surroundings. They should also be trained how to act if they are kidnapped. Best practices include speaking about their personal lives and families so that kidnappers see them as humans and not as a commodity for sale. Those who are kidnapped should avoid speaking about hot-button issues like politics or religion. Companies should also teach employees what to do when they are rescued. For example, employees should not run toward the rescue team because they might be mistaken as being a part of the enemy group. During a kidnapping situation, the company should provide support to the hostage employee's family and keep a low media profile. The media can make things worse, depending on what information gets released and is seen by the kidnappers. Finally, companies should consider purchasing kidnap and ransom insurance, which will help cover the cost of the **ransom** should a kidnapping occur.

ACTIVE SHOOTERS

Preparations for **active shooters** are unfortunately becoming more common and more of a necessity. Similar to any other emergency preparedness plan, the key is having a plan and ensuring that employees know the safety protocol. When developing an active shooter plan, it is prudent for organizations to involve local law enforcement to discuss the plan and coordinate responses. Companies should develop processes and procedures to be able to lock down facilities and prohibit access at the entrances during a lockdown. The active shooter plan should identify areas of the building for visitors or guests to gather during an event, and a critical response team to activate during an incident. As with all emergency plans, this plan should be documented, communicated, and practiced on a regular basis. After each drill, there should be a de-brief and assessments of the strengths and weaknesses of the plan to allow for improvements. If an active shooter event should occur, management should immediately make counseling resources available to the employees.

INSIDER THREATS

The risk of a threat coming from inside the organization is real and serious. An **insider** is anyone who has access to a company's resources, such as data, personnel, information, buildings, equipment, and networks. While many insiders are employees, other insiders include anyone who gained access to a badge, passwords, or access controls such as a vendor, contractor, or repair person. An **insider threat** is a person or persons who use that access to harm the organization. Harm can be intentional or unintentional, but always results in negative consequences to the organization. Insider threats can take the form of:

- Unauthorized disclosure of information
- Sabotage
- Workplace violence
- Corruption
- Espionage

Organizations can make efforts to deter insider threats by developing best practices to define, detect, identify, assess, and manage the risk. The identification and detection of potential risks is the most critical prevention method. Employees must be trained to watch for and report potential incidents or concerns.

DATA BREACHES

A **data breach** is an incident in which unauthorized individuals gain access to sensitive company data such as personnel data, customer data, or financial data. A breach is when that information is viewed or shared without the permission of the organization. There are steps that a company should take to prevent such incidents, including educating employees on proper procedures for protecting data, ensuring that all security standards and systems are up-to-date and documented, continually monitoring the systems and networks for intrusions or issues, ensuring that all data is backed up to allow for restoration, and having information technology experts on staff to set up and monitor security protocols.

In the event that a data breach does occur, the speed at which an organization responds is critical. The breach must be identified, a response plan should be activated, all evidence must be collected and analyzed, attempts at containment or recovery should be executed when appropriate, and affected people and organizations should be notified. When it is over, a post-event analysis should be executed to identify the lessons learned.

WORKPLACE ILLNESS, INJURY PREVENTION, INVESTIGATION, REPORTING, AND ACCOMMODATION

The **Occupational Safety and Health Act** of 1970 mandates that it is the employer's responsibility to provide an environment that is free from known hazards that causes or may cause serious harm or death to employees. The only workers who are not protected by this act are those who are self-employed, family farms where only family members work, and workplaces that are covered by other federal statutes or state and local government. This act is monitored and enforced by the **Occupational Health and Safety Administration (OSHA)**. OSHA ensures that employees have a safe workplace free from recognized hazards. It also requires all employers and each employee to comply with occupational safety and health standards, rules, and regulations. Employers may be found in violation if they are aware or should have been aware of potential hazards that could cause injury or death.

Preventing workplace illness and injury includes training employees, following OSHA standards, and being mindful of and preparing for the potential hazards typically seen in the line of duty.

IDENTIFICATION OF HAZARDS

Every organization has an obligation to identify, inspect, and maintain **hazardous materials** in a way that prevents worker injury or death. OSHA recommends six steps to identify and assess hazardous materials:

1. Collect and maintain current information about all workplace hazards and materials.
2. Inspect the workplace regularly for any safety hazards, concerns, or potential risks.
3. Identify any materials that present a hazard to employee health.
4. Conduct immediate investigations into any incidents or accidents that occur.
5. Identify hazardous materials required for non-routine tasks or emergency situations.
6. Identify control measures and prioritize the hazardous materials for control.

Some hazardous materials, such as cleaning supplies or equipment, may be used on a daily basis. Other materials, such as fire extinguishers or chemicals for annual machine maintenance, may be used only infrequently or in emergency situations. All of these materials must be listed and inspected, and have control mechanisms in place for handling the material in use and handling the fallout of an accident or incident. Above all, the safety of the employees should be the primary concern.

REPORTING OCCUPATIONAL INJURIES

OSHA requires that any occupational injury or illness be **recorded** if it results in medical treatment that goes beyond first aid, restricted work activity or job transfer, time away from work, loss of consciousness, or death. An incident that results in an inpatient hospitalization must be reported within 24 hours, and any incident resulting in an employee's death must be reported to the nearest OSHA office within eight hours. For each recordable injury or illness, an **OSHA Form 301 Injury and Illness Incident Report** must be completed within seven calendar days. Employers are obligated to keep a log of all incidents on an **OSHA Form 300 Log of Work-Related Injuries and Illnesses**, and a concise report of annual incidents should be reported on an **OSHA Form 300A Summary of Work-Related Injuries and Illnesses** at the end of each year. Form 300A must be posted where all employees can find it on February 1 through April 30, and all documentation should be kept for five years so that it is available on request for examination. Any procedure or doctor's visit that can be labeled as first aid does not need to be recorded. However, any needle-stick injury, cut from a sharp object contaminated with another person's blood, or incision that requires stitches should be reported.

SAFETY TRAINING PROGRAMS

Most organizations can follow a series of basic steps to create an effective **safety training program**. First, a safety risk assessment is conducted to determine the safety hazards present in the workplace. Then each hazard is investigated to determine if training will help to eliminate the dangers associated with the hazard. If so, information that each employee needs to know about the hazard should be identified, and a series of training goals and objectives based on these needs can be established. Once training goals have been established, a training program can be created and implemented, and then the results can be evaluated.

WORKPLACE INJURY OR ILLNESS INVESTIGATION

When an employee is injured on the job or becomes ill as a result of completing work duties, the employer must **investigate** the incident to understand why it happened. This investigation should identify ways to prevent similar incidents from occurring in the future. An employer's internal investigation should entail interviewing the sick or injured employee, assessing that employee's immediate work environment, and interviewing other employees who may have witnessed the incident or worked under the same conditions. An **OSHA Form 301 Injury and Illness Incident Report** should be completed for all recordable incidents. In addition, employers may want to document the incident further for internal purposes. If that is the case, they should create a standardized form for collecting the details to ensure that each investigation is conducted in a similar fashion and that no important information gets overlooked. Sometimes, OSHA will investigate an employer. These investigations may occur either onsite or offsite.

APPROACHES TO A DRUG FREE WORKPLACE

Shows like A&E's *Intervention* and recent news of the opioid epidemic address some of the many personal struggles for employees involved in or suffering from **alcoholism and drug abuse**. Moreover, these problems are not temporary, and many people need help correcting these behaviors. Alcoholism is now a **protected disability** under the American with Disabilities Act (ADA). The act does not protect employees who report to work under the influence, nor does it protect them from the consequences of their actions or blatant misconduct.

Problems caused by drug abuse are similar to those caused by alcoholism. However, additional problems associated with drug abuse are the likelihood of stealing due to the high cost of the employee's habit, and its illegal nature. The ADA does not protect current drug use as a disability.

DRUG-FREE WORKPLACE ACT

The **Drug-Free Workplace Act** of 1988 requires that government contractors make a good-faith effort to ensure a drug-free workplace. Employers must prohibit illegal substances in the workplace and must create drug awareness trainings for employees. Any federal contractor with contracts of $100,000 or more must adhere to a set of mandates to show that they maintain a drug-free work environment. Employer responsibilities include:

- Develop a **written policy** prohibiting the production, distribution, use, or possession of any controlled substance by an employee while in the workplace.
- Develop **standards of enforcement**. All employees must receive a copy of the policy and understand the consequences of a violation.
- Implement **drug awareness trainings** to help employees understand the hazards and health risks of drug use.

Although drug testing is not required, employers should have some type of **screening** in place.

CAUTIONARY MEASURES WHEN DESIGNING DRUG TESTING PROGRAMS

Many employers utilize drug testing to screen applicants and, in some cases, current employees. Generally speaking, employers can legally require applicants to pass a **drug test** as a condition of employment or adopt programs that test active employees, as long as the programs are not discriminatory. Due to the controversial nature of drug-testing programs, employers must be meticulously cautious when designing these programs, to ensure that their practices will be upheld if brought to court. *Wilkinson v. Times Mirror Corporation* established the following elements for testing programs:

- Samples are collected at a medical facility by persons unrelated to the employer.
- Applicants are not observed by others when they furnish samples.
- Results are kept confidential.
- Employers are only informed by the medical lab whether the applicant passed or failed.
- Applicants are notified by the medical lab of any portion they failed—in some cases, applicants will haves an opportunity to present medical documentation prior to the employer receiving the results.
- There is a defined method for applicants to question or challenge test results.
- Applicants must be eligible to reapply after a reasonable time.

MEDICAL MARIJUANA

As with drug screening, there are no accommodations required by federal law to allow the use of **medical marijuana**, but some states do have laws in place protecting its use. Employers should review their policies to see if they violate any obligations under state disability accommodation or leave laws. The Americans with Disabilities Act (ADA) requires employers to enter into discussions about reasonable accommodations with workers with disabilities. The goal is to determine if a worker can perform the essential functions of his or her job. The Family and Medical Leave Act (FMLA) requires employers to allow time off for medical treatment for qualified employees. While medical marijuana use is not covered under either the ADA or FMLA and all marijuana use is still deemed illegal under federal law, courts have been reviewing the use of medical marijuana in some states. The initial set of cases have been ruled in favor of employers; however, employers must ensure that corporate drug-testing and screening policies are in line with emerging laws in the states in which they operate. Employers should identify if an employee has appropriate medical certification, if drug test results are tied to medicinal use, and if the use of medical marijuana will pose a risk in the workplace.

TREATMENT OF SUBSTANCE ABUSE

Employers are putting more and more effort into providing resources and other assistance to employees who are dealing with substance abuse problems. Substance abuse costs an organization time and money due to lost productivity, workplace violence, legal liability, and turnover. Some of the ways that employers have responded by expanding resources and services include:

- Expanding existing treatment options through Employee Assistance Programs to lower barriers to seeking care
- Offering telehealth services to ensure easier access to assistance
- Working with their insurance providers to offer physical therapy and chiropractic visits for employees to reduce dependency on pain medication
- Encouraging openness in the workplace to remove the stigma of substance abuse issues by having leaders share stories of past challenges
- Communicating more aggressively and visibly about the resources available to employees
- Working with the corporate health insurance organizations to ensure that there are providers for the employees who are available and seeing new patients
- Expanding coverage options for employees who work remotely to ensure adequate coverage

Substance abuse takes a big toll on the employee and the employer. Employers can create **Workplace Supported Recovery** programs to prevent substance abuse issues or assist employees with treatment. Support for treatment of substance abuse issues needs to be built into the culture of the organization.

Corporate Social Responsibility

HUMAN RESOURCE ACTIVITIES THAT SUPPORT SUSTAINABILITY

HUMAN RIGHTS

There are three mainstays of sustainability:

- Economic viability
- Environmental protection
- Social equity

There is a recognized link between human rights and a safe, healthy environment for employees. **Social equity** is the defense of human rights that includes the protection of access to equal opportunities and the resources required to thrive in society. Organizations work to create policies and services to protect and promote the rights of all individuals regardless of race, sex, nationality, ethnicity, religion, or any other status. Human rights also include the right to work and the right to education. Human resources (HR) has a strong role in embedding social responsibility and human rights into performance objectives ad reviews. HR can also influence the corporate culture to align human rights best practices into employee recruitment, training, and retention, and allow employees to see their connections to the purpose and importance of their work as it supports the greater good.

SAFETY PRACTICES

Creating a safe, healthy environment that protects the most valuable asset of an organization, its people, is a critical element of the company bottom line. The Occupational Safety and Health Administration (OSHA) provides a platform for reimaging concepts to protect workers in partnership with organizations to promote sustainability that can include:

- Partnering with organizations to integrate health and safety sustainability actions
- Training and educating workers with the health and safety community
- Measuring the impact of health and safety performance on business outcomes
- Recognizing employees for efforts to promote and sustain health and safety practices
- Collecting and analyzing data on health and safety efforts that support sustainability

Employers will achieve sustainability when they ensure the health and safety of their employees.

LABOR STANDARDS

If sustainability is achieved through protection of the health and safety of an organization's employees, then **labor standards** must factor into that equation. Labor standards that support the protection of workers will establish:

- **Prohibitions against child labor.** In the words of the International Labour Organization, children must be protected against "work that is mentally, physically, socially, or morally dangerous and harmful," or work that interferes with their education. These protections include minimum age requirements and prohibitions against children performing hazardous work.
- **Prohibition against forced labor.** Forced labor is a modern-day form of slavery in that it involves people being trapped and coerced into working while being held against their will. Forced labor is prohibited under international law.
- **Prohibition against discrimination.** Discrimination in organizations is most often a systemic issue resulting from a lack of policy to combat it or the non-enforcement of a policy. Discrimination can lead to exclusion from the workforce and poverty.

- **Creating equal treatment and the right to collective bargaining.** Sustainable organizations set labor standards to eliminate discrimination and provide equal and equitable treatment to all candidates and employees. Additionally, companies can provide for the right to collective bargaining, such as allowing unions for employees to protect and promote themselves.

PERFORMANCE DEVELOPMENT

Sustainable performance in an organization is demonstrated by employees who are productive, satisfied, flourishing individuals. Company management and HR in coordination can create this environment for their employees, encouraging them to be engaged in envisioning a future for the organization by embracing four mechanisms:

- Create a positive environment
- Promote decision-making at all levels
- Encourage transparency in sharing corporate strategy and information
- Develop a strong performance feedback process

Employees who are actively engaged and contributing to the company vision and mission will welcome constructive, authentic performance feedback. Thriving employees want to learn and grow by conquering new skills and acquiring knowledge. Performance development includes setting goals, providing feedback, and creating opportunities for growth and development, both personally and professionally.

DIVERSITY, EQUITY, AND INCLUSION

Diversity is the incorporation of a wide range of individuals, embracing their differences, identities, and perspectives. **Equity** is a fairness doctrine, which requires understanding the unique challenges that various social identity groups face. **Inclusion** is supporting and welcoming all, not despite of, but because of their differences.

Organizations that want to not only meet current needs but also position themselves to meet the demands of future generations must acknowledge the link between diversity, equity, and inclusion (DEI) and corporate sustainability. What a company does today impacts all future generations. As the composition of the world and workforce change, companies must change with them. The most sustainable organizations will anticipate the requirements of tomorrow's workforce and implement change now. HR can help management think strategically about the future and develop changes to policies and programs that promote DEI in today's work. The workforce of tomorrow seeks to see DEI in corporate policies and programs such as:

- Equality in race, gender, and sexual orientation
- Climate change
- Human rights issues
- Pollution
- Income inequality

COMPENSATION

As a tenet of social equity and non-discrimination, **compensation** is a substantive part of an organization's sustainability. Compensation is a component of an employee's job satisfaction. Equitable compensation is a large part of the DEI and social contract that a company has with its employees and customers. To support sustainability, compensation packages, beyond being fair, should be based on long-term incentives tied to the efforts most important to the company. Compensation can be tied to goals such as conservation of natural resources, DEI goals, reduction of carbon footprint, or other challenges tied to the corporate vision.

Creative compensation can be a powerful tool for recruiting and maintaining employees.

SUPPLY CHAIN MANAGEMENT

An organization's strategic plan to integrate social, financial, and environmental responsibilities should include choosing **supply chain management** strategies that ensure that the company's supply chain plan is congruous with human rights, health, and safety. Sustainable supply chain programs help improve the productivity of the organization while being cost-effective by providing visibility into vendor performance and operations.

The goal of a sustainable supply chain management plan is to create a flow of sustainable practices that build a network that operates smoothly and effectively. In end-to-end supply chains, from raw materials sourcing to "last mile" logistics, there are three approaches to sustainability:

- **Green supply chain:** integration of environmental principles
- **Transparency supply chain:** partnership with businesses to disclose information about the provenance of goods and labor
- **Circular supply chain:** products are disassembled to raw material form and remade into viable new products

ORGANIZATIONAL PHILOSOPHIES AND POLICIES

An **organizational philosophy** is a key element of organizational culture and creates the foundational values, beliefs, and guidelines for doing business. This philosophy cultivates the relationships among the organization, employees, customers, and shareholders. An organization's philosophy is derived from its **mission statement** and describes its set of values, beliefs, and norms. The organizational philosophy may also provide a basis for establishing **departmental philosophies**. Employees and managers need to clearly understand the organizational philosophies, cultures, policies, and procedures so they can all act in alignment with organizational goals and strategies.

DEVELOPMENT

Every organization has a philosophy, whether it is written down and acknowledged or not. While some firms take the time and effort to **develop** and write a philosophy, many small companies have informal and unwritten philosophies. If an organization does try to articulate a philosophy, it should start with the CEO and board of directors. The key elements of a philosophy include:

- The reason for existing as an organization
- The values of the firm
- The goals of the company
- What the end state of the organization should look like
- How the company sees itself
- How the company sees itself in relation to the world
- How the organization approaches business

The philosophy should set the foundation for the mission of the company and should describe the path that the leaders will follow to ensure that the company performs and operates in concert with the philosophy.

INTEGRATION

If an organization makes the effort to develop a formal philosophy, the next step is to **integrate** that philosophy into the business by developing a **mission and vision statement**, a set of values that will guide decision-making, the corporate strategy, and the policies surrounding business practices. Tying the foundational documents together will ensure that the staff lives and works according to the purposeful decisions that the executives have outlined. This integration provides a meaning to the work that employees need to know and feel to be engaged and productive and to strive for creativity in their job.

Organizations should provide actionable feedback to employees on a frequent basis to ensure that they understand their role in relation to the mission and vision, strategy, and goals. Employees who feel connected to work are high performers and rate their work satisfaction as high. Philosophies that are fully integrated into the rest of the foundational documents ensure continuity and strength.

CREATING SHARED VALUES

Organizational culture is often based on a set of **shared values**. Shared values are the principles, traditions, attitudes, and beliefs that influence the members of an organization. Ideally, these values support the vision and mission of the organization. For example, highly competitive industries such as national sports leagues might list assertiveness and emphasizing outcomes as values. Inclusive industries in human services might list traits like fairness, tolerance, respect, and team orientation as values. Many startup and lean environments will list innovation, precision, successful experimentation, and strong task analysis as key values. Regardless of which shared values an organization chooses, these values should be clearly communicated to applicants, employees, and shareholders so that all parties are in alignment for sustainability and success.

STEPS TO IMPLEMENT A CORPORATE SOCIAL RESPONSIBILITY STRATEGY

DEVELOPING A BUSINESS CASE

A **business case** defines the rationale for a corporate strategy. Created by and for executive management, a business case should define why a **corporate social responsibility (CSR)** strategy is an integral part of the overall corporate mission, vision, and strategy. The push for CSR strategies is both philosophical and pragmatic. Philosophically, a CSR strategy needs to evolve past pure economic interests and serve the relationship with its wide swath of stakeholders. Pragmatically, CSR strategies align with the push for organizations to benefit and improve society in a public-facing way.

The business case should cover the following elements:

- A clear link to corporate financial performance
- Cost and risk reductions of implementation and maintenance of a CSR strategy
- The competitive advantage that a CSR strategy would offer the company against competitors
- The benefit to the organization's reputation with customers
- A stewardship model that ties social values and financial goals, recognizing the interdependence between the business and society

There will be no single justification for a CSR strategy, and the business case should articulate how a CSR strategy will improve the bottom line.

OBTAINING EXECUTIVE APPROVAL

While most organizations understand and acknowledge the need and desire for a CSR strategy, it can still be viewed as a financial burden to the company, so securing **executive approval** is challenging but essential. There are four recommended approaches to obtaining buy-in and approval from the executive team:

- Use case studies to demonstrate the success that other organizations have achieved by implementing CSR strategies.
- Emphasize value beyond the financial data to highlight positive results that the CSR strategy will generate.
- Look within the organization to identify areas of improvement that the company can focus on while implementing the CSR strategy to create added value.
- Focus on the raw data using studies that both demonstrate the benefit a CSR strategy can bring and the detrimental effects of an organization that customers consider irresponsible or non-responsive to social responsibilities.

CSR is a business practice that is both ethical and strategic, and executives must buy in to both elements for success.

SELECTING PARTNERS

As organizations implement CSR programs, it is incumbent upon the team to first identify initiatives in areas of work that are congruent with the CSR strategy. Many companies look to opportunities in the sustainability market, such as water stewardship, social justice, environmental sustainability, alternative energy sourcing, and clean technology initiatives. Selection criteria should be created for assessing candidates. When the investment categories are defined, organizations need to do due diligence to identify the best **partners** with whom to work. Several factors should be reviewed and considered, including:

- The partner's mission and vision and how they align with those of the organization
- How the partner and organization can collaborate to meet the CSR strategy and goals in a way that is complementary to both the partner and the organization
- The partner's performance record
- Local partners that can demonstrate value to the communities where the organization is located
- The partner's ability to commit to a long-term relationship
- Partners that are meeting the needs of the local community

Partners should be rated against the established criteria and rank-ordered for selection.

IDENTIFYING AND ANALYZING PERFORMANCE INDICATORS

Overarching **performance indicators** should be designed and developed in the CSR strategy and more in-depth when partners are selected and onboarded. All performance indicators should start with strong and clear goals from the CSR strategy and the partnership agreements. Key criteria developed for each partner to measure the success of the partnership should include:

- **Key performance indicators (KPI)** to measure specific impacts and accomplishments in the environmental or social cause that was established in the plan. These KPIs can be established by:
  - Benchmarks against high performance in the industry
  - Employee perspectives on company performance
  - Adherence to social policies
  - Recognition achieved
  - Number of community members impacted positively
  - Satisfaction ratio (employees, partner, and community)
- Level of transparency on progress toward goals
- Ability to maintain close alignment with the organization's CSR strategy
- Assessment of performance by the community

Measuring CSR performance is critical and should be documented and disseminated both for future improvement and for efforts such as recruitment, investment, and reputational benefits.

RECRUITING AND ORGANIZING PARTICIPANTS

Setting a CSR strategy and even enlisting partners are not sufficient for success. Organizations need to recruit and involve employees and community members to implement the programs and to ensure that the desired impact is recognized by the community. To involve employees, an organization can:

- Implement surveys to ask for employee input on what efforts or partnerships the organization should commit to.
- Ensure that employees are fully informed about the selection of partners and the performance of the programs.
- Ask for donations to include automatic payroll deductions, letting employees select which efforts they would like to support.
- Encourage volunteerism by offering time off to volunteer or organizing corporate outings in support of an effort.

- Ensure management sets an example by personally participating in programs.
- Recognize high performers who work in and contribute to the CSR programs.

To involve the community, an organization can:

- Ask community members to share knowledge, information, and experiences with the company and its employees.
- Ask for contributions to the efforts which helps to increase buy-in and commitment.
- Request feedback on perceptions of performance and areas of improvement.

CSR programs are successful when the preponderance of stakeholders are involved and invested in the success of the program.

APPROACHES TO COMMUNITY INCLUSION AND ENGAGEMENT

Community engagement involves creating partnerships through dedication and community involvement. Both the internal organization and external community are strengthened through an exchange of responsibility, knowledge, and services. As they enter the workforce, members of Generation Z are changing the way businesses strategize to attract and retain younger workers. This group in particular is drawn to organizations that are active in philanthropy and community engagement. Although **community engagement programs** are designed to help the populations they serve, they may also be used to teach staff sensitivity, greater understanding, and leadership skills through employee volunteerism. Advocates of corporate community engagement programs also find that they achieve triple returns, providing benefits to the charity or nonprofit organization in the form of free services, to the employees in the form of useful experience, and to the employer in the form of a more-cognizant workforce. Community engagement can also provide advantages in recruitment, teamwork, morale, retention, corporate brand, reputation, and sales.

REPRESENTATION ON COMMUNITY BOARDS

When local companies contribute executives and specialists to the community within which it operates, it can forge relationships, offer expertise, create partnerships, and forge future plans that are jointly beneficial to the community and the corporation. **Community boards** are a fundamental way for members to govern their communities. Boards have three primary functions:

- Establish policy
- Make strategic decisions
- Oversee community activity

Corporate representatives on a community board should contribute (not run), advise (not manage), and contribute to (not dominate) the discussion and decision-making process. Representatives should be viewed as partners rather than overseers to foster strong relationships and add benefits to the community.

JOINT COMMUNITY PROJECTS

Corporate involvement in the local community can be highly impactful and beneficial to both the community and the organization. There are many avenues that firms can take in establishing **joint projects** with the community. Organizations can identify local issues within the community where the company can advocate for policy change, program development, or resources such as drug treatment programs, after-school programs, or pregnancy crisis centers. Investing in its employees who live in the local community is a strong part of helping employee develop skills and qualifications that can be used outside of work. Companies can embed values of volunteerism in the organizational culture by allowing employees some paid time off to do volunteer work. Better yet, an organization can create group volunteer efforts and sponsor a team to do a community project. Firms can sponsor local events, such as science fairs, that align with the company mission. There are many options, and the organization must take care to be consistent and genuine in their efforts.

EMPLOYEE VOLUNTEERISM

There are many companies that have implemented **volunteer programs** to encourage their employees to participate in charitable activities; some provide employees with supplemental time off during work hours. Employers may also set up community service days when the business closes or runs with a reduced crew and donates time to help the community. This could include stocking shelves in a food pantry, cleaning up a local park, or visiting sick children in the hospital. Leadership may also decide to join the board of directors for community organizations that matter to them. Whereas many companies will create **guidelines** of acceptable activities or reject things like hours spent participating on political campaigns, others might attempt to diversify local, national, and global support. The bottom line is that the firm must decide which causes and organizations to support. Some employers will also impose **exclusions**, such as limiting eligibility to employees with satisfactory performance, or requiring manager approval to ensure that time off will not conflict with scheduling or productivity.

These programs are intended to help the communities they serve, but they also help employees develop **soft skills**. Understanding, sensitivity, empathy, collaboration, communication, and leadership are some desirable workplace traits that are cultivated by volunteer activities. Moreover, organizations that are able to make a connection between volunteer programs and diversity will provide opportunities to build an inclusive workplace, cultural competence, and an ability to get along with individuals from diverse backgrounds. Information about volunteer programs, including how to sign up, and rules for scheduling time to participate in advance, should be clearly communicated. Although participation can be encouraged, human resources (HR) and leadership must keep these programs strictly voluntary and not pressure staff into taking part. The benefits of donating time or money are that it feels good, it puts the firm in a favorable light, and it helps others. Additionally, offering ways to give back can be a morale booster and a means to recruit and retain talent.

CORPORATE PHILANTHROPY AND CHARITABLE GIVING

The elements of **corporate social responsibility** differ greatly; some may emphasize philanthropy, donating a percentage of profits to charity, or volunteering activities. Organizations often find philanthropy and charitable work financially rewarding, especially when synchronizing business strategies to cause agendas. Not only can **corporate philanthropy** increase revenues, but it has also been known to boost morale and employee engagement. The corporate culture surrounding philanthropy and charitable giving should be covered during new-hire orientations. Employees should feel empowered to identify opportunities and explore creative ways to solve challenges efficiently. HR practitioners can support corporate philanthropy to demonstrate good values, build image, and foster a sense of efficiency. Volunteers serve as **philanthropic representatives of the company** in the community and can have a strong impact on the public. However, every company will need to determine the best approach for corporate philanthropy that aligns with organizational goals and values. Employers can set up payroll deductions so that employees can easily donate to causes that they support. The employer may also elect to match the employee's contributions.

US Employment Laws and Regulations

EMPLOYMENT AND AUTHORIZATION TO WORK

IMMIGRATION REFORM AND CONTROL ACT (IRCA)

The **Immigration Reform and Control Act (IRCA)** was passed by Congress in 1986 to reduce the volume of **illegal immigrants** coming into the United States for employment opportunities. The IRCA prohibits any employer from hiring illegal immigrants. Denying employment to these immigrants was considered necessary because border patrols could not handle the flow of unauthorized immigration. The act also prohibits employers with four or more employees from discriminating against applicants based on citizenship or natural origin.

The **Homeland Security Act** of 2002 transferred control of immigration from the Department of Justice to two agencies within the Department of Homeland Security (DHS): Immigration and Customs Enforcement (ICE) and the US Citizenship and Immigration Services (USCIS). New employees of all US employers are required to complete and sign an **I-9 verification form** designed by the USCIS to certify that they are eligible for employment. The form requires two types of **verification**: 1) proof of identity and 2) evidence of employment authorization. The I-9 form must be completely executed by both the employee and employer within three days of hire. Employers must retain these forms for three years or for one year past the date of termination, whichever is longer. Employers need to take proactive steps to make certain that their workforce is lawful. At a minimum, employers should verify employee information with the Social Security Administration (SSA).

FORM I-9 AND E-VERIFY

As part of the IRCA and requirements to verify eligibility to work in the United States, Congress created **E-Verify**. The E-Verify system is operated by the DHS and the SSA. E-Verify is a web-based system used by employers to electronically verify an employee's eligibility to work in the United States. Employers must be registered on the DHS website, a process that includes completing a Memorandum of Understanding, which requires employers to use E-Verify for each hire.

E-Verify requires that an employee's name and Social Security number match the SSA records. If the data is inconsistent, the system will return a tentative **no-match**. A no-match does not mean that a person is in the country illegally or that a W-4 form has been falsified. There are extenuating circumstances, such as a name change or error on the W-4, that could be the cause for the no-match. There are specific requirements and procedures that an employer must follow if the system returns a "non-confirmation" or no-match. The SSA will send a letter to the employer with specific advice on handling a no-match situation. While E-Verify is predominately voluntary for employers, the federal government and some states do require its use.

GREEN CARDS AND VISAS

Work visas are permits that allow a non-immigrant individual to travel to a country other than their home country and work in the new country. Typically, work visas are temporary documents and are required upon entry into a country if the individual intends to seek work. Rules regarding work visas vary country to country. In the United States, the most prominent types of work visas are:

- **H-1B high-tech visas** allow a specialty worker with a bachelor's degree or equivalent to be employed in the US for three years, with an option to renew.
- **H-2B visas** are similar to H-1B, but cover unskilled workers who are willing and able to fill positions that the US employer has been unable to fill within the US. H-2B visas are generally issued for one year and can be renewed.
- **TN visas** are issued under the North American Free Trade Agreement (NAFTA). They are designed to enable Canadian and Mexican professionals to work in the US. TN visas are coordinated through the Department of State.
- **F-1 visas** allow students to come to the US to study full-time at an accredited institution.

Green Cards, or Permanent Resident Cards, allow an individual to both work and live in the United States permanently. Green Cards are administered through the USCIS.

DEFERRED ACTION FOR CHILDHOOD ARRIVALS (DACA)

The **Deferred Action for Childhood Arrivals (DACA)** bill was passed in 2012 to allow eligible young adults who arrived in the United States as children to gain work authorization for a temporary period of time. It provided them with protection against deportation. These individuals must have arrived in the US prior to turning age 16, before June 15, 2007. DACA does not provide a path to citizenship, and DACA recipients are not eligible for many aid programs such as Medicaid, the Children's Health Insurance Program (CHIP), and the health marketplaces for the Patient Protection and Affordable Care Act (PPACA, or ACA). DACA status must be reviewed and renewed every two years for the individual to continue to be covered by the provisions in the act. Employers are required to verify the employee's identity and authorization to work. Employers are not allowed to investigate the employee's immigration status. The I-9 form verifies the right to work and is all the documentation that the employer may request.

EMPLOYMENT-AT-WILL DOCTRINE

The **employment-at-will doctrine** essentially allows both the employer and the employee the mutual right to end the employment relationship at any time. This philosophy of hiring whomever you want for as long as you want was created to protect workers from wrongful terminations. In more recent years, the voluntary relationship has been challenged by state and case laws intended to protect workers. These laws have created exceptions to employment-at-will, including implied contracts, retaliatory discharges, and public policies. **Implied contracts** may be verbal or written promises by an employer to continue an employment relationship. However, some courts have recognized a **promissory estoppel** exception when an employer makes a promise that he or she reasonably expects the employee to rely upon, the employee does rely upon it, and the employee suffers financial or personal injury as a result.

BACKGROUND CHECKS

Before a candidate is onboarded, the employer should perform due diligence on the candidate's background. Some parts of a **background check** can be completed before an offer of employment, and others only after the offer has been extended and accepted. Background checks should be pertinent to the position and can cover such topics as:

- References
- Employment verification from previous employers
- Consumer or credit report
- Criminal conviction check (if warranted for the position and permitted by state law)
- Driving record (if warranted for the position)
- Drug test
- Lie detector test (only after conditional offer has been extended)
- Medical exams (only after hire and only to document support for a requested accommodation or if the employer has reason to believe that the employee will not be able to perform the job)

In some cases, employers who fail to conduct an appropriate background check may be held liable for some actions of the employee, known as negligent hiring.

FAIR CREDIT REPORTING ACT (FCRA)

Federal law regulates the use of consumer and credit report information through the 1970 **Fair Credit Reporting Act (FCRA)**. Credit reports may be used for the purpose of assessing character and general reputation. The FCRA has two goals and five main provisions:

Goals:

- To protect the privacy of an individual's credit data by restricting access to only those who have a legitimate need for the information
- To ensure the accuracy of an individual's consumer report information by giving the individual access and the right to dispute their data and to know whether they have been granted or denied credit by an organization based on their consumer data

Provisions:

- The person being investigated must provide prior written authorization to allow the employers access to and his or her consumer report information.
- Address-checking places the onus on the employer to ensure that the report it receives is actually for the intended employee or candidate.
- If an employer takes an adverse action against an employee or candidate based on the consumer report information, they must notify the employee or candidate with specific information about the agency that provided the information and the specific type of information received and used.
- The employer must limit access to the consumer report information and must destroy the information to prevent unauthorized disclosure to other parties.
- Employers who supply information to a consumer report must ensure that the information is accurate and complete.

COMPENSATION
FAIR LABOR STANDARDS ACT (FLSA)

The **Fair Labor Standards Act (FLSA)** of 1938, also known as the Wagner-Connery Wages and Hours Act, or the Wage Hour Bill, sets minimum wage standards, overtime pay standards, and child labor restrictions. The act is administered by the Wage and Hour Division of the Department of Labor. The FLSA carefully defines employees as "exempt" or "nonexempt" from provisions, requires that employers calculate **overtime** for covered employees at one and one-half times the regular rate of pay (also called "time and a half") for all hours worked in excess of 40 hours during a week, and defines how a workweek should be measured. The purpose of **minimum wage standards** is to ensure a living wage and to reduce poverty for low-income families, minority workers, and women. The **child labor provisions** protect minors from positions that may be harmful or detrimental to their health or well-being and regulates the hours that minors can legally work. The act also outlines requirements for employers to keep records of hours, wages, and related payroll items.

2020 OVERTIME RULE

The Department of Labor established new **overtime rules** and guidelines for classification of exempt employees in 2020. The threshold for an exempt employee was set at $35,568 annually, or $684 per week. Employees under this threshold are non-exempt and must be paid overtime, even if classified as a manager or a professional within the company. Overtime must be paid at a rate of 1.5 times the regular hourly rate for hours worked in excess of 40 hours in a workweek. When this change was put into effect in 2020, employers needed to review their employee statuses and should have reclassified some employees who were previously exempt to non-exempt under the new threshold.

> **Review Video: US Employment Compensation Laws**
> Visit mometrix.com/academy and enter code: 613448

EQUAL PAY ACT

The **Equal Pay Act**, which was passed in 1963, prevents wage discrimination based on gender. It requires an employer to provide equal pay to both men and women performing similar tasks unless the employer can prove that there is an acceptable reason for the difference in pay, such as merit, seniority, or quantity or quality of work performed. This act also establishes the criteria that must be considered to determine whether a particular position is similar. This includes the effort necessary for the tasks related to the position, the level of responsibility associated with the position, the skills required to perform the position, and the working conditions associated with the position.

LEDBETTER V. GOODYEAR TIRE & RUBBER CO.

In 1998, Lilly Ledbetter filed a lawsuit against the Goodyear Tire & Rubber Company. She alleged pay inequality, based on the pay of male counterparts, under the Title VII of the Civil Rights Act of 1964 and the Equal Pay Act. The courts initially found in Ledbetter's favor, stating that her pay inequality claims were upheld and awarding her $360,000 in back pay. However, Goodyear filed a request to vacate the judgment, stating that the claim was too far after the fact, as her employment went back 20 years, and that the lawsuit should not have been allowed. After several rulings back and forth, the case moved to the Supreme Court. The Supreme Court ruled in 2007 that pay discrimination suits must be brought within 180 days of the employer's pay decision.

LILLY LEDBETTER FAIR PAY ACT

The **Lilly Ledbetter Fair Pay Act** of 2009 overturned the 2007 Supreme Court decision in *Ledbetter v. Goodyear Tire & Rubber Co.*, which ruled that the statute of limitations to make a discriminatory pay claim was 180 days from the first discriminatory paycheck. The Lilly Ledbetter Fair Pay Act of 2009 established a law that the statute of limitations restarts with each discriminatory paycheck. The act applies to all protected classes, and covers both wages and pensions. Due to the scope of the act, employers could face claims years after an employee has left the company. This act was designed to make employers more proactive in resolving pay inequities.

EMPLOYEE RETIREMENT INCOME SECURITY ACT (ERISA)

The **Employee Retirement Income Security Act (ERISA)** was passed in 1974 to protect employees who are covered under private pensions and employee welfare benefit plans. ERISA ensures that employees receive promised benefits and are protected against early termination, mismanaged funds, or fraudulent activities. ERISA mandates that employers adhere to eligibility requirements, vesting requirements, portability practices, funding requirements, fiduciary responsibilities, reporting and disclosure requirements, and compliance testing.

Most employees who have at least 1,000 hours of work in 12 months for two consecutive years are eligible to participate in **private pension plans**. Employees have the right to receive some portion of employer contributions when their employment ends. Employees must be allowed to transfer pension funds from one retirement account to another. Sufficient funds must be available from the employer to cover future payments. Employers must appoint an individual to be responsible for seeking ideal portfolio options and administering pension funds. Employers must adhere to extensive reporting requirements, provide summary plan documents, and notify participants of any changes. Employers are required to complete annual minimum coverage, actual deferral percentage, actual contribution percentage, and top-heavy testing to prevent discrimination in favor of highly compensated employees.

FEDERAL WAGE GARNISHMENT LAW

The **Federal Wage Garnishment Law** of 1968 imposes limitations on the amount of disposable earnings that may be withheld from an employee's income in a given pay period to satisfy a **wage garnishment order** for failure to pay a debt. The law restricts the amount that can be withheld to 25 percent of an employee's disposable weekly earnings or an amount that is 30 times the FLSA minimum wage, whichever is less. However, overdue payments to the IRS, child support in arrears, and alimony payments and other exceptions allow for more significant amounts to be withheld. Employers must immediately begin income withholdings upon receipt of a garnishment order, and funds must be sent to the respective agency within seven days. Failure to do so could impose hefty fines and penalties for the employer. Employers may not take disciplinary action or discriminate against employees due to the receipt or obligation to comply with wage garnishment orders.

DAVIS-BACON ACT

The **Davis-Bacon Act** of 1931 applies to federal contracts in excess of $2,000, for the construction, alteration, or repair of public buildings. The act requires that contractors and subcontractors must pay laborers and mechanics no less than the prevailing wage rates and fringe benefits, as determined by the Secretary of Labor, for like work and workers. Wages and fringe benefits are defined to include basic hourly pay and medical/hospital care, pensions upon retirement or death, unemployment benefits, life insurance, disability insurance, vacation and holiday pay, and other bona fide fringe benefits.

WALSH-HEALEY PUBLIC CONTRACTS ACT

The 1936 **Walsh-Healey Public Contracts Act** covers employees who produce, assemble, handle, or ship goods to the US government or Washington, DC on contracts exceeding $10,000. For these contracts, workers must be paid at least federal minimum wage for all hours worked, and 1.5 times their regular rate of pay for all hours worked over 40 in a workweek. This act was created to protect employees from exploitative employers and to improve labor standards.

MCNAMARA-O'HARA SERVICE CONTRACT ACT

The 1965 **McNamara-O'Hara Service Contract Act** covers contractors and subcontractors performing services on prime federal contracts in excess of $2,500. These contractors must pay service employees no less than the prevailing wage found in the locality or rates paid by the predecessor's collective bargaining agreement. The act also covers fringe benefits and vacations and all safety and health standards currently applied to the contract. Overtime provisions of the FLSA are also covered under the act.

EMPLOYEE AND LABOR RELATIONS
NATIONAL LABOR RELATIONS ACT (NLRA)

The **National Labor Relations Act (NLRA)** was passed by Congress in 1935 after a long period of conflict in labor relations. Also known as the **Wagner Act**, after New York Senator Robert Wagner, it was intended to be an economic stabilizer and establish collective bargaining in industrial relations. Section 7 of the NLRA provides employees with the right to form, join, or assist **labor organizations** as well as the right to engage in **concerted activities** such as collective bargaining through representatives or other mutual aid. Section 8 of the NLRA also identifies five **unfair labor practices** and sets rules for employers:

- Employers shall not interfere with or coerce employees from the rights outlined in Section 7.
- Employers shall not dominate or disrupt the formation of a labor union.
- Employers shall not allow union membership or activity to influence hiring, firing, promotion, or related employment decisions.
- Employers shall not discriminate against or discharge an employee who has given testimony or filed a charge with the NLRA.
- Employers cannot refuse bargaining in good faith with employee representatives.

TAFT-HARTLEY ACT

Because many employers felt that the NLRA gave too much power to unions, Congress passed the **Labor Management Relations Act** in 1947. Also known as the **Taft-Hartley Act**, the act sought to avoid unnecessary strikes and impose certain restrictions over union activities. The act addresses **four basic issues**: unfair labor practices by unions, the rights of employees, the rights of employers, and national emergency strikes. Moreover, the act prohibits unions from the following:

- Restraining or coercing employees from their right to not engage in union activities
- Forcing an employer to discriminate in any way against an employee to encourage or discourage union membership
- Forcing an employer to pay for work or services that are not needed or not performed

- Conducting certain types of strikes or boycotts
- Charging excessive initiation fees or membership dues when employees are required to join a union

LANDRUM-GRIFFIN ACT

The government exercised further control over union activities in 1959 by passing the **Labor Management Reporting and Disclosure Act**. Commonly known as the **Landrum-Griffin Act**, this law regulates the **internal conduct of labor unions** to reduce the likelihood of fraud and improper actions. The act imposes controls on five major areas: reports to the Secretary of Labor, a bill of rights for union members, union trusteeships, conduct of union elections, and financial safeguards. Some key provisions include the following:

- Granting equal rights to every union member with regard to nominations, attending meetings, and voting
- Requiring unions to submit and make available to the public a copy of their constitutions, bylaws, and annual financial reports
- Requiring unions to hold regular elections every five years for national organizations, and every three years for local organizations
- Monitoring the management and investment of union funds, making embezzlement a federal crime

> **Review Video: US Employment Law: Employee and Labor Relations (NLRA)**
> Visit mometrix.com/academy and enter code: 972790

NLRB V. WEINGARTEN

As a result of the 1975 Supreme Court case *NLRB v. Weingarten*, union employees have the right to request coworker presence at investigatory meetings that may involve disciplinary action. In 2000, the NLRB (National Labor Relations Board) expanded this protection to nonunion employees. These protections are known as **Weingarten rights**.

LECHMERE, INC. V. NLRB

The 1992 Supreme Court case *Lechmere, Inc. v. NLRB* determined that nonemployee union organizers may solicit employees on private company property if no other reasonable alternative to contact employees exists. This preserves the employees' right to organize.

WARN ACT

The **Worker Adjustment and Retraining Notification (WARN) Act** applies to employers with more than 100 full-time workers or more than 100 full- and part-time workers totaling at least 4,000 hours per week. The WARN Act requires that employers provide a minimum of 60 days' notice to local government and affected workers in the event of a plant closing that will result in job loss for 50 or more employees during a 30-day period. Notification is also required in the event of mass layoffs that will result in job loss for greater than 33 percent of workers, or more than 500 employees, whichever is less, during a 30-day period. There are a few situational exceptions to the WARN Act, including natural disasters and unforeseeable business circumstances.

PRIVACY PROTECTION ACT

The **Privacy Protection Act** of 1974 was passed to protect the privacy of individuals employed by government agencies or by government contractors. Although this act prohibits government agencies from disclosing individual personnel records, the **Freedom of Information Act (FOIA)** requires these agencies to release certain information, like what the organization does or how it is organized. However, requests for information that could constitute a disclosure of personal privacy are exempt from FOIA requests and remain protected.

The Privacy Act also established the **Privacy Protection Study Commission**, which has outlined three main policy goals:

- minimize intrusiveness
- maximize fairness
- create legitimate expectations of confidentiality

The Commission also advocates five basic employee rights regarding procedures:

- notice
- authorization
- access
- correction
- confidentiality

ELECTRONIC COMMUNICATIONS PRIVACY ACT

The **Electronic Communications Privacy Act (ECPA)** of 1986 made it illegal to intentionally intercept a wire, oral, or electronic communication. The act defined *intercept* as "the aural or other acquisition of the contents of any electronic, wire, or oral communication using any electronic, mechanical, or other device." The ECPA covers all telephone conversations, voicemail messages, email (while being transmitted), and live conversations. However, if one of the two parties consents to the intercepts, then it may be recorded, even without the consent of the second or other parties. Some states have laws that require two-party consent, and these are fully enforceable. Telephone equipment used in the course of ordinary business is exempt from the act, which allows companies to record telephone conversations for quality control and verification purposes.

EMPLOYEE POLYGRAPH PROTECTION ACT

The **Employee Polygraph Protection Act** of 1988 was designed to protect individuals seeking employment from being required to submit to polygraph tests. This act specifically forbids private employers from basing hiring decisions on polygraph tests unless the individual is seeking a position involving pharmaceuticals, working in an armored car, or serving as a security officer. This act does not apply to any government agency or federal contractor or subcontractor with the Federal Bureau of Investigation, national defense, or national security contracts. If an employer requires a polygraph test and the position is not related to one of these areas, the company can be fined up to $10,000.

JOB SAFETY AND HEALTH

SEXUAL HARASSMENT

The Civil Rights Act of 1964 bans **sexual harassment** and makes it an employer's responsibility to prevent it. Sexual harassment can be defined as unsolicited sexual advances, requests for sexual favors, and any other conduct of a sexual nature that meets any of the following conditions:

- Obedience to such conduct is construed as a condition of employment either explicitly or implicitly.
- Obedience to or rejection of such conduct is used as the basis for employment decisions affecting an individual.
- Such conduct produces an intimidating, hostile, or offensive working environment or otherwise has the effect of interfering with an individual's work performance.

Sexual harassment is separated into two types: **quid pro quo (this for that) cases** and **hostile environment cases**. Victims do not need to suffer loss, but the harassment needs to be pervasive or severe to be considered a violation. Employees may be offended by any sexual conduct in the workplace, such as lewd comments, jokes, pornographic pictures, or touching. Employees who voice discomfort may request that the environment be changed. If an employer fails to correct the offensive environment, employees may press charges without needing to demonstrate physical or psychological damage.

BREAK TIME FOR NURSING MOTHERS

The **Patient Protection and Affordable Care Act**, often simply called the **Affordable Care Act**, was established in 2010 as an amendment to the FLSA. Employers are required to provide reasonable time for a nursing mother to express breast milk after the birth of a child. Reasonable time is not defined by the FLSA, but the Department of Labor has found that mothers need two to three breaks of between 15 and 20 minutes each in an eight-hour workday. The act covers nursing mothers up until the child reaches age one. Employers are also required to provide a private location for nursing mothers to attend to this need; the space cannot be in a restroom.

HIPAA

The **Health Insurance Portability and Accountability Act (HIPAA)** was passed in 1996 to provide greater protections and portability in healthcare coverage. Some individuals felt locked into current employer plans and feared that they would not be able to obtain coverage from a new employer plan due to preexisting conditions. Some of the **key HIPAA provisions** are preexisting condition exclusions, pregnancy, newborn and adopted children, credible coverage, renewal of coverage, medical savings accounts, tax benefits, and privacy provisions. Employees who have had another policy for the preceding 12 months cannot be excluded from coverage due to a preexisting condition or pregnancy. Newborn or newly adopted children who are covered by credible coverage within 30 days of their birth or adoption are also protected from exclusion due to preexisting conditions. **Credible coverage** involves being covered under typical group health plans, and this coverage must be renewable to most groups and individuals as long as premiums are paid. **Medical savings accounts** were created by Congress for those who are self-employed or otherwise not eligible for credible coverage. Individuals who are self-employed are also allowed to take 80 percent of their health-related expenses as a tax deduction. Finally, HIPAA introduced several regulations that impose **civil and criminal penalties** on employers who disclose employees' personal health information without consent.

> **Review Video: What is HIPAA?**
> Visit mometrix.com/academy and enter code: 412009

EQUAL EMPLOYMENT OPPORTUNITY
EXECUTIVE ORDER 11246

Issued in 1965, **Executive Order (EO) 11246** requires all nonexempt government contractors to take actions to avoid discrimination, including:

- Do not discriminate against an employee or candidate due to race, color, religion, sex, or national origin.
- Take positive affirmative action that candidates and employees are treated without regard to their race, color, religion, sex, or national origin.
- Post notices of the company's obligations under EO 11246, and furnish notices to labor unions with which it has a collective bargaining agreement.
- Include an equal opportunity provision in all employment ads and postings.
- Furnish information and reports as required to the Secretary of Labor.
- Allow the contract to be canceled for noncompliance.
- Include all these provisions in contracts with nonexempt subcontractors and vendors.

EO 11246 is administered within the Department of Labor, by the Office of Federal Contract Compliance Programs.

EQUAL EMPLOYMENT OPPORTUNITY ACT

The **Equal Employment Opportunity (EEO) Act** of 1972, signed by President Nixon, amended Title VII of the Civil Rights Act of 1964 to give the Equal Employment Opportunity Commission (EEOC) authority to conduct enforcement litigation for itself. The act prohibits discrimination in employment terms, compensation, working conditions, and other areas of employment. The act mandates enforcement by the courts instead of juries and provides civil penalties for violations. Penalties can include remedial hiring policies for employers and potential reinstatement with back pay for victims.

REHABILITATION ACT

Also signed by President Nixon, the **Rehabilitation Act** of 1973 was the precursor to the Americans with Disabilities Act of 1990. These laws cover employment discrimination against persons with disabilities. The Rehabilitation Act covers federal contractors and subcontractors whose contracts exceed $10,000. The act also requires an equal opportunity clause in all contracts. Additionally, employers with more than 50 employees or contracts of over $50,000 must have written affirmative action plans for employing people with disabilities. The Act is administered by the Office of Federal Contractor Compliance Programs (OFCCP).

Section 501 of the Rehabilitation Act prohibits discrimination in federal employment on the basis of a disability and requires the Federal Government to proactively use affirmative action in employment for individuals with disabilities.

Section 503 of the Rehabilitation Act prohibits federal contractors and subcontractors from discriminating in employment against individuals with disabilities and requires employers to take affirmative action to recruit, hire, promote, and retain these individuals.

VIETNAM ERA VETERANS' READJUSTMENT ASSISTANCE ACT

Another law signed by President Nixon, this one in 1974, the **Vietnam Era Veterans' Readjustment Assistance Act** applies to federal contractors and subcontractors with contracts over $10,000, and prohibits discrimination against special disabled veterans and veterans of the Vietnam era. A **special disabled veteran** is a veteran who has a 30% or greater disability rating, or who was released from active duty due to a service-related disability. A **Vietnam-era veteran** is defined as a veteran who served in the Vietnam War or who served between the period of August 1964 and May 1975 regardless of location, and who was not dishonorably discharged. Contracts must include an equal opportunity clause. OFCCP administers and enforces this act.

EXECUTIVE ORDER 13672

President Obama issued **Executive Order 13672** in 2014. It prohibits contractors and subcontractors who have contracts greater than $10,000 from discriminating on the basis of sexual orientation and gender identity, and requires that contractors include these two protected categories in their equal opportunity policies and notices.

MCDONNELL DOUGLAS CORP. V. GREEN

The 1973 case **McDonnell Douglas Corp v. Green** established a test for whether discrimination has occurred in the workplace. The plaintiff, Percy Green, filed a complaint with the EEOC that he had been a victim of discrimination. The case then became a lawsuit and eventually went to the Supreme Court. There were two parts to the findings:

1. The onus to prove a "prima facie" case of discrimination falls on the complainant.
2. The burden then falls on the company to prove that there was a legitimate, nondiscriminatory reason for the personnel action put forth by the complainant.

This case created the "burden-shifting" framework for discrimination cases.

EQUAL EMPLOYMENT OPPORTUNITY COMMISSION (EEOC)

The **Equal Employment Opportunity Commission (EEOC)** was created to enforce Title VII of the Civil Rights Act of 1964 and the Americans with Disabilities Act (ADA). The EEOC holds jurisdiction over any charges under those titles and has the power to authorize or bring suit in federal court on behalf of an employee. The EEOC may help an aggrieved party prosecute or issue a "right to sue" notice, giving permission for the person to pursue the case independently. The primary responsibility of the EEOC is to **prevent discrimination** based on race, color, religion, sex, origin, disability, or age. Employers are obligated to furnish any information the EEOC requests, including annual reporting for employers with 50 or more employees. There are **five steps** the EEOC follows when handling discrimination cases: 1) a charge filed within 180 days, 2) an attempt at a no-fault settlement, 3) an EEOC investigation, 4) an attempt to resolve through conciliation, and 5) a recommendation for or against litigation. Drastic remedies may be decreed upon an employer found guilty of discrimination, including but not limited to reinstatement of the employee, back pay, elimination of testing, hiring quotas, and new training programs.

CIVIL RIGHTS ACTS

The **13th and 14th Amendments** address equal protection in employment rights by state and local governments for all citizens. Major prohibitions against racial discrimination in hiring, placement, and continuation of employment contracts by private employers, unions, and employment agencies date back to the early **Civil Rights Acts** of 1866 and 1870. The **National Labor Relations Act** of 1935 indirectly prohibits racial discrimination in labor unions by requiring fair representation for all. New York was the first state to pass additional regulations to eliminate discrimination in state employment due to race, creed, color, or national origin with the **Fair Employment Practices Act** of 1945. This was well before **Title VII of the Civil Rights Act** of 1964 prohibited employment discrimination based on race, color, religion, sex, or national origin for all employers with 15 or more employees. Title VII was amended by the **Equal Employment Opportunity Act** of 1972, which strengthened enforcement and expanded coverage so that one person could file suit on behalf of many affected individuals for equal damages. The act was last revised in 1991 to more clearly define which actions are discriminatory and to outline prosecution procedures for jury trials and monetary damages.

The Civil Rights Act Section 703(e) states that it is **legal to discriminate** on the basis of sex, religion, or national origin in special occasions where the specified characteristic is a "**bona fide occupational qualification (BFOQ)** and reasonably necessary to normal operations and the survival of that particular business or enterprise." It is the employer's responsibility to prove and corroborate a BFOQ and its necessity to business operations and that no other options are available that would have less discriminatory impact. The Supreme Court does not obligate employers to make religious accommodations that could impose upon the rights of other workers, decrease production efficiencies, accommodate unfair perks that would not benefit others, provide undue hardship, or breach a collective bargaining agreement. Moreover, the courts have rejected client preference or traditional BFOQs, and only a select number of cases have upheld race or gender as legitimate BFOQs. Examples of sex being upheld as BFOQs by the courts are 1) when social modesty morals and privacy conflicts are the main concern for clients; 2) when a position requires a defined aesthetic authenticity; or 2) when one sex is biologically unable to perform job duties. **EEOC guidelines** encourage employers to prepare written job descriptions listing the essential functions of a job.

AMERICANS WITH DISABILITIES ACT (ADA)

The **Americans with Disabilities Act (ADA)** was established in 1990 to protect individuals with physical or mental impairments from job discrimination. The law requires that all employers with 15 or more employees make **reasonable accommodations** to employ disabled people who are otherwise qualified. Individuals are considered otherwise qualified if they can perform the essential functions of the job if these accommodations are in place. There may be occasions in which the act does not cover people who have disabilities that might pose a direct threat to themselves or the general public because reasonable accommodations cannot eliminate the potential threat. In addition, if an employer would face undue hardship (generally high cost relative to company size), accommodations can be refused. Employers should engage in an interactive dialog with the employee (or job candidate) to come up with a reasonable accommodation whenever possible.

Amendments to the act broaden the definition of "disability" to include anything that severely limits a major life activity or bodily function. Major life activities include, but are not limited to, seeing, thinking, reading, or working. Further, the EEOC has noted that the following **impairments** can meet the definitions of a disability: deafness, blindness, intellectual disabilities, partially or completely missing limbs, mobility impairments that require the use of a wheelchair, cerebral palsy, diabetes, autism, epilepsy, HIV/AIDS, cancer, multiple sclerosis, muscular dystrophy, major depression, bipolar disorder, posttraumatic stress disorder, obsessive compulsive disorder, and schizophrenia. Additionally, changes to the act prohibit reverse discrimination claims from non-disabled workers.

AGE DISCRIMINATION IN EMPLOYMENT ACT (ADEA)

The **Age Discrimination in Employment Act** (ADEA) was first passed in 1967 to protect job applicants and employees between 40 and 60 years of age. The ADEA applies to all private employers with 20 or more employees, government agencies, and labor unions with 25 or more members. The act also prohibits these parties from **discriminating against older workers** in benefit plan designs. Although the upper age limit was raised to 65 and then 75 in subsequent years, the **Consolidated Omnibus Budget Reconciliation Act** eliminated an upper limit, so that the ADEA covers almost everyone at least 40 years of age, with the exception that certain executives may be forced into retirement at age 65.

PREGNANCY DISCRIMINATION ACT

There are two main clauses of the **Pregnancy Discrimination Act** of 1978. The first clause applies to Title VII's **prohibition against sex discrimination**, which also directly applies to discrimination on the basis of childbirth, pregnancy, or related medical conditions. The second clause requires that employers treat women affected by pregnancy the same as others for all employment-related tasks and similarly in their ability or inability to work. In short, the Pregnancy Discrimination Act makes it illegal to fire or refuse to hire or promote a woman because she is pregnant, force a pregnancy leave on a woman who is willing and able to perform the job, and stop accruing seniority for a woman because she is out of work to give birth.

UNIFORM GUIDELINES ON EMPLOYEE SELECTION PROCEDURES (UGESP)

The **Uniform Guidelines on Employee Selection Procedures (UGESP)**, which were passed in 1978, are actually a collection of principles, techniques, and procedures designed to help employers comply with federal anti-discrimination laws. The primary purpose of these guidelines is to define the specific types of procedures that may cause disparate impact and are considered illegal. The UGESP relates to unfair procedures that make it much less likely that an individual belonging to a protected class would be able to receive a particular position.

GRIGGS V. DUKE POWER CO.

Prior to the 1964 Civil Rights Act, Duke Power Co. segregated employees by race. Once the act passed, the company started requiring a high school diploma and a certain score on an IQ test to qualify for any positions above manual labor. As a result, many African Americans could not obtain the higher-paying jobs. The 1971 Supreme Court case **Griggs v. Duke Power Co.** determined that employers must be able to demonstrate that job requirements are actually linked to an ability to perform the work. It also determined that employers may be charged with discrimination when a protected group appears to have been discriminated against, even if the discrimination was unintentional. This is known as **disparate impact**.

PHILLIPS V. MARTIN MARIETTA CORP.

Linked to the 1964 Civil Rights Act, the 1971 Supreme Court case **Phillips v. Martin Marietta Corp.** ruled that a company cannot refuse to employ women with young children if they employ men with young children unless there is a legitimate business necessity.

GENETIC INFORMATION NONDISCRIMINATION ACT (GINA)

The **Genetic Information Nondiscrimination Act (GINA)** is a 2008 federal law that applies to all employers and makes it illegal for genetic information about a person or a family member to be used to **deny enrollment** in a fully insured or self-insured healthcare plan or to change the individual's premiums or contribution rates. The US Department of Labor has defined **genetic information** as a disease or disorder in an individual's family medical history, the results of an individual's or family member's genetic tests, or the fact that an individual or family member has sought or received genetic services. These protections also include the genetic information of any fetus or embryo connected to the individual's family.

GINA also forbids an employer from requesting or otherwise collecting a person's genetic information unless the information is used in certain wellness programs, inadvertently obtained, or needed to comply with certification requirements or regulations, or when observing biological effects of toxins in the workplace. The information an employer might obtain when requesting medical documentation for extended absences, requested leave, or accommodations is commonly accepted. Court remedies for GINA are similar to those existing for sex and racial discrimination.

LEAVE AND BENEFITS
EEOC V. VERIZON (2011)

In 2011, the **Equal Employment Opportunity Commission (EEOC)** found that Verizon had unlawfully denied reasonable accommodations to hundreds of people with disabilities and then disciplined or fired them for attendance issues. This was a national class-action lawsuit, and the largest settlement in EEOC history for penalties under the Americans with Disabilities Act (ADA). The EEOC found that Verizon failed to make reasonable accommodations for time off as required for employees with disabilities, and used the absences to punish and ultimately fire them. The ADA requires employers to make accommodations such as paid or unpaid leave for employees with disabilities as long as it does not create undue financial hardship to the company. Verizon was fined $20 million in the settlement.

FAMILY AND MEDICAL LEAVE ACT (FMLA)

The **Family and Medical Leave Act (FMLA)** of 1993 is a federal regulation that gives employees the right to a maximum of 12 weeks of **unpaid leave** each 12-month period specifically for the care of medical conditions that affect themselves or immediate family members. To be eligible for FMLA leave, an employee must have worked for a covered employer for the preceding 12 months and for a minimum of 1,250 hours during that time. All private employers, public or government agencies, and local schools with 50 or more employees within a 75-mile radius must adhere to the regulations. Qualifying events covered under FMLA include the following:

- The birth or adoption of a new child within one year of birth or placement
- The employee's own serious health condition that involves a period of incapacity
- An ill or injured spouse, child, or parent who requires the employee's care
- Any qualifying exigency (such as arranging childcare, tending to legal matters, and attending military ceremonies) due to active-duty foreign deployment of the employee's spouse, child, or parent
- The care of an ill or injured covered service member as long as the employee is a spouse, child, parent, or next of kin

Time to care for military personnel or recent veterans has been expanded to 26 weeks in a 12-month period.

The FMLA has undergone some significant amendments, and human resource practitioners should be aware of the following:

- If a company fails to denote an employee's leave as FMLA leave, the employee may be eligible to receive compensation for any losses incurred.
- Prior to 2008, all FMLA disputes required Department of Labor or legal intervention. Now, employees and employers are encouraged to work out any issues in-house to avoid the cost of litigation.
- Light duty does not count toward FMLA leave.
- FMLA covers medical issues arising from preexisting conditions.
- Due to their unique scheduling, airline employees are eligible for FMLA after 504 or more hours worked during the preceding 12 months.

Consolidated Omnibus Budget Reconciliation Act (COBRA)

The **Consolidated Omnibus Budget Reconciliation Act (COBRA)** of 1986 requires that all employers with 20 or more employees continue the availability of **healthcare benefits coverage** and protects employees from the potential economic hardship of losing these benefits when they are terminated, work reduced hours, or quit. COBRA also provides coverage to the employee's spouse and dependents as qualified beneficiaries. Events that qualify for this continuation of coverage include the following:

- Voluntary or involuntary termination for any other reason than gross misconduct
- Reduction in hours that would otherwise result in loss of coverage
- Divorce or legal separation from the employee
- Death of the employee
- The employee becoming disabled and entitled to Medicare
- The dependent no longer being a dependent child under plan rules (older than 26)

Typically, the employee and qualified beneficiaries are entitled to 18 months of continued coverage. There are some instances that will extend coverage for up to an additional 18 months. Coverage will be lost if the employer terminates group coverage, premium payments are not received, or new coverage becomes available.

Uniformed Services Employment and Reemployment Rights Act (USERRA)

The **Uniformed Services Employment and Reemployment Rights Act (USERRA)** of 1994 is applicable to all employers. USERRA forbids employers from denying employment, reemployment, retention, promotion, or employment benefits due to service in the uniformed services. Employees absent in services for less than 31 days must report to the employer within eight hours after arriving safely home. Those who are absent between 31 and 180 days must submit an application for reemployment within 14 days. Those who are absent 181 days or more have 90 days to submit an application for reemployment. Employees are entitled to the positions that they would have held if they had remained continuously employed. If they are no longer qualified or able to perform the job requirements because of a service-related disability, they are to be provided with a position of equal seniority, status, and pay.

The **escalator principle** further entitles returning employees to all of the seniority-based benefits they had when their service began plus any additional benefits they would have accrued with reasonable certainty if they had remained continuously employed. Likewise, employees cannot be required to use accrued vacation or PTO during absences. USERRA requires all healthcare plans to provide **COBRA coverage** for up to 18 months of absence and entitles employees to restoration of coverage upon return. Pension plans must remain undisturbed by absences as well. However, those separated from the service for less-than-honorable circumstances are not protected by USERRA.

Patient Protection and Affordable Care Act (PPACA)

The **Patient Protection and Affordable Care Act (PPACA)**, often referred to simply as the **Affordable Care Act** or **ACA** is a comprehensive healthcare law that was passed in 2010 to establish regulations on medical services, insurance coverage, preventative services, whistleblowing, and similar practices. A few key provisions of PPACA include the following:

- **Individual mandate:** required all individuals to maintain health insurance or pay a penalty; however, it was removed from the statute effective tax year 2019
- **State healthcare exchanges**: provides individuals and families a portal where they can purchase healthcare coverage from a variety of plans
- **Employer shared responsibility:** requires that employers with more than 50 employees provide affordable coverage to all employees that work 30 or more hours per week or pay a penalty
- **Affordable coverage:** does not allow employers to shift the burden of healthcare costs to employees, and imposes a penalty for employees who obtain government subsidies for coverage

- **Flexible spending accounts (FSAs)**: imposes a cap on pretax contributions to FSAs, health reimbursement arrangements (HRAs), and health savings accounts (HSAs)
- **Wellness incentives:** allows employers to provide premium discounts for employees who meet wellness requirements
- **Excise tax on "Cadillac" plans:** was to impose excise tax on employers that provide expensive coverage beginning in 2020; however, it was repealed in 2019.
- **W-2 reporting requirements:** requires employers to report the cost of coverage under employer-sponsored group health plans on each employee's W-2 form
- **Summary of benefits coverage:** requires insurance companies and employers to provide individuals with a summary of benefits coverage (SBC) using a standard form
- **Whistleblower protections:** amends the FLSA to prohibit employers from retaliating against an employee who applies for health benefit subsidies or tax credits

NATIONAL FEDERATION OF INDEPENDENT BUSINESS V. SEBELIUS (2012)

Opponents of the PPACA argued that certain provisions of the law, such as the individual mandate, were unconstitutional. In 2012, in the case *National Federation of Independent Business v. Sebelius*, the Supreme Court ultimately ruled that the PPACA was constitutional, and it remained intact until President Trump reversed the individual mandate effective 2019; the "Cadillac plan" excise tax was also repealed in 2019. All other elements of the PPACA legislation are still currently in place.

Chapter Quiz

Ready to see how well you retained what you just read? Scan the QR code to go directly to the chapter quiz interface for this study guide. If you're using a computer, simply visit the bonus page at **mometrix.com/bonus948/shrmcp** and click the Chapter Quizzes link.

SHRM-CP Practice Test #1

Want to take this practice test in an online interactive format?
Check out the bonus page, which includes interactive practice questions and much more: **mometrix.com/bonus948/shrmcp**

Refer to the following for questions 1 - 2:

> You are a human resources manager for a midsized technology company with a diverse employee group—there are many employees from India, some are from Russia, and others are American. Employees tend to stay within their own cultural groups for socializing and even for project collaboration. This has created a siloed work environment, resulting in minimal communication and inefficient work processes.

1. What would be a creative and effective way to improve communication across the organization?

    a. Pair up individuals from different cultures on specific work assignments.
    b. Require language classes for each of the dialects spoken in the organization.
    c. Offer cultural sensitivity training for the entire organization.
    d. Organize on-site social activities to take place during work hours.

2. What guidance would you give to supervisors/managers for managing teams from different backgrounds?

    a. Consider employees' cultural preferences before assigning work tasks.
    b. Have weekly team meetings and ask employees to share what they're working on for the week.
    c. Get to know each team member and their background to build trust and establish the relationship first.
    d. Facilitate face-to-face discussions among team members during times of conflict.

3. The Fair Labor Standards Act (FLSA) mandates that most employees be paid overtime for more than 40 hours in a week unless they fall under certain criteria. Which is NOT an FLSA exemption?

    a. Outside sales exemption
    b. Computer employee exemption
    c. Creative professional exemption
    d. Advanced engineer exemption

4. Which of the following elements is the most critical when establishing an organizational diversity, equity, and inclusion (DE&I) strategy?

    a. Employee survey data
    b. Leadership buy-in
    c. Budgetary allocations
    d. Training and development

5. Return to Work (RTW) programs are an effective tool to help transition employees back to full duty. When are they used?

    a. An employee experiences an on-the-job injury.
    b. An employee experiences an injury, whether on the job or off duty.
    c. Family and Medical Leave Act (FMLA)-protected leave is denied for the employee.
    d. An employee's physician will not give a medical release.

6. One kind of bias that can occur during an interview is a halo bias. What is a halo bias?

    a. Interviewers tend to rank candidates higher when they are similar to themselves.

    b. An interviewer observes one negative trait in a candidate, and it negatively influences the perception of other traits.

    c. An interviewer observes one positive trait in a candidate, and it positively influences the perception of other traits.

    d. Interviewer base a hiring decision immediately upon their first impression of the candidate.

7. There are many critics of using personality assessments as part of the hiring process. Which of the following is the MOST valid concern that critics have expressed?

    a. Assessments can pigeonhole applicants based solely on personality traits.

    b. Applicants can usually manipulate the results—they choose the option that the organization wants to hear rather than how they feel.

    c. Assessments may ask questions that would identify and exclude disabled individuals.

    d. Disparate impact—protected groups of people may be excluded from consideration based on their responses.

Refer to the following for questions 8 - 9:

> Human resources has been tasked with creating a comprehensive and consistent training program in an organization that has never had a structured program in the past. Previously, training was administered and tracked differently across departments according to their specific needs and requirements.

8. What should be human resource's first task in creating the program?

    a. Taking inventory of each department's training needs and current processes

    b. Researching learning management systems—obtaining quotes, checking references, and so on

    c. Becoming familiar with the legal requirements and best practices of training programs in the industry

    d. Creating an organization-wide training calendar with scheduled training assignments and due dates

9. What criteria is the LEAST important to consider when deciding on training delivery methods and course durations for the new program?

    a. Legal obligations to remain compliant

    b. Current training delivery methods and course durations

    c. Workplace logistics and preferred learning styles of employees—that is, are there field-based employees who may not have easy access to a learning management system, or perhaps employees aren't able to step away from their desks for long durations

    d. The content of the training being delivered

10. In assessing human resources (HR) technology programs, what is an example of a "best of breed" concept?

    a. Selecting an HR/payroll system and a separate third-party learning management system (LMS) with better features

    b. Performing a needs analysis internally to determine the optimal system to streamline current processes

    c. Selecting an all-in-one, integrated solution with HR, payroll, performance management, and learning management capabilities.

    d. Selecting an HR/payroll system that requires the least amount of customization to ensure a fast implementation and simpler future upgrades.

Refer to the following for questions 11 - 12:

You directly manage a team of eight human resource (HR) people, all varying in ages and length of work experience. For example, your senior HR generalist is nearing retirement and has worked in HR for nearly 30 years. Your newest hire, an HR coordinator, is just a few years out from graduating college. As you are aware, managing a multigenerational workforce presents many challenges.

11. What is one challenge that you anticipate your older workers encountering when working closely with younger workers on a high-profile project?
   a. The quality of work from younger workers may not be up to the standards of older workers.
   b. Older workers tend not to take feedback constructively.
   c. Older workers expect more latitude from management, whereas the younger generation needs and expects more guidance at each step of the way.
   d. Older workers expect direct, face-to-face communication, whereas younger workers are content with communication via email, text or, instant messaging.

12. What would be the most effective strategy to engage the younger workers?
   a. Provide a performance-based bonus.
   b. Promote a team-based culture that is heavy on collaboration.
   c. Provide a defined career path with training opportunities to achieve the next step.
   d. Schedule a once-per-week happy hour with the entire team.

Refer to the following for questions 13 - 14:

A long-tenured and valued employee has recently been coming to work late, calling in sick on Mondays, and his/her overall appearance is messy and disheveled. He/she has also been behaving strangely and getting agitated more easily than usual. His/her supervisor suspects that he/she has a drug problem.

13. How would you approach the situation as a human resource representative?
   a. Call the employee's emergency contact on file, and inquire if something has changed with the employee recently.
   b. Pull the employee into a private conference room along with the supervisor. Explain the strange behavior that you and the supervisor have witnessed, and ask for an explanation.
   c. Coach the supervisor to have a conversation with the employee privately.
   d. Require that the employee complete a drug test before any conversation occurs.

14. Assume the employee admitted that he/she began using cocaine about six months ago. He/she says that he/she started using casually, but recently it's gotten out of control, and he/she needs help. What would be your next course of action?
   a. Explain that despite the substance abuse problem, he/she will be held to the same performance standards as any other employee.
   b. Your company has a zero-tolerance policy, so his/her employment should be terminated immediately.
   c. As an active drug addict, he/she is protected under the Americans with Disabilities Act, so work with him/her to find a reasonable accommodation to help him/her get clean.
   d. Offer the employee Family and Medical Leave Act (FMLA)-protected leave to enroll and attend a rehab program.

15. How would you describe employee engagement?

a. An employee who is satisfied with his/her job
b. An employee with commitment to the organization and motivation to perform well
c. Engagement that is generally higher within the first 30 days after hire but that usually fades
d. An employee who is ambitious and works hard but is always looking outside the organization for new opportunity.

Refer to the following for questions 16 - 17:

> Late in the afternoon an account manager, Sharon, knocks on your door and asks to come in. It's clear she's been crying: her face is red and her eyes are swollen. She sits down in your office chair and begins sobbing. Through her sobs she explains that she put a lot of work into building a client relationship within a shared account, but her colleague just took all the credit in a team meeting.

16. What would be the most effective way to calm Sharon down?

a. Say, "She should not have taken credit. I'm sorry you had to go through that."
b. Suggest that she talk to her supervisor about it.
c. Suggest that she take some time to calm down, then speak directly with her colleague, and explain how it made her feel.
d. Guess Sharon's feelings and ask if you're correct. For example, "It sounds like you're feeling a lack of recognition and maybe disrespected by your colleague. Do I have that right?"

17. Sharon has calmed down and says, "Thanks. I feel a lot better. I just needed to vent to someone. Now I can go on about my day and put this behind me." What would you do next?

a. Give a warm smile to Sharon, and say, "My door is open any time." Consider it "case closed." Sharon clearly didn't want this conflict to progress into anything more.
b. Give a warm smile to Sharon, and say, "My door is open any time"; however, after she leaves your office, give her supervisor a call, and explain what had just happened and that she should keep an eye on things between the two.
c. Thank Sharon for confiding in you, but diplomatically explain that it is not human resource's role to be a therapist.
d. Explain to Sharon that anything she says in your office is not confidential and that you may be looking into this further.

Refer to the following for questions 18 - 20:

> Initech is a healthcare company with 500 employees based out of the home office in Seattle. They have 150 employees working remotely from their homes all over the country. The Initech office is always buzzing with activity and events—company meetings, Friday social hour, summer BBQ, and holiday parties for employees and their families. The remote employees have been complaining because they feel disconnected from the home office. Unfortunately, the budget doesn't allow for frequent visits for the remote employees to visit the home office.

18. What would be a creative solution to help the remote employees feel more included while keeping costs low?

a. Post photos of the events on the company intranet so remote employees can see them.
b. Invite the remote employees to attend the holiday party and summer BBQ; however, they would be responsible for covering the cost of their own transportation and lodging.
c. Organize periodic social meet-ups for remote employees who live near one another.
d. Set up a dial-in/web cam for the company meetings and social events so that remote employees can hear and see the activity.

19. What could be the biggest advantage of having a remote workforce from a human resource perspective?

   a.   Lower overhead costs—less office space and equipment required
   b.   No commute for remote employees, resulting in fewer emissions for the environment
   c.   No need for child care for remote employees
   d.   Better overall work-life balance for remote employees, resulting in higher morale and more successful recruitment efforts

20. What is the biggest disadvantage of having a remote workforce?

   a.   Lack of communication between coworkers and employees and managers
   b.   The possibility for employees to misrepresent their work time
   c.   Home-based employees being likely to encounter too many distractions and not being as efficient
   d.   Possible safety and risk concerns for employees to hurt themselves away from the office

21. What is the most significant morale destroyer that middle managers often face as a function of their role?

   a.   Difficult employee relations issues
   b.   Changing directives from upper management
   c.   Low compensation relative to the level of responsibility
   d.   A lack of authority from upper management in application of policies

Refer to the following for questions 22 - 25:

> In response to a labor market-wide rise in turnover rates, the executive team of a large nonprofit decided to raise the wages of all hourly employees by 3%.
>
> Despite the increase in pay, turnover rates remained higher than usual for the company, so the HR team reviewed recent exit interview responses to better understand why employees were leaving. Overall, the interview data was mixed. The company received, in general, high praise for "corporate vision" and "workspace amenities," but it was criticized for "untrustworthy leadership" and "compensation dissatisfaction." Additionally, these were some of the recurring remarks that were mentioned:
>
> - Belief in mission and doing good for others
> - Lack of opportunity for advancement due to favoritism

22. What would be the most effective first step for the HR team following the exit interview review?

   a.   Review performance management practices to assess effectiveness of promotion procedures.
   b.   Launch an internal investigation into all managers to identify toxic leaders.
   c.   Conduct stay interviews to better understand why current employees have chosen not to leave.
   d.   Recommend an additional 5% salary increase for all employees.

23. Reviewing the performance management reports has revealed managers selecting candidates for promotions based on personal similarities instead of on actual performance outcomes. Which of the following tools would be most helpful for tackling performance assessment criteria?

   a.   Job analysis
   b.   Workplace observations
   c.   Job evaluation
   d.   Employee survey

24. Before recommending an additional round of companywide raises, which of the following steps would be most effective at addressing compensation criticisms and the lack of trust in company leadership?

    a. Propose an expanded C-suite to include a chief human resources officer who is best suited to build the trust of the workforce.

    b. Design a pay-for-performance model of compensation to improve the work-to-reward visibility.

    c. Review benefits and how they compare to market standards in relation to what the workforce actually uses.

    d. Conduct a pay audit and publicize the results and any proposed follow-up action.

25. Many of the exit interviews mentioned employees seeking leadership positions outside of the company because they did not possess the education standards required to advance and their hands-on experience was not recognized as an equivalency. What barrier to diversity is most likely at play in these instances?

    a. Disparate treatment

    b. Systemic inequality

    c. Ableist standards

    d. Stereotyping

26. Dependent enrollment with COBRA continuation coverage

    a. is required if the primary beneficiary is enrolled.

    b. is allowed even if the primary beneficiary is not enrolled.

    c. is only permitted if the primary beneficiary is enrolled.

    d. is generally not permitted in any instance.

27. What is a Performance Improvement Plan (PIP) best suited for?

    a. Documentation prior to a termination action

    b. Insubordinate behavior

    c. Quantifiable performance deficiencies with potential for improvement

    d. Unionized workplaces

28. Which of the following workplace behaviors is most likely to be reduced as a result of building diverse teams?

    a. Conflict

    b. Trust

    c. Groupthink

    d. Collaboration

29. Best practice for initial completion of the US Citizen and Immigration Services (USCIS) Form I-9 does NOT include that

    a. the employee should fill out the form no later than the first day of work.

    b. the employer may specify that the employee should supply a passport to verify identify.

    c. the employee may use a translator for purposes of completing the form.

    d. the employer must review the original documentation supplied by the employee.

30. Which question should interviewers avoid asking candidates during an interview?

    a. Are you able to work for our company without immigration sponsorship?

    b. Are you able to perform the work duties without accommodation?

    c. Do you live close to our office?

    d. It sounds like you have an accent. Where are you from?

31. H-1B work visas may only be obtained for employees who

    a. reside in either Mexico or Canada and work in a specialty occupation.

    b. pass a rigorous test to prove their knowledge of the United States.

    c. work in a specialty occupation and have a bachelor's degree equivalency.

    d. are a recent college graduate and wish to work in the same field of study.

32. Why are human resource representatives generally excluded from bargaining unit representation?

    a. They often oversee the work of others in a supervisory capacity.

    b. They act as an advisor and/or representative of management during collective bargaining.

    c. They are responsible for defining organizational policies that may conflict with collective bargaining agreements (CBAs).

    d. They are responsible for enforcing the provisions of the CBAs and policies.

33. Focus groups are an effective means to gather employee feedback. For what are they best suited?

    a. Employees in the same division or department

    b. Specific subjects of discussion

    c. Fewer than five participants

    d. Unstructured brainstorming sessions

34. If a rejected candidate asks for feedback from the employer on how he/she might improve, what is the MOST appropriate response?

    a. A non-specific response like "You just weren't the right fit for our team".

    b. Honest and direct feedback with a list of areas to improve upon.

    c. A standard, generic response, which is given to all candidates: "We decided to move forward with another candidate".

    d. A customized response based on several factors from the level of position, number of candidates interviewed, and whether the candidate is internal or external.

35. What is the primary difference between coaching and mentoring?

    a. Coaching is generally used for a specific reason—either to prepare an individual for a new challenge or to change a specific work behavior.

    b. Coaching is generally conducted in a one-on-one setting.

    c. Coaching is usually used in the case of pending, or as a result of, a disciplinary action.

    d. Coaching is more instructional with job-related training.

36. Under the Patient Protection and Affordable Care Act (PPACA), an employer may utilize the look-back measurement method to determine

    a. if an employee will be expected to work more than 30 hours per week.

    b. if an employee has received health insurance coverage over the past year.

    c. if an employee has worked more than 130 hours in a month.

    d. if an employee's pay is low enough that he/she qualifies for a subsidy.

Refer to the following for questions 37 - 38:

    A supervisor reports to you that he/she is having some personality clashes on his/her team. Specifically, there is one employee who is particularly forceful in his/her opinion and tends to dominate the weekly team meetings. He/she openly complains about routine tasks that all human resource team members have to complete because he/she feels that they're "beneath" him/her. Other employees have expressed frustration when working with this individual.

37. What advice would you give to this supervisor?

  a. Have a direct conversation with the employee. Explain how this behavior has been putting off others on the team.
  b. Be specific in the feedback—explain how talking over others in a meeting makes others feel like they don't have a voice.
  c. Tailor the employee's work assignments so that they're more challenging and complex.
  d. Provide conflict resolution training to the employee and others on the team.

38. Another employee on the team has poor attendance. He/she always seems to be having one personal crisis after another, from personal medical conditions to taking care of family members to a sick dog. He/she is not private about any of these details and will share these ailments with anyone who will listen. How would you guide the supervisor to handle this employee?

  a. Meet with the employee privately and hear him/her out. Understand the issues he/she is facing, and remain empathetic.
  b. Try your best to avoid discussing any personal issues in the workplace. Change the subject when the employee begins to over share about his/her personal life and stick to talk about work.
  c. Focus on the attendance issue. Hold the employee accountable for being late, and request a doctor's note the next time he/she calls in sick.
  d. Facilitate a 360-degree performance evaluation for the entire team in hopes that feedback from others on the team will help give the employee some self-awareness.

39. In the context of Fair Labor Standards Act (FLSA), which statement is true regarding the concept of workers being "engaged to wait" versus "waiting to be engaged"?

  a. An employee who is "engaged to wait" is effectively on duty and must be paid for that time.
  b. An employee who is "waiting to be engaged" is usually required to remain at the workplace or nearby in case they are needed.
  c. An employee who is "engaged to wait" is generally on call and can use his/her time freely as long as they're able to make it to the workplace in the event they are called.
  d. An employee who is "engaged to wait" is relieved of duty, so he/she does not need to be paid unless he/she is called to work.

40. Under Fair Labor Standards Act (FLSA) guidelines, what are employees entitled to?

  a. One 30-minute lunch and two 15-minute breaks for every eight hours worked
  b. No required lunch or rest periods
  c. One hour lunch and two 10-minute breaks for every eight hours worked
  d. One 30-minute lunch break for every four hours worked

41. Under the North American Free Trade Agreement (NAFTA), what do Canadian professionals need to work in the United States?

  a. A TN visa
  b. An H-1B visa
  c. The appropriate documentation (i.e., offer letter, proof of Canadian citizenship) presented at the US border
  d. US permanent residency (green card)

42. Currently, 28 states in the United States are considered "Right to Work" states. What are Right to Work laws?

  a. Legislation that forbids unionizing among employees.
  b. Legislation that allows for an employee to be terminated for any reason as long as it is not illegal
  c. Legislation that provides a choice to employees with respect to union membership
  d. Legislation that ensures employment opportunities for permanent resident aliens

43. How would you respond to the email?

An employee emails you, as a designated human resources (HR) representative, with a complex explanation of his/her medical history and explains that he/she has an upcoming surgery. It's clear from the tenor of the email that he/she is stressed about missing work time. He/she wanted to know what the next steps are to prepare for the upcoming leave. You don't know the answer to the question off the top of your head, and the HR person who specializes in leaves is out of the office for a week.

a. First, explain that the employee should not send any protected health information over an unsecure network. Request that he/she come into the office and meet with the human resource (HR) specialist face-to-face upon his/her return from vacation.
b. Thank the employee for the email, and explain that the HR specialist who is the point of contact is out of the office. Offer to explain the situation to him/her when he/she is back and have him/her touch base with the employee at that point.
c. Research the information he/she is seeking on your own, and respond back to the employee within the day.
d. Reply to the employee with a CC to the HR leave specialist, explaining that the HR specialist will reach out to the employee upon his/her return to the office.

44. Critics of utilizing key performance indicators (KPIs) to measure goal attainment say that instead of fostering collaboration, they often times promote

a. competition.
b. micromanagement.
c. slow progress.
d. unachievable standards.

45. How would you handle this complaint?

A supervisor, John, gives you a call and says, "I have an issue. Another supervisor, Steve, made a joke to one of my employees that made her feel uncomfortable." John goes on to describe the insensitive joke about a "black Santa" that Steve told to the African American employee, Karen. John finishes with, "So what do I do?" Steve is a well-liked supervisor who has never crossed the line before. According to John, Karen and Steve are friends, and she doesn't want him to "get into trouble," but she thought she should at least mention it.

a. Thank John for bringing this to your attention, and ask that he let you know if it ever happens again. Take no further action because this was an isolated incident with Steve
b. Document the interaction between Steve and Karen based on the facts presented by John. Save it in case another questionable scenario with Steve ever comes up.
c. Speak with Karen directly, and document the conversation. Ask her how she wants you to proceed.
d. Have an informal but stern conversation with Steve. Explain that his joke was inappropriate and should never happen again.

46. When an employee is injured on the job, what is the first thing supervisors and managers should be instructed to do after stabilizing the employee?

a. Draft a statement of what happened.
b. Contact human resources.
c. Collect witness statements.
d. Address the cause of the injury, and fix it if possible.

47. A job hazard analysis is a tool that Occupational Safety and Health Administration (OSHA) recommends to prevent workplace injury, illnesses, or accidents. When performing a job hazard analysis, who is it most important to consult with?
   a. The employees who are performing the work
   b. The supervisor of the employees who perform the work
   c. OSHA
   d. The organization's safety officer

Refer to the following for questions 48 - 49:

> In a municipal government workplace, a supervisor oversees a 10-person team of permit technicians who are mostly stationed at the front counter and greet customers. Two permit technicians, Jane and Susan, are like oil and water. They argue in team meetings, roll their eyes at each other, and don't respond to each other's emails. The supervisor is fed up and has come to you for guidance.

48. What would your advice be to the supervisor?
   a. Rearrange the counter schedule so that Jane and Susan never work together.
   b. Organize a face-to-face meeting between the two with the supervisor acting as a facilitator.
   c. Pull Jane and Susan aside separately; explain that the expectation is that their behavior remain professional.
   d. Organize a conflict resolution training for Jane and Susan to attend.

49. What is the type of conflict that best describes the interaction between Jane and Susan?
   a. Dysfunctional conflict
   b. Functional conflict
   c. Task conflict
   d. Bullying behavior

Refer to the following for questions 50 - 52:

> One of your direct reports, Peter, is quiet, conscientious, and detail oriented. He doesn't speak often in team meetings, but when he does, his responses are logical and fact based. Conversely, another direct report, Jason, almost never stops talking. He likes to exaggerate and always has a funny story to tell. He is creative, easygoing, and excellent at problem-solving.

50. Given Peter's personality, how would you go about delivering a work assignment to him?
   a. No different than any other team member, it would be discussed in the regular weekly team meetings.
   b. You would bring it up in your next weekly one-on-one meeting with the opportunity for Peter to ask follow-up questions.
   c. Send an email with the work assignment details, with the explanation that you will discuss it at your next regularly scheduled one-on-one meeting.
   d. In your next regularly scheduled one-on-one meeting, ask for his input on which assignment he'd like to work on. Give him the assignment of his choice.

51. You have a high-visibility performance review overhaul project that you need your team to deliver. How would you go about dividing the work between Peter and Jason?

a. Encourage both Peter and Jason to get out of their comfort zones—assign the research and data analysis to Jason, and Peter can create the communication pieces and deliver the presentations.

b. Determine the overall project plan, strategy, and tasks together. Then let them divvy up the work directly with each other, keeping you apprised of any important decisions.

c. Have Jason determine the overall project plan and the strategy of the program. Peter can conduct best practice research and analyze applicable data.

d. Have both of them work together on the same tasks—both complete research, put together the project plan, and deliver presentations to employees and leadership.

52. While working on this project together, what could be a potential conflict between Peter and Jason?

a. Conflicting roles

b. Competing priorities

c. Conflicting perceptions

d. Conflicting styles

Refer to the following for questions 53 - 54:

A team of five customer service representatives (CSRs) works in a call center. They usually sit for the entirety of their eight-hour shifts, answering calls and speaking to customers with a headset. One CSR has severe back issues so has requested a stand-up desk to help with back pain.

53. How would you handle this request?

a. Provide the stand-up desk to the employee as it's a reasonable request.

b. Perform an ergonomic assessment of the workstation before making any determinations if a modification is needed.

c. Ask for a doctor's note. If the doctor states that he/she requires a stand-up desk to perform the essential functions of the job, provide it.

d. Back pain does not qualify as "disability" under the American's with Disabilities Act, so no accommodation needs to be made.

54. After you provide the stand-up desk to the CSR, another employee complains about unfair treatment. He/she would like a stand-up desk as well, not for disability reasons, but for health and wellness. There may be budget to purchase two to three more stand-up desks but not for all five CSRs. How would you handle this request?

a. Explain that the reason the other CSR was given a stand-up desk was for a disability, and this was an accommodation under the Americans with Disabilities Act. For that reason, he/she will not be given one unless he/she too has a doctor's note.

b. Purchase the stand-up desk. If anyone else asks for one, provide it as well until the budget is exhausted. Work to obtain more budget the following year to provide the desks to all five CSRs.

c. Set up a program in which the highest-performing CSR of the quarter is awarded with a stand-up desk until the budget is exhausted.

d. Offer to help set it up if he/she purchases the equipment using his/her own money.

55. What is a "top-heavy" 401(k) plan?

a. A plan with an average deferral by highly compensated employees at 2% greater than non-highly compensated employees

b. A plan with more than 60% participation by executives

c. A plan with greater than 60% of its total value in the accounts of "key" employees

d. A plan with less than 60% participation by non-highly compensated employees

56. Which is NOT a best practice for Form I-9 retention?

    a. Retain the form three years after hire date or one year after termination date, whichever is later.
    b. Restrict Form I-9 access to supervisors and managers.
    c. Shred the forms once an employee reaches the three-year employment anniversary.
    d. File terminated employees' forms separately from active employees' forms.

57. For an employer to hire an unpaid intern, the internship must meet several criteria. Which option is NOT a criterion to qualify for an unpaid internship?

    a. The intern receives academic credit for completion of the internship.
    b. The intern's work does not take away work from another paid employee.
    c. The intern must work less than 20 hours per week.
    d. The intern receives relevant and valuable on-the-job training.

Refer to the following for questions 58 - 59:

> You are a human resource manager supporting the northwest division of a nationwide electronics store. The majority of your employees work directly with customers, either helping them decide which television to purchase in the store, or they travel to a customer's home to help setup or troubleshoot an electronic product purchased in the store. On occasion, customers will report that they noticed something missing from their home after a visit from an employee. Usually there's no way to definitely prove that an employee stole anything.

58. How would you go about preventing this from happening in the future?

    a. Remove the temptation—request that customers secure their valuables prior to a visit from one of your employees.
    b. Conduct a thorough background check before hiring, and reject anyone with a criminal record.
    c. In new hire orientation, conduct ethics training and threaten criminal prosecution if an employee is caught stealing.
    d. Pair up employees who visit customer homes so that they can hold each other accountable.

59. An employee comes to your office one day and nervously tells you he/she has knowledge of another employee who stole an item from a customer's home. He/she doesn't want to tell you who it is until you guarantee him/her anonymity. How would you handle this?

    a. Explain that you can never guarantee anonymity and that he/she is obligated to give the name of the accused now that you have knowledge of these events.
    b. Promise that his/her name will remain anonymous and the employee in question will never know who complained.
    c. Tell him/her that you will do your best to ensure his/her name is kept confidential, but you can't make any guarantees.
    d. Explain the importance of finding the person who stole the item and that you need his/her help.

60. What is the style of negotiation that aims to meet the needs of both parties and leverage collaboration to come to an agreement called?

    a. Principled bargaining
    b. Positional bargaining
    c. Distributive bargaining
    d. Composite bargaining

61. Which type of employee must be excluded from bargaining units as per the National Labor Relations Act (NLRA)?

a. Supervisors
b. Employees who work in the private sector
c. Part-time employees
d. Seasonal employees

62. Which is the provision that does NOT typically describe a health savings account (HSA)?

a. "Use it or lose it"—funds expire at the end of the plan year.
b. Both employees and employers may contribute to the account on the employee's behalf.
c. Employees may reduce their taxable income by contributing funds to an HSA.
d. HSA funds are portable—if an employee leaves the organization, he/she can take the funds.

63. Under "coordination of benefits" rules, how are insurance claims processed?

a. Charges are first allocated to the primary payer, and then residual charges are submitted to a secondary payer.
b. Claims are processed only at an "allowable amount" as determined by the insurance company, and any residual cost is an out-of-pocket charge to the employee.
c. Out-of-pocket expenses are deducted directly from the employee's flexible spending account.
d. Charges are split evenly between the primary and secondary payers.

64. What would be the next course of action for you to get this position filled?

As a recruiter, you are having a difficult time filling a civil engineer position that has been open for a few months. Few qualified individuals have applied, and the passive candidates who you've contacted haven't returned your calls. You've been aggressive in your advertising approach (in fact you've exceeded your advertising budget), but it's proving to be difficult to find quality candidates in this competitive market.

a. Re-assess the salary and benefit package for the position.
b. Work on obtaining additional budget, and post more job advertisements.
c. Have a brainstorming session with the hiring manager, and ask for ideas and suggestions.
d. Change the requirements for the job: it could be that they are hindering potential applicants from applying.

65. The expectancy theory of motivation explains that an individual's choice is driven by

a. an intrinsic desire for personal growth.
b. the desire to avoid the alternative.
c. how desirable the outcome is.
d. the essential needs of the individual.

66. What is the practice of storing, managing, and processing data in remote, Internet-based servers commonly referred to?

a. Cloud computing
b. Locally hosted computing
c. Software as a Service (SaaS)
d. E-commerce

Refer to the following for questions 67 - 68:

Acme Corp is experiencing a rapid increase in new projects and, in turn, revenue. Because of this influx of new work, the hiring pace has quickened as well. The employee headcount is projected to grow from 500 employees to 600 over the course of the year. Unfortunately, turnover seems to be increasing at the same rate, and it seems to be mostly newer employees leaving the organization.

67. What would be the most impactful action human resources could take to identify the cause of this increase in turnover?

    a.   Conduct exit interviews with each employee who leaves the organization. Identify trends in the reasons mentioned.

    b.   Speak with the managers of each exiting employee. Ask if they have any insight on why the individuals are choosing to leave the organization.

    c.   Analyze the recruitment strategy and interview notes when the employee was hired. Because they're often new employees who leave quickly, it's likely that the wrong hiring decision was made.

    d.   Send out an employee satisfaction survey to all employees. Identify areas of discontent among current employees.

68. The exit interview comments have shown that employees feel overwhelmed and burnt out—this is causing employees to quit within their 90-day probationary period. What would be a possible solution human resources could take to reduce turnover?

    a.   Speak with managers and supervisors, relay this information, and request that they lighten the workload for all employees.

    b.   Introduce every Friday as a work-from-home day to improve work-life balance.

    c.   Implement realistic job previews during the interview process to give candidates a better idea of what will be expected of them.

    d.   Improve new hire orientation and training, ensuring that new hires are able to get up to speed quickly.

Refer to the following for questions 69 - 70:

You are the vice president of human resources for a small start-up software company. The bulk of your employees are young, highly educated hard workers and smart when it comes to technology but not so much when it comes to healthcare benefits, retirement, and other employment-related details. For most, this is their first job out of college. The CEO is a visionary and has expressed that he/she wants the company to always be cutting edge and a desirable place to work to attract only the best software developers in the country.

69. Given the information in the scenario, what proposed initiative or program would you include in your annual strategic human resources plan?

    a.   Unlimited paid time off (PTO)

    b.   An onsite health clinic for employees and their dependents

    c.   An employee recognition program with cutting-edge technology as rewards

    d.   A structured career path program with learning and development opportunities

70. The career path program was a hit with the software developers. The next step in creating that cutting-edge workplace reputation is embracing flexible/remote work opportunities. Your CEO doesn't like the idea and thinks it would negatively impact productivity. However, you're confident that it's the way of the future. How would you sell the idea to the CEO?

    a.   Provide positive case studies from other organizations that have embraced remote assignments.

    b.   Suggest that you allow it for a maximum of once per week as a trial. Monitor the remote work output, and expand the program if successful.

    c.   Remind the CEO that remote work assignments would expand your recruitment reach into other hot technology markets, not just local to your headquarters office.

    d.   Remind the CEO that not only is telecommuting cutting edge, but it allows software developers to focus better and in turn produce higher-quality work.

71. How would you deliver the feedback to this employee?

You are a supervisor who manages a small team of three professionals. One in particular is a high performer with a great attitude. Unfortunately, he/she made a huge error on his/her most recent client report, which ended up costing the organization a significant amount of money. It is an error that you need to address with, but you don't want to dampen his/her spirits as he/she tends to be sensitive to negative feedback.

   a. Remain neutral and state the facts of the mistake in the report. Ask for feedback on how to avoid these mistakes in the future.
   b. Send an email with the details of the mistake to be less confrontational.
   c. Explain the mistake and the impact it had on the company. Warn him/her that if it happens again, he/she might be disciplined.
   d. Document the event in the details of his/her next performance review.

72. To meet eligibility for Family and Medical Leave Act (FMLA)-protected leave, an employee and employer must meet specified criteria. Which criterion is NOT an FMLA qualifier?

   a. The employee must have worked for the employer for at least 12 months.
   b. The employee must have worked at least 1250 hours in the past 12 months.
   c. The employer must employ at least 50 employees within a 75-mile radius.
   d. The employee must give the employer at least 30 days' notice of an upcoming leave.

73. Which is NOT an example of an unfair labor practice?

   a. An employer declining to participate in collective bargaining
   b. An employer not making concessions during collective bargaining
   c. An employer offering benefits to employees who decline participation in a union
   d. An employer closing down a location upon unionizing activity by employees

74. According to Maslow's Hierarchy of Needs, what follows the need for feeling valued and respected as the highest step in the pyramid?

   a. Safety and security
   b. Love and belonging
   c. Physiological (i.e., hunger and thirst needs)
   d. Self-actualization

75. What does the Worker Adjustment and Retraining Notification (WARN) Act require?

   a. An employer must provide affected employees with 60-days' notice of an impending layoff of more than 50 employees.
   b. An employer must provide employees who are over the age of 40 with a revocation period after signing a severance agreement.
   c. An employer must provide affected employees with 60-days' notice of an impending layoff of any size.
   d. An employer must publicly release the names of each person affected by a layoff.

76. When preparing to make an offer to a candidate, recruiters must consider several factors before deciding how much to offer within the applicable pay scale. What factors should NOT be considered?

   a. The candidate's expectations
   b. Internal equity—how much the other incumbents are being paid for the same job
   c. The candidate's current compensation
   d. The candidate's potential commute

77. What types of organizations are required to maintain an affirmative action program (AAP)?

a. Federal government contractors or subcontractors, as mandated by the Office of Federal Contract Compliance (OFCCP)
b. All organizations with more than 50 employees, as mandated by the Equal Employment Opportunity Commission (EEOC)
c. None, rather it is best practice for all organizations to remain informed of minority and female representation
d. All federal, state and local government agencies

78. A compensation philosophy is influenced by many factors. Which factor should have the LEAST amount of impact when defining an organization's compensation philosophy?

a. Number of employees in the organization
b. Industry in which the organization works
c. Current employee expectations
d. Availability of talent in the market

79. Psychologist Bruce Tuckman developed the "Forming, Storming, Norming and Performing" concept to describe the team formation process. Oftentimes, teams may move back and forth between which two stages when faced with a new task?

a. Forming and storming
b. Storming and norming
c. Performing and forming
d. Norming and performing

80. What is the most important action to take before initiating recruitment efforts to fill an open position?

a. Determine where the position will be advertised.
b. Build a candidate pipeline.
c. Define the skills needed for the position.
d. Determine the appropriate compensation level for the position.

81. Which statement does NOT describe unlawful harassment?

a. Unwelcome conduct that is based upon the victim's protected status
b. Behavior that is severe and pervasive enough that a reasonable person would find it hostile or abusive
c. Enduring offensive conduct becomes a condition of employment
d. Any type of bullying or unwelcome conduct from a supervisor

82. After a lengthy investigation concludes, a sexual harassment complaint is determined to be unfounded. What is the most appropriate course of action?

a. Disciplinary action for the complainant—there were no grounds for the complaint.
b. Disciplinary action should be taken only if the reason was malicious.
c. Disciplinary action would be considered retaliation if the complainant were to be disciplined for making a complaint.
d. Initiate a gentle conversation with the complainant and subject together to describe the results of the investigation.

83. In selecting a new human resource information system (HRIS), what is the first step in the process?

a. Determine the available budget.
b. Define organizational needs versus wants in a new system.
c. Determine if the selection process will be conducted by a consultant or internal resources.
d. Collect quotes and proposals from prospective HRIS vendors.

84. Under the Myers-Briggs Type Indicator (MBTI) personality assessment, people are categorized as introverted versus extroverted, sensing versus intuitive, and so on. In total, there are how many different combinations of personality types?

    a. 4
    b. 5
    c. 16
    d. 64

85. When conducting a strengths, weaknesses, opportunities and threats (SWOT) analysis, what portion may be accomplished by a political, economic, social and technological (PEST) analysis?

    a. Weaknesses and threats
    b. Strengths and weaknesses
    c. Strengths and opportunities
    d. Opportunities and threats

86. When conducting market research for compensation studies, which is a best practice?

    a. Consider the job title and level of the position at other organizations.
    b. Contact other organizations directly for pay information as the information is more accurate.
    c. Leverage employee-reported salary figures through online tools.
    d. Utilize at least one market survey with aggregated salary information.

87. How long is an H-1B visa valid?

    a. An indefinite period of time
    b. Three years, then renewable for another three years, for a total of six years
    c. Three years
    d. One year, then renewable each subsequent year

Refer to the following for questions 88 - 89:

> A supervisor has reported a situation about one toxic employee in a team of six. His/her work performance is bad, he/she puts others down and rolls his/her eyes in team meetings, and his/her attendance is poor as well. He/she calls in sick frequently and comes in late. He/she has stated that he/she has a medical condition, so the supervisor is afraid to confront him/her about the behavior for fear of a retaliation claim.

88. How would you advise the supervisor to handle this problem employee?

    a. The supervisor should send an email to him/her summarizing the disrespectful behavior and specific attendance issues. This would serve as valuable documentation later if needed.
    b. The supervisor should focus on the medical condition and refer the employee to human resources to discuss an accommodation or possible Family and Medical Leave Act (FMLA) leave.
    c. The supervisor should have a direct conversation with the employee focused on his/her performance and attendance. Going forward, the supervisor should begin documenting each instance of bad behavior.
    d. The supervisor should focus on supporting the other team members. Thank them for picking up the slack, and let them know they can stop by any time to discuss concerns.

89. Six months later, the employee is still a challenge. He/she will improve just enough to avoid discipline and seems to be on his/her best behavior around the supervisor, but one team member is reporting "mean" behavior—passive aggressive comments, scoffs and eye rolls, and whispering with other employees. The complainant is shy but well respected and normally has a great attitude. The supervisor doesn't feel a direct conversation between the two will help the situation. What should the next course of action be for the supervisor?

   a. Separate the two employees physically. Move their desks, and make it so that none of their work assignments are dependent upon each other.
   b. Move forward with a disciplinary action for the offending employee as this is bullying behavior.
   c. Pull the offending employee aside privately and explain what has been reported. Inform him/her that bullying is not tolerated in the workplace.
   d. Keep a watchful eye on the situation. Check in frequently with the employee who feels targeted and ask the employee to keep a log of each incident.

90. What is an advantage of hiring externally rather than from inside the organization?

   a. It brings a fresh perspective and creativity to the organization.
   b. It can be less expensive for recruitment efforts.
   c. It causes less conflict among coworkers.
   d. External candidates are likely to be more competent.

Refer to the following for questions 91 - 94:

A small marketing firm within a niche tech industry is facing some growing pains following its initial business successes.

The organization's initial achievements were attributed to the cooperative culture among its team members and the high transparency practiced by company leadership in decisions and operations. As a result of the early successes, the company began to experience substantial growth; after a series of acquisitions and expansions, it now has several hundred employees in both domestic and international offices.

In an attempt to harness the people power of a diverse employee base, the chief operations officer tasks the division leaders with creating virtual teams of employees who specialize in specific skills or knowledge to help solve pervasive operational challenges. These focus teams consist of employees across a wide range of geographical regions, and they are tasked with discussing and proposing solutions for several operational, strategic, financial, and systematic challenges facing the growing organization.

Six months after tasking the division leaders, the COO checks in with each of the focus teams to gauge their progress and gather feedback; however, the COO is disappointed to learn that the majority of groups fail to meet on a regular basis and that, even when they do, they struggle to agree on a focus or direction for which challenges to address or what possible solutions might look like.

In response to the follow-up meetings, the COO seeks the guidance of the organization's HR director for assistance in improving the efficacy of the focus teams.

91. After the focus teams are up and running with renewed leadership buy-in and clearly defined timelines and goals, the HR director checks in with the COO to see how his vision is playing out. The COO is grateful for the director's initial observations and course correction suggestions but observes that since the teams have been working more closely together, there has been a rise in conflicts due to misunderstandings between team members from different regions and cultures. Which of the following actions that the HR director could recommend would be most effective?

    a. Issue a "celebrate diversity" online training for all team members to take.
    b. Design a team-building activity that connects members to common work goals and values.
    c. Let the misunderstandings play out naturally to encourage the evolution from conflict to collaboration.
    d. Assign conflicting team members to different teams or projects to ease the tension.

92. After collecting data from the focus teams, the HR director discovers one of the major obstacles to consistent meetings is the time zone differences. Which of the following solutions would be most effective to suggest?

    a. Team meetings should be scheduled several months out in advance to enable team members to plan accordingly.
    b. The teams should only use collaborative technologies that allow them to discuss and contribute in a running thread.
    c. Teams should be redistributed to keep all group members within no more than two time zones of each other.
    d. Team members who are unable to participate in the meetings should be removed from the project.

93. Which of the following action steps should the HR director take first in assisting the COO?

    a. Sit in on the next focus teams' meetings to observe discussions and interactions.
    b. Design an employee feedback survey to better understand the perspectives of the focus teams.
    c. Facilitate a meeting between the COO and the division leaders to discuss obstacles and future timelines.
    d. Meet with the division leaders to gauge their understanding of the focus teams and challenges they have experienced.

94. During the HR director's initial meeting with the COO, which of the following questions would be most effective in helping the director determine possible root causes for the initial shortcomings of the focus teams?

    a. How many focus teams were created?
    b. What type of timeline was provided to the division leaders for this project?
    c. Where would you like the focus groups to be in six months?
    d. How often and for how long do the focus teams meet?

95. What is the model of transactional leadership characterized by?

    a. Rewarding high performers with tangible rewards
    b. Working to change the organization with innovation and new ideas
    c. Leaders "serving" their employees
    d. Giving authoritative direction and demanding excellence

96. What is one provision of the Affordable Care Act (ACA) regarding preventive care?

    a. Characterize all women's health treatments as preventive.
    b. Preventive care shall be covered at 100% and is not subject to co-pays, deductibles, or coinsurance.
    c. Insured members shall receive $1 million in coverage for preventive care.
    d. The out-of-pocket cost for preventive care shall be capped at a percentage of the federal poverty level.

Refer to the following for questions 97 - 98:

A CEO of a midsized technology company has gained a reputation for berating others in meetings, firing employees who make minor mistakes, and micromanaging his/her senior leadership team.

97. How would you describe the likely culture of the company and its employees?
a. Fear based with minimal contribution from employees
b. Competitive among employees with a cutthroat mentality
c. Tight-knit—employees commiserate about their experiences with the CEO
d. High performing—employees wanting to prove the CEO wrong by doing their best work

98. As a human resource (HR) leader in this organization reporting to the CEO, how would you propose fixing this leadership challenge?
a. Clearly communicate with your own HR staff and other employees in the organization that you're aware of the issue and are working to resolve it. Offer an open door to anyone who needs to talk about their challenges.
b. Hire a third-party consultant to conduct a leadership assessment with the entire executive team, including the CEO.
c. Launch an internal investigation into inappropriate behaviors by the CEO. Interview multiple employees across the organization about their unpleasant interactions.
d. Begin looking for another job. The CEO runs the company how he/she wishes and will likely not be receptive to feedback or any attempts to correct behavior. It's best to begin looking for a better work environment elsewhere.

99. What does Title II of Genetic Information Nondiscrimination Act (GINA) prohibit?
a. Discrimination of employees or applicants based on genetic information
b. Discrimination of employees or applicants based on gender identity
c. Unauthorized sharing of protected health information
d. Discrimination of applicants based on disability status

100. When calculating the rate of turnover in an organization, which is most helpful?
a. Separate out involuntary terminations from voluntary terminations.
b. Include both voluntary and involuntary terminations in the calculation.
c. Consider the prior year's headcount when dividing by the number of employee exits.
d. Consider the prior year's total number of employee exits when dividing by average headcount.

101. Which is a step that is NOT a part of the evidence-based decision-making (EBDM) process?
a. Identify and frame the situation.
b. Gather evidence from internal and external sources.
c. Ask for factual feedback from stakeholders.
d. Consider the opinions of applicable subject matter experts (SMEs).

Refer to the following for questions 102 - 103:

Your organization is opening its first international office in Chennai, India. It will start as a relatively small office with mostly software developers, but there is a need to have a human resource (HR) person located there. You will oversee the work of this India-based HR manager in addition to your US-based team of five.

102. What would be your first step in helping open the India office?

a. Conduct a political, economic, social and technological (PEST) analysis through a human resource (HR) lens.
b. Travel to Chennai, see the landscape, meet the location contacts, and begin recruiting for the HR manager.
c. Conduct a strengths, weaknesses, opportunities and threats (SWOT) analysis through an HR lens.
d. Begin collecting sample employee handbooks, forms, and policies from India companies.

103. Six months later, you have a promising human resources manager on board, and the India office seems to be running smoothly. However, as expected, there are some minor challenges with communication between the two offices. What would be the most effective practice to adopt to improve daily communications?

a. Institute regular video conference calls for all virtual meetings
b. A reminder to the US location to use clear language in emails and eliminate the use of slang
c. A daily 15-minute status call at a time that is convenient for both time zones
d. Training provided at both locations regarding customs of the other culture—India culture training at the US location and American culture training at the Chennai location.

Refer to the following for questions 104 - 105:

ABC Corp has a large number of millennial employees joining the company in entry-level positions. Most of these individuals show great promise and ambition upon hire, but after a few months, they struggle with the steep learning curve of ABC's complicated product lineup and proprietary sales techniques. They become frustrated and are leaving the organization at a high rate. Because of this, human resources has decided to implement a mentoring program in the hopes that pairing more senior sales leaders and executives with these entry-level employees will help retain millennials. The problem is that a good mentoring program needs a budget, and ABC is conservative with nonessential spending.

104. How would you appeal to senior finance leadership and convince them of the importance of this program?

a. Put together a comprehensive document that defines eligibility requirements, high-potential employees who may participate, a timeline, marketing material, and a communication plan.
b. Put together a succinct, finance-centered document with the total budget needed, how the budget will be spent, the expected impacts on employee retention, and in turn, cost savings.
c. Start a six-month pilot program, which costs much less than the full program, and hope that its success will justify the money spent thus far.
d. Give a presentation to the senior finance leadership, and give several case studies of other organizations that had success with mentoring programs. Explain the employee morale-boosting benefits, and answer any questions they have.

105. Assuming you were given the budget for the mentoring program, you finalize the details and launch the program. So far, you've had plenty of mentors and mentees who are eager participants. What is the LEAST important consideration when pairing mentors and mentees?

a. Similar goals for the mentoring relationship
b. Similar career aspirations and field of work
c. The seniority and experience level of the mentor
d. The mentor and mentee's preference of match

106. What happens if an employee on leave submits a medical certification and human resources questions the validity of diagnosis and the professional's credentials?

    a. Human resources (HR) should contact the medical professional for more information about the employee's medical condition.

    b. HR must make the best determination of its validity based on the information provided to maintain the employee's privacy.

    c. HR may require a second opinion from another healthcare provider.

    d. HR may not contact the medical professional but should contact the employee for more information on the health condition.

107. What does PEST stand for in relation to analysis framework?

    a. Political, electronic, social, taxation

    b. Political, economic, social, technological

    c. Pop culture, economy, strategy, technology

    d. Political, environmental, social, technological

108. 401(k) plan auto-enrollment for new hires

    a. is a great strategy to boost participation and encourage financial responsibility among employees.

    b. is not legal.

    c. is not advisable from an employee relations standpoint; employees tend to feel deceived.

    d. is a requirement of most retirement plans.

109. A nine-box grid is an effective tool that compares an employee's performance with his/her potential for advancement. What is it most commonly used for?

    a. Disciplinary documentation

    b. Succession planning

    c. Talent acquisition

    d. Compensation planning

110. What is an advantage of using a business partner model in an organization rather than the generalist model?

    a. A human resources (HR) business partner is able to become more familiar with specific lines of business, thus acting as a strategic partner to the designated group.

    b. An HR business partner can focus on a designated area of expertise and become an advanced subject matter expert.

    c. An HR business partner has a wide range of skills and abilities, so he/she is able to provide guidance in almost any scenario.

    d. The business partner model allows for better consistency in policy application across departments in the organization.

111. How is an organization's vision statement different from the mission statement?

    a. It is a set of core principles that guides the organization's decision-making.

    b. It is forward looking and higher level, describing the organization's strategic direction.

    c. It remains constant throughout the organization's life cycle.

    d. It is more specific, describing how business is conducted.

112. According to the Thomas-Kilmann Conflict Mode Instrument chart, as the importance of a goal/assertiveness and the importance of a relationship/cooperation both increase, an ideal conflict resolution style is "collaborating." Under the same model, as the importance of a goal/assertiveness increases and the importance of a relationship/cooperation is minimal, what is the likely response?

    a. Avoiding—"I don't want to deal with it"
    b. Competing—"It's my way or the highway"
    c. Accommodating—"Whatever you want is OK with me"
    d. Compromising—"Let's make a deal"

113. What is an employee's right to have union representation during a disciplinary interview at the workplace called?

    a. Loudermill rights
    b. Weingarten rights
    c. Garrity rule
    d. Right to counsel

114. When presented with a harassment complaint from an employee, which statement should human resources avoid saying to the victim?

    a. "Thank you for bringing this to our attention; however, this does not sound like harassing behavior."
    b. "Please keep any investigation details confidential."
    c. "We do not tolerate retaliation."
    d. "The information you're giving me today is completely confidential."

115. To comply with the Age Discrimination in Employment Act (ADEA), what should severance agreements include for employees over age 40?

    a. A 21-day consideration period plus a seven-day revocation period after signing
    b. A seven-day consideration period plus a 21-day revocation period after signing
    c. A waiver of any type of complaint to the Equal Employment Opportunity Commission (EEOC)
    d. A minimum of 30 days' health insurance coverage

116. How would you describe the most effective approach to diversity recruitment?

    a. Hire more diverse employees into the workplace.
    b. Alter workplace practices to appeal to multiple generations of employees—leverage technology where appropriate, and train older workers on this technology.
    c. Train hiring managers and other interviewers on appropriate, and inappropriate, questions to ask during an interview.
    d. Expand advertising sources to include diversity-focused professional organizations and websites.

117. Under the Patient Protection and Affordable Care Act (PPACA), what is the period of time during which an employer must offer coverage to those employees who are considered full time called?

    a. The measurement period
    b. The stability period
    c. The administrative period
    d. The standard measurement period

Refer to the following for questions 118 - 120:

The CEO of your organization recently decided to launch a comprehensive company-wide employee engagement survey. Included in the survey were questions regarding satisfaction with internal services such as information technology, operations, and human resources (HR). Unfortunately, HR scored the lowest among all internal services, indicating employee dissatisfaction with HR interactions. The CEO is concerned and asked you, the HR director, how you will handle this.

118. How would you respond to the CEO?

a. Explain that although unfortunate, this is a common response from employees when asked how they feel about human resources (HR). HR's role is to be an enforcer of laws and policies, and that is usually not well received.

b. Explain that you will be looking into this further by conducting an audit of all HR processes and protocols to see what needs to be improved.

c. Based on the results it's clear that your HR staff needs to work on their customer service skills—tell the CEO that you'll be mandating customer service training for all HR staff immediately.

d. Tell the CEO that you will be issuing another company-wide survey; this time it will be regarding only HR internal services to identify the exact source of dissatisfaction.

119. What will be your first steps in initiating a human resources (HR) audit?

a. Identify the key HR staff for interviews and feedback.

b. Create a comprehensive audit checklist.

c. Collect benchmark data for comparison to findings.

d. Determine the scope of the audit.

120. Given the original reason for the human resources (HR) audit, what would be the MOST appropriate type of audit?

a. An audit to ensure all HR functions are aligned with best practices

b. An audit to ensure compliance with applicable regulations

c. An audit to ensure HR function is aligned with organizational goals

d. An audit focused on employee relations

Refer to the following for questions 121 - 122:

You are a human resources manager for a small software start-up company. The organization is relatively flat with several software engineers reporting to one lead and all five leads reporting to the director. A common complaint among the engineers is that there is no opportunity for advancement. In fact, this is prompting some high performers to look for jobs elsewhere.

121. What approach would you take to address this source of discontent?

a. Spearhead a significant wage increase for all engineers in the company to make up for the fact that they may never receive a promotion.

b. Make it clear to engineers that promotions are difficult to come by in smaller organizations and instead emphasize all the perks that they enjoy by working for a small, dynamic company.

c. Encourage engineers to identify the gaps in their skills in relation to the lead position and improve upon those skills to prepare for a potential promotion.

d. Train the leads to encourage the engineers to assess and communicate their needs and act—pursue learning opportunities and set goals.

122. What types of human resource metrics would you calculate to quantify the severity of the issue?

a. Time since last promotion

b. Turnover rate

c. Retention rate

d. Performance and potential

123. What guideline does the "4/5 rule" refer to?

a. Affordability for healthcare insurance under the Patient Protection and Affordable Care Act (PPACA)
b. Potential disparity in recruitment and selection of protected classes
c. Eligibility for labor union membership
d. An employee's ability to perform the essential functions of his/her job

124. In which domain is workforce planning and employment a focus?

a. The employee life cycle
b. Organizational strategy
c. Human resource operations
d. Managing performance

125. What does the SMART goal acronym stand for?

a. Smart, metric-driven, actionable, relevant, and time bound
b. Specific, measurable, accurate, relative, and time bound
c. Specific, measurable, achievable, relevant, and time bound
d. Specific, masterful, achievable, relevant, and time bound

126. How would you handle this situation?

A new father, who has not exhausted his Family and Medical Leave Act (FMLA) leave for the year, has requested the next 12 Fridays off to care for his new baby. He cites "baby bonding time" under the FMLA law and feels that this intermittent leave qualifies. His supervisor has expressed the challenge this will present his department as they usually have a time-sensitive report to submit each Friday.

a. Decline the employee's request as this would clearly present a hardship on his department.
b. Approve the employee's request as he still has Family and Medical Leave Act (FMLA) leave available.
c. Speak with the supervisor to see if other employees in the department would be able to work overtime on Fridays to cover the absence of this employee. If so, allow the request.
d. Require that the employee uses vacation time or paid time off as this would not qualify for FMLA.

127. Which is an example of a Bona Fide Occupational Qualification (BFOQ)?

a. A job applicant supplying documentation of his/her college degree
b. A fast-food restaurant with Christian values only hiring Christian employees
c. An airline only hiring attractive female flight attendants to draw in more male passengers
d. A sheriff's office refusing to hire police deputies over the age of 50

128. Which is the provision that does NOT typically describe a flexible spending account (FSA)?

a. "Use it or lose it"—funds expire at the end of the plan year (or at the end of the grace period).
b. Both employees and employers may contribute to the account on the employee's behalf.
c. Employees may reduce their taxable income by contributing funds to an FSA.
d. FSA enrollment is mandatory for employees with a Section 125 plan.

129. What is the biggest risk in conducting an employee satisfaction survey?

a. Skewed results because only the most satisfied employees respond
b. The potential for employees to not be truthful in their responses
c. The potential for the responses to not be anonymous
d. No employer follow-through on the results gathered from employees

130. In the instance of Family and Medical Leave Act (FMLA)-protected leave, new mothers' and fathers' rights differ in what way?

    a. New mothers can take the entire 12 weeks; new fathers may only take leave for bonding purposes.

    b. New mothers can take the entire 12 weeks; new fathers may only take leave to care for their spouse during the period of disability, which ranges from six to eight weeks.

    c. They have the same rights; however, they may not take the leave at the same time.

    d. They have the same rights—both can take time for bonding with the newborn, and the mother can take time for the period of disability. A new father can take the time to care for his spouse during the recovery period.

131. If an employee requests a day off, citing a religious holiday that he/she wishes to observe, is the employer obligated to grant the request?

    a. The employer should if the employee has enough vacation time or paid time off.

    b. If it is not a company-observed holiday, the employer is not required to allow the day off.

    c. The employer should grant the request if it does not present undue hardship.

    d. To avoid claims of discrimination, an employer should allow the request no matter the circumstances.

Refer to the following for questions 132 - 133:

> A common recruitment practice of your organization is to attend career fairs to attract a variety of different candidates for multiple open positions. You usually attend the fairs, as well as two to three other recruiters. You enjoy speaking with attendees and sometimes find some quality candidates. The CFO (your boss) has come to you and expressed his concern that the career fairs are very costly, and he's not sure if they're worth it.

132. What metric would you use to either verify the CFO's concerns or prove that the career fairs are worth the expense?

    a. Cost per hire

    b. Cost per candidate by source

    c. Applicants per opening

    d. Source of hire

133. Assume you've crunched the numbers and discovered that the career fairs are producing more candidates than other sources such as online job postings or employee referrals. How would you convey to the CFO that he was wrong?

    a. Choose your battle. Don't tell the CFO that he was incorrect, but simply stop registering for career fairs and instead focus on improving other recruitment methods.

    b. Casually mention it at the next regularly scheduled team meeting when the topic of recruitment comes up.

    c. Schedule a meeting with him and bring a print-out showing the data. Ask him what he'd like you to do, given this information.

    d. Schedule a meeting with him, and bring a print-out showing the data. Suggest that you continue attending but perhaps reduce the number of other company representatives to reduce the cost.

134. What is an ineffective approach for a supervisor to deliver feedback to a struggling employee?

    a. The supervisor should list each area of deficiency and how it impacts the team and/or organization.

    b. The supervisor should provide specific examples of instances in which the employee had a misstep.

    c. The supervisor should make performance expectations clear.

    d. The supervisor should provide some praise around the things the employee is performing well.

Answer Key and Explanations for Test #1

1. D: Encouraging social connections will help work interactions as well. If the social activities occur on site during work hours, employees are more likely to attend than if they are offsite or on employees' own time.

2. C: Direct confrontations and group meetings where people are expected to share updates can be uncomfortable for some cultures. Supervisors and managers should focus their time and energy on establishing trust with each individual on their team.

3. D: There is no specific advanced engineer exemption. The Fair Labor Standards Act (FLSA) exemptions apply only to white collar-type employees who fall under the salary and duties test that include executive, administrative, professional (learned and creative), computer, outside sales, and highly compensated employees.

4. B: Each of the listed elements are important to a successful DE&I strategy, but leadership buy-in is one of the essential first steps. It will lead to the effective collection and use of employee survey data (A), appropriate financial resources to fund action steps (C), and impactful training and development (D) opportunities. Leadership buy-in serves as both a practical step to secure tangible support for financial and personnel-driven resources and as a cornerstone for the more intangible support elements such as trust-building and role modeling across an organization.

5. B: Return to Work (RTW) programs can be used for on-the-job injuries or off-duty injuries as well.

6. C: A halo bias is when interviewers or recruiters base their assessment of a candidate solely on one positive characteristic. A horns bias is the opposite: one perceived negative trait sours the entire interaction. A similarity bias is when interviewers are drawn to a candidate who is similar to themselves, and a first impression bias is when interviewers makes a hiring decision based solely on their initial thoughts and feelings of the person.

7. A: The other concerns listed can usually be assuaged with a legitimate assessment provider. But no matter how buttoned up the assessment tool is, great applicants might be eliminated from the process based solely on their personality type.

8. A: Understanding the current state of training and the needs for each department will help human resources (HR) determine where the gaps are and what training needs to be eliminated, added, changed, or maintained. At that point, HR can verify that legal obligations are being met and best practices are being followed, and a plan can begin to take place.

9. B: Current training delivery methods and course durations should not be an important factor in deciding how to structure the new training program. Human resources should factor in legal obligations and logistical requirements. In addition, some training content is best delivered in person rather than online—for instance, training that needs discussion or opportunities for learners to ask questions.

10. A: "Best of breed" is a term used to describe the process of selecting only the best software system for a specific need of the organization, which often means not choosing an all-in-one system, which may have system limitations in various areas.

11. D: Older workers tend to value direct communication and lengthier, personal-type conversations. This can present challenges with a younger generation, who tend to prefer quick, work-related conversations to accomplish the objective. They also tend to be more familiar with modern communication technology like texting and instant messaging.

257

12. C: The millennial generation wants to know how to get to that next step in their career and feel engaged when they are provided with development opportunities.

13. B: Suspected drug users who are acting erratically should never be confronted alone. Also, supervisors are often not trained to handle a conversation of this magnitude, so it is best to have both a human resource representative and the supervisor present. Also, presenting the employee with a drug test prior to any conversations could cause the employee to panic and risk a negative outcome for the situation.

14. D: The most appropriate course of action would be to offer Family and Medical Leave Act (FMLA)-protected leave so the employee can attend rehab. You might also verify with your insurance to see if, and how, it is covered. Although it is true that he/she could be held to the same standards as other employees, it is important to first provide the tools for the employee to get clean. Once he/she is recovered, you may hold him/her to that standard. Additionally, current drug users are not protected under the Americans with Disabilities Act, but recovered addicts are.

15. B: An engaged employee is one who is loyal to the organization, speaks highly of the organization to friends and family, knows what work needs to be done to make a positive impact, and does it. Job satisfaction and employee engagement are not the same thing; job satisfaction is usually driven by extrinsic factors such as pay, benefits and time off, whereas intrinsic motivators and strong leadership drive engagement.

16. D: When an individual is in the "red zone," an effective technique is to guess an employee's feelings and/or needs that aren't being met. This can help them articulate his/her feelings while focusing on the facts. Advice in any form to an individual in this state is usually not well received. Once he/she has calmed down, you might ask if you can give them some advice.

17. B: This conflict does not rise to the level of any type of harassment or even bullying; it sounds like normal workplace conflict between two colleagues. For this reason, there is no need for a formal investigation; however, the supervisor should be made aware of the situation so that the conflict does not escalate.

18. C: Organizing a social meet-up for remote employees to connect with one another would encourage strong working relationships and a kind of support group where they can share remote working experiences and tips. Posting photos would probably make remote workers feel even more left out of the fun. Also, if given the choice, remote workers would probably prefer not to attend the company party if it meant paying for travel and lodging. The dial-in and webcam would not be a bad idea but, again, may make the remote workers feel more left out.

19. D: The biggest advantage is offering a better work-life balance for employees. Overhead costs may be slightly less for a remote worker; however, the employer should still pay for home office supplies and equipment. A lack of commute does have a positive impact on the environment, but that is not necessarily the focus from a human resource perspective. Last, a remote work arrangement is not a substitute for child care as the employee's focus should be on working, not tending to other responsibilities.

20. A: Although the other options could be potential downsides of having a remote workforce, the biggest disadvantage is the impact on communication and work relationships. Employees and managers must be more proactive in communication efforts with remote workers—a simple face-to-face chat is not an option.

21. D: According to research, middle managers are among the most unhappy in the workplace, and a primary reason is a lack of authority from upper management and having to enforce policies that they may not agree with.

22. A: By reviewing the performance management processes, measurable work outcomes are set as the center of the investigation. While this review may lead to eventual investigations of certain managers for unethical practices (B), putting the work outcomes as the focus clearly communicates the ultimate goals of the review and any follow-up actions. Stay interviews (C) can be useful to recognize what the company does well and what it should continue to do with respect to retention; however, getting to the root of any possible favoritism or discrimination is of a higher priority when data from the exit interviews can serve as a starting point for key retention factors. Recommending an additional salary increase (D) may eventually be part of the solution but increasing salaries without additional data about compensation decisions like starting rates, compensable factors, bonuses, and merit increases may lead to inefficient spending.

23. C: A job evaluation is used for assessing each position's relative worth to organizational outcomes. Job evaluations are critical tools to define what roles and responsibilities are of highest value to the organization. This data can then be utilized to design performance management processes and outcomes that are based on quality of work rather than personal similarities. Job analysis tools (A) can be useful for more accurately defining what a job actually does and how it functions within a team or organization but do not necessarily get to the root of responsibility value within the context of performance management. Workplace observations (B) and employee surveys (D) can be useful tools to better understand performance review priorities but are typically used within the job evaluation process rather than on their own as standalone tools.

24. D: Pay audits assess the actual compensation rates of employees in comparison to each other and to their worth to the company. Pay audits can be an incredibly useful tool to root out disparate treatment or disparate impact in compensation practices. This data can then be used to right any wrongs that may be occurring across the organization rather than raising pay rates across-the-board. By publicizing the data, the company is displaying the transparency in operations that is critical when building trust with the workforce. A benefits review (C) or performance-pay adjustments (B) may end up being productive steps forward but conducting a pay audit first will more directly address the root of complaints about compensation practices. Expanding the C-suite to include the HR function (A) at the top levels of leadership may assist in long-term human management operations; however, this could also cause tension in the short term if the company is trying to expand the reach of leadership while the leadership is already considered untrustworthy.

25. B: Systemic inequality (oftentimes manifested as systemic racism and/or systemic classism) refers to the societal histories, policies, and disenfranchisement that can lead to disadvantages for certain dimensions of people. Lack of access to affordable higher education can force those who grew up in less economically stable communities to seek employment instead of a college education; this lack of formal schooling can be a barrier even in situations where the experience in the field may be more valuable than the diplomas their more privileged peers have earned. It is essential for companies to review and assess the job descriptions and promotion specifications to ensure that the job requirements are truly required and not just preferred. Unintentional discrimination in the job descriptions like this situation is likely to amount to disparate impact as opposed to disparate treatment (A). Ableist standards (C) may be at play in the event that an employee was not physically or mentally able to complete a college education; however, this explanation is less likely to affect many experienced individuals at once. Stereotyping (D) is a barrier to diversity but is not overtly present in this scenario.

26. B: Dependents may enroll with COBRA continuation coverage even if the primary beneficiary (employee or former employee) is not enrolled.

27. C: PIPs are best for specific and measurable problems with an employee's performance that may be turned around with guidance and training. Insubordinate behavior is not generally resolved with a PIP. And last, although PIPs are sometimes the final step before a termination, it is best for managers and supervisors to issue a PIP with the intent that the behavior can be improved.

28. C: Groupthink is a group behavior trend in which a group's members speak and behave in ways that preserve social cohesion over production and outcomes; the team functions well together but may not have the most effective or creative outputs. Trust (B) in the workplace can be complex to manage and may increase or decrease depending on the communication that accompanies team building and operations. Conflict (A) in the workplace is likely to increase with an influx of differing perspectives and experiences, but if appropriately managed, collaboration (D) can be the conflict style that experiences the greatest increase. Collaboration in the workplace also depends on high levels of trust and creative thinking to design new solutions and create new value.

29. B: The employer should provide a comprehensive list of acceptable documentation to an employee and allow him/her to choose the documentation that meets the criteria. Requiring a new hire to supply a passport would discriminate against those who are not US citizens.

30. D: Even if a candidate appears to be originally from the United States, interviewers should not ask where the candidate is from, as national origin is a protected class. If not selected, a candidate could claim discrimination based on this criterion.

31. C: H-1B visa applicants are eligible if they possess a bachelor's degree or foreign equivalent and work in a specialty occupation as defined by the US Citizen and Immigration Services (USCIS).

32. B: Human resources is usually in the role of preparing for, and participating in, collective bargaining. This falls under the "confidential employee" exemption with the National Labor Relations Act (NLRA).

33. B: Focus groups with employees are optimal when they pertain to specific topics, such as feedback on the benefit plan or succession planning. Around eight to 10 participants are best, and they should be a diverse group of employees to more accurately represent opinions across the organization. Although employees should feel free to voice their opinions openly, the facilitator should bring some semblance of structure to the focus group. He/she should give an introduction, ask open-ended questions to participants, and be prepared to summarize the discussion at the conclusion.

34. D: A response to a candidate asking for feedback on how to improve can vary based on multiple factors. If there is a reason to foster a relationship with a candidate, it can be worthwhile to provide constructive but carefully worded and concise feedback.

35. A: Coaching is used in specific instances for individuals—to help them prepare for a leadership role or an upcoming assignment or to help them develop a specific skill or stop exhibiting a certain behavior. Mentoring is usually in the case of a formal or informal program and can help individuals pursue their personal or professional goals.

36. A: The look-back measurement period is a method of determining eligibility for coverage. The employer looks at a defined period of time that the employee has worked and averages the weekly hours. If the average is 30 hours or more per week, the employee would likely be eligible for coverage.

37. B: Feedback is best delivered in a specific format. Describe the exact behavior that needs to stop and what needs to start happening. In this case, the employee needs to stop talking over people in meetings. Providing more complex work assignments to the employee may further alienate others on the team as they'd see the poor behavior rewarded with more advanced assignments.

38. C: Although this employee may be going through a series of personal crises, it's important to focus on his/her work performance and attendance issues. If the attendance issues are not addressed, they can have a negative impact on the others on the team.

39. A: An employee who is "engaged to wait" is one who must stay at the workplace until his/her work assignment is given; therefore, he/she must be paid for that time as he/she is effectively on duty. An employee who is "waiting to be engaged" is relieved of his/her work duties, and can use his/her time freely, but must return to the workplace if a work assignment requires his/her presence.

40. B: Federal law does not require lunch or rest periods for employees; however, many states do have these provisions.

41. C: Canadian citizens, unlike Mexican citizens, do not need a TN visa to work in the United States. They need only present proof of Canadian citizenship, a written job offer from the prospective employer, and proof of qualification for the position at the US border. They are generally then admitted as a TN nonimmigrant.

42. C: In a Right to Work state, employees are able to decline union membership if they choose.

43. C: As the employee is noticeably anxious about the health condition and missing work, it is best to respond to the email with a response as soon as possible rather than deferring to the HR Specialist who is not in the office.

44. A: Key performance indicators (KPIs) are relatively controversial, with some experts claiming they foster competition rather than collaboration.

45. C: Based on the facts that Karen and Steve are friends, Steve is in good standing with the company and has never been in trouble before, and Karen clearly has a desire to maintain the friendship, it would be best to let her make the decision on the next course of action.

46. B: Once the injured employee is helped and stabilized, the first call should be to human resources (HR) before taking any witness statements or writing up a summary of events. It could be dangerous to fix the cause of the injury, so again, it is best for supervisors to consult with HR before handling anything themselves.

47. A: Although a supervisor may also be a good resource in assessing the dangers of the job, employees have the best familiarity with the potential hazards of their everyday responsibilities.

48. B: A direct, facilitated conversation is best in the instance of workplace conflict. That way Jane and Susan can hear each other's perspectives and make strides in repairing the relationship. It is best to address the situation before it continues to get worse.

49. A: Dysfunctional conflict among employees is a detriment to the workplace and can cause absenteeism and/or turnover—this is the best descriptor of the interactions between Jane and Susan. Functional conflict is actually a beneficial type of conflict and can actually promote problem-solving and creative ideas. Bullying behavior is generally one-sided, and task conflict is isolated to a certain project or task.

50. C: Individuals who are thoughtful and fact based typically prefer to "digest" information before asking questions or responding. Sending an email ahead of the one-on-one meeting would allow Peter the time to consider all his questions or concerns before having a direct conversation. Also, it is not always feasible or equitable to dole out work assignments based solely on employee preference.

51. B: As the manager of the group you should be involved in the strategic discussions and overall project plan. From there, if Jason and Peter are able to decide collaboratively which tasks they feel most comfortable with, they will have more buy-in for the project itself.

52. D: Peter and Jason have different working styles. Peter may resent Jason's attention-seeking and flashy style, and Jason may feel that Peter needs to speak up if he has questions, concerns, or generally any information to share.

53. C: The CSR's medical professional should make the determination of the need for the stand-up desk. You should not try to determine the legitimacy or severity of a disability; rather, focus on the reasonableness of the accommodation request. And in this case, the request is reasonable.

54. B: Employers should never divulge another employee's personal health information, even to justify the reason for an accommodation. Although the performance-based program is creative, an employee's comfort should not be dependent on how well he/she performs on the job. The best course of action in this case is to work to obtain a budget to eventually offer stand-up desks to all employees who sit for extended periods of time. This can be treated as a perk of the job and may end up preventing future health issues for employees.

55. C: A "top-heavy" 401(k) plan is one in which more than 60% of the entire plan's value resides in the accounts of "key" employees. A key employee is defined as an employee with major ownership of the company and/or in a decision-making role.

56. C: Forms for active employees should never be destroyed. The retention requirement is three years after hire date or one year after termination date, whichever is later.

57. C: The Department of Labor has issued seven criteria that qualify an internship to be unpaid. There are no restrictions for weekly hours.

58. D: Pairing up employees when they visit customers' homes is a creative solution that would provide a safer situation for everyone—customers and employees. It is unwise to make a uniform disqualification for anyone who has a criminal record as this can result in disparate impact. Although it is a good idea to inform new hires of the organization's expectations when it comes to ethics, threatening criminal prosecution is not exactly a warm welcome! Last, telling customers to secure their valuables prior to a visit conveys that they should not trust the employee visiting the home, which may have a negative impact on future business.

59. B: Generally, in the case of a harassment complaint, you cannot promise anonymity. However, this is a complaint regarding criminal activity of the accused, and there is no need for the complainant's name to be disclosed.

60. A: The principled negotiation style is an interest-based bargaining technique that aims to identify a mutually beneficial agreement, also known as "win-win."

61. A: Supervisors are to be excluded from bargaining units under the National Labor Relations Act (NLRA) if they have independent judgment to make personnel decisions such as hiring, terminating, or promoting.

62. A: HSA funds never expire, and employees who leave the organization do not lose access to the funds.

63. A: Coordination of benefits rules require that the insurance plan listed as primary will be charged first, and any residual charges will be processed by the secondary payer.

64. C: The hiring manager knows the position and the industry best, he/she can give expert insight into the next steps in the recruitment strategy.

65. C: The expectancy theory of motivation hypothesizes that individuals make the choices that they do based on the likelihood and importance of the outcome.

66. A: Cloud commuting is a practice of storing, managing, and processing data in remote servers rather than a locally hosted server.

67. A: Although each option presented could help identify different causes of turnover, the best way to pinpoint the top reason would be to conduct exit interviews with each exiting employee and identify trends.

68. C: Realistic job previews would give candidates a realistic glimpse into what the job would entail on a daily basis. It would encourage them to self-select out of the hiring process if they aren't a good fit rather than waiting until after they're hired.

69. D: The software developers in this scenario are young and hardworking, so unlimited paid time off (PTO) may not resonate with them as much as other perks. Additionally, unlimited PTO has plenty of pitfalls and risks, so ultimately it may not be worth the potential issues. These employees also seem to have minimal interest in anything related to health care or insurance benefits. Millennials typically have a strong desire to remain challenged and advance quickly in their careers—a career path program would allow them to constantly learn, evolve, and move to the next level when the time is right.

70. B: The most effective method of gaining leadership buy-in is to show, rather than tell. If the CEO is willing to agree to a trial period, he/she will see the intangible benefits of allowing employees to work from home. Trial periods are effective methods of testing out a workplace program without a full commitment. The CEO is more likely to agree to this.

71. A: Direct, timely feedback is always the best approach with employees. Asking for feedback on how to avoid mistakes in the future makes him/her feel invested in the solution.

72. D: Although 30 days' advance notice of an upcoming leave is ideal, in many instances it will not be feasible for an employee to give any advance notice. If no advance notice is given, it is not an adequate reason to deny Family and Medical Leave Act (FMLA) leave.

73. B: Both the employer and the union must participate in the collective bargaining process and display good faith bargaining efforts; however, neither party is required to make concessions.

74. D: The need for self-actualization is the final stop in the pyramid. Once an individual has met his/her basic hunger and thirst needs, he/she looks to fill the need for safety, then feeling a sense of belonging. Next is the need for feeling esteem from others and, finally, the need for a sense of purpose, or self-actualization.

75. A: The Worker Adjustment and Retraining Notification (WARN) Act requires that for a layoff affecting 50 or more employees at one location, employees must be given 60 days' notice prior to their employment ending.

76. C: Many states and local legislatures are banning the practice of asking for a candidate's current compensation as basing an offer on current pay can have disparate impact on protected classes. The salary offer should be based primarily on the candidate's level of experience, but other factors such as potential commute, candidate requirements, internal equity, and others may be considered as well.

77. A: Federal contractors and subcontractors are required by the OFCCP to annually review and update their AAPs, which include a report and documentation of affirmative actions such as outreach efforts and training programs.

78. C: Current employee expectations should not be a driving factor when defining an organization's compensation philosophy. Although it is important to pay a fair and equitable amount for the work being performed, employee expectations are often higher than the wage commensurate with the work performed.

79. B: Teams often will relapse from the norming stage back into storming when faced with new challenges.

80. C: The most important first step before beginning a recruitment process is defining the needed skills an incumbent should have to be successful in the role. Once this list is established, that will help define compensation, optimal advertising sources, and finally, qualified candidates.

81. D: According to the Equal Employment Opportunity Commission (EEOC), petty slights, annoyances, and isolated incidents will not rise to the level of illegality.

82. B: A harassment claim that is found to be malicious should result in discipline for the complainant. It is never a good idea to discuss an investigation and its results with the complainant and subject in the same room.

83. C: The first step in the process of selecting a new human resource information system (HRIS) is to determine if the organization will conduct the vendor selection process internally or if a third-party consultant will be hired to perform the search. Once that decision is made, the other steps will follow.

84. C: There are 16 different personality type combinations using the four pairs of Myers-Briggs Type Indicator (MBTI) preferences: introverted versus extraverted, sensing versus intuitive, thinking verses feeling, and judging versus perceiving.

85. D: A political, economic, social and technological (PEST) analysis is a method of obtaining and reviewing data from external influences to the organization.

86. D: Organizations should not contact other organizations directly for specific compensation amounts as this may lead to antitrust violations. Also, job titles and levels can vary across organizations; the actual duties and responsibilities should be taken into account when determining the similarity of positions. Last, employee-reported salary amounts are not always accurate.

87. B: The initial issuance of an H-1B visa is valid for three years and is renewable for another three years for a total duration of six years.

88. C: The supervisor should focus solely on the employee's performance and attendance. A blend of direct face-to-face feedback and documentation is best to illustrate that the supervisor is following protocol and no unfair treatment based on his/her medical condition is taking place.

89. A: This employee's bad behavior is just under the radar and is not quite egregious enough to rise to the level of discipline. A direct conversation from the supervisor may only make matters worse for the other employee. In this case it would be best to separate the two employees in hopes that the situation can be diffused over time.

90. A: External candidates can bring new ideas and approaches to an organization, whereas an internal candidate is influenced by the current organizational mind-set.

91. B: Misunderstandings and conflict are to be expected on newly formed global teams due to clashes between the external cultures and beliefs that each member brings to the team. Team building intent on highlighting the common ground of skills and organizational goals and values can help to build an internal team culture. A strong internal team culture uses trust and mutual respect to turn conflict into collaboration and takes advantages of the individual differences of its members. Online trainings (A) can be a useful part of the puzzle when managing a diverse team, but they are not as effective as interactive, values-based activities. Allowing conflict to play out (C) without intervention may work but may also cause resentment and mistrust. Automatically assigning conflicting team members (D) elsewhere does not get to the root of the challenges and weakens the teams as members were initially chosen for their specialty knowledge that may not translate as well on different teams.

92. A: Scheduling meetings in advance enables the groups to rotate the days and times of the meetings so that group members can share the burden of inconvenient time zones. In addition, scheduling meetings in advance can give group members an adequate amount of time to schedule their professional and personal responsibilities accordingly so they will be able to participate. Collaborative technologies that allow for passive discussion and group work (B) are great as a supplemental component to global teams but can negatively impact group progress when decisions must be made or discussions require real-time feedback or consensus. Redistributing teams according to the members' respective time zones (C) would take away from the project's initial vision to take advantage of the combination of specific skills and global perspectives to solve challenges. Eliminating a team member solely due to lack of meeting participation (D) is an extreme reaction if the rest of his or her contributions are of high quality, and he or she is otherwise communicative and responsive. Before eliminating a team member, the team and its leaders should first seek feedback from that member to learn what his or her desire to take part in the team is and what individual barriers he or she may experience in attending the meetings.

93. D: The division leaders are the linchpin between the COO's vision and the focus groups themselves and will provide the most insight on the practical side of the project's launch and progress. By targeting the division leaders for data collection, the HR director will better understand the progression from executive idea to leadership design to ground-level execution. With the information from the division leaders, the HR director will be better equipped to then observe the focus groups (A), collect data from group members (B), and facilitate future meetings or plans of action to improve focus group outcomes (C). Additionally, data collection at the division leaders' level may help to uncover other tensions or misunderstandings that could have developed as a result of recent organizational globalization.

94. B: Leadership buy-in is one of the most critical elements of any successful DE&I project or initiative. Leadership buy-in must be more than a one-time occurrence, and it must be highly visible and consistent. It is important for the HR director to dig further into why and how the first project check-in by the COO occurred a full six months after its launch. By establishing timelines with clear deadlines for goals and objectives, the COO can remain present with the project to guide and support both the division leaders and the focus group members. The future goals of the focus groups (C) are important to consider when planning the next action steps, but without digging into the root causes of the project's initial challenges, progress and positive change will be limited.

95. A: Transactional leadership is a style of leadership that is objective driven, in which leaders incentivize wanted behavior with tangible rewards and discourage unwanted behavior with punishment. Transactional leadership is an opposing model from transformational leadership, in which leaders look to inspire and motivate to change the status quo. Transactional leadership is best in the instance of emergency operations or when there is a high-priority objective.

96. B: As part of the Affordable Care Act (ACA), preventive care, vaccines, and screenings are no longer subject to copayments, deductibles, or coinsurance. There are also expanded protections for women's health services.

97. A: The most likely resulting culture in the organization would be fear based. Employees would likely be fearful of making contributions as they may make a mistake and would be fearful of losing their jobs or speaking up in meetings.

98. B: It's best to hire a neutral third-party expert to come in and make an unbiased assessment. The CEO is more likely to be receptive to feedback from a professional who has made a thorough analysis of the organization's leadership.

99. A: Under Title II of the Genetic Information Nondiscrimination Act (GINA), it is illegal for employers to base any type of hiring decision (promotions, hiring, and/or firing) based on genetic information such as family medical history or the likelihood that they may contract a disease or illness.

100. A: When determining the cause of employee turnover, it is best to separate out involuntary terminations from voluntary terminations. Counting involuntary terminations in the calculation will skew the separation rate and will not help determine the cause for attrition.

101. D: The evidence-based decision-making (EBDM) process is a concept that is based solely on research and facts, so thoughts and feelings, even from a subject matter expert (SME), are not generally factored in when making a management decision.

102. A: Before traveling to Chennai or collecting sample documents, a political, economic, social and technological (PEST) analysis should be conducted from a human resources viewpoint. Political, economic, social and technological factors will influence most decisions that need to be made, so thorough research and analysis is critical.

103. C: The most effective approach to improving daily communication is a short status call that occurs every day. The attendees can discuss pressing topics for the day or just catch up, and this allows attendees to build relationships and feel connected.

104. B: Senior leaders who are focused in finance are usually most interested in how much things will cost and what the return on investment will be. Furthermore, usually their time is short and valuable, so a more succinct delivery of this information is better.

105. C: A successful mentor does not necessarily need to be the most senior. Even a less experienced mentor can provide insight and guidance to a mentee in an area the mentee is not familiar with.

106. C: Although human resources (HR) may contact the medical professional to confirm the validity of the certification and ask clarifying questions, to protect the employee's privacy, they may not ask for more information about the condition. HR may require a second or third opinion at the employer's expense.

107. B: A PEST analysis is conducted as part of a strategic market analysis of several factors: political, economic, social and technological.

108. A: Automatic enrollment in a 401(k) for new hires, although not a requirement, is a recommended strategy to boost participation in the plan. There is not usually backlash from employees against this provision; however, communication to new hires and current employees is essential to avoid mistrust.

109. B: A nine-box grid is a matrix with three degrees of performance on one axis and three levels of potential on the other axis. Names are generally plotted in the different grid squares to identify individuals who have potential to move into leadership roles in the organization.

110. A: Answer B describes a specialist role, answer C describes a generalist role, and answer D is actually a common disadvantage of utilizing the business partner model. Different business partners across the organization who support different divisions tend to reflect inconsistency in practice as compared to their counterparts.

111. B: A vision statement should be aspirational and strategic, describing where the organization wants to be in the future and how they plan to achieve that goal.

112. B: During a conflict between two individuals, when the relationship is of minimal importance and the goal is of high importance, often the response between the two parties is competitiveness.

113. B: A union member has the right to union representation in an investigatory interview that may result in discipline, and this right is known as "Weingarten."

114. D: Human resources should never guarantee confidentiality to complainants. In the case of an investigation, details of the complaint will likely need to be shared with the accused and/or witnesses.

115. A: The Age Discrimination in Employment Act (ADEA) requires an employee over 40 to receive 21 days to review a severance agreement before signing. Once the employee signs the agreement, he/she has seven days from the date of signature to change his/her mind and revoke the agreement. Agreements should not contain any type of language that would prevent employees from filing a complaint with the Equal Employment Opportunity Commission (EEOC).

116. D: Organizations should never base any hiring decision on race, gender, age, or any other protected visual attributes, even if the intent is to "hire for more diversity." Also, whereas the other two suggestions would help create a more inclusive workplace, the most effective strategy is to expand the reach of recruitment efforts toward underrepresented groups.

117. B: The stability period is the duration of time that coverage must be offered to all full-time employees. This period of time must be at least six months and not less than the defined measurement period.

118. B: In this instance, you should gather more information before instituting a plan of action. The cause of the poor ratings could be anything from bad internal customer service to inefficient processes. Another survey would probably give employees survey fatigue, so it's best to launch an internal audit.

119. D: The first step in a human resources audit is to determine the type and scope of the audit. Will you focus on one specific function, such as recruiting or employee relations? Or will it be more exhaustive of all processes? Will it be strategic or compliance-oriented, or will it identify best practices?

120. A: This audit should address all human resource (HR) functions, not just employee relations. The poor survey results could be prompted by other processes such as performance reviews, benefits enrollment, promotional opportunities, and so on. Although compliance is important, it is not the goal of this audit. Industry best practice will provide a useful benchmark to identify deficiencies in the HR function.

121. D: In this situation, you don't want to imply that the engineers only need to improve upon their skills to get a promotion, but you also don't want to stifle their ambition. The leads should work with the engineers to identify exactly what they need—is it just more money? More recognition? More responsibility? More autonomy? Perhaps some of these needs can be met with a creative solution rather than a promotion.

122. A: The best way to quantify this situation is to calculate the time since last promotion for each employee and average it out across the organization. Whereas a turnover rate may indicate a problem with higher-than-average employee exits, it will not identify the reason for exits.

123. B: The "4/5 rule" and "80% rule" are commonly used phrases that describe the ideal selection rate for protected classes, as defined by the Equal Employment Opportunity Commission (EEOC). The selection rate of minorities should be at least 80% of the selection rate of nonminorities.

124. C: Workforce planning and employment are a human resources domain that is operationally focused, with emphasis on recruitment/selection, retention, and separation. Although similar to the employee life cycle, workforce planning and employment are less comprehensive.

125. C: A SMART goal is specific, measurable, achievable, relevant, and time bound.

126. A: Intermittent Family and Medical Leave Act (FMLA) leave is not mandated for baby bonding time; however, an employer may allow it. In this particular instance, it would present a hardship on the department, and asking others to work extra hours to fill in for this employee would likely be perceived as unfair.

127. D: A Bona Fide Occupational Qualification (BFOQ) is only legitimate if it is a criterion (e.g., gender, religion, or national origin) that is required for business operations. There is a business need and safety consideration for hiring police officers and deputies who are younger than 50.

128. D: FSA participation is optional for employees. During open enrollment, each employee decides how much money, if any, to contribute to an FSA. Employers may contribute to a flexible spending account (FSA) on behalf of their employees. The funds generally do expire at the end of the plan year; however, many plans offer a three-month grace period that allows employees to access the funds into the following year.

129. D: The biggest organizational risk when conducting an employee satisfaction survey is the potential for not taking any action based on the findings of the survey. This may backfire and create ill will among employees.

130. D: Both new mothers and new fathers have the same rights under Family and Medical Leave Act (FMLA)—that is 12 weeks of job and benefit protection following the birth or adoption of a child. This includes bonding time, physical incapacity from the delivery, and/or care for the spouse who is recovering.

131. C: It is a good idea to grant the employee's request but only if it does not present undue hardship to the employer. Some examples of undue hardship could be cost, staffing shortages, or a decrease in workplace efficiency.

132. B: Cost per candidate by source is calculated by dividing the total cost of the source (in this case, the total cost of the career fairs) by number of candidates generated by the source. This metric can then be compared to the cost of alternate sources of generating candidates to prove its efficiency.

133. D: Because you report to the CFO, you should tread lightly when telling him he's wrong but still have a direct and private conversation about it. It's obvious that he's concerned about cost, so it's best to provide a solution to mitigate those costs while still meeting your objective of attending the career fairs.

134. A: When providing feedback, a supervisor should limit the focus to one or two areas of deficiency. Otherwise, it tends to make the employee feel defensive.

SHRM-CP Practice Test #2

1. How should a risk that is slowly but surely going to happen be handled?

    a. Prepare
    b. Act
    c. Park
    d. Adapt

2. A technology company hires three new information technology professionals. To fill the positions, the company incurs both internal and external costs totaling $60,000. The total first-year compensation of the three new hires is $300,000. What is the Recruitment Cost Ratio?

    a. 2%
    b. 5%
    c. 20%
    d. 50%

Refer to the following for questions 3 - 5:

> A growing online travel agency has 1,500 employees in three offices working in a fun, but fast-paced environment. The small HR team is trying to keep up with the demands of a busy and growing company.

3. Each year, for compliance purposes, the HR team instructs all employees to review and sign a one-page sexual harassment policy. Their managers are supposed to review the information with them in a one-on-one meeting before they sign the document. The HR business partner is well aware that the managers do not spend time reviewing the information, and most employees do not read it before signing and turning the document in. She is concerned about the lack of effective harassment prevention training the company is conducting. But when she raises her concerns, the leadership team makes it clear that they cannot spend any extra time on this. What can the HR business partner do?

    a. Advise the leadership team of the significance of the training, and insist on improving the current process by conducting in-person trainings for all employees.
    b. Instead of the managers, have the HR generalist review the document with employees one-on-one before asking them to sign.
    c. Eliminate the training because it wastes valuable resources but does not yield the desired outcome.
    d. Develop a series of short online training modules that employees are asked to complete each year.

4. As part of their flexible working environment, the company put all employees on salary and classified them as exempt. This allows them to complete their work on a flexible schedule. The HR business partner reviews results of an internal audit, and discovers that not all employee groups meet the requirements to be exempt. For example, the customer service partners do not fall into any of the exemptions and often work overtime. What is the next step the HR business partner should take?

    a. Set up a meeting with the leadership team, inform them of the findings, and present a solution to change the compensation structures.
    b. Because the current pay structure emerged from the company's culture, it is not subject to the exemption rule, and no further steps are needed.
    c. Inform employees and their respective managers that no one is allowed to work any overtime going forward.
    d. Modify the job duties of the employees in question so that they meet the exemption requirements.

5. After growing for the last couple of years, the company is now considered to be in the maturity state of its life cycle. What should the HR business partner focus on during this stage?

    a. She should conduct job assessments to improve and correct job descriptions.

    b. She should help maintain the company's agile and creative spirit.

    c. She should contribute to creating a compelling company culture in alignment with its mission and vision.

    d. She should provide support to employees who experience stress due to ongoing change.

6. A person is described as being single and a recent college graduate from San Francisco. What layer is this description referring to?

    a. Internal dimension

    b. Organizational dimension

    c. External dimension

    d. Personal dimension

7. Which of the following tools would be most useful in correcting the historically pervasive discrimination in compensation?

    a. Compensation survey

    b. Pay audit

    c. Job analysis

    d. Performance evaluations

8. What tasks needs to be performed continuously throughout the entire risk management process?

    a. Invest and set direction

    b. Reevaluate and direct

    c. Monitor and review

    d. Engage and motivate

Refer to the following for questions 9 - 11:

> A brewing company employs 1,200 people across four breweries. The VP of HR works at the headquarters and has four HR generalists reporting to her. There is one HR generalist on site at each of the breweries. One of them recently got promoted to training manager, and a new HR generalist was hired for the position.

9. The VP of HR asks the new HR generalist to prepare a 30-day action plan and then meets with her for an initial development meeting. What should the HR generalist include in her action plan?

    a. Schedule a one-on-one meeting with each manager she will be supporting.

    b. Observe current processes instead of asking too many questions.

    c. Make suggestions to improve work processes and procedures.

    d. Implement best practices learned from her previous positions.

10. During her first week, the new HR generalist spends time observing different workgroups to understand the business better. She overhears a supervisor say to a pregnant employee that she's been forgetful lately because of her "baby brain." The comment stays on the HR generalist's mind, and she is unsure if she should say something. What is the BEST thing for her to do?

    a. Consult with a peer to determine if the comment is acceptable or not.

    b. Report her observations to the VP of HR.

    c. Continue learning about the company culture to understand the context.

    d. Approach the pregnant employee to ensure the comment did not upset her.

11. The supervisor of the pregnant employee comes to the HR generalist with a request for a written warning. Despite multiple verbal warnings, the employee keeps using her cell phone during work time for personal text messaging and playing games. The HR generalist has also had several conversations with the employee about this. However, the HR generalist is sympathetic because the employee reminds her of herself when she was pregnant. She does not think that the employee should receive a written warning and consults with her supervisor, the VP of HR. What should the VP of HR do?

    a. Allow the HR generalist to deny the manager's request for a written warning if she does not agree with it.

    b. Ask the HR generalist to prepare a written warning according to the manager's request.

    c. Review the employee's file to determine if there have been previous performance management issues.

    d. Find out why the HR generalist does not agree with the written warning.

Refer to the following for questions 12 - 14:

A federal credit union prides itself on creating a positive workplace culture for its 600 employees. They offer benefits like a free gym membership, paid volunteer opportunities, movie nights, and excellent health insurance. The CEO meets with the VP of HR to discuss the costs of the employee perks. While he wants to maintain the benefits, the company also needs to find cost savings. After further discussion, they decide that renegotiating their benefits premiums will be the best strategy to lower costs.

12. The VP of HR is under pressure to negotiate lower benefits premiums and is preparing for a tough price negotiation with the benefits vendor. What will be the BEST strategy to start off the negotiation?

    a. Convey the company's firm position on reducing costs.

    b. Create a welcoming atmosphere that makes the benefits vendor feel comfortable.

    c. Set goals for the meeting and lay out the company's negotiation strategy.

    d. Focus on understanding the benefits vendor's side.

13. As the VP of HR prepares for the negotiation meeting, she reviews some points with the company's controller. At the end of their meeting, the controller wishes her good luck and jokes that she should wear her sexy, low-cut blouse for the negotiation. How should the VP of HR react?

    a. Smile and walk away because it is important to maintain a good relationship.

    b. Follow his recommendation because he knows the vendor and what it will take to win the negotiation.

    c. Ask the controller to please refrain from making sexual jokes.

    d. Schedule a follow-up meeting with the controller to address the situation.

14. To find further cost savings, the VP of HR wants to eliminate the benefits and perquisites that employees rarely use. The company has not been tracking usage data. How should she go about determining which ones are underutilized?

    a. Conduct a company-wide employee survey.

    b. Conduct interviews with individual employees.

    c. Review statistical data on what company benefits employees generally use and do not use.

    d. Review stay and exit interviews to determine which benefits are most frequently and infrequently mentioned.

15. What can someone improve on to become an impactful communicator?

    a. Giving feedback

    b. Multitasking

    c. Vocal qualities

    d. Emotional intelligence

16. An Indian citizen moved to the United States for a job in the information technology industry. What is the term for money he regularly sends back to his family in India?

   a. Global diaspora
   b. Global disbursement
   c. Global remittances
   d. Global support payments

Refer to the following for questions 17 - 19:

> A company that develops and sells household products is going through firm-wide change initiatives. Their goal is to become a leader in corporate sustainability by developing green, nontoxic household products and using recycled packaging.

17. The CHRO keeps a pulse on how the employees feel while changes are being implemented. At first, she hears positive feedback. But later, employees start to express that the company is not doing enough. Digging deeper, she finds out that employees feel like the company is talking a lot about sustainability but not really living up to their vision. What should the CHRO do with this information?

   a. With the approval of the CEO, gather employee feedback and ideas, and organize them to formulate suggested solutions.
   b. Sell the employees on the company's vision, and engage them more in the change initiatives.
   c. Ask employees to be patient and wait for the changes to be completed before making judgments.
   d. Improve communication to employees through frequent updates on the company's internal website.

18. The company decides to focus on utilizing the creativity, skills, and knowledge of its employees to achieve their long-term goal of becoming a leader in corporate sustainability. To accomplish these goals, the company needs to retain their top talent. The CEO asks the CHRO to develop a retention strategy and wonders if offering substantial pay increases will be necessary. What suggestion should the CHRO make?

   a. Give employees a pay increases each time the company reaches one of their strategic goals.
   b. Develop an aggressive lead market compensation strategy.
   c. Improve company benefits in addition to a moderate pay increase for all employees.
   d. Conduct an employee survey and focus group to determine what motivates the team.

19. In a meeting with the executive team, the CEO lays out the revised second phase of the change initiative aligning their day-to-day business operations with the company's vision of becoming a leader in corporate sustainability. The CEO asks each department head how they will support the upcoming changes. What contribution can the CHRO make?

   a. Implement changes within the HR team before they are rolled out to the rest of the company.
   b. Review the change proposal to streamline processes and remove any redundancies.
   c. Analyze the effects of the change initiative on employees and departments.
   d. Build a candidate pool focusing on candidates with experience in corporate sustainability.

Refer to the following for questions 20 - 21:

> An electric utility company operates four petroleum-fired power plants that provide the majority of the electricity for the region. Recent legislative changes require the company to make substantial shifts away from petroleum and towards renewable sources of energy. Although the CEO has a future vision for the company and is ready to lead the company through the transition, many of the company's managers are set in their ways and reluctant to change.

20. In a meeting with the upper management team, opinions are voiced that the company should resist change and stick to the old ways that have been working for so many years. The CEO and the CHRO meet separately after this meeting to discuss how to move forward. The CEO is concerned that the company does not have leaders with experience in the renewable energy sector or the ability to lead related change initiatives. What initial suggestion should the CHRO make?

   a. Start building a talent pool and hiring managers with knowledge in the renewable energy sector.
   b. Develop leadership training seminars to prepare the managers for leading change initiatives.
   c. Review the performance of each manager, and suggest which managers should be terminated because they are unlikely to support the upcoming change initiative.
   d. Conduct an assessment of the current talent within the organization, and forecast which talent will be needed to determine hiring and training needs.

21. The CHRO wants to make sure the HR team is prepared to fully support the change initiative. What steps can she take to prepare her team?

   a. Ask her team to review job descriptions in preparation for necessary revisions and updates.
   b. Delegate one initiative-related responsibility to each member on the team.
   c. Enroll HR employees in a refresher seminar on employee communications.
   d. Identify how the individual HR employees will be affected by the changes.

22. What contributes to an employee's motivation, according to Vroom?

   a. Likelihood to get promoted if one puts in effort
   b. Transparent communication from managers to employees
   c. Working in a motivated and driven team environment
   d. Having a manager with good leadership skills

23. What is arbitration?

   a. A third party assists in the decision-making process.
   b. An executive employee makes a decision.
   c. A neutral agent determines a resolution.
   d. Negotiation among the involved parties.

24. What is the final step when putting a knowledge management system in place?

   a. Training employees on how to access and use the knowledge database
   b. Integrating the knowledge database into the company's information technology system
   c. Creating a dashboard for easy information access
   d. Revising and adding new information on an ongoing basis

25. A company decides to outsource part of the human resources function. What is the next step after a contractor has been selected?

   a. Monitor the project schedule
   b. Negotiate a contract
   c. Define goals
   d. Create an RFP

26. An HR manager wants to determine if there is a correlation between an employee's score on a pre-hire assessment test and their sales performance as measured by the number of closed sales in the last quarter. What tool can he use?

   a. Trend diagram
   b. Pie chart
   c. Scatter diagram
   d. Pareto chart

27. While at work, two employees get into a serious argument that results in a physical altercation on company property. The employees have a clear understanding that this violates company policy. The manager pulls both employees into the office to terminate their employment. What step should the manager have taken beforehand?

a. Establish a baseline for the termination.
b. Review the company's performance management system.
c. Interview the employees as part of an investigation.
d. Consult with legal counsel.

28. A new marketing manager is assigned a mentor by the human resources (HR) department. The mentor is a senior business partner of the company with many years of experience. They are meeting once a month, and the mentor prepares for the meetings by setting learning objectives and creating training material for the mentee. Why might this mentorship NOT be successful?

a. Meetings should take place weekly.
b. Communication should be a two-way street and objectives set together.
c. The mentor should be a peer and not a senior colleague.
d. The mentor should not be assigned by HR, but selected by the mentee.

29. Which of the following contains an instruction for how the federal government should operate?

a. Administrative protocol
b. Agency guideline
c. Statute
d. Executive order

30. Sarah is a carpenter on a construction crew tasked with framing a series of residential houses. As the only female on the team, Sarah feels pressured to avoid wearing makeup at work or talking about her young children in an attempt to secure respect from her team and supervisors. This scenario is a demonstration of which of the following barriers to success for diverse workers?

a. Imposter syndrome
b. Microaggressions
c. Identity covering
d. Cultural taxation

Refer to the following for questions 31 - 33:

A pharmaceutical company motivates its employees to work hard through offering big sales incentives. With sales booming, many employees work 60 to 80 hours per week to earn the bonuses.

31. The HR business partner becomes aware of high turnover throughout the organization. It has created so many vacancies that the recruiting team is not able to keep up with filling them. However, the CEO is pleased with the company's sales performance and says the turnover is the nature of the business and the recruiting team needs to work harder to fill the openings. What should the HR business partner do?

a. Focus all efforts of the HR team on filling the open positions.
b. Outsource recruiting requests that the in-house recruiters are unable to fill.
c. Review exit interviews to determine the root cause of the retention problem.
d. Provide training and development opportunities for employees to improve retention.

32. The CEO announces plans to expand the company and gathers data to draft a business plan for the expansion strategy. What should the HR business partner do because he is aware that the company is already short-staffed?

    a. Advise the CEO to hold off with expansion efforts until the staffing situation has been improved.

    b. Set up an employee referral program with strong incentives to boost talent acquisition efforts for the expansion strategy.

    c. After assessing the current workforce, research temporary staffing agencies that can provide the needed talent, and provide a cost estimate to the CEO.

    d. Motivate employees with the CEO's vision for the expansion, showcasing all of the new career opportunities that will come with it.

33. The HR team checks in with the different sales teams to gather feedback on implemented changes as a result of the expansion efforts. Although most teams give positive feedback, one team displays low employee morale. To find out more, the HR team conducts interviews with representatives from this team. They find out that the sales team manager often makes inappropriate comments and derogatory remarks about older employees. The HR business partner reports these findings to the head of sales. In their discussion, the head of sales urges the HR business partner to not upset the team manager because he has close relationships with major accounts that the company cannot afford to lose. What should the HR business partner do next?

    a. Provide coaching and training to the manager to improve his communication and leadership style.

    b. Report the findings to the CEO, conduct an investigation, and take the necessary steps to stop the manager's behavior.

    c. Recommend hiring additional sales staff to decrease stress and pressure on the team.

    d. Keep a close eye on the manager to see if further incidences occur.

34. What is an important prerequisite for successful networking?

    a. Firm handshake

    b. Elevator speech

    c. Business cards

    d. Having expertise

35. In what type of interview would the following question MOST likely be asked? "Tell me about a time when your team failed to accomplish a goal. How did you lead your team to achieve the goal in the end?"

    a. Behavioral interview

    b. Stress interview

    c. Case interview

    d. Unstructured interview

36. New procedures are being rolled out from the company headquarters to offices located all over the country. The communications director created a detailed slide show presentation to share with all general managers virtually. What type of groupware is intended to be used for this purpose?

    a. Web conferencing

    b. Video presence

    c. Virtual meeting

    d. Network seminar

37. In what stage of a workforce analysis would a flow analysis be conducted?

    a. Supply analysis

    b. Demand analysis

    c. Gap analysis

    d. Solution analysis

38. What pay system rewards long-term employment instead of high performance?

   a. Merit pay
   b. A straight piece-rate system
   c. A differential piece-rate system
   d. Time-based step-rate pay

39. What is a characteristic of a polycentric talent acquisition orientation?

   a. Each country has its own unique talent acquisition approach.
   b. Headquarter staffing policies are mimicked in other countries.
   c. The company has a global talent acquisition plan.
   d. Each region establishes its own staffing policies.

Refer to the following for questions 40 - 42:

> A transportation company operates shuttle buses that bring guests from the airport to a number of hotels. The company has 60 employees. There are four buses running at any given time, picking guests up every 10–15 minutes.

40. Bus driver A, whose personality is to operate very much by the book, always sticks to the exact bus schedule. Bus driver B, who is known to be more of a free spirit, keeps his bus going with the flow, often ends up well ahead of schedule, and occasionally overtakes the other shuttles. This leads to regular conflict between the two drivers. Bus driver A decides to report the situation to the HR generalist. What should she do?

   a. Arrange a meeting with both bus drivers to facilitate communication.
   b. Observe both bus drivers by spending time riding on each of the buses.
   c. Prepare a written warning for the bus driver not following the exact bus schedule.
   d. Collect data on customer satisfaction regarding their shuttle service.

41. The company is planning to change the bus routes to service the hotels more efficiently. The general manager asked the HR manager to inform all company employees of the changes. The majority of bus drivers are well-tenured and older. Most of the sales representatives are newer to the workforce. The company's management team oversees both groups. What is the best way for the HR manager to roll out the new information?

   a. Create a short video that illustrates the new bus routes, and send it to all employees via email.
   b. Set up a conference call for the managers, send an email to the sales representatives, and schedule a workgroup meeting for the bus drivers.
   c. Meet with each employee one-on-one to discuss the new routes and answer their questions.
   d. Utilize the company's intranet, and create a space for all information regarding the new routes. Then, send an email to all employees directing them to check the intranet.

42. One bus driver, who has been working for the company full-time for 25 years, is clearly unhappy about the introduced changes to the routes. A week later, he meets with the HR generalist, and informs her that he needs to take a leave of absence due to a serious health condition. He turns in an FMLA medical certification form that his doctor completed. The HR generalist reviews the information, determines that he qualifies for the leave of absence, and informs his manager that he will be out for a certain amount of time. The manager responds that the bus driver only requested the time off because he is unhappy with the changes and HR should not approve his leave. What should the HR generalist do?

   a. Tell the manager that the employee qualifies for FMLA and therefore has a right to take the requested leave.
   b. Deny the employee's leave request based on the manager's argument.
   c. Advise the manager to terminate the bus driver's employment. That way, he can fill the position with a new employee.
   d. Decide to compromise. Inform the employee that the maximum amount of time he can be off is two weeks.

43. A company is experiencing low productivity and therefore plans to restructure its workflows. A team of organizational and employee development (OED) specialists develops a plan for the restructure and implements it. After the change initiative has been completed, the company notices employees resisting the changes. What is likely to be the reason for their resistance?

   a. The changes were implemented too quickly.
   b. The restructure was developed with insufficient data.
   c. Employees were not included in the development.
   d. No feedback was provided after the implementation.

44. What is the MOST significant reason why a company would want to invest in leadership development and succession planning?

   a. It results in higher employee engagement and lower turnover.
   b. A competitive labor market makes it difficult to hire leaders externally.
   c. Employees are more likely to meet and exceed performance expectations.
   d. Sharing leadership responsibilities allows companies to succeed in a rapidly changing environment.

45. A recently formed team is beginning to develop good working relationships. Employees are starting to work together and help each other. What should the manager do to support the team?

   a. Promote communication and assist in decision-making processes.
   b. Communicate expectations clearly.
   c. Motivate employees and give praise for achievements.
   d. Establish guidelines for team interactions.

46. What should organizational and employee development (OED) specialists be aware of during the entire OED process?

   a. Organizational structure
   b. Employees' emotional reactions
   c. Leadership succession plans
   d. Institutionalized practices

47. A pharmaceutical company that employs 1,000 sales representatives determines during a supply analysis that its current attrition rates are at 16%. Conducting a demand analysis, they set a future goal of attrition rates being at 6% or less. What is the attrition gap that they need to close to accomplish their goal?

    a.   6%
    b.   10%
    c.   16%
    d.   37.5%

Refer to the following for questions 48 - 50:

> The new CEO of a clothing retail store is looking to increase sales. The company has storefronts in twenty different US states. At the moment, all associates are paid hourly and there are no sales incentives. The CEO finds out that sales performance has not been tracked in the past. Each store has its own sales techniques, and product knowledge varies vastly.

48. The HR manager is asked to develop a sales incentive plan. What should he do first?

    a.   Conduct a series of sales trainings to increase the product knowledge and sales abilities of the associates.
    b.   Communicate the new sales incentive plan to associates and address their questions and concerns.
    c.   Develop an incentive program with monetary as well as nonmonetary sales incentives.
    d.   Analyze the current sales performance of individual stores and associates, and benchmark it against market data for other retail stores.

49. In order to effectively lead the new sales-driven culture that the general manager wants to see in stores, the store managers need some sales and leadership training. The CEO comes across free online training modules that he wants the HR team to roll out to the store managers. However, the HR manager believes an in-person custom training would be the best option to achieve the desired results. What should he do?

    a.   Gather information about the free online training, and develop a plan to roll it out to the store managers.
    b.   Research different training options, conduct a cost-benefit analysis of the top choices, and then meet with the general manager to recommend the most effective training option.
    c.   Meet with the store managers to find out which training option they would prefer to participate in.
    d.   Develop an in-house training program that is cost-effective but delivers more value than the free online training modules.

50. The company decided to change the current employee pay structures to a competitive sales incentives-based pay structure. What would be the best way for the HR manager to communicate the new pay structure to all employees?

    a.   Conduct a conference call with store managers to prepare them to answer employee questions and concerns. Then, send a concise, but comprehensive email to all associates.
    b.   Conduct face-to-face meetings with associates in each store to address their questions and concerns in person.
    c.   Because the individual store managers know their associates best, put them in charge of communicating the changes to their employees.
    d.   Send a detailed letter to each associate that explains the changes, including the rationale behind them. Make sure that the associates have ample time to review the letter.

Refer to the following for questions 51 - 53:

Over the last decade, a telecommunications company has been struggling financially as the demand for landline phones continues to diminish. They have been incorporating other business lines, some more successful than others, but have not been able to turn around their financial performance as much as they had hoped. The executive team decided to implement significant organizational changes that include a number of layoffs, department restructuring, and moving the administrative offices to a smaller location.

51. They are discussing ways to implement the changes successfully. What is the first thing that they should do?
a. Communicate a clear vision to the workforce.
b. Encourage employees to take action.
c. Behave with urgency on a daily basis.
d. Ask the workforce for feedback on the proposed changes.

52. The information technology (IT) department is not affected by any of the layoffs. One employee was recently terminated for poor performance. Despite management assuring the IT staff that the department is not participating in the layoffs, rumors circulate that the terminated employee was laid off and that there might be more terminations coming. One employee questions the IT manager about the reason for their coworker's termination. How should the manager respond?
a. Explain that the coworker's termination was due to performance issues.
b. Inform the employee that he is unable to discuss his coworker's termination.
c. Direct the employee to the HR department for an answer.
d. Request that the employee stop spreading rumors within the department.

53. The majority of the company's software developers are contractual employees from the Philippines. Based on their distinct cultures, should the change initiative be communicated differently to them than to their US counterparts?
a. Yes, because US employees tend to be more open to change than their Filipino counterparts.
b. Yes, because the Filipino employees tend to be more open to change than their US counterparts.
c. No, because cultural differences do not influence how employees perceive change.
d. No, because they both perceive change similarly.

54. How should diversity and inclusion (D&I) strategies be put into effect?
a. Strategies should be put into effect identically.
b. Strategies should be put into effect justly.
c. Strategies should be put into effect simultaneously.
d. Strategies should be put into effect consecutively.

55. What is an example of cultural relativism?
a. An organization's goal to contribute to social justice
b. Not utilizing a vendor because they engage in child labor
c. Expressing that ant soup offered in the employee cafeteria sounds unappetizing
d. A company built on values of respect and honesty

Refer to the following for questions 56 - 58:

A satellite communication firm recently added specialty broadband services to their line of offerings. As a result, they have been growing rapidly. This has led to a number of internal promotions, bringing in many new hires, and extending contracts with third-party staffing partners.

56. A former assistant manager was promoted to lead his own department. One of his first goals is to get to know his team and find out ways to motivate individual employees. What can the manager do to motivate one of his employees who he regards as affiliation-oriented?

    a. Create a collaborative work environment.
    b. Create a competitive work environment.
    c. Create an innovative work environment.
    d. Create a flexible work environment.

57. The HR manager attends a legal seminar that covers recent lawsuits involving third-party staffing arrangements. Because the company has been increasingly using third-party employees, he is concerned that some of the arrangements could potentially pose a legal risk for the firm. What steps should he take?

    a. Recommend that the company not sign any further agreements with third-party contractors.
    b. Extend company benefits to all third-party employees.
    c. Research the company's use of third-party employees, and seek clarification from legal counsel.
    d. Ensure that no third-party employee works more than twenty hours per week.

58. With the growth of the company, the executive team is discussing changing the organizational structure to group departments under its main product divisions. How can the HR manager best support this effort?

    a. Research types of organizational structures, and present the advantages and disadvantages of each to the executive team.
    b. Communicate the restructure to all affected employees, addressing any questions and concerns.
    c. Meet with department heads to hear their opinions and concerns regarding the company's restructure.
    d. Develop employee engagement initiatives for each step of the change process.

59. What protects a company from having to pay for legal costs and settlement fees in case an employee sues?

    a. COBRA
    b. ADR
    c. EPLI
    d. EAP

60. A manager interviews a candidate who demonstrates that she possesses the knowledge and skills required for the position. However, the interviewee has a large tattoo on her arm. The manager doesn't hire her because he feels that she appears irresponsible. What bias is this?

    a. Contrast effect
    b. Halo effect
    c. Cultural noise
    d. Nonverbal bias

61. As a step to reduce workplace accidents, a company assesses how many workers are wearing personal protective equipment. What kind of indicator are they studying?

    a. A preceding indicator
    b. A leading indicator
    c. A dominant indicator
    d. A lagging indicator

62. A company introduces a new human resources system that allows managers to view and generate reports, write employee reviews, and process transfers, leaves, and terminations in one application. What kind of system is this?

a. Decision-maker service
b. Employee self-service
c. Service point application
d. Manager self-service

63. What is an important task of the HR department when a company expands outside of its home country?

a. Prepare the workforce for global transfers and assignments.
b. Balance the need of standardization with the necessity for localization.
c. Research and identify HR vendors in each country.
d. Restructure the HR department to mirror the global business structure.

64. A company operates in an area that is subject to a reoccurring tornado and earthquake risk. As part of their disaster preparedness plan, they set up an employee text alert system that will allow the company to quickly communicate information to all employees in case of emergency. What is this risk strategy called?

a. Transfer
b. Alleviate
c. Mitigate
d. Enhance

65. A company was recently certified as a B Corp. What stage of the corporate social responsibility (CSR) maturity curve is the firm in?

a. Adaptation
b. Integration
c. Assimilation
d. Transformation

66. What is the C-suite?

a. Cloud that stores human resources data
b. Coaching seminar
c. Employee appreciation celebration
d. Executive management

67. Which organization focuses on challenges brought about through globalization?

a. Organization for Economic Co-operation and Development
b. UN Global Compact
c. World Trade Organization
d. International Labor Organization

Refer to the following for questions 68 - 70:

> The CEO of a growing software company has been noticing a recent decline in productivity. When talking to the project directors, they learn that the majority of junior developers are not living up to their anticipated potential.

68. In a meeting with the executive leadership team, a strict performance management system with the goal of terminating underperforming employees is being discussed. How should the HR manager, who is attending the meeting, react when asked to implement the new system?

    a. The HR manager should discuss employee engagement initiatives that can improve employee performance.

    b. The HR manager should implement the system as asked by the executive leadership team.

    c. The HR manager should address the lack of communication between the developers and their managers as a potential reason for the performance issues.

    d. The HR manager should point out the difficulty of hiring new developers, and challenge management to look at the underlying reasons for the low performance.

69. The senior management team agrees that one of the steps to address the performance issues is to update their current performance management system, which is based on annual reviews. The CEO tasks the HR manager with developing a new performance management system based on continuous feedback and regular check-ins with the employees. What is the first step that the HR manager should take?

    a. Conduct a company-wide employee opinion survey to determine the reason(s) behind the junior developers' low performance.

    b. Meet with the project directors to develop an understanding of what improvements they want to see as a result of the new performance management system.

    c. Develop a thorough communication plan to inform all employees of the upcoming changes to the performance management system.

    d. Gather data, including the projected return on investment, to demonstrate the value of rolling out a new performance management system.

70. After implementing a new performance management system and other changes, the company sees an increase in productivity. The performance of most of the developers has improved significantly. However, four developers were terminated for continuously failing to meet performance standards. The HR department is now tasked with filling the four open positions. What is an important step the HR team should take?

    a. Meet with the project directors to determine the knowledge, skills, and abilities a candidate needs to be successful.

    b. Update current job descriptions to reflect the implementation of the new performance management system.

    c. Utilize internet recruiting to build a large pool of both active and passive candidates.

    d. Build a strong employment brand to position the company as an employer of choice.

Refer to the following for questions 71 - 73:

> It is the busy holiday season for a hotel, so the hotel's CEO wants to see strong sales and steep profits. As an incentive, front desk receptionists receive a commission whenever they sell a room upgrade to a customer. The hotel front office manager noticed that some of the receptionists are giving customers vouchers for a free night's stay when they purchase an upgrade. Those vouchers should only be given out to address serious customer complaints. The hotel front office manager, who tends to avoid confrontation, is content that sales numbers are looking good. They do not want to address the issue and possibly upset their employees.

71. What should the HR manager do when he becomes aware of this practice?

   a. Because the hotel front office manager is aware and approves of the practice, HR does not need to act.

   b. The HR manager should talk to the front desk receptionists to find out how common the practice is.

   c. The HR manager should make the hotel front office manager aware that the practice is problematic and needs to be addressed.

   d. HR should recommend eliminating the voucher program to prevent misuse.

72. During the busy holiday season, many high-performing employees resign. This time of year is especially stressful for front desk employees who have to serve a large number of customers quickly. The HR manager overhears some of the best-performing front desk receptionists say that they are thinking about resigning. What should he do after informing the front office manager about what he just heard?

   a. Identify the exact reasons for the high turnover, and develop strategies to eliminate them.

   b. Hire employees with high stress tolerance, and build a candidate pool in case of further resignations.

   c. Help the front office manager create employee schedules to ensure that there is enough coverage for adequate rest breaks.

   d. Train the front office manager on strategies to increase employee engagement during the busy season.

73. The HR department is in the process of filling an open front office lead position. Two candidates made it to the final interview stage and are scheduled to meet with a panel of managers next week. The front office manager approaches the talent acquisition manager and hands him a résumé. He says that he found a highly qualified candidate that he thinks would be a much better fit for the open position than the other two candidates. The talent acquisition manager reviews the résumé and agrees that the candidate appears to be highly qualified. When he asks the front office manager where he received the résumé, he says that the candidate is his cousin. How should the talent acquisition manager handle this situation?

   a. The manager should interview the candidate.

   b. The manager should inform the front office manager that all candidates need to complete an online application in order to be considered for a position.

   c. The manager should schedule a phone screen with the candidate to determine if he truly is as qualified as his résumé seems to indicate.

   d. The manager should inform the front office manager that he is unable to consider the candidate.

74. What is a feature of an asynchronous learning environment?

   a. Employees can access learning modules using different types of technology.

   b. Employees receive real-time feedback.

   c. Employees can study anywhere and anytime.

   d. Employees interact with each other in real time.

75. What would indicate that a company's business manager has a global mindset?

   a. The manager recommends a cultural seminar to the staff.

   b. The manager is not afraid of change and welcomes it.

   c. The manager trusts that the company's structure will produce the desired results.

   d. The manager has experience applying headquarter policies to subsidies.

76. A manager tells his employee that he will be demoted if he votes for the union. What are possible consequences if the employee reports the incident?

   a. The National Labor Relations Board (NLRB) will investigate the charge.

   b. The union and employer will engage in mediation.

   c. The NLRB will file a complaint on behalf of the employee.

   d. There will be no consequences because the employer can demote, but not terminate, the employee.

Refer to the following for questions 77 - 79:

> A local coffee shop chain has a promote-from-within culture. The company hires management trainees that are later promoted to assistant store managers after successfully completing the training program. A formal mentorship program is part of the training program.

77. An employee has successfully passed the training and is getting ready for his new role as assistant store manager. He meets with his mentor to get advice on how to lead the team of the new store he has been assigned to. The mentor knows the team well as he previously managed that exact location. What advice can the mentor give when asked by the mentee how he should approach his new employees?

   a. Because the mentor has in-depth knowledge of the particular store, he should pass as much knowledge as possible on to the new assistant manager.
   b. The mentor should review situational leadership theories with the mentee to prepare him for his new leadership role.
   c. The mentor should ask the mentee to take the employees' perspective, and think about how he would want a new assistant manager to approach him.
   d. Because the mentee has completed the training program, the formal mentorship relationship is ending. Therefore, the mentor should spend the last meeting celebrating the promotion and closing the mentoring relationship.

78. A new trainee is hired at the store, and the assistant manager is put in charge of her training. What should he focus on first?

   a. Support the new trainee in making decisions and finding solutions.
   b. Provide guidance and direction, keeping a close eye on her.
   c. Delegate tasks to the new trainee and empower her.
   d. Coach and motivate the new trainee.

79. The assistant manager has four trainees directly reporting to him. His trainees attend quarterly training seminars at the corporate office and are asked to prepare for the next one by setting a professional goal. The assistant manager meets with each of them before the training to review the goals that they set. Which of the employees should the assistant manager encourage to change their goal?

   a. Employee A: My goal is to successfully complete the training program by September.
   b. Employee B: My goal is to increase my add-on sales by 10% over the next three months.
   c. Employee C: My goal is to submit three employee referrals to talent acquisition before the end of the year.
   d. Employee D: My goal is to double the store's profitability over the next six months.

80. What is an advantage of a functional human resources (HR) structure?

   a. Alignment with organizational strategy
   b. Ensuring compliance and confidentiality
   c. Consistency across the entire organization
   d. Accessibility of the HR department for employees

81. What is a key benefit of conducting stay interviews?

   a. Improved retention
   b. Development of performance objectives
   c. Not needing exit interviews
   d. Data gathered for performance appraisals

82. A call center is looking to fill some of their open management positions. They receive a total of 250 applications, of which 100 are from female candidates. What is the yield ratio of female applicants to total applicants?

    a. 20%
    b. 25%
    c. 40%
    d. 60%

83. Why is it essential that a company works hard to build a comprehensive diversity and inclusion program?

    a. Because it has a direct impact on the company's profitability
    b. Because it is necessary for building a positive company reputation
    c. Because it helps employees and managers approach situations from different perspectives
    d. Because it is difficult to change deeply held beliefs, assumptions, and habits

84. After a diversity council has been established, what is part of the next step in the Diversity and Inclusion (D&I) Strategic Process by Gardenswartz and Rowe?

    a. Build a diverse candidate pool through targeted recruiting initiatives.
    b. Assemble an employee resource group.
    c. Assess the results achieved by the diversity council.
    d. Develop a diversity immersion program for managers and employees.

Refer to the following for questions 85 - 88:

> A nationwide organization operates with leadership and management teams working remote or from one centralized location and then with small teams of a handful or fewer employees working at service locations across the country.
>
> After a visit from the off-site manager and other leadership figures to a small service location, an on-site team member is let go for misuse of company property and gross negligence. Two months later, a new staff member is selected as a replacement and starts working. The new staff member is a woman in her late twenties, and her coworkers are two men in their mid-to-late fifties.
>
> Almost immediately, the new staff member begins reporting back to the management team regarding condescension and inflexibility from her coworkers. Over the course of six months, she reports instances of disregard for organizational directives, discriminatory side comments, and, eventually, feeling uncomfortable in the workplace. After several incidents, the off-site manager seeks guidance from the team's HR representative for best practices and next steps.

85. Which of the following would be the most effective first step for the HR representative to present for the manager?

    a. The manager should relocate his or her office to be able to work on-site and better understand the working dynamic.
    b. The manager should design and implement a performance improvement plan for the male team members to improve overall morale.
    c. During the next team meeting, the manager should join virtually to remind staff members of the organizational values.
    d. The manager and the HR representative should schedule one-on-one meetings with each of the team members individually to better understand the workplace dynamics.

86. Which of the following is more likely to be positively correlated with a highly performing, diverse team?

    a. Psychological safety

    b. Disparate impact

    c. Conflict-free collaboration

    d. Team dissatisfaction

87. After meeting with each of the on-site team members, the manager and HR representative discover that some of the miscommunications likely stem from the differences in life experiences and expectations that come with team members being from different generations. How should the manager most effectively coach a multigenerational workforce?

    a. Assign tasks that align with the generational strengths of each employee, such as computer work for the younger employee and mentoring roles for the older employees.

    b. Determine each team member's individual strengths and challenges through individual coaching sessions and set goals for each individual to use his or her strengths to contribute to the team.

    c. Observe team meetings and when miscommunication arises, mediate the conversation to aid each team member in better understanding the other.

    d. Assign projects that force each team member to work one-on-one with the other in order to fast-track communication strategy development.

88. Which of the following DE&I tools would be most effective at creating a sense of belonging for employees of a diverse workforce who are spread across the country?

    a. Employee surveys

    b. Unconscious bias training

    c. Employee resource groups

    d. Performative allyship

89. Data is being gathered during the strategy implementation phase of a project. What is the BEST way to communicate the results to senior managers after analyzing the data?

    a. By organizing the data in a spreadsheet

    b. By providing the full raw data

    c. By presenting bulleted slide show presentation slides

    d. By telling a story backed by the data

90. An organization decides to partner with two employment service agencies for a temp-to-lease program. HR is asked to write the staffing contract. What best practice should they keep in mind?

    a. Refrain from pricing negotiations.

    b. Utilize a standard contract.

    c. Consult with legal counsel.

    d. Specify an end date of service in the contract.

91. What was the court ruling in Lechmere, Inc. v. NLBR?

    a. If an employee misses time worked due to union-related activities, the company cannot hold it against him in his attendance record.

    b. A company does not have to allow union representatives to campaign on company property if they are not employed by the company.

    c. A company is allowed to continue business operations during a strike by hiring new employees or temporary workers.

    d. Employees have the right to bring a third person into the room if they are being questioned as part of an investigation.

Refer to the following for questions 92 - 95:

After a string of discrimination-related incidents and consistently low workplace culture scores, a medium-sized financial advising firm launched a series of unconscious bias trainings in an attempt to create a more inclusive workplace.

The trainings consisted of six 30-minute virtual sessions with interactive capabilities and a short answer debrief at the end of each session to gauge participant experience. Employees were instructed to attend a minimum of four out of the six trainings, which were scheduled across the span of nine months.

After the final training, the HR team met to review participation metrics, the debrief answers, and updated workplace culture scores.

92. When developing the next phase of unconscious bias trainings and DE&I programs, which of the following actions would be the most effective?
   a. Increase the number of trainings offered and required to improve exposure.
   b. Eliminate the unconscious bias training due to poor participation rates and negative debrief results.
   c. Demand a higher rate of participation among organizational leaders during the next series of trainings.
   d. Link the virtual trainings to supplemental in-person follow-up sessions within each facility.

93. In addition to adding in-person elements to the training, the HR team is also tasked with improving the virtual portion of the unconscious bias training. After analyzing the first iterations of the training, which of the following steps should come next?
   a. Implementing a pilot training prior to a companywide launch
   b. Developing effective and appropriate content to fill training sessions
   c. Evaluating the results of the first training through surveys and focus groups
   d. Designing an efficient delivery structure that is scheduled with respect to its participants work responsibilities

94. Consider the chart below detailing the number of employees who participated in the training series stratified by organizational function.

Trainings completed	Financial Advisors	Loan Officers	Accounting Specialists	Marketing Team Members	Team & Facility Leaders	Executive Leadership
0	2	9	0	1	5	2
1-3	7	13	1	2	4	1
4	75	14	8	9	9	3
5-6	4	0	3	3	2	1
Total:	*88*	*36*	*12*	*15*	*20*	*7*

Which of the following conclusions would be most appropriate to draw from the available data?
   a. The loan officers are the likely root cause of the discriminatory behaviors and sentiment within the organization.
   b. Current and future DE&I programs and policies will likely benefit from stronger leadership buy-in.
   c. The strategy used to achieve the accounting specialists' participation rates should be duplicated for underperforming groups.
   d. The unconscious bias training was most effective among the teams with fewer employees.

95. In collaboration with facility leaders, the HR team launches the next series of unconscious bias trainings with a reduced requirement for the virtual session attendance but with added elements of in-person, unconscious bias team reflections and activities. Which of the following business outcomes would be most effective to track immediately following these changes that could suggest the actual impact of the new training design?

    a. Employee engagement rates
    b. Net facility income
    c. Employee retention rates
    d. Performance management scores

96. What conflict resolution technique aims to find a solution that both parties view as a success?

    a. Integrate
    b. Compromise
    c. Accommodate
    d. Collaborate

97. A manufacturing company produces finished goods for a multinational technology company with whom they have an agreement. The technology company incorporates these goods into its product lines and owns the marketing, customer service, and all sales. What type of growth strategy is this for the technology company?

    a. Contract manufacturing
    b. Joint venture
    c. Strategic alliance
    d. Greenfield operation

98. What approach can be used to evaluate HR's performance and alignment with organizational strategy?

    a. Internal customer satisfaction rate
    b. Employee retention rate
    c. Human capital return on investment
    d. Balanced scorecard

99. What is one advantage of a group interview?

    a. More candidate comfort during the interview
    b. Elimination of unqualified candidates
    c. Increased control for the interviewer
    d. Time-savings for both companies and job seekers

Refer to the following for questions 100 - 102:

A home improvement retailer has been reporting negative cash flow due to low sales numbers and high expenses. The senior leadership team develops a new organizational strategy to turn around the company's financial performance, and all departments are asked to take immediate action.

100. The CEO asks the CHRO how the HR department will contribute to the strategy. What is the best suggestion the CHRO can make after brainstorming with the HR department?

    a. Because the HR department does not generate revenue, they will provide their support to the revenue-generating segments of the company.

    b. Suggest a reduction in force, and develop severance packages for laid-off employees.

    c. Analyze current sales commission thresholds and evaluate company spending on perquisites and employee appreciation initiatives.

    d. Temporarily enact a hiring freeze of all nonessential positions to reduce costs.

101. The new organizational strategy affects all employees, and the executive team is discussing ways to communicate it to the store and warehouse personnel. They decide to hold staff meetings with each workgroup. What can they do to ensure that the meetings are successful?

    a. Start the meetings off with an icebreaker activity.

    b. Provide lunch for employees while presenting a detailed slide show presentation.

    c. Conduct focus groups within the meetings.

    d. Choose a presenter who understands the audience's needs and perspectives.

102. One of the store managers in charge of implementing a number of changes is known to be a "country club manager." What kind of advice can the HR manager give him to be successful?

    a. Create a collaborative team environment.

    b. Delegate tasks to the team as much as possible.

    c. Hold employees accountable.

    d. Encourage employees to accomplish goals.

103. A company recently went through an organizational and employee development (OED) intervention. How can HR help the company promote and support adherence to the new processes?

    a. Utilize HRIS to track data.

    b. Support leaders through ongoing training and development initiatives.

    c. Ensure new processes and goals are reflected in performance reviews.

    d. Establish a mentorship program.

104. A group of seven managers is meeting to discuss restructuring the geographic areas that their sales teams support. They make a list of factors that will support the restructure as well as a list of what might hinder it. They then rate each factor depending on its importance. What kind of decision-making tool are they using?

    a. Cost-benefit analysis

    b. SWOT analysis

    c. Multi-criterion decision analysis

    d. Force-field analysis

105. What can be said about good governance at an organization?

    a. It is introduced by the governance board.

    b. It is free of any contradictions.

    c. It originates at the leadership level.

    d. It applies equally to the host and home country of the organization.

106. What are the three components of sustainability?

    a. Social, economic, environmental

    b. Local, regional, international

    c. Resources, infrastructure, production

    d. Equality, justice, ethics

Refer to the following for questions 107 - 109:

> Previously, a car manufacturer has been successful in hiring managers in training and then quickly promoting them after the training period. However, they recently noticed a majority of the managers in training leaving the company as soon as their training was complete, often taking positions with competitors. The talent manager reviews the reasons behind the resignations, and concludes that the majority of employees left because they were dissatisfied with their rate of pay.

107. The vice president of human resources meets with the talent manager to discuss the retention challenges. What's the best course of action?

    a. Ensure that a realistic job and pay preview is provided to candidates during the hiring and onboarding process.

    b. Research competitor pay rates, obtain other market compensation data, and establish new, more competitive pay plans.

    c. Give all employees a cost-of-living pay increase and add nonmonetary incentives to pay plans.

    d. Position the company as an employer of choice by offering perquisites such as company cars, a wellness program, and gym memberships.

108. The headquarters of the car manufacturer is located in the United States, whereas the manufacturing units are spread across different countries. A manager with a successful career at headquarters receives a promotion to vice president and will run the company's motor vehicle assembly plant in India. He is popular amongst his direct reports for being engaging and for sharing both responsibilities and recognition with them. What challenges is he likely to face in his new position?

    a. He might have to adjust project deadlines because employees tend to be late.

    b. His new direct reports might not appreciate him distributing important tasks within the team.

    c. His new employees are likely to challenge his authority.

    d. He might experience difficulties creating harmony within the new team he is leading.

109. What can the new VP do to be successful in running the company's motor vehicle assembly plant in India?

    a. He should attend social events outside of work to build relationships.

    b. He should create a competitive work environment.

    c. He should only expect employees to participate in company events during the regular workday.

    d. He should expect that employees will be productive in their roles, despite any personal differences.

110. What is a common reason behind an employee's resistance to change?

    a. Because it is outside of the employee's comfort zone

    b. Worry that change will result in unexpected costs

    c. Belief that change is not possible

    d. Fear that he or she will not be able to meet new performance expectations

111. A consulting firm determines that the average annual salary for project analysts in their area is $60,000. They are looking to hire a new project analyst and post the position with an annual pay rate of $70,000. What pay strategy does the company pursue?

    a. Top market competition

    b. Match market competition

    c. Lead market competition

    d. Lag market competition

112. What task is performed by a leader compared to a manager?

   a. Schedule and plan the open enrollment benefits meetings.
   b. Design informational handouts to be distributed at the open enrollment benefits meetings.
   c. Organize speakers on health topics for the open enrollment benefits meetings.
   d. Motivate the team to exceed benefits enrollment goals.

113. What are the four common phases of the employee life cycle according to the Society for Human Resource Management (SHRM)?

   a. Attraction, onboarding, retention, separation
   b. Recruitment, integration, development, transition
   c. Application, selection, training, compensation
   d. Talent acquisition, performance, payroll, offboarding

114. What is an example of a business outcome that can be measured to gauge the effectiveness of an employee engagement initiative?

   a. Employee problem-solving abilities
   b. Employee motivation
   c. Managerial skills
   d. Employee absences

115. What is an important part of administering an employee survey to avoid employees becoming disappointed and disengaged?

   a. Conducting surveys at regular intervals, for example, annually
   b. Using online surveys for higher response rates
   c. Communicating the results to the employees
   d. Asking primarily open-ended questions in the survey

116. Which of these is most important for having a successful focus group?

   a. Encourage discussion.
   b. Have an agenda.
   c. Recognize conflicts early on.
   d. Summarize statements.

Refer to the following for questions 117 - 119:

> The new CHRO of an insurance agency notices that the company is struggling to hire, develop, and hold onto its human capital. In particular, she notices low retention, low employee morale, excessive absenteeism, and a lacking talent pipeline.

117. The CHRO studies recent exit interviews and conducts a series of stay interviews that all point to a lack of management support. She is convinced that the managers would benefit from training but heard that the CEO does not want to spend money on training and development initiatives. What could the CHRO do to address the problems?

   a. Use the data and insights gained to present a business case to the CEO indicating the importance of investing in managerial training and development.
   b. Develop a cost-efficient employee engagement initiative to address low employee morale.
   c. Meet with managers one-on-one to review the company's performance management process.
   d. Research literature on management best practices, provide it to the managers, and encourage them to study the material.

118. The new CHRO is aware that hiring top talent in the insurance sector is a challenge because it is often not the industry of choice for many recent graduates. She also knows that unemployment is low and the labor market is highly competitive. What can the CHRO do to improve hiring efforts?

a. Research and study recruiting metrics for the insurance sector.
b. Review job postings and rewrite ads to attract more candidates.
c. Build rapport with local college career services personnel.
d. Sign up for several local job fairs to meet candidates in person.

119. The company recently introduced a new state-of-the-art software program that transforms the way insurance agents put together portfolios, calculate rates, and create presentations for customers. Due to the complexity of the new software, the company had all insurance agents go through a one-day training to become familiar with the new tool. After a couple of weeks, the CHRO notices that some of the more tenured agents are struggling with using the new software program and have decreasing sales. What should the CHRO do?

a. Hold agents accountable for their decreased performance, setting clear expectations.
b. Prepare for increased turnover by building a talent pool.
c. Arrange for all agents to attend a second day of training on the new software program.
d. Offer additional training to agents whose performance has decreased.

120. What are the three key qualities of a leader that are crucial for leading a learning organization, according to Peter Senge?

a. Designer, steward, teacher
b. Mentor, change agent, motivator
c. Manager, trainer, strategist
d. Planner, visionary, communicator

121. Two employees sit on the board of directors and have full voting power. What system is that?

a. Mixed system
b. Single-tier system
c. Matrix system
d. Dual system

122. An employee has been selected for a global assignment and is getting ready to move in the coming weeks. What is an important step in preparing the assignee for departure?

a. Determining a competitive pay rate for the employee while on assignment
b. Analyzing the return on investment
c. Identifying how the assignment fits with the employee's career aspirations
d. Attending a cultural awareness training program

Refer to the following for questions 123 - 125:

A bank, who had a conservative image in the past, decides to update their employment brand to attract a younger and more diverse customer and candidate base. The CHRO is in charge of updating the recruiting website. To gather ideas, she holds a brainstorming session with the HR team.

123. What is the best idea that the CHRO should look into further?

   a. Highlight the bank's affirmative action plan in the new employment brand.

   b. Conduct a series of stay interviews to gather managers' views on diversity within the organization.

   c. Ask several employees to each make a short video showing what diversity in the workplace means to them.

   d. Launch a quick diversity and inclusion project that can be used as the basis for the new employment brand.

124. The CHRO asks the HR manager to work together with the marketing manager on one aspect of the new recruiting website. The HR manager is from New York, direct, task-focused, and efficient. The marketing manager is from Peru, creative, relationship-oriented, and enthusiastic. They set up a meeting to discuss the project, but are both frustrated afterward. The HR manager feels like they did not make any progress and wasted time. The marketing manager is offended by his harsh tone and feels like he does not like her. After a couple of meetings with no success but growing frustration on both sides, the HR manager seeks the advice of the CHRO. What should she do?

   a. Break up the project. The HR manager and marketing manager will each work on one aspect of the website without having to collaborate.

   b. Sit in on their next meeting, and mediate between the two parties by having each of them explain the other's perspective.

   c. Explain to the HR manager that this behavior is unacceptable. In his position, he needs to show more cultural sensitivity.

   d. Inform both parties that even though they are not friends, they are still expected to work together professionally and complete the assigned project.

125. The marketing department consists of eight employees who have been working together for many years. They are very tight-knit. A new content marketing lead is hired and joins the department. The marketing manager notices that there is tension between the old employees and the new hire. The tension disrupts their work and resulted in a missed deadline. How should she handle the conflicts within her team?

   a. Talk to employees one-on-one to understand what causes the tension.

   b. If the new employee does not fit into the department's culture, it is best to reassign her to a different team.

   c. Schedule a team meeting, and facilitate a team discussion to solve the problems.

   d. Wait to intervene until the team moves from the storming to the norming phase.

Refer to the following for questions 126 - 128:

> A car rental company offered only two-way rentals in the past, where customers pick up and drop off their rental car at the same location. The company's strategic goal is to expand business to include one-way rentals so customers can return their car at a different location from where they rented it. The vice president of HR is tasked with preparing branch employees for the new business process. He is aware that each branch currently operates independently and in competition for profit with each other. Therefore, they are likely to resist the change. The new one-way rental program will require branches to work collaboratively and communicate frequently.

126. Since the vice president of HR has significant experience with leading change initiatives, the executive team asked him what they can expect from employees once this change initiative is rolled out. What advice can he give?

- a. There is likely to be an initial drop in performance.
- b. There is likely to be an initial increase in turnover.
- c. There is likely to be an initial decrease in customer satisfaction.
- d. There is likely to be an initial lack of trust in leadership.

127. What suggestion can the vice president of HR make that will help prepare the teams working at the different branches for the new business process?

- a. Schedule in-person meetups between each of the branches so teams can build relationships.
- b. Host a video conference to roll out the new process and introduce the teams to each other.
- c. Encourage the different branches to communicate via the company's intranet, and develop an app that connects employees on the go.
- d. Communicate strict performance management steps for employees who do not cooperate with other branches.

128. After the new process has been rolled out, the vice president of HR conducts an assessment of how well it has been implemented and embraced. He finds out that all branches are working together well with the exception of one region called region X. Region X is managed by a senior regional manager who is known for being the cause of conflict and ongoing disagreements among the other regional managers. How should the VP of HR handle this?

- a. Advise the CEO to restate clear expectations of how branches and regions are to collaborate with each other.
- b. Take performance management steps to correct the regional manager's behavior.
- c. Reintroduce the change initiative to region X, and work alongside the regional manager to roll out the new process.
- d. Meet with regional managers to determine the underlying issues for the disagreements, and encourage communication to find solutions.

129. A company introduces a new product and needs its call center employees to go through extensive product training so that they can answer customer questions. The training is conducted through an online learning portal, set up as a labyrinth, that employees have to navigate through. Along the way, they learn about different aspects of the product, take quizzes, collect points, and move up levels to access more information. What type of learning is this?

- a. Scenario-based learning
- b. Maze product training
- c. Gamification
- d. Play-based learning

Refer to the following for questions 130 - 132:

> A local grocery retailer employs 2,000 employees in its 25 stores. The company is family owned, and the current CEO is the founder's son. Many of the managers and employees are related to the CEO and his family.

130. The company recently hired a new HR manager. The CEO briefs the HR manager that the company is looking to cut costs where possible. Therefore, he would like him to find a more affordable benefits vendor as premiums have been steadily increasing. The HR manager, who has many years of experience in managing employee benefits, reviews the current benefits package. He concludes that premiums are already on the low-end and there would be no significant cost savings by switching vendors. What alternative can he suggest to the CEO?

a. Inform the workforce of rising benefits costs and ask them to use their benefits wisely.
b. Continue research until a more affordable benefits vendor has been located.
c. Organize a reoccurring health fair for employees where vendors offer free BMI measurements, blood pressure checks, and tips for a healthy lifestyle.
d. Consider reducing the employees' hours so that they are no longer eligible for benefits.

131. The new HR manager spends time observing different employees to learn about the business. He notices that the maintenance supervisor, who is the CEO's cousin, appears unqualified when working on a defective fridge. When talking to the maintenance supervisor, the HR manager finds out that he has no training in performing the work required by his position. He further hears other employees saying that the maintenance supervisor often calls in favors from friends when he cannot complete the job himself. The HR manager is concerned about the maintenance supervisor's performance but also knows that he is close to the CEO. The CEO does not like to hear his family members being criticized. What should the HR manager do?

a. He should give the CEO a hint to observe the maintenance supervisor's work himself.
b. Because the maintenance department and the HR department are separate from each other, the HR manager does not need to act.
c. He should conduct an investigation to find out how the maintenance supervisor got his position without having the necessary qualifications for it.
d. He should inform the CEO of his findings and concerns.

132. One day the HR manager is informed that a department of labor representative is at the reception desk looking to talk to her. What should she do?

a. Talk to the representative and provide the information the department of labor is requesting.
b. Ask the representative to have a seat in her office while she calls the company's attorney.
c. Ask the representative to come back later so she has time to collect files and find out if there is any potential legal exposure.
d. Inform the representative that she is happy to meet with him, but he would first need to schedule an appointment.

133. What tool can you use to make sure all of the firm's risk management strategies and processes are compliant with local laws?

a. Attestation
b. Audit
c. Risk analysis
d. Security report

134. A company aims to reduce occurrences in which employees violate company policy and have to be disciplined. What steps can they take?

a. Implement strict disciplinary actions as a deterrent.
b. Monitor employees closely throughout their shifts.
c. Take away employees' company discounts if violations occur.
d. Create a company culture of open two-way communication.

Answer Key and Explanations for Test #2

1. D: In the PAPA model, this risk falls in the adapt category because the event is approaching slowly but surely. The organization is certain that it is going to happen but has time to adapt to the circumstances.

2. C: The Recruitment Cost Ratio is calculated by dividing the total amount of recruitment costs ($60,000) by the total first-year compensation of new hires in a given time period ($300,000) and then multiplying the result by 100. $60,000/$300,000x 100 = 20%.

3. D: The HR business partner displays the leadership and navigation competency by recognizing and modifying ineffective practices. Converting the training from paper forms to online training modules is a creative solution to promote compliance while accommodating business needs. The proposed training design gives employees the flexibility to complete the training modules when they find time to do so. It also ensures that they actually receive the information instead of signing a document without reading it.

4. A: The HR business partner displays the consultation competency by recognizing an area of improvement the company has and advising the leadership team of solutions to remedy the problem. Falsely classifying employees as exempt can have serious legal consequences for a company. Therefore, the HR business partner has to research and present lawful alternative compensation options that will align with the company culture to the leadership team.

5. B: The HR business partner displays the business acumen competency by being aware of where the company is in its life cycle. A company's life cycle includes: introduction, growth, maturity, and decline. One of HR's responsibilities during the maturity stage is to keep the company's agile, competitive, and creative spirit alive, which can be challenging due to its larger size.

6. C: According to the layers of diversity model by Gardenswartz and Rowe, the external dimension includes a person's marital status, education, and place of residence.

7. B: Pay audits are designed to assess the rates of pay for all comparable positions and their compensable factors devoid of the individuals performing the job. Pay audits can help to identify pay discrepancies that may have been persisting for an individual because of past pay inequities, and they can identify pay practices to be corrected. Pay audits are most useful in correcting historical pay inequities as they are designed to identify when those inequities may have started and occurred. Compensation surveys (A) and market data about compensation trends can be useful for a company when setting pay rates for future hires or in times of pay restructuring. A job analysis (C) can be a useful tool prior to conducting pay audits to affirm that job descriptions and duties are accurate across different positions. Performance evaluations (D) are important within the context of pay equity to reward employees in clear, tangible ways that directly correlate to their work performance.

8. C: Throughout the entire risk management process, it is important that strategies are monitored and reviewed to ensure alignment with the process' goals and the organization's overall strategy.

9. A: The HR generalist displays the relationship competency by focusing on getting to know the managers and department heads she will be supporting in her new position. To successfully support the locations, she needs to build strong relationships with the leaders and get to know them to build mutual trust. The meetings will also help her learn about the business and build her business acumen competency.

10. B: The HR generalist displays the global and cultural effectiveness competency by recognizing that the pregnant employee is being stereotyped by her supervisor. The HR generalist should take action. Since she is new in her role, she should consult with her supervisor, the VP of HR, on the company procedure to address these kinds of inappropriate comments.

11. D: The VP of HR displays the critical evaluation competency by being aware of biases that can occur and asking further questions to determine if the HR generalist's sympathy is due to a similar-to-me error. If the reason for not agreeing with the written warning turns out to be because she sees herself in the employee, then the VP of HR can address the bias. Then, they can train the HR generalist on how to act objectively and identify and remove bias in similar situations.

12. B: The VP of HR displays the relationship competency by preparing for a successful negotiation. Before going into a negotiation, it is important to prepare and be clear about what one would like to accomplish. Upon starting the meeting, one should create a welcoming and comfortable atmosphere to build a trusting relationship with the negotiation partner. This forms the foundation of a successful meeting and discussion.

13. C: The VP of HR displays the global and cultural effectiveness competency by recognizing this comment as an inappropriate gender stereotype. The right thing for her to do is to speak up, make the controller aware of the implication of his joke, and ask him to refrain from gender stereotyping in the future.

14. A: The VP of HR displays the critical evaluation competency by being knowledgeable on how to best gather data. The best data collection method in this case is an employee survey. Conducting interviews is too time intensive and would not survey the entire workforce. Reviewing stay and exit interviews is unlikely to provide the needed information. Reviewing data from outside the organization would not answer the question of which benefits the company's employees are using and not using.

15. C: Being an impactful communicator involves effective listening, integrity, trustworthy appearance, good eye contact, good posture, a well-projected voice, and appropriate gestures.

16. C: Global remittances are funds that migrant workers send to support their families back in their home countries.

17. A: The CHRO displays the leadership and navigation competency by seeing potential for the company to improve, finding innovative solutions, and taking action to implement them. Through keeping a pulse on the employees, the CHRO finds out early on that employees feel like the company is not walking their talk. The CHRO takes their input seriously and uses it to develop solutions that can support the company's strategy and contribute to organizational success.

18. D: The CHRO displays the communication competency by not assuming that the rate of pay is the only thing that motivates employees. Instead, the CHRO seeks to develop an understanding about what employees truly want. Focusing company resources on what truly motivates employees will be more successful in retaining them than just increasing their pay. An employee survey and interviews will be a good foundation to develop a successful retention strategy.

19. C: The CHRO displays the consultation competency by showing awareness how the HR team can best contribute to the successful implementation of the proposed changes. One responsibility of the HR department in managing change is to keep a pulse on the workforce and analyze the effects that the changes have on employees and departments. This allows the HR department to identify if there are additional training needs and to determine if there is effective communication to and from employees.

20. D: The CHRO displays the business acumen competency by studying the talent and knowledge that exists within the organization and forecasting what will be needed in the future. Assessing the company's current talent resources is an important first step, followed by forecasting what the company will need to successfully implement the upcoming changes. By contrasting these two, the CHRO can put together a recommendation for the CEO about which talent gaps need to be filled through either hiring or training.

21. C: The CHRO displays the consultation competency by knowing what skills are needed to successfully support organizational change. Expertise in channels of communication will be critical for the HR team to support the company changes.

22. A: According to Vroom's expectancy theory, an employee is motivated by three factors: expectancy, instrumentality, and valence. For example, an employee will be motivated if he can expect to get a desired promotion by working hard.

23. C: Arbitration is a contract negotiation tool available to both the union and the company. If the two parties cannot reach an agreement, a third party, the arbitrator, is tasked with determining a resolution. Both parties must adhere to the arbitrator's decision.

24. D: The final step in creating a knowledge management system is to update, revise, and add information on an ongoing basis to keep the database relevant and current.

25. B: There are nine steps in the outsourcing process. Choosing a contractor is the sixth step, followed by negotiating a contract. Defining goals is part of the first step. Creating an RFP (request for proposal) is the third step. Monitoring the project schedule after the project has been implemented is the eighth step.

26. C: A scatter diagram is used when one wants to determine if there is a correlation between two variables. One axis would be the test scores, and the other axis the number of closed sales. The diagram will show a dot for each employee. If the dots resemble a line, it would suggest that there is a correlation between the two variables.

27. C: The company should conduct a thorough investigation before making the decision to terminate an employee. As part of the investigation, the manager should interview each of the employees to hear their side of the story. The employees should then be suspended pending investigation. This will give HR time to research and review all relevant information, including any prior similar instances, before making a final decision.

28. B: A successful mentorship is a two-way street in which both parties exchange knowledge and learn from each other. The mentee must help shape the overall mentoring relationship, and goals should be set together. The frequency of meetings can vary. Generally, a mentor is a senior colleague or a peer. In a formal mentorship, the mentor and mentee are usually paired by HR. In an informal mentorship, the mentee often selects someone as a mentor for themselves.

29. D: An executive order issued by the US president is an order for how the federal government is to act, operate, or collaborate.

30. C: Identity covering occurs when a worker feels the need to downplay or hide part of their personality or personal life in order to better fit in with the majority. Identity covering can prevent employees from feeling like they truly belong in the workplace and can prevent them from reaching their true potential. Imposter syndrome (A) is the phenomenon in which an employee doubts their abilities or feels as if they are not qualified for the role. Microaggressions (B) are intentional or unintentional comments or behaviors that have a discriminatory effect. Cultural taxation (D) is the burden borne by minority employees to participate in DE&I initiatives and to represent others of the same diversity dimension.

31. C: The HR business partner displays the critical evaluation competency by collecting and reviewing data and using it to identify the root of the problem within the organization. Once the core of the problem has been identified, he can develop solutions to improve the company's retention. He knows that solving staffing shortages in the long term requires improving retention - not hiring more employees who will likely leave quickly.

32. C: The HR business partner displays the business acumen competency by collecting data, analyzing the current workforce, identifying solutions that will support the company's strategy, providing a recommendation, and supplying the CEO with the necessary data for the expansion business plan.

33. B: The HR business partner displays the ethical practice competency by reporting and investigating the accusations right away. Unethical behavior and inappropriate comments can damage the company's reputation, result in employees leaving the organization, and lead to costly legal ramifications. Even though the head of sales is hesitant to address the issue, the HR business partner does the right thing by stopping the inappropriate behavior.

34. D: Keys for successful networking include meeting people that can help you, having expertise or other resources that you can contribute, and the willingness to put in time and effort to maintain the relationship.

35. A: This question is asking how the interviewee handled a particular situation in the past. The idea behind a behavioral interview is that you can predict how a candidate will behave in the future based on how he behaved in the past. A stress interview aims to put a candidate on the defense to determine how he responds to pressure. In a case interview, a candidate is given a business problem and asked to solve it. An unstructured interview is characterized by casual, spontaneous, and open-ended questions.

36. A: Web conferencing allows a presenter to share presentation slides on each participant's computer. The participants can see the slide show presentation slides on their device and can hear the presentation over their computer's speakers or headphones. They also have the opportunity to directly communicate with the presenter through a webchat or their computer's microphone.

37. A: A flow analysis looks at how employees move around in the company. It follows each team member throughout the employee life cycle, including any promotions, demotions, or transfers. It is a critical part of evaluating the skill and talent that exists within the organization (supply analysis). The demand analysis forecasts future talent needs of the company. The gap analysis contrasts the demand against the supply to identify possible talent shortfalls. During the solution analysis, a company identifies ways to fill any talent gaps.

38. D: Time-based step-rate pay rewards tenure over performance. Pay increases are granted on a previously established timeline. On the contrary, merit pay, also called performance-based pay, grants pay increases based on an individual's performance. With a straight or differential piece-rate system, an employee is paid a base wage plus additional pay for completed work up to an established standard. They may receive a premium for work accomplished that exceeds this standard.

39. A: In a polycentric organization, each country has its own unique talent acquisition approach. In an ethnocentric organization, headquarter staffing policies are mimicked when expanding into other countries. A geocentric organization has a global talent acquisition plan. Each region establishes its own staffing policies in an egocentric organization.

40. A: The HR generalist displays the relationship management competency by mediating between the two bus drivers and guiding them to find a solution to their disagreement. Instead of imposing a solution, the HR generalist allows the employees to come to one on their own, helping them gain a better understanding of their coworker's perspective. This understanding will lead to better collaboration in the long term.

41. B: The HR manager displays the communication competency by adjusting the communication method depending on the audience. Managers need to be informed through a communication medium that allows them to ask questions and prepares them to address issues that their bus drivers might bring up. A conference call would be ideal for this. The sales representatives also need to know about the change. However, since they are tech-savvy, and the change does not affect them much, an email is sufficient. The bus drivers are most affected by the change and should be informed in person. A workgroup meeting is a good choice because all of their questions and concerns can be addressed in real-time.

42. A: The HR generalist displays the ethical practice competency by granting the employee his right to take FMLA. He protects the company from legal exposure by complying with the law. Terminating the bus driver's employment would be against the law. The employee has a right to take up to 12 weeks of leave if he qualifies for it due to a serious health condition.

43. C: The employees affected by the change were not included in the development of the restructure, which can lead to resistance.

44. D: Succession planning and leadership development are imperative because the environment in which organizations operate changes rapidly. Shared leadership, in contrast to having single leaders, allows for quicker and more efficient responses to external change.

45. A: The team is in the norming stage of Tuckman's ladder of team development. The leader's role is to promote communication among the team members and guide them in decision-making processes. In the forming stage, leaders need to communicate expectations clearly. In the storming stage, it is important for leaders to establish guidelines for team interactions. Once the team moves past the norming stage to the performing stage, leaders should motivate employees and give praise for achievements.

46. B: During the entire OED (organizational and employee development) process, the specialists should be aware of the employees' emotional reactions to proposed and implemented changes. They should also find ways to improve their ability to adapt to the changes.

47. B: The company has determined that 16% of their sales representatives are leaving the firm. Their goal is to reduce this number to 6%. Therefore, the gap between the current attrition and the future targeted attrition is 10% (16%-6%). Given that the company has 1,000 sales representatives, this change would result in only 60 employees leaving the organization (6%), rather than 160 (16%).

48. D: The HR manager displays the critical evaluation competency by first gathering and analyzing the data. He needs to determine where sales numbers are currently at and then set realistic goals by comparing those numbers to market data. This enables him to develop a sales incentive plan that challenges the sales associates while still being achievable. Developing an understanding of this data and setting realistic goals is the foundation for creating and communicating the new sales incentive plan. That understanding is also critical for developing effective training programs.

49. B: The HR manager displays the relationship management competency by researching and gathering data before meeting with the CEO to make a recommendation. By looking at the problem through the CEO's eyes and comparing options for cost and effectiveness, he can prepare to answer any questions the CEO might have. Then, the HR manager can gain the CEO's support in choosing the best available training option for the management team. Rolling out the free online training modules might not be in the best interest of the company. Asking the store managers for their preferences also does not help HR find the most effective training option. It's unknown if the HR team has the resources and abilities to develop an in-house training program.

50. A: Impactful communication starts with understanding the audience's perspective, drafting a clear message, and delivering it effectively. A conference call gives managers the opportunity to ask questions and prepare answers to questions they might get. A concise but comprehensive email communicates the message consistently to all associates. Conducting face-to-face meetings is not realistic with a dispersed workforce. The company would want the message to be consistent across all stores and therefore would not want to leave all communication up to the individual store managers. The message should be understandable and complete but at the same time brief and to the point. Providing too much information in a letter can lead to a communication overload for many employees.

51. C: The first step in Kotter's Change Model is to create a sense of urgency. Establishing a sense of urgency will demonstrate the need for change. Providing a clear vision is the third step. Over-communicating and encouraging feedback are part of the fourth step.

52. B: The information technology manager displays the ethical practice competency by maintaining confidentiality. Neither he nor the HR department should share any details regarding an employee's termination. Asking the employee to stop spreading rumors would not address his question.

53. D: Both the US and the Philippines generally have a short-term orientation in Hofstede's dimensions of culture. Therefore, people in both countries typically value tradition and resist change. They also tend to focus on quick, short-term results in both their professional and personal lives.

54. B: Diversity and inclusion (D&I) strategies need to account for differences in cultural backgrounds, organizational departments, and geographical locations. Therefore, they should not be put into effect identically across the entire organization. It is important that the implementation is adaptable, just, and fair, taking into account the uniqueness of individuals and teams.

55. C: This is an example of cultural relativism because a judgment is made based on the person's own cultural perspective. Someone from Laos is likely to regard it as tasty, whereas a European visitor might find the idea disgusting. The other answer choices are examples of ethical universalism.

56. A: According to McClelland's Three Needs Theory, there are three intrinsic needs that determine how an employee can be motivated: achievement, affiliation, and power. An affiliation-oriented employee is motivated by teamwork and building relationships. An achievement-oriented employee is motivated by meaningful and challenging work. A power-oriented employee is motivated by competition.

57. C: The HR manager displays the business acumen competency by applying information he learned in the legal seminar to improve the company's operations. Conducting further research on the company's use of third-party employees and seeking the assistance of a legal counsel shows that he takes the necessary steps to limit the company's legal exposure.

58. C: The HR manager demonstrates the relationship management competency by meeting with each department head and listening to their concerns. The meetings give the HR manager a broad understanding of how the restructure will impact the different departments, including what they will need in terms of support during the process. Involving leaders on different levels of the organization in the decision-making process will contribute to a successful restructure and ensure that their concerns are addressed early on. One possible need could be developing employee engagement initiatives, but it is too early to determine this yet. Communicating the restructure to employees should take place once the plans are concrete. Because the executive team has already decided on the organizational structure, there is no need to research alternatives.

59. C: EPLI (employment practices liability insurance) is insurance for companies that protects them in case they get sued by an employee. It covers legal costs and settlement fees related to the suit.

60. D: This is an example of a nonverbal bias. The manager draws conclusions based on her personal appearance and interprets her tattoo as a sign that she is irresponsible.

61. B: Wearing personal protective equipment is considered a leading indicator because it affects the rate of future workplace accidents. The opposite is a lagging indicator, which had an impact on the number of workplace accidents that occurred in the past.

62. D: This is an example of a manager self-service (MSS) application. It allows managers to handle the HR part of their role through one portal. It can be used for reporting and the performance management process. Tasks that are traditionally handled by the HR department can now be performed by the managers themselves.

63. B: Finding the right balance between standardization and localization is an important part of HR's role in supporting the company's globalization efforts. Some policies, processes, and procedures will be consistent across the entire company. However, others will need to be adjusted to reflect the local culture of the host country.

64. C: This is an example of risk mitigation. The company reduces the severity of the potential consequences by creating a plan to quickly communicate with employees and share information that will help keep them safe.

65. D: There are three stages on the corporate social responsibility (CSR) curve: compliance, integration, and transformation. The company is at the transformation stage. They have successfully integrated sustainability into their core strategy by receiving the B Corp certification. A company can obtain this certification if they meet a number of environmental and social performance standards.

66. D: The C-suite refers to the executive management team of the company and often includes the CEO, CFO, COO, CHRO, and CIO.

67. A: The Organization for Economic Co-operation and Development (OECD) sets goals, formulates policies, and supports its member states on issues brought about through globalization and global trade.

68. D: The HR manager displays the leadership and navigation competency by guiding the senior management team to look at the problem from a different angle, considering factors they might have previously overlooked. Even though the HR manager should aim to align the HR strategy with the company's strategic goals, he has to evaluate the decisions of the executive leadership team to be sure that they are in the best interest of the company. The HR manager does not know if low employee engagement or a lack of communication are reasons for the low performance, so addressing these would not be helpful.

69. B: By meeting with and listening to the project directors, the HR manager displays the relationship management competency. The first step is to understand the needs of the project directors to make sure that the new performance management system achieves their desired results. Conducting an employee survey is not a necessary step in developing a new performance management system. Communicating the change to the performance management system should take place after it has been developed. Because the decision to update the performance management system has already been made, there is no need to make a case for doing so.

70. A: The HR team displays the business acumen competency by seeking information about the position that they are asked to fill. Knowing exactly what knowledge, skills, and abilities are needed helps HR recruit the right candidates. After the HR team has gained an understanding of what the ideal candidate looks like, they can utilize recruitment strategies including internet recruiting. The question does not indicate that job descriptions are outdated or whether the company already has an employment brand in place.

71. C: The HR manager displays the ethical practice competency by recognizing the behavior as unethical and taking the necessary steps to investigate and address it. The receptionists receive a commission percentage for a successful upgrade sale. However, enticing customers to buy an upgrade with a voucher that is not intended for that purpose should not be rewarded with a sales incentive.

72. A: HR displays the consultation competency by identifying the reasons for the high turnover and working with the team to address the issue. This can involve developing strategies to help the employees reduce stress and deal with the large workload during the season. It has not been determined if a lack of breaks or low employee engagement are the reasons for the high turnover. Before building a candidate pool, the HR manager should find out what kind of skills and abilities a qualified candidate needs rather than assume that high stress tolerance is the most important characteristic.

73. D: The talent acquisition manager displays the ethical practice competency by explaining to the front office manager that he is unable to consider the candidate. It would be unethical towards the two candidates that made it to the final interview to add in another candidate who did not have to go through the same initial selection process. It would also be unethical to give preferential treatment to a family member of the front office manager.

74. C: E-learning, which is learning conducted via electronic media, can be either synchronous or asynchronous. Asynchronous learning means that employees can access the material anytime and anywhere. With synchronous learning, employees go through the training material at the same time and communicate with each other in real time.

75. B: One characteristic of someone who acquired a global mindset is that they are not afraid of change and uncertainty. They welcome it and see it as a chance for improvement.

76. A: Telling an employee that he will be demoted if he votes for the union is an unfair labor practice (ULP). After the employee reports the ULP to the NLRB, the NLRB will investigate the allegation.

77. C: The mentor displays the communication competency by giving his mentee tools that will allow him to find his own solution. Instead of giving him the answer, the mentor assists him in discovering the answer for himself. This helps prepare him for his new leadership role. Passing on knowledge is helpful, but teaching the mentee how to find solutions and develop his own leadership style will have a bigger impact. Ending the training program does not necessarily end the mentoring relationship. If both parties agree, they can continue the mentoring relationship.

78. B: According to the Hersey-Blanchard Situational Theory of Leadership, employees go through different stages, and leaders should adjust their leadership style accordingly. The first stage is "telling," in which the leader should provide guidance and direction, keeping a close eye on the new employee. The second stage is "selling," in which a leader should focus on coaching and motivating. The third stage is "participating," in which the leader should provide support when the employee is making decisions and finding solutions. The fourth stage is "delegating," in which a leader should empower the employee.

79. D: According to the goal-setting motivation theory, goals need to be precise, clear, measurable, challenging, and attainable. The goals of employees A, B and C fit this criterion. Employee D's goal is not likely to be attainable by a trainee, and therefore the assistant manager should encourage him to rephrase the objective.

80. C: An advantage of a functional HR structure is that HR practices are uniformly applied throughout the entire organization. Accessibility of the HR department for employees is an advantage of a decentralized HR structure. No matter what the structure of the HR department is, it should be in alignment with the organization's strategy while maintaining compliance and confidentiality.

81. A: Stay interviews can improve retention by allowing managers to find out early on if an employee is happy and satisfied or unhappy and disengaged. If the employee is unhappy or disengaged, the manager has an opportunity to address their concerns. With exit interviews, it's usually too late to prevent the employee from resigning.

82. C: The yield ratio is calculated by dividing the number of female applicants by the number of total applicants: 100/250 = 40%.

83. D: It is important for a company to invest in a comprehensive diversity and inclusion program because the goal is to change deeply held beliefs, assumptions, habits, and processes, which is a difficult undertaking. If the company does not truly care about making these difficult changes and putting in the necessary effort, the initiative will not be successful. Further, the company will not be able to profit from the advantages of a diverse workforce.

84. A: Establishing a diversity council is part of the third step of creating a diversity and inclusion (D&I) infrastructure. The next step (fourth step) is taking action and implementing the planned initiatives. This includes making changes to talent acquisition, onboarding, career advancement opportunities, and remuneration.

85. D: In a working environment where management and team members are geographically dispersed, it is important that dialogue with each employee is conducted to better understand the team dynamics and motivations and to separate facts from emotions. Conducting conversations with both the manager and HR representative demonstrates to employees that their complaints are being addressed, and it also allows each team member to communicate his or her point of view without any interruptions. Relocating the manager on-site (A) would be an extreme reaction that could take away from other sites he or she manages and other organizational responsibilities he or she oversees. While performance improvement plans (PIP) may be required after further conversation (B), immediately placing just the employees of one gender on PIPs without additional investigation may cause backlash and additional discrimination claims. The manager joining the team meetings to discuss organizational values (C) can be a positive action, but it fails to address the specific behaviors that are causing the tension among the team.

86. A: Diverse teams, even high-performing diverse teams, typically experience higher levels of conflict due to the differences in experiences, beliefs, and behaviors. Psychological safety is the critical element in which, despite the differences among team members, everyone feels comfortable offering opposing ideas, trying new things, adjusting their point of view, and taking risks. Disparate impact (B) (or unintentional discrimination) and team dissatisfaction (D) are less likely to be found positively correlated with high-performing, diverse teams. Collaboration (C) in and of itself is a style of conflict that leads to new solutions and added value.

87. B: It is important for managers to not get lost in the stereotypes of generational differences (A) and recognize each employee for his or her individual strengths and challenges. Those strengths may or may not align with generational expectations, and they will vary by individual and must be addressed as such. By focusing on the strengths of each employee, the manager can help the team to see the value in each other and lean into each member's strengths in order to improve the work outcomes of the site. As an off-site manager, mediating all conversations (C) is inefficient and unlikely to be effective. Forcing conflicting team members to work together (D) without addressing the challenges at hand can end up exacerbating the conflicts and lead to more drastic negative outcomes.

88. C: Employee resource groups can serve as an important tool to bring together groups of employees with a common trait to feel as if they are truly part of a team. These groups can go beyond just social gatherings, as they can discuss issues and challenges facing the organization and propose solutions to improve the working experiences for a diverse workforce. Employee surveys (A) are important tools for understanding how the workforce feels and views the company, but they do not necessarily pull employees together. Unconscious bias training (B) can be a useful tool, but it can be difficult to effectively plan and map the belonging metrics that result. Performative allyship (D) is a negative phenomenon in which companies say the right thing in support of diverse workforces while neglecting to take actual action.

89. D: The best strategy to communicate results is to tell a story based on the data. A large quantity of data that is presented in bulleted slides or pages of spreadsheets can overwhelm many audiences.

90. C: HR should consult with legal counsel when writing a staffing contract. They should avoid setting end dates in the contract so it can be terminated in case of dissatisfaction. They should also stay away from generic contract forms. Finally, they should negotiate the price of the staffing company's service.

91. B: In Lechmere, Inc. v. NLBR, the court ruled in favor of the company. Lechmere, Inc. did not allow union representatives on company property to solicit and distribute materials because they were not employees of the company and had no other business reason to be on the property.

92. D: Unconscious bias trainings are at higher risks of failure if they are used as stand-alone bandages that simply check a "DEI training" box. In general, DEI trainings benefit from a variety of modalities, interactions, and workplace-specific applications. Simply adding additional trainings (A) runs the risk of backfiring if employees refuse to attend or feel their time is being wasted. Eliminating the trainings altogether (B) could also cause backlash from employees because they may view the action as an abandonment of DEI strategy.

Higher leadership participation (C) can be a helpful change to the next series of trainings, but the participation must be due to a genuine desire to contribute to DEI advancement and not due to threats or demands.

93. D: In the ADDIE method of training design and evaluation, the design stage comes after the analysis stage (analyze, design, develop, implement, evaluate). Designing prior to developing (B) is important in this scenario because without knowing how many sessions the training will include, the length of each session, and the capabilities of the virtual platform, the development stage lacks the context for the depth and breadth of topics to be covered. Evaluating the results of the first training (C) occur as part of the analysis portion that has already been conducted; formal training evaluations will be held again after the next training sessions.

94. B: Nearly half of the team leaders, facility leaders, and executive leadership members failed to meet the standards set for the organization. Whether the leaders felt they were above the training, were not the problem, or were too busy, this lack of participation can be observed by lower-level employees, and thus the lack of commitment demonstrated by organizational leadership can be detrimental to the future participation and buy-in from the rest of the workforce. While the numbers for the loan officers are discouraging (A), it is not possible to discern from the data if the reason the participation rate was low was because of discrimination or because of other issues inhibiting employees from attending the trainings. While the accounting team's participation rates (C) are encouraging, the strategy used to mobilize a team of 12 is not likely to have the same effect when duplicated for a team of 36 or 88. While the smaller teams may have recorded higher levels of participation (D), participation rates are not equivalent to training effectiveness, and additional follow-up and measurements are required to make such conclusions.

95. A: Unconscious bias trainings are not intended to change beliefs necessarily but to influence behaviors and improve the interactions between employees, customers, and stakeholders. Tracking the employee engagement rates through volume of communication, opened emails, and communication maps can be evidence of shifting behavioral patterns. Net facility income (B) may be measured as a long-term outcome, but unconscious bias trainings are unlikely to affect financial outcomes immediately. Employee retention rates (C) and performance management scores (D) may shift in response to unconscious bias training, but the short-term changes to these metrics can be misleading. For example, employee retention may decrease, which can be read as a negative outcome of the trainings, but the employees leaving may be those who do not support a diverse workforce. Thus, in the long run, the turnover results in positive outcomes.

96. D: A collaborative conflict resolution seeks to find a mutually agreed-on solution that both parties view as a success. This process can take time and effort, but it allows for maintaining a valuable relationship.

97. A: Contract manufacturing is characterized by one company having another company manufacture its products as a means of controlling costs. In a joint venture, two companies set up a new company that they own together. A strategic alliance is formed when companies share resources. A Greenfield operation is building a new facility altogether.

98. D: A balanced scorecard shows if the HR strategy is in alignment with and supports the company's strategic direction. It can be used to assess the performance of the HR department and gauge the value it provides for the organization.

99. D: In a group interview, one or several managers interview a number of job candidates. They can be conducted as either team interviews or panel interviews. The main advantage is that they reduce the time spent on the interview and candidate selection process.

100. C: These projects demonstrate the CHRO's business acumen competency by taking steps to align the HR strategy with the organizational strategy. They demonstrate that the CHRO understands how the HR department can contribute to cost savings and improving the company's financial performance. Supporting the revenue-generating sections of the company does not necessarily lead to improved financial performance. Laying employees off or enacting a hiring freeze might not be in the best interest of the company.

101. D: An impactful communicator is most likely to successfully communicate the message. He should be engaging and credible, understand the employees' needs and perspectives, and communicate a clear message. An icebreaker activity would not be appropriate for this kind of meeting. Providing a detailed slide show presentation can overwhelm the employees with information. Focus groups are also not the right medium to communicate the change because they are used to gain information rather than disseminate it.

102. C: According to Blake-Mouton's theory, a "country club manager" is highly concerned about his people but has a low concern for tasks. He tends to be encouraging and creates a collaborative environment. But he often fails to hold employees accountable and avoids giving negative feedback to his subordinates. In order for him to become a team leader, he would need to develop an equal amount of concern for tasks. "Impoverished managers," with a low concern for both tasks and people, tend to delegate their work.

103. C: HR professionals can support adherence to new processes by incorporating goals that reflect those processes into performance reviews. Performance objectives should be transparent and easy for employees to understand. They should also reflect the new goals and responsibilities that resulted from the change initiative.

104. D: The managers are conducting a force-field analysis and identifying factors that help and hinder the proposed restructure. As a result, the team can determine which possibilities they should pursue further and which ones to stay away from.

105. C: Good governance starts with a company's leadership team. The top company officials need to exhibit it in everything that they do. It then must be obviously displayed at all other levels of the organization.

106. A: There are three main parts of sustainability: social, economic, and environmental. The social aspect addresses social inequalities and advocates for the fair treatment of all individuals. The economic aspect focuses on how to operate a business and use resources conscientiously to achieve profits. The environmental aspect addresses the consequences of one's actions on the environment, to include climate change.

107. B: The VP of HR and the talent manager demonstrate the critical evaluation competency by seeking out market pay rate data that allows them to evaluate how their company's pay system compares to other companies. This data has to be collected before determining if employees should be given pay increases, incentives, or perquisites. The lack of a realistic job preview does not seem to be the cause for the retention problem.

108. B: According to Hofstede's dimensions of culture, the United States is a country with low power distance, whereas India is a country with high power distance. The VP's approach of sharing responsibilities and recognition with his employees is not likely to be well received because Indian employees would expect a manager to complete important tasks himself.

109. A: According to Trompenaars's and Hampden-Turner's cultural dilemmas, India has a diffuse culture, which means that their personal and work lives intertwine. Therefore, to be successful, one has to attend work-related social events and build relationships. The United States is the opposite and has a specific culture, where work and personal lives are kept separate. In the United States, forming relationships is unnecessary to work together successfully. The US is also an individualist culture that values competition, and India is not.

110. A: One common reason an employee might express resistance to change is that he fears new and unfamiliar processes that are outside of his comfort zone. This is called the fear of the unknown.

111. C: To attract the best talent, the company pursues a lead market strategy and offers higher wages than the market. A match market strategy would be to offer pay rates similar to other companies. A lag market strategy would aim to save on personnel costs by offering lower-than-average wages.

112. D: A leader has a strategic vision. They motivate and encourage a team to reach and exceed goals. A manager focuses on transactional activities. They schedule, organize, plan, and compile resources.

113. B: The recruitment phase is the beginning of the employee life cycle (ELC). Then comes integration, which includes onboarding and the employee's introduction to their new role. The third phase, development, includes training and performance management. The last phase, transition, is when the employee leaves their position due to a promotion, termination, or transfer.

114. D: The employee absence rate is a measure that can be calculated and used to assess the effectiveness of an engagement action plan. Problem-solving abilities, employee motivation, and managerial skills are not outcomes that can be measured explicitly.

115. C: Employee surveys are a tool to increase employee engagement. But it is important that managers communicate the results honestly to their employees, take the feedback seriously, and respond in a meaningful manner. The greatest mistake companies can make with employee surveys is ignoring or not responding to the survey results. This can lead to frustrated and disengaged employees.

116. A: The leader of a focus group should put his emphasis on drawing out information from the participants. He can do this by involving all of them equally and encouraging deep discussion of the topic.

117. A: The CHRO displays the critical evaluation competency by using the data and insights she gained to build a business case. A business case that is well-researched and backed up by solid data has the best potential to convince the CEO to invest in the necessary training and development for his managers. Properly trained managers will have a positive impact on the company's operations. A cost-efficient employee engagement initiative, one-on-one meetings, and literature for self-study can be quick fixes in the interim. However, they do not adequately address the manager's training needs.

118. C: The CHRO displays the relationship management competency by building rapport with external contacts that can help create a talent pipeline for the company. Working directly with colleges and their career services centers will improve hiring efforts in the long term.

119. D: The CHRO displays the ethical practice competency by promoting fairness when she notices that the new technology has become a disadvantage for the more tenured and less computer-savvy employees. She shows awareness that new technology can lead to performance gaps between the younger and older workforce. To give all employees a fair chance, the company needs to offer more training and support to the less computer-savvy employees.

120. A: In a learning organization, leaders are designers, stewards, and teachers. As designers, they create the vision, values, and processes of the organization. They have a sense of stewardship for their employees as well as for the company's mission. As teachers, they encourage others to discover and seek new possibilities.

121. B: Involving employees in the company's decision-making process is called codetermination. One form of this is the single-tier system in which one or more employees sit on the board of directors and have the right to vote. Other possible forms of codetermination are a dual system or a mixed system.

122. D: Once the employee has been selected for the global assignment, it is important for him to learn about the local culture. This will prepare him for a successful start overseas. Setting pay rates, analyzing the potential return on investment, and assessing fit with the employee's career aspirations should take place well before selecting an employee for the assignment.

123. C: This suggestion displays the global and cultural effectiveness competency by taking advantage of the diverse perspectives that exist within the organization and involving employees in the development of a new employment brand. Efforts and views should come from the employees and managers themselves and not originate solely within the HR department. Diversity and inclusion programs generally take time to develop and cannot be expected to bring quick results.

124. B: The CHRO displays the global and cultural effectiveness competency by recognizing the cultural differences as the root cause of their problem working together. Therefore, she is able to mediate between both parties and use the situation as a learning lesson about how to overcome cultural differences by seeing the other person's perspective. This will allow them to understand each other better and improve their working relationship going forward.

125. A: The marketing manager displays the communication competency by having one-on-one conversations with all team members to find out why the new employee does not fit in with the rest of the team. If the current employees are a close group that has worked together for a long time, they might need support to adjust to the new team member. It is important to get to know the new employee to see if they have any conflicts with the company culture.

126. A: When change is introduced, there is likely to be some initial decline in performance, which is known as the "J curve." Employees often react to change with resistance and rejection. As a result, productivity declines. If the change initiative is managed well, then employees will come to accept the change, and performance will ideally increase above the initial level.

127. C: The VP of HR displays the business acumen competency by using his understanding of the business to identify solutions to organizational challenges. His suggestion to utilize the intranet for communication aligns HR strategy with the company's strategic goals by enabling employees to communicate and collaborate on a daily basis. A one-time meeting in person or virtually would be a good start. However, it does not support the need for ongoing interaction and collaboration. Strict performance management steps would not be appropriate at this time because the company first needs to create a platform that enables employees to successfully collaborate with each other.

128. D: Because the working relationship with Region X's manager is an ongoing problem, the VP of HR needs to get to the bottom of the issue. He does this by displaying the relationship management competency which involves meeting with each regional manager to gain a full understanding of the problem. Once the root of the problem is uncovered, he can encourage open communication among the regional managers and find a permanent solution. Solving this disagreement and improving the relationships between the regional managers will result in improved cooperation and better overall performance.

129. C: This is an example of gamification, a form of mobile learning (m-learning), where educational material is delivered in the form of a game. It is intended to make learning more fun and the material more engaging.

130. C: The HR manager displays the critical evaluation competency by recognizing that switching to a cheaper vendor, if available, would not have the desired results. That's because the new vendor's premiums are likely to increase year after year as well. He knows that there is a direct link between the health of the employees and how much the company is paying in healthcare premiums. Therefore, his strategy of focusing on preventative health is a good long-term solution to reduce premium increases.

131. D: The HR manager displays the leadership and navigation competency by speaking up even if it is something that the CEO would rather not hear. It is necessary for the HR manager to voice his concerns because improper maintenance can have costly consequences for the company.

132. B: The HR manager is displaying the communication competency by knowing when to talk to someone and when to seek expert advice first. Even though the company has nothing to hide, it is important to follow the attorney's recommendations when dealing with the department of labor. The attorney can provide guidance regarding what information has to be shared and what files need to be turned over.

133. B: Conducting a compliance audit at the last step of the risk management process will ensure that all implemented changes comply with applicable regulations and laws.

134. D: Companies that want to minimize having to discipline their workforce should practice open communication with their employees. It allows employees to develop a good understanding of company policies and expectations. And, managers who are in regular communication with their employees understand reasons for their behavior and can correct it before a violation occurs.

SHRM-CP Practice Tests #3 and #4

To take these additional SHRM-CP practice tests, visit our bonus page:
mometrix.com/bonus948/shrmcp

How to Overcome Test Anxiety

Just the thought of taking a test is enough to make most people a little nervous. A test is an important event that can have a long-term impact on your future, so it's important to take it seriously and it's natural to feel anxious about performing well. But just because anxiety is normal, that doesn't mean that it's helpful in test taking, or that you should simply accept it as part of your life. Anxiety can have a variety of effects. These effects can be mild, like making you feel slightly nervous, or severe, like blocking your ability to focus or remember even a simple detail.

If you experience test anxiety—whether severe or mild—it's important to know how to beat it. To discover this, first you need to understand what causes test anxiety.

Causes of Test Anxiety

While we often think of anxiety as an uncontrollable emotional state, it can actually be caused by simple, practical things. One of the most common causes of test anxiety is that a person does not feel adequately prepared for their test. This feeling can be the result of many different issues such as poor study habits or lack of organization, but the most common culprit is time management. Starting to study too late, failing to organize your study time to cover all of the material, or being distracted while you study will mean that you're not well prepared for the test. This may lead to cramming the night before, which will cause you to be physically and mentally exhausted for the test. Poor time management also contributes to feelings of stress, fear, and hopelessness as you realize you are not well prepared but don't know what to do about it.

Other times, test anxiety is not related to your preparation for the test but comes from unresolved fear. This may be a past failure on a test, or poor performance on tests in general. It may come from comparing yourself to others who seem to be performing better or from the stress of living up to expectations. Anxiety may be driven by fears of the future—how failure on this test would affect your educational and career goals. These fears are often completely irrational, but they can still negatively impact your test performance.

Elements of Test Anxiety

As mentioned earlier, test anxiety is considered to be an emotional state, but it has physical and mental components as well. Sometimes you may not even realize that you are suffering from test anxiety until you notice the physical symptoms. These can include trembling hands, rapid heartbeat, sweating, nausea, and tense muscles. Extreme anxiety may lead to fainting or vomiting. Obviously, any of these symptoms can have a negative impact on testing. It is important to recognize them as soon as they begin to occur so that you can address the problem before it damages your performance.

The mental components of test anxiety include trouble focusing and inability to remember learned information. During a test, your mind is on high alert, which can help you recall information and stay focused for an extended period of time. However, anxiety interferes with your mind's natural processes, causing you to blank out, even on the questions you know well. The strain of testing during anxiety makes it difficult to stay focused, especially on a test that may take several hours. Extreme anxiety can take a huge mental toll, making it difficult not only to recall test information but even to understand the test questions or pull your thoughts together.

Effects of Test Anxiety

Test anxiety is like a disease—if left untreated, it will get progressively worse. Anxiety leads to poor performance, and this reinforces the feelings of fear and failure, which in turn lead to poor performances on subsequent tests. It can grow from a mild nervousness to a crippling condition. If allowed to progress, test anxiety can have a big impact on your schooling, and consequently on your future.

Test anxiety can spread to other parts of your life. Anxiety on tests can become anxiety in any stressful situation, and blanking on a test can turn into panicking in a job situation. But fortunately, you don't have to let anxiety rule your testing and determine your grades. There are a number of relatively simple steps you can take to move past anxiety and function normally on a test and in the rest of life.

Physical Steps for Beating Test Anxiety

While test anxiety is a serious problem, the good news is that it can be overcome. It doesn't have to control your ability to think and remember information. While it may take time, you can begin taking steps today to beat anxiety.

Just as your first hint that you may be struggling with anxiety comes from the physical symptoms, the first step to treating it is also physical. Rest is crucial for having a clear, strong mind. If you are tired, it is much easier to give in to anxiety. But if you establish good sleep habits, your body and mind will be ready to perform optimally, without the strain of exhaustion. Additionally, sleeping well helps you to retain information better, so you're more likely to recall the answers when you see the test questions.

Getting good sleep means more than going to bed on time. It's important to allow your brain time to relax. Take study breaks from time to time so it doesn't get overworked, and don't study right before bed. Take time to rest your mind before trying to rest your body, or you may find it difficult to fall asleep.

Along with sleep, other aspects of physical health are important in preparing for a test. Good nutrition is vital for good brain function. Sugary foods and drinks may give a burst of energy but this burst is followed by a crash, both physically and emotionally. Instead, fuel your body with protein and vitamin-rich foods.

Also, drink plenty of water. Dehydration can lead to headaches and exhaustion, especially if your brain is already under stress from the rigors of the test. Particularly if your test is a long one, drink water during the breaks. And if possible, take an energy-boosting snack to eat between sections.

Along with sleep and diet, a third important part of physical health is exercise. Maintaining a steady workout schedule is helpful, but even taking 5-minute study breaks to walk can help get your blood pumping faster and clear your head. Exercise also releases endorphins, which contribute to a positive feeling and can help combat test anxiety.

When you nurture your physical health, you are also contributing to your mental health. If your body is healthy, your mind is much more likely to be healthy as well. So take time to rest, nourish your body with healthy food and water, and get moving as much as possible. Taking these physical steps will make you stronger and more able to take the mental steps necessary to overcome test anxiety.

Mental Steps for Beating Test Anxiety

Working on the mental side of test anxiety can be more challenging, but as with the physical side, there are clear steps you can take to overcome it. As mentioned earlier, test anxiety often stems from lack of preparation, so the obvious solution is to prepare for the test. Effective studying may be the most important weapon you have for beating test anxiety, but you can and should employ several other mental tools to combat fear.

First, boost your confidence by reminding yourself of past success—tests or projects that you aced. If you're putting as much effort into preparing for this test as you did for those, there's no reason you should expect to fail here. Work hard to prepare; then trust your preparation.

Second, surround yourself with encouraging people. It can be helpful to find a study group, but be sure that the people you're around will encourage a positive attitude. If you spend time with others who are anxious or cynical, this will only contribute to your own anxiety. Look for others who are motivated to study hard from a desire to succeed, not from a fear of failure.

Third, reward yourself. A test is physically and mentally tiring, even without anxiety, and it can be helpful to have something to look forward to. Plan an activity following the test, regardless of the outcome, such as going to a movie or getting ice cream.

When you are taking the test, if you find yourself beginning to feel anxious, remind yourself that you know the material. Visualize successfully completing the test. Then take a few deep, relaxing breaths and return to it. Work through the questions carefully but with confidence, knowing that you are capable of succeeding.

Developing a healthy mental approach to test taking will also aid in other areas of life. Test anxiety affects more than just the actual test—it can be damaging to your mental health and even contribute to depression. It's important to beat test anxiety before it becomes a problem for more than testing.

Study Strategy

Being prepared for the test is necessary to combat anxiety, but what does being prepared look like? You may study for hours on end and still not feel prepared. What you need is a strategy for test prep. The next few pages outline our recommended steps to help you plan out and conquer the challenge of preparation.

STEP 1: SCOPE OUT THE TEST

Learn everything you can about the format (multiple choice, essay, etc.) and what will be on the test. Gather any study materials, course outlines, or sample exams that may be available. Not only will this help you to prepare, but knowing what to expect can help to alleviate test anxiety.

STEP 2: MAP OUT THE MATERIAL

Look through the textbook or study guide and make note of how many chapters or sections it has. Then divide these over the time you have. For example, if a book has 15 chapters and you have five days to study, you need to cover three chapters each day. Even better, if you have the time, leave an extra day at the end for overall review after you have gone through the material in depth.

If time is limited, you may need to prioritize the material. Look through it and make note of which sections you think you already have a good grasp on, and which need review. While you are studying, skim quickly through the familiar sections and take more time on the challenging parts. Write out your plan so you don't get lost as you go. Having a written plan also helps you feel more in control of the study, so anxiety is less likely to arise from feeling overwhelmed at the amount to cover.

STEP 3: GATHER YOUR TOOLS

Decide what study method works best for you. Do you prefer to highlight in the book as you study and then go back over the highlighted portions? Or do you type out notes of the important information? Or is it helpful to make flashcards that you can carry with you? Assemble the pens, index cards, highlighters, post-it notes, and any other materials you may need so you won't be distracted by getting up to find things while you study.

If you're having a hard time retaining the information or organizing your notes, experiment with different methods. For example, try color-coding by subject with colored pens, highlighters, or post-it notes. If you learn better by hearing, try recording yourself reading your notes so you can listen while in the car, working out, or simply sitting at your desk. Ask a friend to quiz you from your flashcards, or try teaching someone the material to solidify it in your mind.

STEP 4: CREATE YOUR ENVIRONMENT

It's important to avoid distractions while you study. This includes both the obvious distractions like visitors and the subtle distractions like an uncomfortable chair (or a too-comfortable couch that makes you want to fall asleep). Set up the best study environment possible: good lighting and a comfortable work area. If background music helps you focus, you may want to turn it on, but otherwise keep the room quiet. If you are using a computer to take notes, be sure you don't have any other windows open, especially applications like social media, games, or anything else that could distract you. Silence your phone and turn off notifications. Be sure to keep water close by so you stay hydrated while you study (but avoid unhealthy drinks and snacks).

Also, take into account the best time of day to study. Are you freshest first thing in the morning? Try to set aside some time then to work through the material. Is your mind clearer in the afternoon or evening? Schedule your study session then. Another method is to study at the same time of day that you will take the test, so that your brain gets used to working on the material at that time and will be ready to focus at test time.

STEP 5: STUDY!

Once you have done all the study preparation, it's time to settle into the actual studying. Sit down, take a few moments to settle your mind so you can focus, and begin to follow your study plan. Don't give in to distractions or let yourself procrastinate. This is your time to prepare so you'll be ready to fearlessly approach the test. Make the most of the time and stay focused.

Of course, you don't want to burn out. If you study too long you may find that you're not retaining the information very well. Take regular study breaks. For example, taking five minutes out of every hour to walk briskly, breathing deeply and swinging your arms, can help your mind stay fresh.

As you get to the end of each chapter or section, it's a good idea to do a quick review. Remind yourself of what you learned and work on any difficult parts. When you feel that you've mastered the material, move on to the next part. At the end of your study session, briefly skim through your notes again.

But while review is helpful, cramming last minute is NOT. If at all possible, work ahead so that you won't need to fit all your study into the last day. Cramming overloads your brain with more information than it can process and retain, and your tired mind may struggle to recall even previously learned information when it is overwhelmed with last-minute study. Also, the urgent nature of cramming and the stress placed on your brain contribute to anxiety. You'll be more likely to go to the test feeling unprepared and having trouble thinking clearly.

So don't cram, and don't stay up late before the test, even just to review your notes at a leisurely pace. Your brain needs rest more than it needs to go over the information again. In fact, plan to finish your studies by noon or early afternoon the day before the test. Give your brain the rest of the day to relax or focus on other things, and get a good night's sleep. Then you will be fresh for the test and better able to recall what you've studied.

STEP 6: TAKE A PRACTICE TEST

Many courses offer sample tests, either online or in the study materials. This is an excellent resource to check whether you have mastered the material, as well as to prepare for the test format and environment.

Check the test format ahead of time: the number of questions, the type (multiple choice, free response, etc.), and the time limit. Then create a plan for working through them. For example, if you have 30 minutes to take a 60-question test, your limit is 30 seconds per question. Spend less time on the questions you know well so that you can take more time on the difficult ones.

If you have time to take several practice tests, take the first one open book, with no time limit. Work through the questions at your own pace and make sure you fully understand them. Gradually work up to taking a test under test conditions: sit at a desk with all study materials put away and set a timer. Pace yourself to make sure you finish the test with time to spare and go back to check your answers if you have time.

After each test, check your answers. On the questions you missed, be sure you understand why you missed them. Did you misread the question (tests can use tricky wording)? Did you forget the information? Or was it something you hadn't learned? Go back and study any shaky areas that the practice tests reveal.

Taking these tests not only helps with your grade, but also aids in combating test anxiety. If you're already used to the test conditions, you're less likely to worry about it, and working through tests until you're scoring well gives you a confidence boost. Go through the practice tests until you feel comfortable, and then you can go into the test knowing that you're ready for it.

Test Tips

On test day, you should be confident, knowing that you've prepared well and are ready to answer the questions. But aside from preparation, there are several test day strategies you can employ to maximize your performance.

First, as stated before, get a good night's sleep the night before the test (and for several nights before that, if possible). Go into the test with a fresh, alert mind rather than staying up late to study.

Try not to change too much about your normal routine on the day of the test. It's important to eat a nutritious breakfast, but if you normally don't eat breakfast at all, consider eating just a protein bar. If you're a coffee drinker, go ahead and have your normal coffee. Just make sure you time it so that the caffeine doesn't wear off right in the middle of your test. Avoid sugary beverages, and drink enough water to stay hydrated but not so much that you need a restroom break 10 minutes into the test. If your test isn't first thing in the morning, consider going for a walk or doing a light workout before the test to get your blood flowing.

Allow yourself enough time to get ready, and leave for the test with plenty of time to spare so you won't have the anxiety of scrambling to arrive in time. Another reason to be early is to select a good seat. It's helpful to sit away from doors and windows, which can be distracting. Find a good seat, get out your supplies, and settle your mind before the test begins.

When the test begins, start by going over the instructions carefully, even if you already know what to expect. Make sure you avoid any careless mistakes by following the directions.

Then begin working through the questions, pacing yourself as you've practiced. If you're not sure on an answer, don't spend too much time on it, and don't let it shake your confidence. Either skip it and come back later, or eliminate as many wrong answers as possible and guess among the remaining ones. Don't dwell on these questions as you continue—put them out of your mind and focus on what lies ahead.

Be sure to read all of the answer choices, even if you're sure the first one is the right answer. Sometimes you'll find a better one if you keep reading. But don't second-guess yourself if you do immediately know the answer. Your gut instinct is usually right. Don't let test anxiety rob you of the information you know.

If you have time at the end of the test (and if the test format allows), go back and review your answers. Be cautious about changing any, since your first instinct tends to be correct, but make sure you didn't misread any of the questions or accidentally mark the wrong answer choice. Look over any you skipped and make an educated guess.

At the end, leave the test feeling confident. You've done your best, so don't waste time worrying about your performance or wishing you could change anything. Instead, celebrate the successful completion of this test. And finally, use this test to learn how to deal with anxiety even better next time.

> **Review Video: Test Anxiety**
> Visit mometrix.com/academy and enter code: 100340

Important Qualification

Not all anxiety is created equal. If your test anxiety is causing major issues in your life beyond the classroom or testing center, or if you are experiencing troubling physical symptoms related to your anxiety, it may be a sign of a serious physiological or psychological condition. If this sounds like your situation, we strongly encourage you to seek professional help.

Additional Bonus Material

Due to our efforts to try to keep this book to a manageable length, we've created a link that will give you access to all of your additional bonus material:

mometrix.com/bonus948/shrmcp

Made in the USA
Monee, IL
11 June 2024